The Troubled Pregnancy

Mason looks at the legal response to those aspects of the troubled pregnancy which require or involve medico-legal intervention. The unwished-for pregnancy is considered particularly in the light of the Abortion Act 1967, s.1(1)(d) and the related action for so-called wrongful birth due to faulty antenatal care. The unexpected or uncovenanted birth of a healthy child resulting from failed sterilisation is approached through an analysis of the seminal case of *McFarlane* and associated cases involving disability in either the neonate or the mother. The disabled neonate's right to sue for its diminished life is discussed and the legal approach to the management of severe congenital disease is analysed - thus following Baroness Hale in believing that care of the newborn is an integral part of pregnancy. Aspects are considered from historical and comparative perspectives, including coverage of experience in the USA, the Commonwealth and Europe.

Cambridge Law, Medicine and Ethics

This series of books was founded by Cambridge University Press with Alexander McCall Smith as its first editor in 2003. It focuses on the law's complex and troubled relationship with medicine across both the developed and the developing world. In the past twenty years, we have seen in many countries increasing resort to the courts by dissatisfied patients and a growing use of the courts to attempt to resolve intractable ethical dilemmas. At the same time, legislatures across the world have struggled to address the questions posed by both the successes and the failures of modern medicine, while international organisations such as the WHO and UNESCO now regularly address issues of medical law.

It follows that we would expect ethical and policy questions to be integral to the analysis of the legal issues discussed in this series. The series responds to the high profile of medical law in universities, in legal and medical practice, as well as in public and political affairs. We seek to reflect the evidence that many major health-related policy debates in the UK, Europe and the international community over the past two decades have involved a strong medical law dimension. Organ retention, embryonic stem cell research, physician assisted suicide and the allocation of resources to fund health care are but a few examples among many. The emphasis of this series is thus on matters of public concern and/or practical significance. We look for books that could make a difference to the development of medical law and enhance the role of medico-legal debate in policy circles. That is not to say that we lack interest in the important theoretical dimensions of the subject, but we aim to ensure that theoretical debate is grounded in the realities of how the law does and should interact with medicine and health care.

General Editors
Professor Margaret Brazier, *University of Manchester*
Professor Graeme Laurie, *University of Edinburgh*

Editorial Advisory Board
Professor Richard Ashcroft, *Queen Mary, University of London*
Professor Martin Bobrow, *University of Cambridge*
Dr Alexander Morgan Capron, *Director, Ethics and Health, World Health Organization, Geneva*
Professor Jim Childress, *University of Virginia*
Professor Ruth Chadwick, *Cardiff Law School*
Dame Ruth Deech, *University of Oxford*
Professor John Keown, *Georgetown University, Washington, D.C.*
Dr. Kathy Liddell, *University of Cambridge*
Professor Alexander McCall Smith, *University of Edinburgh*
Professor Dr. Mónica Navarro-Michel, *University of Barcelona*

Marcus Radetzki, Marian Radetzki, Niklas Juth
Genes and Insurance: Ethical, Legal and Economic Issues
978 0 521 83090 4

Ruth Macklin
Double Standards in Medical Research in Developing Countries
978 0 521 83388 2 hardback   978 0 521 54170 1 paperback

Donna Dickenson
Property in the Body: Feminist Perspectives
978 0 521 86792 4

Matti Häyry, Ruth Chadwick, Vilhjálmur Árnason, Gardar Árnason
The Ethics and Governance of Human Genetic Databases: European Perspectives
978 0 521 85662 1

Ken Mason
The Troubled Pregnancy: Legal Wrongs and Rights in Reproduction
978 0 521 85075 9

Daniel Sperling
Posthumous Interests: Legal and Ethical Perspectives
978 0 521 87784 8

Keith Syrett
Law, Legitimacy and the Rationing of Health Care
978 0 521 85773 4

The Troubled Pregnancy

Legal Wrongs and Rights in Reproduction

J. K. Mason

MD (Cantab.), LLD(Edin.), FRC Path, FRSE
Professor (Emeritus) of Forensic Medicine and Honorary Fellow,
School of Law in the University of Edinburgh

CAMBRIDGE
UNIVERSITY PRESS

CAMBRIDGE UNIVERSITY PRESS
Cambridge, New York, Melbourne, Madrid, Cape Town, Singapore, São Paulo

Cambridge University Press
The Edinburgh Building, Cambridge CB2 8RU, UK

Published in the United States of America by Cambridge University Press, New York

www.cambridge.org
Information on this title: www.cambridge.org/9780521850759

First published 2007

Printed in the United Kingdom at the University Press, Cambridge

A catalogue record for this publication is available from the British Library

ISBN 978-0-521-85075-9 hardback
ISBN 978-0-521-61624-9 paperback

This book is dedicated to the 'gang'
Graeme, Sharon and Geoff
with great affection.

Contents

Preface

The origin of this book lies in a series of articles I wrote, mainly for the *Edinburgh Law Review*, following upon the ground-breaking House of Lords ruling in *McFarlane* v. *Tayside Health Board* in 2000. I admit to being amongst those who found that unanimous decision hard to accept and I followed its fallout with increasing interest. Cambridge University Press were kind enough to agree to a proposal that we consolidate the results into a coherent monograph and this has resulted in *The Troubled Pregnancy*. It will, however, be apparent that what started as a relatively simple fancy rapidly became a major academic exercise. The more I looked at the individual index cases, the more I became involved with the subject both on a historical and an international basis. The result was a major expansion of the anticipated text.

Inevitably, then, the book has taken some time to write – and this has not been helped by the acquisition of the occasional metal joint and of a serious bout of two-fingered repetitive strain injury. It has, therefore, been particularly prone to the well-known hazard that medical law is a moving target. At the same time, it has provided a welcome opportunity to reflect on what has gone before or, so to speak, to 'learn on the job' – to put it in perspective, I still think *McFarlane* was wrong but I doubt if it was as wrong as I thought it was five years ago! I must, therefore, ask the reader's forgiveness if, at times, it looks as though I have changed my mind between Chapters 1 and 8 – indeed, I may well have done so. In the end, however, I hope I have painted a fair picture of an area of jurisprudence in which decisions must be made that cannot, by their very nature, please everyone.

I have had the enormous privilege of spending some twenty years in the Edinburgh School of Law where I have received unfailing kindness and help from my legal colleagues; I owe them, collectively, a debt of gratitude for giving me what turned out to be a third career. As to this particular project, I would like to thank Mrs Elspeth Reid, lately editor of the *Edinburgh Law Review*, for her encouragement of my research; Dr Parker Hood and Ms Joelle Godard for their help in the Australian and European ambiences respectively; Dr Alexis Tattis for early assistance and Dr Sharon Cowan for valuable guidance in the feminist field. My truly profound thanks, however, go, firstly, to Mr Geoff Pradella, one of my recent postgraduate students, who undertook some prodigious research for me and also read and commented on several chapters; and, secondly – and as always – to Professor Graeme Laurie who encouraged me throughout, read and constructively criticised some chapters and, on more than one occasion, saved the manuscript from the flames! Finally, I must thank Cambridge University Press for their forbearance over the months and for giving me the long-sought opportunity to publish under the auspices of my alma mater. I hope the book does them justice.

Edinburgh
JKM
August 2006

Table of cases

Table of statutes

1 The nature of the troubled pregnancy

Introduction

Most academics have difficulty in writing their monographs and I must certainly count myself among that majority. I can, however, go one stage further and admit to having had a comparable difficulty in finding a title. In planning their families, most people would opt for an ideal number of ideal children. Life, however, is far from ideal and my aim has been to collate and review the development of the law as it now relates to human reproduction that has gone contrary to plan – contrary in the sense that the problems have strayed beyond those that can be settled within the doctor/patient relationship and which, as a result, require some legal control of the outcome.

Inevitably this implies that there is, at source, some form of conflict between the three principals – the pregnant woman, her fetus and her medical adviser. One's consequent reaction is to see these as encompassed within the mantle of 'unwanted pregnancy' and, certainly, a very large number of pregnancies are genuinely unwanted. At the same time, by far the greater proportion of these will be resolved between the woman and her doctor within the abortion clinic and I should make it clear that, while I consider lawful termination of pregnancy at considerable length in this book, I do so with some reluctance insofar as I am not concerned with abortion per se – and certainly not with abortion on what are often described as the 'social grounds'.[1] Rather, I am concerned with abortion as a potential and lawful solution to many of the other problems of the complicated pregnancy.

Most persons who wish to avoid pregnancy will, however, surely see contraception as being preferable to abortion as a means to that end. Given that they are using contraceptive methods under expert medical guidance and that they believe that, as consumers, they are protected from the hazards of defective production, they will expect a satisfactory outcome. The vagaries of contraceptive methods are such, however, that

---

[1] Abortion Act 1967, s.1(1)(a).

the possibility of failure is to be anticipated and, when it occurs, the chances of that failure being attributable to an individual's negligence are, in general, very slender.[2] The situation changes, however, when a person has expressed his or her aversion to parenthood by way of the ultimate contraceptive method – that is, sterilisation. The intention is obvious, the persons responsible for the treatment are readily identifiable and the individual's right to competent treatment is clearly recognisable. A pregnancy following sterilisation is, in every way, the paradigm 'unwanted' pregnancy which fits well within the stated remit of this book.

This, however, is only half the story. What concerns many couples is not so much the fact of pregnancy but, rather, the resultant parenthood. The greater part of that concern will be based on economics – can we afford to be the good parents that the child deserves? As Peter Pain J put it in an early example of unwanted pregnancy:

[E]very baby has a belly to be filled and a body to be clothed. The law relating to damages is concerned with reparation in money terms and this is what is needed for the maintenance of a baby.[3]

Clearly, then, if that extra expense results from someone's negligence, there is a prima facie case that compensation is payable. At the same time, however, it is important to appreciate that, in seeking such compensation, there is no *necessary* denigration of the child's status.

On the other side of the coin, however, a sizeable minority will be concerned for the type of child they will be parenting. Such concern may, again, be double-edged. On the one hand, many will want the 'perfect baby' and, such are the advances of modern medicine that, while the so-called designer baby cannot, at present, be produced to order, it is increasingly possible to ensure that imperfection is predictable – and, given the consumer/provider nature of much modern medical practice, increasing numbers of prospective parents expect those predictions to be made and to be made available for evaluation. At the same time, perhaps even more will, either for good or for unsustainable reasons, be positively worried lest the woman be carrying an imperfect child.

Thus, in many cases involving 'unwanted' pregnancy and birth, it is not *a* baby that is unwanted but, rather, that *particular* baby – or, to put it more bluntly, a child that is disabled. That is a harsh thing to say – harsh because, insofar as it is almost universally held that it is a mark of a civilised society that all its members are treated equally and are afforded

---

[2] *Richardson* v. *LRC Products Ltd* (2001) 59 BMLR 185, [2000] Lloyd's Rep Med 280 is an unusual case involving a defective condom which proves the point.

[3] In *Thake* v. *Maurice* [1986] QB 644 at 666. Discussed in greater detail at p. 102 below.

the same respect, it touches upon the moral conscience of society as a whole. This is not to condemn or even criticise those who, say, faced with an unexpectedly disabled neonate, will initially reject it. In practice, it is remarkable how few unexpectedly disabled children are committed to institutional care; rather, it is noticeable that many are accepted into a loving and caring family. Nonetheless, it is an inescapable fact that, while the upkeep of children costs money, the upkeep of a disabled child costs not only more money but also a great deal of hidden expenditure in the form of extra care and attention. Thus, the economic problems of pregnancy are intimately bound with the health of the resultant child.

A further aspect of the 'unwanted' pregnancy that deeply troubles the public conscience is that, so often, the logical disposal of the unwanted is by way of death. Again, then, we are restrained by an innate adherence to the principle of the 'sanctity' of human life – a principle that recurs again and again in the pages that follow. The result may well be a conflict of conscience – an unwanted pregnancy may turn into an unwanted abortion. Equally dramatically, an originally rejected disabled neonate has become deeply loved and a new conflict arises – that between, on the one hand, the parents' desire to support their child and, on the other, that child's best interests in abandoning his or her struggle for existence. And we will see that the judiciary, when asked to decide between these parental options, have their own problems to overcome – an added dimension being that an individual case decision will, as likely as not, be taken to represent public policy. Thus, the outcome of a case may well depend upon whether the individual or the majority on the bench are motivated primarily by moral or by legal principles.

There are, indeed, so many aspects – and so many nuances within those aspects – to the subject matter of this book that I decided it was best described by the neutral overall term 'the troubled pregnancy'. Having said which, I should say that it is implicit – though, perhaps, not obvious[4] – that I am confining discussion to those troubles which have both an ethical and a legal dimension. The obstetric management of birth may, for example, be negligent and, as a result, be a potent source of neonatal disability; but it is a purely technical matter and contains no ethical element. Similarly, the purist might well say that an adulterous pregnancy is likely to be troubled; but, again, this is not a book on family law.

It is not difficult to appreciate that, as a result of this selection, one of the main difficulties in writing on it – and one of the major dilemmas influencing the courts once they become involved – has lain in the

---

[4] A pregnancy can, of course, be 'troubled' by the various patho-physiological problems associated with the state and there is no intention to include such purely medical matters.

intensely emotional nature of the subject. Indeed, insofar as the law in this field has been established over the years on something of an ad hoc basis, it could be said that its ethical component has proved to be more basic and significant to its evolution than has strict legal principle. That being so, it is hard to keep one's personal interpretation of the ethical conditions out of one's analysis of the many variations on the theme of troubled reproduction that arise – and it will become evident that this goes as much for judges as it does for authors. Rather surprisingly, the dilemmas facing the former have been demonstrated most recently – and most vividly – in the Australian courts[5] and this is one reason why I have devoted considerable space to the Australian cases. As to the latter, it cannot be said that an author's personal views are in the same league of significance as those of the judiciary and, while I have some strong views on many of the topics addressed in the body of the text, I hope I have succeeded in being reasonably objective. At heart, then, this book concerns the growth of the common law in these difficult areas rather than an analysis of the community's moral response to that lead – although, from what has been said, it is clear that the two are, mutatis mutandis, inseparable.

This book can be regarded as a triptych. At one side, and beginning the saga, we have the troubled conception and its intensely ethical association with abortion. On the other, and completing the picture, we have the extension of the troubled pregnancy into the realm of troubled parenthood as exemplified by the management of the disabled neonate – and I justify this inclusion because, whether intended or unintended, parenthood is the *natural* concomitant of pregnancy. The core of the book, however, is concerned, as in the title, with the origins and management of the troubled pregnancy and 'troubled', here, has been defined in the terms which have come into widespread usage over recent years:

- 'wrongful pregnancy' – generally taken as meaning an 'uncovenanted' pregnancy[6] resulting from defective contraceptive advice or surgical intervention;
- 'wrongful birth' – which implies the birth of a disabled child as a result of inadequate antenatal management; and

---

[5] I regard the case of *Cattanach* v. *Melchior* (2003) 188 ALR 131 as the most significant example of the moral/legal debate to be found in the contemporary era.

[6] This expression was first used in this context by Kennedy J in *Richardson* v. *LRC Products Ltd*, n. 2 above. It is used in Scots law to describe an event that was not so much unexpected as one which was not contemplated by the parties concerned and is, therefore, aptly applied to a pregnancy following, say, a sterilisation operation. I am anxious to perpetuate it as it avoids applying the pejorative, and often inaccurate, adjective 'unwanted' to a child.

- 'wrongful life' – essentially, a claim *by the neonate* that he or she is suffering because his or her mother was wrongly advised as to continuation or termination of the pregnancy.

Since these terms are central to the text – and because they are not universally agreed – it will, I believe, be helpful to discuss their implications in some detail in this introduction.

Categorisation of the troubled pregnancy

It is, in fact, difficult to establish their precise origins. One thing is, however, certain – they were born in the United States[7] where the three-pronged concept of antenatal tort has been around for at least thirty years.[8] It is equally true that the terms have been plagued by uncertainty as to their meaning since their inception while, at the same time, they have been subject to conceptual criticism at both academic and judicial level. In a relatively recent review, Strasser[9] goes to some lengths to describe the difficulties of placing a particular event in a *particular* cause of action – a matter which is, perhaps, of special significance in the United States with its many different jurisdictions and, consequently, varied interpretations. Should, for example, a failed sterilisation operation resulting in the birth of a disabled child be categorised as a wrongful pregnancy or a wrongful birth? Or, should the extent of the doctor's knowledge of the facts make any difference to the nature of the action? Categorisation, as Strasser points out, allows for different states to allow or deny different actions while the mere categorisation of an action may result in the award of different damages in circumstances that are, essentially, similar. In short, 'jurisdictions do themselves and each other a disservice when focusing attention on factors other than the negligent action and the resulting harm'.[10] And it cannot be denied that the courts of the United Kingdom, the Commonwealth and of the European Union are faced with similar difficulties.

---

[7] There is, of course, a mass of literature on the subject of 'birth-related torts'. The most recent, and very helpful, review of the subject that I have found is content to accept their relevance: Mark Strasser, 'Yes, Virginia, There Can Be Wrongful Life: On Consistency, Public Policy, and the Birth-Related Torts' (2004) 4 *Georgetown Journal of Gender and Law* 821–61.

[8] For an exhaustive survey of the predominantly 1970s cases, see Marten A. Trotzig, 'The Defective Child and the Actions for Wrongful Life and Wrongful Birth' (1980) 14 *Family Law Quarterly* 15–40.

[9] n. 7 above.

[10] ibid., at 823. It will be seen later, for example, that California recognises only two relevant torts – actions for wrongful life brought by the resultant child and actions for wrongful birth brought by the parents (*Turpin* v. *Sortini* (1982) 31 Cal 3d 220).

As to uncertainty within these terms, first, both 'wrongful conception' and 'wrongful pregnancy' are used fairly indiscriminately to describe the situation in which a child is born to a couple who did not want any or any more children and had received expert advice or treatment designed and expected to prevent that happening. Although it is clear that the two represent a continuum, I would prefer, in the context of 'a wrong done', to speak only of wrongful pregnancy. Conception, per se, does a woman no harm – countless pre-implantation embryos are lost without their existence being noted.[11] Only the resulting pregnancy can cause the woman harm or wrong and, to that extent, 'wrongful pregnancy' can hardly be said to be a misnomer – although we will see that it may not be accepted as a term of art.

The same cannot be held in respect of an action for 'wrongful birth' which is raised *by and/or on behalf of the parents* and is, here, taken to mean the birth of a disabled, but otherwise wanted, child which could have been prevented had the defect been detected *in utero* and had the woman, as a consequence, elected for a legal termination of her pregnancy.[12] Clearly, there is nothing wrongful about the birth of a disabled child – indeed, it could be held that, from the implications alone, the retention of the phrase does a disservice to medical jurisprudence as a whole. What are wrongful – and, as we will see later, something may be wrong but still not actionable – are the defective antenatal care and the resulting denial of choice to the pregnant woman. Thus, 'wrongful birth' is not only a misnomer but the action itself fully represents the dangers of particularising a general principle – that of medical negligence. This is certainly not a new criticism. As long ago as 1979, we have the influential American academic, Professor Capron, writing:

[I]t would be easier to recognize a case arising from the birth of a child with a preventable genetic defect as one for appropriate general and special damages to parents and child along the customary lines of tort law if our vision were not impaired by the distorting lenses of 'wrongful life'.[13]

---

[11] Some commentators positively distinguish a 'wrongful conception' from a 'wrongful pregnancy' when the former has been negatived by lawful termination – and this seems a reasonable distinction as the argument as to the allocation of damages may be very different. Even so, any *dolor* derives from the pregnancy. See Bernard Dickens, 'Wrongful Birth and Life, Wrongful Death before Birth and Wrongful Law' in Sheila A. M. McLean (ed.), *Legal Issues in Human Reproduction* (Aldershot: Dartmouth, 1989), chapter 4.

[12] It has to be remembered that, while the majority of jurisdictions world-wide now allow for termination of pregnancy on the grounds of maternal health, not all accept fetal disability of itself as a justification.

[13] Alexander Morgan Capron, 'Tort Liability in Genetic Counselling' (1979) 79 *Columbia Law Review* 618–84 at 634, n. 62. This quotation, of itself, proves the potential confusion

An outstanding recent criticism of the phrase has been voiced by the Supreme Court of Indiana:

It is unnecessary to characterize the cause of an action here as 'wrongful birth' because the facts alleged in the Johnsons' complaint either state a claim for medical malpractice or they do not. Labeling the Johnsons' cause of action as 'wrongful birth' adds nothing to the analysis, inspires confusion, and implies the court has adopted a new tort.[14]

And I would go further – it seems to me that the phrase 'wrongful birth' is frankly confusing as it is applied in the present context.

Yet, of these three basic concepts, it 'wrongful life' that has attracted the greatest controversy and criticism – and it is not only inevitable but it is, surely, right that this should be so. An action for 'wrongful life' is brought by a disabled child who is claiming, basically, that he or she would not have achieved a separate existence were it not for the negligence of the doctor[15] managing the pregnancy.[16] The clear implication of the phrase is that there must be a corrective 'rightful death'. It, therefore, takes us immediately into the moral and emotional minefields of fetal and, by extension, neonatal euthanasia where, for many, the values underlying the importance of human life and the protection of the vulnerable are challenged.[17] It is small wonder that judicial opinions have been influenced by non-legal considerations when dealing with such claims and that the relevant jurisprudence has become distorted. The backlash has, accordingly, been considerable – we have, for example, the Australian High Court Judge Kirby[18] quoting the label of 'wrongful life' as 'unfortunate',[19]

---

as, interestingly, the nomenclature at the time was different. 'Wrongful birth' was said to be associated with the unplanned birth of a *healthy* child; 'wrongful life' concerned the child who was socially or, later, physically disabled and stemmed from the claim of being disabled by virtue of being born illegitimate: *Zepeda* v. *Zepeda* 190 NE 2d 849 (Ill., 1963).

[14] *Bader* v. *Johnson* 732 NE 2d 1212 (Ind., 2000) at 1216, referring back to similar criticism in *Greco* v. *United States* 893 P 2d 345 (Nev. 1995) at 348. The additional point in *Bader* v. *Johnson* is that it was argued from the other side that actions for wrongful birth were barred in Indiana. I admit to having chosen to quote *Bader* for the additional reason that it is the only case I know that refers to 'the troubled pregnancy' (at 1219).

[15] The largely theoretical possibility of an action against the parents is discussed at p. 195 below.

[16] It will be seen that there is very little conceptual difference between actions for wrongful birth and those for wrongful life. The important practical difference is that the former is bought by the parents and the latter by the disabled child. The theory and practice of each, thus, overlap and the two actions are commonly taken in parallel.

[17] As Harvey Teff put it many years ago: 'One is not instinctively attracted to the cause of someone who appears to be impugning life itself', in 'The Action for "Wrongful Life" in England and the United States' (1985) 34 *International and Comparative Law Quarterly* 423–4, at 425.

[18] In *Harriton* v. *Stephens* [2006] HCA 15 at [8].   [19] Quoting Teff, n. 17 above, at 425.

'ill-chosen',[20] 'uninstructive'[21] and 'misleading and decidedly unhelpful'.[22] In his view, its use, even as a shorthand phrase should be avoided – the underlying reason being that, while a neonatal action in negligence might sound, an action under the title of wrongful life is more or less doomed to failure (see Chapter 7).

In short – and we will expand on the theme throughout this book – the three adopted pre-natal torts have been widely criticised almost since their inception. Why should this be so? I doubt if one can answer this better than by quoting from the Supreme Judicial Court of Massachusetts:

> These labels are not instructive. Any 'wrongfulness' lies not in the life, the birth, the conception, or the pregnancy, but in the negligence of the physician. The harm, if any, is not the birth itself but the effect of the defendant's negligence on the parents' physical, emotional, and financial well-being resulting from the denial to the parents of their right, as the case may be, to decide whether to bear a child or whether to bear a child with a genetic or other defect.[23]

Thus, even if it is only to state the obvious, the factor common to all three expressions is negligence on the part of health carers. If, then, we are to derive coherence from what is, essentially, a trans-Atlantic formulation – and if, perhaps, we could prevent its permeating the United Kingdom jurisprudence in its present state[24] – the logical approach is to regard all three as mere facets of medical negligence and apply the general rules of tort law rather than to presume we are dealing with unique entities which must be disentangled from one another. This study has convinced me that this is the correct approach despite the fact that, almost in order to make the point, and in deference to popular usage, I am still using the three categories as a framework for discussion throughout the text.

That being the case, it is inevitable that, despite the fact that much of it is common knowledge, we must, by way of a preface, take a brief look at the current state of the general law related to medical negligence. Those aspects which are of particular significance in pregnancy will be addressed in the relevant chapters.

---

[20] Quoting Joseph S. Kashi, 'The Case of the Unwanted Blessing: Wrongful Life' (1977) 31 *University of Miami Law Review* 1409–32 at 1432, although it is clear that this author interpreted 'wrongful life' in a wider sense.

[21] *Harriton* v. *Stephens* [2002] NSWSC 461 at [8].

[22] Quoting *Lininger* v. *Eisenbaum* 764 P 2d 1202 (Colo., 1988) at 1214.

[23] *Viccaro* v. *Milunsky* 551 NE 2d 8 (Mass., 1990) at 9, n. 3.

[24] We will see that, although the formula has gained some acceptance, it is certainly not consistently implemented – see, for example, the 'post-*McFarlane*' cases discussed at p. 90 below.

An overview of medical negligence

In order to prove medical negligence, it is, as is well known, necessary to demonstrate the three essential elements:

- that the health care professional owed the complainant a duty of care – and this is a *legal* duty which is a matter for the courts to decide;
- that there was a breach of that duty to the extent that the standard of care provided fell below the standard required by the law – thus, although, by definition, this is a legal concern, the courts must, and do, defer to *professional* standards; and
- that, because of that breach, the patient suffered a legally recognisable harm – the problem of *causation*.

This book makes no pretence of covering the subject of medical negligence fully. At this point, little more will be attempted other than to isolate some aspects which have particular relevance to the troubled pregnancy. Their more detailed application will, hopefully, become clear in the following chapters.

The duty of care

Normally, there would be little to say under this heading in the context of medical practice. A woman (or a man) requires medical help; she seeks this from a registered medical practitioner;[25] the practitioner, by agreeing to see her in that capacity, assumes a duty of care. On the face of things, that settles the matter.

However, the situation is surprisingly unclear in the case of the pregnant woman where the question arises as to whether the practitioner owes a coincident duty of care to the fetus. The unborn child, one feels, must have rights of some sort and certainly has interests[26] – but can a person owe a duty of care to a fetus which has no legal persona? The topic arises in several chapters including, paradoxically, that concerned with a fetal interest in *non*-survival.

The standard of care

The basics of the modern standard of care required by the law originate in England and Wales in *Bolam*[27] and in Scotland in *Hunter*

---

[25] It is to be remembered that it is the fact of registration from which the doctor derives both privileges and responsibilities.

[26] The question is crystallised in the European Court of Human Rights case of *Vo* v. *France* (2004) 79 BMLR 71, for which see p. 44 below.

[27] *Bolam* v. *Friern Hospital Management Committee* [1957] 1 WLR 582, (1957) 1 BMLR 1.

v. *Hanley*.[28] Both arrive at much the same conclusion and it will be convenient for present purposes to consider only the former and to refer to the '*Bolam* test'.

The Bolam *test*

The *Bolam* test, which, rather surprisingly for a principle that has had such an impact on medical jurisprudence, originated in a judicial instruction to a jury at first instance,[29] is in two parts. The first deals with standards of care in general:

The test is the standard of the ordinary skilled man exercising and professing to have that special skill. A man need not possess the highest expert skill at the risk of being found negligent. It is well-established law that it is sufficient if he exercises the ordinary skill of an ordinary competent man exercising that particular art.[30]

This, then, defines the professional standard of care which, perhaps surprisingly, is of relatively minor concern to us here. The second part, however, runs:

A doctor is not guilty of negligence if he has acted in accordance with a practice accepted as proper by a responsible body of medical men skilled in that particular art.[31]

This delineates the *legal standard of care* owed by the health care worker to his or her patient and it is a test that, almost perversely, has been accepted unreservedly by the courts of the United Kingdom for almost half a century – and has even been extended from the realm of duty to that of causation.[32] It is a useful test in that it provides a simple benchmark for the courts, whose officers seldom have medical training. Clearly, however, it exposes the possibility that the medical profession is dictating the law to the courts and this cannot be a good thing when medical practitioners are parties to the relevant actions. Moreover, it is open-ended insofar as it does not, for example, limit the 'responsible body of medical

---

[28] 1955 SC 200, 1955 SLT 213.

[29] However, both *Bolam* and *Hunter* were fully supported in the House of Lords in *Maynard* v. *West Midlands Regional Health Authority* [1985] 1 All ER 635.

[30] n. 27 above, per McNair J at WLR 586, BMLR 4.

[31] ibid., at WLR 587, BMLR 5. In respect of the Scottish decision in *Hunter*, McNair J opined that there would be no quarrel as to that expression of opinion not according with English law – 'it is just a question of expression'. Hence, there is no doubt that, despite some minor academic quibbling, the foundation of the law is similar on both sides of the Border.

[32] See *Bolitho* v. *Hackney Health Authority* [1998] AC 232, (1998) 39 BMLR 1, HL.

men' to a majority of medical men.[33] There have, as a result, been a number of attempts to restrict the test. The most significant of these was in *Bolitho*[34] where Lord Browne-Wilkinson said:

[I]f in a rare case, it can be demonstrated that the professional opinion is not capable of withstanding logical analysis, the judge is entitled to hold that the body of opinion is not reasonable or responsible.[35]

While many, including the present writer, would suppose that this was nothing new and was always the case, *Bolitho* was generally considered to represent at least a weakening of the *Bolam* bonds.[36] Even so, it seems to have had very little effect on the lower courts[37] – possibly because the judiciary have retained greater faith in the medical profession than have the politicians:

[I]t is quite impossible for a court to hold that the views sincerely held by doctors of such eminence cannot logically be supported at all ... and the views of the defendants' witnesses were views which could be logically expressed and held by responsible doctors.[38]

Nevertheless, the courts have, simultaneously, sought to restrict the *Bolam* test in a more practical and effective way by limiting its influence to establishing whether or not a course of medical action is founded on responsible practice. For example:

[The *Bolam* test] is a necessary, but not sufficient, condition of treatment in the patient's best interests ... [Medical opinion] is relevant to the question whether

---

[33] Sir John Donaldson MR sought to restrict the interpretation to a body 'rightly regarded as responsible' in *Sidaway* v. *Board of Governors of the Bethlem Royal Hospital and the Maudsley Hospital* [1984] QB 493, [1984] 1 All ER 1018, CA, but got little support from the rest of the court.

[34] n. 32 above.   [35] n. 32 above, at AC 243, BMLR 10.

[36] For a thorough review of the current situation, see Margaret Brazier and José Miola, 'Bye-bye *Bolam*: A medical litigation revolution?' (2000) 8 *Medical Law Review* 85–114. See also John Keown, 'Reining in the *Bolam* Test' (1998) 57 *Cambridge Law Journal* 248–50.

[37] Post-*Bolitho* cases of relevance have been extensively researched by Alasdair Maclean, 'Beyond *Bolam* and *Bolitho*' (2002) 5 *Medical Law International* 205–30. Three 'transition' cases which the interested reader may find useful are: *Wisniewski* v. *Central Manchester Health Authority* [1998] Lloyd's Rep Med 223; *Marriott* v. *West Midlands Regional Health Authority* [1999] Lloyd's Rep Med 23; and *Penney* v. *East Kent Health Authority* (2000) 55 BMLR 63, [2000] Lloyd's Rep Med 41. Unfortunately, none of these provides a straightforward answer to the status of *Bolam* at the time.

[38] Per Brooke LJ in *Wisniewski* v. *Central Manchester Health Authority*, n. 37 above. *Wisniewski* is a very useful case for consideration of the test of logic. It is to be noted that Lord Browne-Wilkinson himself made very similar observations at a general level: 'I emphasise that, in my view, it will very seldom be right for a judge to reach the conclusion that views genuinely held by a competent medical expert are unreasonable': *Bolitho*, n. 32 above, at AC 243, BMLR 10.

it is in the patient's best interests or medically necessary, but it is no more than that[39]

and we will note several further examples in the main text.

The patient's decision

Modern medicine is, however, no longer a matter of selection and imposition of a form of treatment on a receptive patient. Professional practice has always been governed by ethical principles but, in the past, these have largely been formulated by the health-caring professions themselves. In recent times, however, medical ethics have been increasingly subject to outside control and can now be said to be mainly structured under the rubric of 'principlism',[40] of which the concept of the autonomy of the individual is undoubtedly currently the most demanding – it has, indeed, become the governing principle of medical law. Choice is an integral part of autonomy which, in the present context is, essentially, the right to control what is done to one's body and the ability to make an autonomous choice depends upon being adequately informed.

The result has been that the provision of information by way of which the patient can make an intelligent choice of – and, hence, a valid consent to – treatment is now established as a major aspect of medical care. Failure in a duty can, as we have seen, result in actionable negligence and, as consequence of the amalgam of all these factors, a very distinct jurisprudence has built up in the last half century under the general heading of information based negligence. Medical negligence is, therefore, no longer a simple matter of sub-standard technique but is also one of inadequate communication with the patient.

Despite its now major contribution to medical law in general, negligent communication in the compass of this book is so much a matter of ante-natal counselling that I propose to delay discussion of the principles until we get to that subject in Chapter 3. Even so, there will be few areas in the book as a whole where the modern importance of doctor/patient communication is not self-evident.

Causation

Once again, the intricacies of the construct of causation within the tort of negligence are very considerable and it would be out of place here to

---

[39] *R. (on the application of N)* v. *Doctor M and others* [2003] 1 FLR 667, (2002) 72 BMLR 81 at [29]. This was a case of disputed treatment rather than of negligence.

[40] For which, see T. L. Beauchamp and J. F. Childress *Principles of Biomedical Ethics* (New York: Oxford University Press, 5th edn 2001).

attempt more than a reminder of these. Put at its simplest, it means that the patient who has sustained a recompensable injury as a result of negligence must show that the negligence *caused* the injury if he or she is to be successful in an action – in short, can the injured claimant prove that he or she would now be normal *but for* the health carer's negligence? On the face of things, this should raise few problems; in practice, it often presents as the major hurdle to be overcome. A few examples will suffice.

First, it may be asked: did the admitted negligence make any difference? *Bolitho*, which has been mentioned above, was a case in point. In that case, the house officer failed to attend an emergency. Medical opinion – at least, in *Bolam* terms, a responsible body of medical opinion – was, however, to the effect that inaction was the treatment of choice, thus, causation could not be shown. A more apposite example in the present context is to be found in the doctor who fails to diagnose the possibility of intra-uterine fetal viral infection; the fetus is born severely disabled – but can the doctor be said to have *caused* the injury? Analysis of this question occupies a major part of Chapter 6. Alternatively, is it possible to distinguish between the effects of the patient's condition and those of his or her treatment? Is, for example, a child's deafness due to the meningitis from which s/he was suffering or to the excess penicillin that was negligently used in treatment?[41] Can we say with probability that a fetal disability was *due* to the medication prescribed to the mother?[42] How do we choose the cause of an injury when there are several competing possibilities?[43] The list is close to endless but, for present purposes, perhaps the most important example relates specifically to information-based negligence whereby, before she can succeed in her action, the complainant must show that she would have *acted on the information* had it been properly presented – and it may be a difficult task to convince a judge who has, so to speak, 'been there before'. For these reasons, further consideration of the causation issue is, again, deferred until Chapter 3.

Having reminded ourselves of these general principles, we can now go forward to discuss how they apply in the particular context of the troubled pregnancy.

---

[41] See, for example, *Kay's Tutor* v. *Ayrshire and Arran Health Board* [1987] 2 All ER 417, 1987 SLT 577, HL.

[42] The well-known thalidomide case was argued for several years in Germany and was eventually settled out of court: Pamela R. Ferguson, *Drug Injuries and the Pursuit of Compensation* (London: Sweet & Maxwell, 1996) at 127.

[43] Although unrelated to reproductive medicine, *Wilsher* v. *Essex Area Health Authority* [1988] AC 1074, [1988] 1 All ER 871, HL, gives a good example of the arguments that can be developed.

2 Voluntary and involuntary termination of pregnancy

Introduction

One cannot help feeling that the topic of abortion has been argued for so long and with such intensity that there can be nothing new left to say – and this leads to some doubt as to the value of a chapter on the subject in this book. Nevertheless, it is one that still arouses intense emotions and there are few people who, when challenged, will not express strong opinions on the ethical and sociological expedience of voluntary termination of pregnancy. As a result, personal attitudes tend to be polarised.[1] We can, however, say, with a sense of relief, that the abortion issue leads to less conflict in the United Kingdom than it does in many other parts of the world. But this is not because we have adopted a middle view – indeed, it is doubtful if it is possible to do so. Rather, there is a sense of war-weariness accompanied by something of a tacit agreement to stop fighting about it, an attitude that helps to explain the paucity of case law that abortion, per se, has spawned in this country.[2] Even so, strongly held views that are suppressed are dormant, not deceased. They can be aroused whenever a new situation arises and, given the intense activity in the field of reproduction that is so much a feature of modern medical innovation, relevant new questions are likely to arise at any time – as is evidenced by the flurry of intellectual and parliamentary activity, albeit at an unofficial level, which arose in early 2006, particularly in relation to late terminations.[3]

---

[1] There are very few other topics about which one could read in a prestigious journal: 'On [X]'s view, abortion is almost never permissible; on my view, abortion is almost always permissible' – M. T. Brown, 'A Future Like Ours Revisited' (2002) 28 *Journal of Medical Ethics* 192–5.

[2] This contrasts with the American experience where physical violence combines with continued legal action which includes accusations of racketeering and extortion: *Scheidler* v. *National Organization for Women, Inc.* 537 US 393 (2003). For a general comparison, see Colin Francome, *Abortion in the USA and the UK* (Aldershot: Ashgate Publishing, 2004).

[3] By reason, generally, of 'the advances in modern neonatal care since 1967'. See BBC News 'Cardinal Urges Abortion Rethink', 21 June 2006 at http://news.bbc.co.uk/2/hi/health/5099362.stm.

This brings us to a second reason why we must start this book with a basic look at abortion legislation and practice – that is, that it is intimately associated with almost every current medico-legal problem that is discussed in the following chapters. Voluntary termination presents as an available alternative, or a significant factor, in the management of the troubled pregnancy in all its forms and it is, of course, the ultimate expression of the unwanted pregnancy. For good or for bad, it lies at the heart of this book and, at the risk of covering too much old ground, it must be addressed before any other of the several topics that follow.

Definitions

It is important that we are clear as to the nature of the subject insofar as there is particular confusion between the expressions 'miscarriage' and 'abortion'. The great majority of readers would, I believe, regard a miscarriage as the natural loss of an early fetus.[4] A difficulty here, however, is that the Offences Against the Person Act 1861, sections 58 and 59, in which the core abortion law in England and Wales is to be found, describe the offence of 'procuring the miscarriage of a woman' – the word 'abortion' occurs only in a marginal note. Procuring a miscarriage is, however, decriminalised in certain circumstances which are defined in the Abortion Act 1967; it is, therefore, reasonable to assume that the law makes no distinction between the two terms.

Even so, the 1967 Act is itself coy in the use of the word 'abortion', which appears only indirectly in relation to other 'law relating to abortion'. Elsewhere, the Act speaks only of 'termination of pregnancy' and it is worth remembering that the 1967 Act was born and nurtured until the last moment as the Medical Termination of Pregnancy Bill.[5] I myself think that the volte-face was unfortunate. The word 'abortion' – together with its correlate 'abortionist' – has strong criminal associations, whereas the 1967 Act has, at best, a minimal criminal interest and is, essentially, a decriminalising instrument. Nonetheless, although I prefer, where possible, to refer to therapeutic termination of pregnancy in those terms, the synonymous use of the word 'abortion' is so widespread that it cannot be avoided.

---

[4] An *early* fetus because the loss of a fetus in the third trimester of pregnancy might equally be regarded as a premature birth.

[5] The change of name was a 'last ditch' stratagem designed to satisfy those who saw the measure in terms of women's rights rather than as a medical treatment.

The fetal persona

Definition, however, goes deeper than that and the abortion debate hinges essentially on the further definition of what it is that is being removed when pregnancy is terminated. It is certainly human tissue – that is a mater of fact. Beyond that, is it a mere adjunct of its mother or is it a human entity having its own humanity? And, if we say that it is the latter, we must go still further and ask is it a human being or is it a human person? These questions have, of course, been argued in depth by an infinite number of commentators[6] and no attempt at a detailed analysis is to be attempted here. In particular, I will ignore the philosophy which tells us that no human being is entitled to the respect due to a human person until he or she is capable of what is, essentially, a cognitive existence[7] – simply because it represents, at the same time, a further invitation to infanticide.[8] At the same time, I take it as read that a fetus, being human and in being, is a human being. The popular answer to that dogmatic approach, it seems, is that it depends on the age of the fetus at the time of the termination – the so-called 'gradualist' approach to the abortion dilemma, by which the fetal claim to recognition strengthens as the organism itself develops.

I return to this later on but, presently, and without prejudice to the outcome of the debate, I find this a difficult position to accept in logic. Fetal development is a slow process which demonstrates no dramatic changes related to moments in time. There is no essential developmental distinction between the fetus in the third stage of labour and the neonate; the fetus that has quickened is indistinguishable from one that is awakening; the embryo immediately before implantation does not differ from one that has just embedded in the uterine mucosa. In short, while one can think and speak of stages in fetal development, they remain stages in the development of *the same* fetus and there is no logical reason to accord it a

---

[6] Of which the following is a cross-section: Baruch Brody, *Abortion and the Sanctity of Human Life: A Philosophical View* (Cambridge, Mass.: MIT Press, 1985); Michael Tooley, *Abortion and Infanticide* (Oxford: Clarendon Press, 1983); R. N. Wennberg, *Life in the Balance* (Grand Rapids: W. B. Eerdmans, 1985); Norman M. Ford, *When Did I Begin?* (Cambridge: Cambridge University Press, 1991); Bonnie Steinbock, *Life before Birth: The Moral and Legal Status of Embryos and Fetuses* (New York: Oxford University Press, 1992). Probably the most publicised early article is that by Judith Jarvis Thomson, 'A Defense of Abortion' (1971) 1 *Philosophy and Public Affairs* 47–66.

[7] For which Tooley, n. 6 above is probably the best known advocate. See also Daniel Callahan, *Abortion, Law, Choice and Morality* (New York: Macmillan, 1970).

[8] Used in its popular sense. In strict English law, infanticide is the killing of a child aged less than one year by its mother when she is in a state of diminished responsibility.

different respect based on its age. The only point at which there is a major and immediate change in status is when it is formed – that is, at fertilisation of the ovum. There is, therefore, much to be said for adopting the conservative Roman Catholic view that human life begins at conception.

I make no secret of my moral support for the recognition of an individual fetal identity which carries with it individual fetal rights. Even so, the clear difficulty with the above analysis is that it takes no account of potentiality. If we accept it, we must also attribute full human existence to the embryo in vitro and, while one must agree with the Warnock Committee that the human embryo in the Petri dish ought to have a special status,[9] that seems to carry the proposition too far. It does, for example, place the death of a genetically abnormal embryo during pre-implantation diagnosis on a par with the abortion of a genetically abnormal fetus – and comparatively few would agree that this is, in fact, the case.[10] The in vitro embryo has no future in itself; left undisturbed, its only destiny is death – in short, it cannot have a human existence, or what has been called a 'future of value',[11] without a change of ambience. The same applies to the embryo in its passage to the uterine environment and, in either case, the critical change occurs at implantation. Thus, while admitting that it carries an element of pragmatism, I conclude that it is at the point of implantation that meaningful human life begins.[12]

Such a view may go some way to satisfying the doubts one may have as to the morality of assisted reproduction as currently practised, but it has no practical effect on the abortion debate. The concept of undertaking a termination of pregnancy before implantation is absurd[13] and it follows that any distinction between the theories that place the beginning of human life at conception and at implantation is inconsequential in the present context. Moreover, I have already argued the case for regarding the *moral* status of the implanted fetus as being unaffected by its

[9] Dame Mary Warnock (Chairman), *Report of the Committee of Inquiry into Human Fertilisation and Embryology* (1984), Cmnd. 9314.

[10] For discussion, see C. Cameron and R. Williamson 'Is there an Ethical Difference between Preimplantation Genetic Diagnosis and Abortion?' (2003) 29 *Journal of Medical Ethics* 90–2. I return to this point later.

[11] The deprivation of a future of value has been cited as a major reason for regarding abortion as unacceptable: Don Marquis, 'Why Abortion is Immoral' (1989) 86 *Journal of Philosophy* 183–202. For a critique, see J. Savulescu, 'Abortion, Embryo Destruction and the Future of Value Argument' (2002) 28 *Journal of Medical Ethics* 133–5.

[12] For a recent criticism of this view, see Margot Brazier,'Human(s) (as) Medicine(s)' in Sheila A. M. McLean (ed.), *First Do No Harm: Law, Ethics and Health Care* (Aldershot: Ashgate Publishing, 2006), chapter 12.

[13] And is legally untenable – see *R (on the application of Smeaton)* v. *Secretary of State for Health* [2002] 2 FLR 146, (2002) 66 BMLR 59.

maturity.[14] It follows that I regard abortion at any stage of gestation as the taking of human life – the problem, then, is to establish how this can be justified within the twin sets of principles of medico-legal ethics and medical law.

Opposition to abortion does not, of itself, constitute an attack on a woman's right to respect for privacy in her life. No-one would deny that such rights exist. We have, however, seen that, despite the fact that the law bestows no *legal rights* on the unborn fetus,[15] it is difficult, and undesirable, to avoid accepting that the fetus has at least some *moral rights*.[16] The problem, then, is to decide whether a woman's right to privacy is to be regarded as one that is absolute or qualified.

The orthodox feminist position adopts the former view, and this is, at least in part, supported by the legal presumption as to fetal rights. In effect, it can be argued that there is no such thing as maternal/fetal conflict because a conflict involves two persons – and the fetus is not a person.[17] The 'rights discourse' is, however, relatively unimportant in the context of this book which is, essentially, based on the law as it stands. Even so, the law in the United Kingdom, in guarding our rights, undoubtedly adopts a Janus-faced position on this particular issue. True, the fetus has no legal rights and, as we will discuss briefly later on, there is no such offence as feticide; yet, specifically and uniquely, it qualifies a woman's right to determine her own bodily integrity – and, in so doing, indirectly protects fetal life – by prohibiting her securing her own miscarriage or enlisting the help in doing so of anyone other than a registered medical practitioner.[18] Paradoxically, however, it is the very attempt to resolve this dichotomy by way of a balancing act that provokes the strongest criticism. To quote Professor McLean:

[14] Popular usage has it that an embryo becomes a fetus at eight weeks' maturation – see *Smeaton*, n. 13 above at [143–7]. I can see no logical or physiological reason for making such a distinction and throughout this book I reserve the term 'embryo' for the pre-implantation stage of development; thus, an implanted embryo becomes, terminologically, a fetus.

[15] This scarcely needs supporting evidence but see, inter alia, *Paton v. British Pregnancy Advisory Service Trustees* [1979] QB 276; *Attorney-General's Reference (No. 3 of 1994)* [1998] AC 245; *Hamilton v. Fife Health Board* 1993 SC 369.

[16] The abortion debate is dissolved if you consider the fetus to be a human non-person – see John Harris, 'Consent and End of Life Decisions' (2003) 29 *Journal of Medical Ethics* 10–15. A cognitive personhood theory, however, also involves regarding the neonate as a non-person – a position that is legally unsustainable.

[17] Of a mass of feminist literature, the reader is referred to the succinct account in Sheila McLean, *Old Law, New Medicine* (London, Pandora Press, 1999); the argument quoted above is to be found at p. 51.

[18] Offences Against the Person Act 1861, ss. 58 and 59 as interpreted by the Abortion Act 1967. The 1861 Act does not run to Scotland where the position is covered by common law. It is extremely unlikely that a woman would be prosecuted for procuring her own miscarriage in Scotland.

Showing respect for the embryo/foetus at the expense of women's rights is a monumental misunderstanding of the concept of respect and a perverse interpretation of the value of human rights. It is to the law's shame that it has in the past colluded in this to the detriment of women.[19]

Clearly, then, we must look more closely at the problem – and from both sides. First, we will consider the nature of fetal status.

Recognition of fetal status

Although, as already explained, I find it hard to see any moral distinction on the basis of fetal maturity in respect of fetal protection – and I am not entirely alone in this respect[20] – it is almost inevitable in practice that the weight given to fetal interests in the balance should be held to depend, in some measure, on the stage of fetal development – for it is this which dictates its potential for an independent existence. Inevitably, then, the discussion reverts, primarily, to the concept of fetal viability.

The viable fetus. Viability is essentially an American concept stemming from the seminal Supreme Court decision in the historic case of *Roe* v. *Wade*.[21] Here, as is only too well known, the Court laid down its 'three trimester' rule which can be summarised:

- In the first trimester, the possibility of a termination was a matter to be resolved solely between the pregnant woman and her physician;
- During the second trimester, the state could intervene by reason of its interest in the health of the mother;
- Once the fetus was viable – a point which the court assessed as lying between the twenty-fourth and twenty-eighth week of pregnancy – the state had a compelling interest in the preservation of life and could, therefore, intervene on its behalf except when the conditions threatened the life or the health of its mother.

Consequent upon the several definitional doubts left open by the ruling, the American case law on abortion has become massive.[22] For present purposes, however, we can extract two points which are of immediate

---

[19] McLean, n. 17 above, at 69.

[20] In *Re F (in utero)* [1988] Fam 122, [1988] 2 All ER 193, an attempt was made to ward a child *in utero*; it was conceded that this could only apply to a viable fetus. Balcombe LJ had this to say: 'While I understand the practical reasons for this concession, it does not appear to me to rest on any logical basis ... If there is jurisdiction to protect a foetus ... I do not see why that jurisdiction should start only at a time when the foetus is capable of being born alive' (at Fam 142, All ER 199).

[21] 410 US 113 (1973), 98 S Ct 705 (1973).

[22] A recent review is to be found in Francome, n. 2 above.

interest from the United Kingdom perspective. First, the American juris-prudence is founded very largely on American constitutional law and, particularly, on the right to privacy that it embraces.[23] It has, therefore, had very little influence on the United Kingdom situation. Second, its concentration on viability certainly preserved some rights for the fetus but at the same time, left these ill-defined as to the limits of enforcement[24] – this being because viability is something of an artificial construct.

There are two complementary reasons for this. First, although the correlation of fetal development with its gestational age is remarkably consistent, not all fetuses will have a similar capacity for life despite being of similar gestation. More importantly, there comes a time when viability depends not only on fetal anatomo-physiology but equally, or even more so, on the neonatal environment – and, in particular, on the quality of medical assistance that is available after birth. These led the Justice of the Supreme Court, O'Connor, to the now famous truism:

The lines drawn [in *Roe*] have become blurred ... The State can longer rely on a 'bright line' that separates permissible from impermissible regulation ... Rather, the State must continuously and conscientiously study contemporary medical and scientific literature in order to determine whether the effect of a particular regu-lation is to 'depart from accepted medical practice'.[25]

And, as we have already noted, it is the reality of such medical and scientific progress that has recently rekindled the abortion debate in the United Kingdom where it has, in effect, lain dormant for decades.

Despite its American origins, the concept of viability is not entirely foreign to United Kingdom law. The offence of child destruction was defined in the English Infant Life (Preservation) Act 1929 as intentionally causing the death of a child capable of being born alive before it had an existence independent of its mother.[26] Live birth has been defined as a child:

that is breathing and living by reason of its breathing through its own lungs alone, without deriving any of its living or power of living by or through any connection with its mother.[27]

---

[23] Based on the interpretation of the 14th Amendment and the protection of liberty and privacy in particular. Are the resultant 'rights' absolute or must they yield to compelling State interests even if the right, itself, is, in US terms, 'fundamental'?

[24] Indeed, the Supreme Court refused to be drawn on the point leaving the assessment to the physicians in individual cases.

[25] In *Akron (City of)* v. *Akron Center for Reproductive Health* 462 US 416 (1983) at 455–6.

[26] The original Abortion Act 1967, s.5(1) described the 1929 Act as 'protecting the life of a viable foetus'; this sentence has, however, now been deleted: Human Fertilisation and Embryology Act 1990, s.37(4).

[27] *Rance* v. *Mid-Downs Health Authority* [1991] 1 QB 587, (1991) 5 BMLR 75, per Brooke J at QB 621, BMLR 92.

Theoretically, therefore, a distinction is to be made between 'live birth' and 'viability' insofar as there is no time requirement imposed on the former whereas the term 'viable', if for no reason other than popular usage, implies survival for a reasonable, albeit undefined, time.[28] Brooke J, however, disposed of this quibble in holding that the statutory use of the word 'viable'[29] was no more than 'a convenient shorthand for the words "capable of being born alive"'.[30] To this extent, therefore, viability does have a place in the English jurisdiction; the temporal limitations on legal termination of pregnancy are, therefore, very similar on both sides of the Atlantic and are probably so, at least, throughout the Anglophone world. It is, however, to be remembered that the fetal lung is morphologically incapable of oxygenating the blood until development is reasonably advanced – Brooke J's definition, thus, clearly sets a limit on viability irrespective of the state of medical technology,[31] and that watershed can be placed at approximately 22 weeks' gestation.

For present purposes, however, we must concentrate more closely on the *overall* significance of viability in the abortion debate and one can legitimately separate this into moral and practical components. As to the former, it is clear from what has gone before, that I cannot see that viability provides us with any morally significant division between what is an acceptable and what is an unacceptable termination of an apparently normal pregnancy. The fetus that is just non-viable is the same fetus as will be viable in the near future; there is no moral difference in destroying it at either side of the, admittedly, ephemeral dividing line. The difficulty, however, is that, as we have already discussed, the same can be said of the fetus at *any* stage of development following implantation. The logical conclusion is that termination of pregnancy at any time, other than for recognisable medical reasons,[32] must be regarded as morally offensive. While this, roughly speaking, represents my personal stance, it disregards the many arguments in favour of legalised abortion – to which we will return briefly below; moreover, we live in a community and the 1967 Act has withstood the test of time – there is no doubt that, rightly or wrongly, the majority of the community support the policy that has been adopted by successive governments and is firmly entrenched within the legal system. But, in so saying, we have moved from deontological considerations to those governed by policy – or, perhaps, to a form of

---

[28] It was also so defined as 'capable of meaningful life outside the womb' in *Roe* v. *Wade* at 410 US 163.

[29] *Rance*, n. 27 above.   [30] ibid., at QB 622, BMLR 93.

[31] See also Sir John Donaldson MR in *C* v. *S* [1988] QB 135 at 151, (1992) 2 BMLR 143 at 157.

[32] The sophistry of the Abortion Act in this respect is discussed further below.

communitarian ethics. Put another way: 'to believe that most (if not all) abortions are immoral is not necessarily to believe that a legislature should criminalize most abortions'.[33]

In essence, the viability 'standard' is one expression of the violability justification of abortion. Under this mantle, we start from the premise that human life is inviolable[34] – that is to say a human being is 'not to be violated: not liable or allowed to suffer violence: and to be kept free from ... assault'.[35] Since it is admitted that the fetus is a human being, the ethical key to the impasse lies in establishing that there is a period in fetal development when it is not inviolable – in other words, it has not achieved some property that distinguishes a mass of human tissue from a human being.[36] The difficulty then becomes that of identifying that necessary property.

The most tangible of these, physiologically speaking, is the appearance of the primitive streak, which represents the incipient formation of the central nervous system; it is only at this point that we can be certain that we are dealing with an individual being.[37] But, while this is of major importance in the management of the embryo in vitro, it has negligible significance in the abortion debate.[38]

The other clear candidate for endowing the fetus with the non-violable status is viability or, as defined in English law, a capacity to be born alive.[39] In theory, at least, it is impossible to make a moral distinction between the viable fetus and the pre-term neonate given, again, the point that the only physical difference between them lies in their environment. It would be wrong to treat them differently,[40] and both are protected by law.[41] The particular significance here, however, is that the equation of

---

[33] Michael J. Perry, *Under God?* (Cambridge: Cambridge University Press, 2003), p. 99. I am much indebted to chapter 6 – 'Religion, Politics and Abortion' – in this relatively recent book.

[34] Though, in all fairness it has to be said that the justification for this is based on no more than that the being *is* human. Some, for example, question whether it is proper to distinguish humans from other animals on this shaky foundation – e.g. Peter Singer, *Rethinking Life and Death* (New York, St. Martin's Press, 1995).

[35] *Perry*, n. 33 above, at 102.

[36] See, for example, Stanley Rudman, *Concepts of Person and Christian Ethics* (Cambridge: Cambridge University Press, 1997).

[37] As is well known, this is why the *Report of the Committee of Inquiry into Human Fertilisation and Embryology*, n. 9 above, chose this 'property' as the point beyond which a human embryo should not be maintained alive in vitro and unfrozen.

[38] It would be significant were the discussion related to so-called menstrual extraction or contragestation techniques. Abortion, however, refers in common usage to the termination of a *diagnosed* pregnancy.

[39] *Rance*, n. 27 above.

[40] As will be seen in Chapter 7, where the management of the disabled neonate is discussed.

[41] The Infant Life (Preservation) Act 1929 does not run to Scotland where the validity of an offence comparable to child destruction is uncertain.

inviolability and viability lends moral justification to the current move to lower to 22 weeks, at least, the basic gestational age beyond which termination of pregnancy, other than to preserve the life of the mother, would be unlawful.[42] But, of course, this concession to the fetal interest can, and will do little to satisfy those who regard viability as no more than one stage in the development of an existing human being.

To define what may *not* be done is, however, a negative approach – something of an apologia. It is intellectually more honest to define an 'acceptable' abortion in positive terms – always, of course, assuming that there is such an entity – and to decide when a termination on 'social' grounds would be morally and legally permissible. Arguably, in the light of the previous discussion, the answer could be the termination of any pregnancy involving a non-viable fetus and this, as we will see, is effectively the position adopted in the United Kingdom. Other jurisdictions – indeed, possibly the majority of those that do not disapprove abortion outright other than to avoid danger to the life of the mother[43] – are more restrictive and adopt a gestational age of 10 to 12 weeks as the point at which the inviolability of the fetus is accepted, at least to a modified extent. But, if we follow my argument as outlined above, it follows that there is no reason to presuppose a change in fetal status at this stage. Wherein, then, lies the justification of what appears to be a policy decision?

First, of course, there is the undoubted instinctive distaste for the deliberate mutilation of a fetus that has all the physical attributes of a human being – witness, as a special case, the repugnance with which termination by so-called 'partial birth' has been greeted in the United States.[44] That, of itself, however, would be unlikely to provide sufficient reason in a pluralistic society by which to make a logical case for separating attitudes to the termination of early and late non-viable fetuses. An alternative and more likely ground would be to consider the effect on the pregnant woman insofar as late terminations are associated with significant maternal morbidity while, by contrast, it is everywhere agreed that an early termination carries less risk to the mother than does a normal pregnancy. This, in effect, is to apply the *Roe* v. *Wade* trimester test which, both in practice and, at best, paralogic, results in termination on demand in the first twelve weeks of pregnancy.

---

[42] In fact, less than 1 per cent of terminations are currently carried out between 22 and 24 weeks' gestation: (2005) 206 *Bulletin of Medical Ethics* 6.

[43] Which, within the European Union, includes the Republic of Ireland, Poland, Malta, Andorra, San Marino and Liechtenstein.

[44] See *Stenberg* v. *Carhart* 530 US 914 (2000) and the consequent passage of the Partial-Birth Abortion Ban Act 2003 through Congress.

Maternal status

The purpose behind this discussion of fetal status has been an attempt to balance the abortion debate in terms of what is loosely called 'human dignity' as it applies to the developing fetus. Inevitably, such an approach must favour the fetus in that it stresses the value of fetal life. There is no reference to fetal rights insofar as there are no such things in legal terms[45] save those that arise indirectly by way of restriction of the rights of others. Those rights that are most likely to be circumscribed in relation to pregnancy are those of the pregnant woman; we must therefore consider, if only briefly, the nature of those rights and to what extent they are infringed by the Abortion Act.

The starting point for this must be the unarguable right of any person to the integrity of his or her body. Personal autonomy is now so deeply entrenched as a guiding principle in medical law as to be accepted almost without question[46] – the most impressive example in recent years lying in the case of *Ms B*[47] in which a hospital was actually fined, albeit nominally, for refusing to disconnect, on the demand of the patient, apparatus on which her life depended. For present purposes, however, the more important exemplar case is that of *Re MB*[48] in which the Court of Appeal upheld the right of a pregnant woman to refuse treatment even though this would result in the death of a full-term fetus.[49] It is, therefore, apparent that, outside the Abortion Act, the pregnant woman's autonomy takes precedence over the well-being even of a *viable* fetus. To evaluate the significance of this, we must look at the wording of the relevant section of the 1967 Act as modified by the Human Fertilisation and Embryology Act 1990, section 37.

---

[45] The concept of value is well argued by Rosamund Scott, 'The English Fetus and the Right to Life' (2004) 11 *European Journal of Health Law* 347–64.

[46] Although there is a noticeable undercurrent of increasing respect for the community's values: Onara O'Neill, *Autonomy and Trust in Bioethics* (Cambridge: Cambridge University Press, 2002); G. M. Stirrat and R. Gill, 'Autonomy in Medical Ethics after O'Neill' (2005) 31 *Journal of Medical Ethics* 127–130; Katherine O'Donovan and Roy Gilbar, 'The Loved Ones: Families, Intimates and Patient Autonomy' (2003) 23 *Legal Studies* 332–58.

[47] *B* v. *NHS Hospital Trust* [2002] 2 All ER 449, (2002) 65 BMLR 149.

[48] *Re MB (an adult: medical treatment)* [1997] 8 Med LR 217, (1997) 38 BMLR 175, CA. Similar reasoning was followed in *St George's Healthcare NHS Trust* v. *S, R* v. *Collins, ex p S* [1998] 3 All ER 673, (1998) 44 BMLR 160.

[49] Thus overriding Lord Donaldson who had previously opined that the only situation in which a doctor might treat in the face of a valid refusal was when that choice might lead to the death of a viable fetus: *Re T (adult) (refusal of medical treatment)* [1992] 4 All ER 649 at 652–3, (1992) 9 BMLR 46 at 50, CA.

The Abortion Act 1967

In summary, section 1(1) now states that a person shall not be guilty of an offence under the law of abortion when termination is performed by a registered medical practitioner and two registered medical practitioners are of the opinion, formed in good faith –

(a) that the pregnancy has not exceeded its twenty-fourth week[50] and that the continuance of the pregnancy would involve risk, greater than if the pregnancy were terminated, of injury to the physical or mental health of the pregnant woman or any existing children of her family; or

(b) that the termination is necessary to prevent grave permanent injury to the physical or mental health of the pregnant woman;[51]

(c) that the continuance of the pregnancy would involve risk to the life of the pregnant woman greater than if the pregnancy were terminated;[52] or

(d) that there is a substantial risk that, if the child were born, it would suffer from such physical or mental abnormalities as to be severely handicapped.[53]

Termination under the Act may be carried out in National Health Service hospitals or in places approved for the purpose by the Minister or the Secretary of State (s. 1(3)). It is this clause which legalises abortions performed privately and for a fee.

It is very doubtful if much further discussion of grounds b) and c) is necessary. No jurisdiction gainsays the absolute right of the pregnant woman to preserve her life should it be jeopardised by continuance of the pregnancy. My information is that mainstream Roman Catholic teaching will also accept the rule when the situation arises – the doctor is entitled to follow good medical practice, subject, of course, to the proviso that he or she is morally bound, by Catholic teaching, to attempt to save both mother and child if that is possible. And that, in practice, will likely be everyone's choice.

It is to be noted, however, that terminations under heading (c) will, generally, be late; the woman concerned has wanted her baby, she has carried it to near term and its loss is a tragedy, albeit necessary – they pose

---

[50] As amended by Human Fertilisation and Embryology Act 1990, s.37(1).

[51] It is to be noted that s. 1(1)(b) contains no comparative element – there simply has to be a risk.

[52] Subsections (b) and (c) are not restricted by requiring the opinion of two registered medical practitioners; single practitioners may act on their own initiative in such circumstances.

[53] Discussion of this last ground will be postponed until Chapter 3.

problems that are wholly different from those associated with what is generally understood as an abortion. Much the same applies to reason (b) although the termination may, of course, be indicated far earlier in the pregnancy. However, although they are of a special character, subsections 1(1)(b) and (c) are significant in the present context in that they impose no restriction on the woman's right to control her own body. The doctor/ patient relationship is on a normal one-to-one footing and she can make her choice without undertaking any enforced balancing act between fetal and maternal interests. Thus far, then, the Act is consistent with the rulings in *Re MB* and *St George's Healthcare NHS Trust* v. *S.*[54]

It is, however, section 1(1)(a), which lies at the heart of the abortion debate, and it is there that we need to consider seriously the impact of the 1967 Act on women's rights. It would be possible to fill a large book doing no more than reviewing the literature on this single point. Collaterally, it is extremely difficult to extract an individual view to represent the so-called 'pro-choice' lobby and which will be regarded as fairly chosen. Because of our very close academic association over many years, I turn to Professor McLean who puts the problem succinctly:

> The liberty to decide may or may not in fact result in a truly free choice, but it is certain that a free choice will never be possible unless reproductive liberty (including the right to terminate pregnancies) is seen as an issue which transcends clinical 'facts' and medical capacities and becomes focussed on the real issue – namely, women's freedom from the biological lottery.[55]

The attack on the Abortion Act is, thus, two-pronged. Firstly, it is condemned as not being 'rights based'[56] and, secondly, as a corollary, it has transferred the right to self-determination from individual women to the medical profession – 'scientific cant has reduced a matter of human rights to one of medical monopoly'[57] – and both these criticisms can be legitimately levelled at section 1(1)(a). At the same time, given that the former depends upon the latter, they are indivisible – and this gives rise to some contradictory and inconsistent results.

On the one hand, for example, medicalising abortion places it firmly within the general management of pregnancy and, as such, it is governed by ethical medical practice as a whole. Thus, third party intervention

---

[54] n. 48 above.

[55] McLean, n. 17 above at 83. The more deeply interested reader should study Emily Jackson, *Regulating Reproduction: Law, Technology and Autonomy* (Oxford: Hart Publishing, 2001).

[56] Jackson, n. 55 above, believes that the passage of the 1967 Act depended largely on 'the reformers' astute presentation of legal abortion as a measure designed to promote public health, rather than an issue of women's rights' (at 84).

[57] McLean, n. 17 above, at 91.

within a doctor/patient relationship is inadmissible[58] and the matter of termination is one to be resolved between the patient and her doctor. So far so good, but, almost uniquely by modern day standards – and inconsistently with *Re MB* and *St George's Healthcare* – the woman does *not* have the last say in arranging her treatment; instead, two doctors must form the opinion that termination is the *right* treatment – at least in a prophylactic sense. As Brazier crystallises the position: 'Abortion in England is a privilege granted or withheld at the doctor's discretion.'[59]

The paradox here lies in the fact that, although the 'women's choice' movement rails against this power, it can be said to strengthen its case insofar as it removes the argument from the potentially confrontational ambience of *women's rights* and places it firmly within the universal sphere of *patients' rights*. And this brings us back to the beginning of what is rapidly becoming a circular argument: given that abortion is regarded as part of the medical management of pregnancy, it is difficult to counter the argument that the procedure should – indeed, perhaps must – be controlled by the medical profession.[60]

Nevertheless, it is apparent that a powerful theoretical case can be made to the effect that the Abortion Act makes substantial inroads into female patients' rights. The question is – can the same be said of a corresponding practical impact? We can consider this question, again, from the singular aspect of section 1(1)(a).

The Abortion Act, section 1(1)(a) in practice

In contrast to comparable legislation in many other jurisdictions, the terms of the 1967 Act are very wide and were probably so designed *in order to* preserve medical control.[61] However, the result is an Act that is so devoid of teeth as to make it, in the opinion of many – and certainly in that of the present author – virtually meaningless as a measure of control.

---

[58] For example, the woman's husband can play no decisive role in what is her medical treatment. See *C* v. *S* [1988] QB 135, [1987] 1 All ER 1230; for Scotland, *Kelly* v. *Kelly* 1997 SC 285, 1997 SCLR 749.

[59] Margaret Brazier *Medicine, Patients and the Law* (London: Penguin Books, 3rd edn 2003) at 320. Note that, in the event that the woman lacks capacity to consent to a termination, her doctors have discretion under the Act to proceed on the basis of a 'best interests' test without recourse to the courts: *Re SG (adult mental patient: abortion)* [1991] 2 FLR 329, sub nom *Re SG (a patient)* (1992) 6 BMLR 95. The courts must be involved if there is any doubt: *D* v. *An NHS Trust (Medical treatment: consent: termination)* [2004] 1 FLR 1110 – and they may not always decide in favour of termination: *Re SS (an adult: medical treatment)* [2002] 1 FLR 445.

[60] The alternative concept of a trade of 'abortionist' is bizarre if for no other reason that medical expertise is essential in the event of complications.

[61] J. Keown, *Abortion, Doctors and the Law* (Cambridge: Cambridge University Press, 1988) provides a good analysis of the history of the Act.

The first important feature to note is that section 1(1)(a) is comparative. No degree of 'risk of injury to the physical or mental health of the pregnant woman or any existing children of her family' imposed by the pregnancy is defined as sufficient to justify a termination – it has simply got to be greater than that associated with the procedure. Moreover the risk does not have to be imminent or even likely; it has only to exist as a hypothetical possibility – and such a risk is inherent in the state of pregnancy. It is now almost trite[62] to say that, although the close-to-negligible tangible risks of an early termination do vary with the age and parity of the mother, the *potential* risks of a full-term pregnancy will always be greater. We can be more specific. Even if she is not at risk of physical injury, a woman wanting to terminate her pregnancy must almost always be in a state of mental anxiety which can only be – or, at least, will most probably be – exaggerated if the pregnancy persists. The fact that, as those opposed to abortion on request will rightly say, the woman may regret her decision to terminate, merely adds to the strength of the argument – it is always possible that the resultant anxiety will, in the end, be *less* than it would have been had the pregnancy been terminated – but, again, the *risk* that it will be greater is always there.

As to the future well-being of other existing children of the family, it is yet another near-certainty that there is a risk of sibling jealousy. In similar vein, no one could deny that the appearance of a new mouth to feed and a body to clothe poses a risk to the economic – and, hence, physical – health of the existing family; again, the fact that there may also be happiness in the appearance of a new brother or sister is immaterial to the argument. Finally, we must note that the Act states that, in coming to their conclusion, the certifying doctors may take account of 'the pregnant woman's actual or reasonably foreseeable environment',[63] a condition which effectively legalises abortion even on the grounds of fetal sex,[64] for there is nothing in the Act that limits the risks to those directly associated with the condition of pregnancy.

The point that I am trying to make is that it is practically impossible to perform an early termination of pregnancy illegally in Great Britain[65] so long as the administrative formalities are completed. Moreover, the

---

[62] I, for example, have expressed this argument for some time: J. K. Mason, *Medico-Legal Aspects of Reproduction and Parenthood* (Aldershot: Ashgate, 2nd edn 1998) at 116 – and similar observations have been made by many commentators.

[63] S.1(2).

[64] The significance of this within the ambience of some ethnic cultures hardly needs airing.

[65] The 1967 Act does not extend to Northern Ireland. where abortion law is largely governed by the historic decision in *R* v. *Bourne* [1939] 1 KB 687, [1938] 3 All ER 615 in which, effectively, the therapeutic concessions of the Infant Life (Preservation)

wording of the Act is such that it is equally difficult to form an opinion as to its lawfulness in 'bad faith'. The operation may be *performed* badly or unsympathetically, but the opinion cannot be gainsaid save, perhaps, in the unlikely scenario that it is reached in disregard of the woman's wishes. This seems to have accounted, at least in part, for the fact that there has been only one relevant conviction reported since the 1967 Act came into force.[66] Interestingly, Dr Smith in that case was charged under the Offences Against the Person Act 1861, section 58, thus emphasising that the 1967 Act is *enabling* in its purpose, despite the fact that section 5(2) states: 'For the purposes of the law relating to abortion, anything done with intent to procure a woman's miscarriage . . . is unlawfully done unless authorised by section 1 of this Act' – which suggests that a charge under that Act and section might be more appropriate.[67]

This extreme paucity of criminal reports[68] supports my contention and leads one to ask – is the 'medicalisation of women's rights' argument very much more than a storm in a teacup? Given that an early termination is always available, is it too much of a constraint to require it to be authorised by a doctor? – given, again, that it is a doctor who will carry out the procedure. It will be said – and is widely expressed in the feminist literature – that the 'conscience clause' in the Act[69] puts another hurdle in the way of the woman seeking a termination, but this is a doubtful objection; the doctor who has a conscientious objection to the taking of fetal life is professionally and legally bound to refer the patient to a colleague who is not so constrained.[70] Indeed, in this respect access to medical treatment by way of abortion is treated no differently from other medical treatment. Most practices are well alert to the position and it is

---

Act 1929 were extended, and amplified, so as to apply to the non-viable fetus. The Channel Islands have adopted legislation that is similar to, though rather more strict than, that of Great Britain – e.g. Termination of Pregnancy (Jersey) Law 1997.

[66] *R* v. *Smith (John)* [1974] 1 All ER 376, 58 Cr App Rep 106. In an unreported case (*R* v. *Dixon*, Nottingham Crown Court, 21 December 1995), a gynaecologist who removed an 11-week fetus during a hysterectomy was acquitted of a charge under the Offences Against the Person Act 1861, s.58; the main reason for prosecution appears to have been the lack of consent on the part of the woman: Clare Dyer, 'Gynaecologist Acquitted in Hysterectomy Case' (1996) 312 *British Medical Journal* 11–12.

[67] Scarman LJ considered obiter that, although the point had not been tested, s.5(2) of the Act implies that s.1 supersedes and displaces the existing common law (in *R* v. *Smith* n. 66 above, at All ER 378).

[68] And only two cases have been considered by the General Medical Council since the Act came into force.

[69] Abortion Act 1967, s.4.

[70] Royal College of Obstetricians and Gynaecologists, *The Care of Women Requesting Induced Abortion: Guideline* (2000), para. 2.3; *Barr* v. *Matthews* (2000) 52 BMLR 217 per Alliott J at 227. It is probable that the same applies to the doctor who regards termination as *medically* inappropriate in the circumstances: General Medical Council, *Good Medical Practice* (2001).

doubtful if it makes any significant contribution to delays in treatment.[71] In fact, it is surprising that the 'Hippocratic (or professional) conscience'[72] has been so easily set aside. It must be well-nigh impossible to prove the point one way or the other, but it is suggested that the continued reliance on the 'post-code' distribution of abortion services as evidence of undue medical influence is little more than a throw-back to the 1970s, when doctors were being asked to discard what had been a fundamental element in their training.

Jackson suggests that the majority even of those who are morally opposed to termination of pregnancy as a matter of 'right' have 'implicitly accepted that a blanket prohibition upon abortion is not a realistic or achievable goal',[73] and it must be apparent that I have to be counted among that group. No-one could claim that that represents a high moral platform; nonetheless, in the face of the powerful arguments that can be deployed in either side of the debate, it is not wholly unreasonable. Very few people would now support a ban on termination in the face of genuine medical need – and probably the majority would extend this to genuine social need. What offends those who defend a moral status for, or a value in, the fetus is the assumption that abortion is justifiable on the basis that it is no more than a corrective of failed contraception – and even more offensive is the sophistry of the Act which attempts to hide that fact behind a false façade of medical paternalism.

A need for reform?

It can, of course, be argued that it is the sheer simplicity of the 1967 Act that has spared Great Britain the continuing – and sometimes violent – discord that is so evident, say, in the United States;[74] we have no need to

---

[71] In 1990, the House of Commons Social Services Committee concluded that it was far from clear that the conscience clause was a significant factor in the variation of the provision of abortion services: John Warden, 'Abortion and Conscience' (1990) 301 *British Medical Journal* 1013.

[72] The Hippocratic Oath includes 'Nor will I give a woman a pessary to procure abortion' – version reproduced in J. K. Mason and G. T. Laurie, *Mason and McCall Smith's Law and Medical Ethics* (Oxford: Oxford University Press, 7th edn 2005), Appendix A. It is inevitable that this clause is deleted in those graduation ceremonies which include profession of a form of the Oath – and even these are few and far between.

[73] n. 55 above, at p. 90. Interestingly, since this chapter was written, the state of South Dakota has attempted to do just that in its Women's Health and Human Life Protection Act 2006. Under this Act, deliberate termination of pregnancy is unlawful save when it is intended to save the life of a pregnant woman. Other states may well follow suit but, despite the political uncertainties as to the future membership of the court, one suspects that the Supreme Court will declare the Act unconstitutional.

[74] n. 2 above.

fan the flames with repeated visits to the courts on points of constitutionality. In which case, one can properly ask – why tamper with it?

I have already expressed my doubts as to the logic of lowering the age above which termination will be lawful only when the life or the health of the pregnant woman is in serious jeopardy; the current value of this proposal is that it reminds us that we cannot lose sight of the value of fetal life – but it does not alter that value. Rather, it seems to me, we might look again at the Act in terms of a balancing operation – does it or does it not achieve its purpose in this way? And, importantly, is it honest?

And I have to admit that, in concentrating on *comparative* risks as between termination and continuance of the pregnancy, it is less than honest in entrusting the decision to doctors. If any specialty is involved, it must be the statisticians but, as has been already pointed out, the odds in favour of greater risks in continuance of the pregnancy are, from all angles, so obvious in the first trimester that it becomes a matter of self-determination – 'I want my pregnancy terminated' becomes a sufficient reason for doing so. If that is the case, then let us say so. The corollary, however, is that, in so saying, we are, at the same time denying the less than 12-week fetus *any* intrinsic value, and it is difficult to see how even the most determined advocate of women's rights could extend that denial to the mid-term fetus. Although I have argued that the fetus of 10 weeks' gestation has the same *intrinsic* moral value as its 20 week counterpart, it would be unreasonable to maintain that there is no comparative difference – at any rate in the eyes of the ordinary man or woman. My quid pro quo would be to distinguish the 12 to 24 week fetus as a separate entity. In that case, I would eliminate any comparative criteria and legalise termination only in the event of a *significant* risk to the physical or mental health of the woman. The difficulty here, of course, is that 'significant' is ill-defined and, possibly, undefinable – but that problem is common to the whole of abortion jurisprudence, and much of the common law tradition, and is, perhaps, an inevitable consequence of attempting a balancing exercise.[75] We might end up in much the same situation as we are now, but we would do so by a more honest route.

[75] A generalised shift towards some recognition of fetal *values* is, I believe, becoming evident despite the rigid rejection of fetal *rights*. See, for example, Lord McCluskey in *Hamilton* v. *Fife Health Board* 1993 SLT 624 at 629. More significant is the cautious rejection of 'absolute' women's rights by the European Court of Human Rights in *Brüggemann and Scheuten* v. *Federal Republic of Germany* [1977] 3 EHRR 113. The opinion is old but has not been overtaken.

And, after all the argument and soul-searching that has surrounded abortion prior to and following the passing of the 1967 Act, would that be all that bad a result? We may well be doing wrong but, at the same time, doing the right thing.[76] In any event, the proposition is, effectively, sterile as, despite the murmurings of parliamentary discontent, the government does not intend to reopen the issue[77] – an evasive policy which, as we will see later, is adopted by the majority of jurisdictions and their courts.

We have, of course, not yet addressed the problems of termination of pregnancy due to fetal abnormality. Discussion of this, which I believe involves wholly different principles, will be found in Chapter 3.

Age and termination of pregnancy

Although the subject is, to an extent, parenthetical, age and access to abortion is so much a feature of the morality of the procedure that a mention of the legal aspects of 'under-age' termination of pregnancy can scarcely be avoided. Moreover, it is more than an academic exercise. Legal terminations were performed on 157 girls under the age of 14 in England and Wales in 2004.[78]

There is no mention of any effect of age of the woman in the 1967 Act; thus, one result of the medicalisation of abortion is that it will be subject to the normal rules governing medical confidentiality and consent to treatment in respect of minors. As to the former, it is recognised that the duty of confidentiality to minors, other than those who are so young as to be wholly in the hands of their parents, is the same as that owed to any other persons. As to the latter, the overall benchmark position is that parents must give consent to medical treatment for a minor below the age of 18 but, as is well known, this is subject to considerable modification depending on the actual age and mental capacity of the minor. In England and Wales, consent to treatment by a minor aged 16 or more will be as effective as if he or she was of adult status.[79] Below that age, however, the

---

[76] An idea uplifted, with acknowledgement, from Ann Furedi, 'Wrong but the Right Thing to Do: Public Opinion and Abortion' in Ellie Lee (ed.), *Abortion Law and Politics Today* (London: Macmillan Press, 1998), chapter 10.

[77] Ann Treneman, 'Sex and Relationships Muddy the Debate' (2005) *The Times*, 20 July, p. 28. See also n. 3 above.

[78] 'Abortions at Record Level' (2005) *The Times*, 28 July, p. 11. These were part of a record 185,415 terminations during the year. Adult sexual activity with a girl (or boy) below the age of 16 is, of course a criminal offence: Sexual Offences Act 2003, s.9; Criminal Law (Consolidation) (Scotland) Act 1995, s.5. At least a few of these instances must have been associated with the more serious offence of rape of a child below the age of 13.

[79] Family Law Reform Act 1969, s.8.

situation is governed by the historic decision in *Gillick*[80] which, in essence, states that a minor below the age of 16 can give valid consent to treatment provided that the doctor has made every effort to persuade the minor to involve his or her parents and provided the doctor is satisfied that the minor has sufficient understanding to appreciate the implications and risks of the procedure – including those associated with refusal of treatment.[81] Clearly, this includes a correlative right to confidentiality which, in turn, includes confidentiality in relation to the minor's parents.[82]

The *Gillick* decision was originally related to providing advice as to the use of contraceptives but it has since been extended to include *all* medical and surgical treatment – indeed, the '*Gillick*-competent' child is now an accepted medico-legal entity. There is, therefore, no reason to suppose that the formula does not include abortion. On the other hand, until recently, there was no positive legal authority indicating that it *did* so and there are many – including myself – who see, on the one hand, a major moral divide between contraception and abortion as methods for the control of pregnancy and, on the other, positive reasons for isolating abortion from other forms of 'treatment' in that it is unique in *always* involving the unrepresented fetus.

The matter has now been put to rest in *R (on the application of Axon)* v. *Secretary of State for Health*,[83] in which the claimant, a divorced mother of five children who had herself undergone a termination, sought a declaration to the effect that, since a doctor owed no duty of confidentiality to a minor in respect of advice and proposed treatment related to contraception, sexual health and abortion, he or she could not provide such

---

[80] *Gillick* v. *West Norfolk and Wisbech Area Health Authority* [1986] AC 112, [1985] 3 All ER 402. A similar situation has been reached in Scotland by way of the Age of Legal Capacity (Scotland) Act 1991, s.2(4). In fact, insofar as the 1991 Scottish Act refers to medical 'procedures' and the English 1969 Act to 'treatments', the position in the present context is clearer in Scotland where the question of whether or not abortion is a medical treatment is irrelevant. For ease of description, I am confining the remaining discussion to the position in England and Wales.

[81] This introduces another level of medical control insofar as it is the doctor who assesses the standard of understanding and, hence, the degree of confidentiality the minor is allowed. Nevertheless, most girls of 15 will probably satisfy the conditions laid down in *Gillick* and it is likely that many of the 2500 or so terminations carried out each year on girls aged less than fifteen are performed without parental knowledge.

[82] It is of interest that 34 of the US states have statutes imposing parental involvement in abortion decisions concerning minors, the constitutionality of which was confirmed in *Planned Parenthood of Southeastern Pennsylvania* v. *Casey* 112 S Ct 2791 (1992). All, however, must have a system of 'judicial by-pass' to which the minor can resort: Carol Sanger, 'Regulating Teenage Abortion in the United States' (2004) 18 *International Journal of Law, Policy and the Family* 305–18. A large proportion of recent US cases relate to the use of this process – e.g. *In re BS* 74 P 3d 285 (Ariz., 2003).

[83] (2006) 88 BMLR 96.

without the consent of the minor's parents; Ms Axon also sought a declaration that guidelines issued by the Department of Health which failed to acknowledge this exception to the general rule were unlawful. This claim seemed doomed from the start and was, in fact, rejected essentially on the grounds that, to accept it would involve overturning the House of Lords in *Gillick*. In anticipation of this, the claim was amended, in the alternative, to apply to abortion only and it is this aspect of the case which is of immediate concern to us here.

Silber J recognised the distinctive aspects of abortion to which I have already alluded and also accepted that about one third of terminations in England and Wales involving girls under the age of 16 were carried out without at least one parent being informed (at [83]). In the end, however, he fell back on Lord Fraser in *Gillick*, who pointed out that the medical professional was only justified in proceeding without parental consent or knowledge if he or she is satisfied that 'the girl will understand his advice', and on Lord Scarman:[84]

It is not enough that she should understand the nature of the advice which is being given; she must also have a sufficient maturity to understand what is involved.

In other words, the *Gillick* test is a moving test that can be adjusted so as to apply to the precise circumstances; the more intricate or significant in the long term is the treatment to be given, the more mature must be the minor before she can be entrusted with her own destiny. Which does not, perhaps, allay one's misgivings as to the unique nature of abortion but which, nevertheless, makes perfect logic so long as *Gillick* represents the relevant law.[85]

The courts will, no doubt, be asked to intervene in the event of conflict between parent and child when parental consent is required and is refused. Some parents may have a passionate desire to become grandparents but this must be a rare source of disagreement. Religious, or other moral, conviction is the more likely cause and, since the courts *must* bow to the minor's best interests,[86] her wishes are most likely to be followed with little argument involved. As a result, reported cases are few and far between and I have been able to discover only one such apposite example[87] since the landmark case decided by Butler-Sloss J

---

[84] At [1986] 1 AC 188 [1985] 3 All ER 424.
[85] Ms Axon also claimed that her rights under the European Convention on Human Rights, Article 8 were violated by the guidelines but this claim was dismissed in a lengthy judgment which is not directly relevant to this chapter – which is not to suggest that it does not merit careful analysis elsewhere.
[86] Children Act 1989, s.1.
[87] *Re B (wardship: abortion)* [1991] 2 FLR 426 – in which a mother opposed the termination of her 12-year-old daughter's pregnancy.

in 1982.[88] The pity is that contraceptive advice – not excluding absti-
nence – is so poorly followed and that under-age pregnancy is, consequently, so common.

Prevention and reversal of implantation

It was proposed, with some misgiving, at the beginning of this chapter
that, for practical purposes, meaningful human life begins at the point of
implantation. Whether this be generally approved or not, it would surely
be agreed on both sides in the abortion 'debate' that prevention of an
unwanted pregnancy is to be preferred to its termination and that, if it has
not been prevented, its termination before the pregnant state was recognised would be preferable to – or less offensive than – termination of an
established pregnancy.

Other than to illustrate this near-truism, contraception per se has no
place in a book concerned with pregnancy.[89] Despite the fact that it
sparked off the massive move towards the recognition of individual privacy in the United States,[90] it now has no legal connotations.[91] Moral
objections, based on the inseparability of the unitive and procreative
functions of marriage, are now virtually confined to ultra-conservative
followers of Islam and Roman Catholicism;[92] we can reasonably ignore
the subject in the present context. The same cannot be said, however, in
respect of the 'grey areas' of family planning – the interceptive and
displanting methods of contraception.

Interceptive methods – or post-coital contraception – are designed to
prevent the fertilised egg implanting in the uterine wall.[93] The most
important techniques involve the insertion of an intrauterine device
(IUD) following sexual intercourse, or, more commonly, the use of
the contragestational or, popularly, 'morning after' pill. Somewhat

---

[88] *Re P (a minor)* (1982) 80 LGR 301, [1986] 1 FLR 272 which established the concept of
the 'mature minor' in respect of abortion decisions; the patient was aged 15.

[89] Though it may yet have a place in the abortion debate – Don Marquis, 'Abortion and the
Beginning and End of Human Life' (2006) 34 *Journal of Law and Medical Ethics* 16–25.

[90] *Griswold* v. *Connecticut* (1965) 381 US 479, (1965) 85 S Ct 1678.

[91] The use of a contraceptive does not, for example, invalidate consummation of a marriage:
Baxter v. *Baxter* [1948] AC 274. The somewhat peripheral but distinct problem of the
failed contraceptive is revisited in Chapter 4.

[92] Douwe A. A. Verkuyl, 'Two World Religions and Family Planning' (1993) 342 *Lancet*
473–5. The present author believes that, insofar as contraception facilitates love-making,
it positively supports the institution of marriage.

[93] Since conception has already occurred, we should, strictly, speak of contragestation
rather than contraception. Post-coital contraception is, however, a term of popular
usage.

controversially, albeit with wide medical support,[94] the government decided to allow the provision of these by the pharmacist without the need for a doctor's prescription;[95] intuitively, while hopefully decreasing the number of unwanted pregnancies, this seems likely to increase promiscuity among young people, and it was this possibility which served to reopen the question[96] of whether emergency contraception was governed by the Offences Against the Person Act 1861, section 58 and was, at the same time, not covered by the Abortion Act.[97]

The whole subject was examined by Munby J in a truly remarkable exposition of the history and current literature on contraception.[98] Clearly, the answer to the problem lay in the interpretation of the word 'miscarriage'. On the one hand there was academic opinion to the effect that it involved the removal of a fertilised egg from its natural habitat irrespective of implantation.[99] On the other, numerous authorities were quoted which contended that pregnancy began at implantation and that there could be no 'carriage' – and, hence, no miscarriage – before implantation.[100] Munby J's tour de force needs to be read in full; suffice it to quote, here, that:

[S]ince the morning-after pill is used before the process of implantation has even begun, and because it cannot make an implanted egg de-implant, the morning-after pill cannot as a matter of law bring about a 'miscarriage'.[101]

[94] E.g. James Owen Drife, 'Deregulating Emergency Contraception' (1993) 307 *British Medical Journal* 695–6.

[95] Prescription Only Medicine (Human Use) Amendment (No. 3) Order 2000 (S.I. 2000/ 3231).

[96] Previously, the Attorney-General had said: 'the phrase "to procure a miscarriage" cannot be construed to include the prevention of implantation', 41 Official Report (6th series) col. 239, 10 May 1983. This has been confirmed on at least two occasions by ministers in the House of Commons (see *Smeaton*, n. 98 below, at [41]).

[97] Amongst other things, the Abortion Act refers to an opinion as to 'a pregnancy'. Moreover, you cannot assess the effects of a pregnancy unless you know that the pregnancy exists.

[98] *R (on the application of Smeaton on behalf of Society for the Protection of Unborn Children)* v. *Secretary of State for Health and others as interested parties* [2002] 2 FLR 146, (2002) 66 BMLR 59.

[99] Predominantly I. J. Keown, '"Miscarriage" A Medico-Legal Analysis' [1984] *Criminal Law Review* 604–14; Victor Tunkel, 'Modern Anti-Pregnancy Techniques and the Criminal Law' [1974] *Criminal Law Review* 461–71.

[100] Amongst others: I. Kennedy, 'Legal and ethical implications of postcoital birth control' in *Treat Me Right* (Oxford: Oxford University Press, 1988), chapter 3, 32–41; Andrew Grubb, 'Abortion Law in England: The Medicalization of a Crime' (1990) 18 *Law, Medicine & Health Care* 146–61; Mason, n. 62 above, pp. 58–61; Kenneth Norrie, 'Postcoital Anti-pregnancy Techniques and the Law' in A. Allan Templeton and Douglas Cusine (eds.), *Reproductive Medicine and the Law* (Edinburgh: Churchill Livingstone, 1990), chapter 2, pp. 11–17.

[101] *Smeaton*, n. 98 above, at [18].

And, legal considerations apart, it is suggested that, since the fate of the unimplanted embryo is that of 'large numbers of fertilised oocytes which are believed to be lost during the normal menstrual cycle',[102] only those who maintain that human inviolability begins at conception need to have moral qualms as to the process. From every aspect, prevention of implantation seems preferable to abortion of the established fetus; on this view, it would be morally retrograde to prohibit the practice.[103]

The same cannot be said for displanting methods which are designed to remove any potential embryo[104] that may have established its natural habitat; in present circumstances, this involves some mechanical process such as the euphemistically termed 'menstrual extraction' or the insertion of an intrauterine device. Since this involves an implanted embryo, it lies clearly within the concept of an abortion and, accordingly, is subject to the Offences Against the Person Act. Importantly in practical terms, it will be seen that the IUD can be used as above, to prevent implantation or to displant a pregnancy; the timing of its use is, therefore critical in respect of the law.

This is well shown in *R* v. *Dhingra* which is the most apposite United Kingdom case to date.[105] In that case, a doctor inserted an IUD into his secretary, according to the newspaper report, 11 days after they had had intercourse – which happened to be 17 days into her menstrual cycle. In the light of the evidence available to him, Wright J, having concluded that a woman could not be said to be pregnant until the fertilised ovum was implanted in the uterine wall – and that this could not occur, at the earliest, until the twentieth day of a normal 28 day cycle – withdrew the case from the jury on the grounds that implantation could not have occurred during the time available.

While this may clarify the law in a general sense, it is obvious that it is very difficult to put into practice because of the variability of a biological process. Munby J, for example, put the time between intercourse and meeting of sperm and egg at anything from a matter of hours to six days; the resulting embryo enters the uterus between four and six days after fertilisation which is, itself, a lengthy process; and implantation is a

---

[102] J. O. Drife quoted, ibid., at [133]. And, more precisely, 'Fewer than 15% of fertilised eggs will result in a birth' (P. Braude quoted, ibid., at [129]).

[103] The relatively draconian Women's Health and Human Life Protection Act 2006 of South Dakota (n. 73 above) still allows for pre-implantation contraception. It also seems to admit of displanting methods involving the early embryo (s.3).

[104] Which distinguishes the process from a medical abortion using antiprogesterones, the function of which is to displant an *established* pregnancy.

[105] *R* v. *Dhingra* (1991) *Daily Telegraph*, 25 January, otherwise unreported. The case is, however, considered at length in *Smeaton*.

process extending from the eighth to the eleventh day after commencing fertilisation.[106] In short, it would be very difficult to prove an established pregnancy in any but a very obvious case.[107]

The rather similar case of *R* v. *Price (Herbert)*[108] might well have provided such an instance. Here, the doctor inserted an IUD into a woman who was ten weeks pregnant. However, it raises the other essential element if disimplantment is to be considered a criminal act – that an offence under section 58 is one of intent. Dr Price maintained that he did not believe the patient was pregnant and could not, therefore, have intended to procure her miscarriage. He was, in fact, convicted but this was quashed on appeal due to a misdirection as to the weight to be placed on the conflicting uncorroborated evidence of the patient – in effect, an accomplice. It is interesting to speculate what would have happened had Dr Dhingra gone to trial, for an offence is possible under section 58 'whether the woman be or not be with child'. One fancies that, again, it would have been, and always would be, extremely difficult to prove intent in such cases but, for reasons already given, one can also doubt the desirability of their successful prosecution. The second difficulty, as we have also seen, is that it is currently impossible to harmonise the use of an IUD or of menstrual extraction with the Abortion Act and its associated regulations as they stand.

Negligence and abortion

A duty to the mother

Very few cases of a simple failed abortion due to obstetric negligence are reported. The majority that are will either fall into the categories of wrongful pregnancy or of wrongful birth – conditions which are described and discussed in Chapters 4 and 3 respectively. Occasionally, however, the fact that a pregnancy has not been terminated goes by unnoticed at the time and these form something of a separate category of unwanted pregnancies – if for no other reason than that the fact of pregnancy itself is appreciated only relatively late. This may mean that the deadline beyond which a remedial termination that can be justified under section 1(1)(a)

---

[106] *Smeaton*, n. 98 above, at [126].
[107] It is clear that, if one transposes Munby J's figures to *Dhingra*, the case for withdrawing the charge in the latter case is far from obvious – although, as argued above, a conviction would have been unlikely. But it does illustrate the importance of the improvements in medical science over a period as short as a decade.
[108] [1969] 1 QB 541, [1968] 2 All ER 282.

has passed; equally often, the pregnancy has reached such a stage that the woman is no longer prepared to proceed to termination.

Just such a situation occurred in *Scuriaga* v. *Powell*[109] which is an old and poorly reported case but is, nevertheless, important in the present context for two reasons. First, it laid the grounds, albeit tenuously, for allowing recovery for the uncovenanted birth of a healthy child and, second, it established that a doctor whose negligence has caused such a pregnancy cannot rely on the woman retrieving the situation by way of termination and we will see in Chapter 4 how significant this can be.

Failure to carry out an abortion within the parameters of good medical practice will, of course, be judged on the normal criteria for establishing negligence. Thus, in the County Court case of *Chissel* v. *Poole Hospital NHS Trust*,[110] the obstetrician failed to remove a twin whose presence was unsuspected. The court held, however, that there was nothing to suggest, or to lead Ms Chissell's doctors to suspect, that she was bearing twins and the chances of one twin fetus surviving lawful abortion were slim; the case, however, failed mainly on the grounds that the experts called disagreed as to whether or not the follow-up of the case satisfied a 'reasonable degree of care' – it, thus fell foul of the *Bolam* test.[111] The fact that Ms Chissell refused a second termination on the grounds that it was now too late to use the simple technique of endometrial suction did not count against her. While one may regret the judge's enforced position in such a case – and there is little doubt his hands would be tied by the jurisprudence of the time[112] – the principles as to a duty to the mother are reasonably clear.[113] What is less clear is whether he has any duty to the fetus. This secondary question was fully examined in the interesting Canadian case of *Cherry* v. *Borsman*.[114]

---

[109] [1979] 123 SJ 406.   [110] [1998] Lloyd's Rep Med 357.

[111] *Bolam* v. *Friern Hospital Management Committee* [1957] 2 All ER 118, (1957) 1 BMLR 1. The current significance of the case has already been discussed in Chapter 1. The corresponding test in Scotland is to be found in *Hunter* v. *Hanley* 1955 SC 200, 1955 SLT 213.

[112] *Maynard* v. *West Midlands Regional Health Authority* [1985] 1 All ER 635, [1984] 1 WLR 634.

[113] The result can be compared with that in a recent Canadian case: *Roe* v. *Dabbs* 2004 BCSC 957. Here, the woman already had an IUD embedded in the uterine wall. The Court considered that the obstetrician should have, as a result, been particularly careful. In particular, the doctor failed to meet the necessary standard in failing to consider the negative post-operative pathology report – no products of conception were discovered in the curettings. The duty of care owed to the patient was, thereby, breached. For further illustration of the importance of the histology report, and the additional question of negligence on the part of the pathologist, see *Crouchman* v. *Burke* (1998) 40 BMLR 163.

[114] (1990) 75 DLR (4th) 668, BCSC; (1992) 94 DLR (4th) 487, BCCA.

Here, a negligently performed abortion, followed by a remarkably lax follow-up, resulted in a severely disabled neonate. It was held, and confirmed on appeal, that, insofar as a negligently performed abortion can cause foreseeable harm to the fetus, the practitioner owed a duty to the fetus to prevent that harm; accordingly, he was liable to the neonate in negligence. This case appears to be unique. No-one would deny that the doctor caused the injuries but he did so in the process of trying to kill the fetus. Given that the law considers the greatest injury to be death, it is a little difficult to see how mitigating that injury can be tortious – or, indeed, how the traditional approach to compensation of restoring the plaintiff to the position he or she would have been in but for the negligence would be anything but absurd. An analysis of the case leads strongly to the conclusion that the court in *Cherry* was anxious to recompense the newborn child and was, therefore, concerned to avoid the case being labelled as one of so-called 'wrongful life' when, as we will see later, recovery would have been very difficult. The decision in *Cherry* may, thus, be seen as an ingenious piece of legal legerdemain and we will return to the case in detail in Chapter 6.

The idea of a duty to the fetus raises a conceptual problem insofar as a dead fetus cannot bring an action; a doctor can only be liable to the fetus if it survives as a neonate.[115] If, therefore, we are speaking about legally actionable fetal injury we should, in fact, be referring to some such entity as the 'neonate-to-be'. It is important that we bear in mind the well-known fact that the fetus has no *positive* legal rights.[116] The words of Sir George Baker in *Paton*:

[t]here can be no doubt, in my view, that, in England and Wales, the foetus has no right of action, no right at all, until birth[117]

have been followed ever since in virtually every Anglophone jurisdiction.[118] It is for this reason that I have couched the discussion of the *morality* of abortion in terms of fetal *values*. This lack of rights depends on

---

[115] And, in England and Wales, it must survive for a minimum of 48 hours: Congenital Disabilities (Civil Liability) Act 1976, s.4(4).

[116] As we have seen, the *viable* fetus has a negative right not to be killed intentionally: Infant Life (Preservation) Act 1929.

[117] *Paton* v. *British Pregnancy Advisory Service Trustees* [1979] QB 276 at 279, [1978] 2 All ER 987 at 989. For Scotland, see *Kelly* v. *Kelly* 1997 SC 285, 1997 SCLR 749, per Cullen LJ-C at SC 291, SCLR 755.

[118] In England, the importance of avoiding maternal/fetal conflict was first emphasised in *Re F (in utero)* [1988] Fam 122, [1988] 2 All ER 193. But, even so, circumstances alter cases; *Re F* was, for example, specifically rejected in the remarkable New Zealand case *Re an Unborn Child* [2003] 1 NZLR 115 where it was proposed that the birth of a child be included in a pornographic film.

a legal denial of personhood for the fetus which is, thereby, also denied protection against criminal or negligent activity – at least in the pre-viable stage. There may, therefore, be times when the mother is deprived of a child she wishes to keep and, while this is, strictly speaking, distinct from the abortion debate, it is certainly an aspect of troubled pregnancy which merits discussion at this point.

Involuntary termination of pregnancy

We have seen that the fetus that dies *in utero* as a result of criminality or negligence has no right – or, indeed, possibility – of action per se; moreover, since it cannot have either a guardian or an executor, no action can be taken on its behalf. At the same time, most people would, it is imagined, hope that the distress of the deprived mother would be adequately recognised.

In practice, this is remarkably difficult and the courts have to use all their wiles to achieve a fair result. The case of *Bagley*[119] is very much in point. Here the pregnancy appears to have been complicated by Rhesus-incompatibility but the mother was negligently denied an early induction and was delivered of a stillborn child. Damages under the Fatal Accidents Act 1976 were expressly disallowed because the child was not live-born but Simon Brown J was able to recognise the loss of satisfaction in bringing up a healthy child as a recoverable head of damages. Recompense under the other heads that he identified – namely the consequent reduced ability or inability to have another child and a recognisable illness brought about by the misfortune – would, however, be contingent upon the precise conditions of the case. Thus, maternal recovery for the 'wrongful death' of her fetus will, at best, depend on something of a lottery.

The difficulty was exemplified by the New Zealand Court of Appeal in the five-judge hearing of *Harrild* v. *Director of Proceedings*.[120] The precise nature of the case concerned the interplay of the New Zealand Health and Disability Commissioner Act 1994 and the Injury Prevention, Rehabilitation, and Compensation Act 2001 but, for present purposes, the issue can be seen as whether or not the death of a fetus *in utero* due to medical negligence could be construed as compensatable injury to the mother who was, in fact, unharmed. Elias CJ concluded that severance of the physical link between mother and fetus that occurs when the fetus dies

[119] *Bagley* v. *North Herts Health Authority* [1986] NLJ Rep 1014. *Bagley* is, in fact, virtually the only UK case available; *Grieve* v. *Salford Health Authority* [1991] 2 Med LR 295 is similar but is less instructive.
[120] [2003] 3 NZLR 289.

in utero constitutes a personal injury to the mother – and this was the majority view.[121]

There is no doubt that, underlying the opinion in *Harrild* was an anxiety to preserve what was described as the 'non-niggardly' attitude to compensation that has been established in New Zealand and which most people would, one feels, applaud, particularly in the context of the death of a baby due to negligence. The alternative logical conclusion that:

> [t]o deny a stillborn recovery for fatal injuries during gestation . . . would make it more profitable for the defendant to kill the plaintiff than to scratch him[122]

is hardly an attractive construct – albeit posing a legal conundrum that persists in the United Kingdom. The almost unique decision in *Amadio* was made in very specific circumstances and, insofar as it is directly in contrast to the House of Lords decision in *Attorney-General's Reference (No. 3 of 1994)*,[123] it is very unlikely that it could be maintained in the United Kingdom. But the opinion in the latter case derived from a consideration of the criminal law and it is that to which we must now turn.

Fetal death, fetal status and the criminal law

Attorney-General's Reference No. 3 concerned the case of a man who stabbed his pregnant girlfriend; at the same time the knife penetrated the abdomen of her viable fetus.[124] Following a premature delivery, the baby died at the age of four months and the man was charged with its murder although it was agreed that he had no intention to kill the fetus.

Inevitably, the trial judge ruled that there was no case to answer. When the case was referred to the Court of Appeal, however, it was held that, in

---

[121] The dissent, of course, maintained that the fetus and the mother must be regarded as separate entities in both biological and practical terms.

[122] *Amadio* v. *Levin* 501 A 2d 1085 (Pa., 1985). 'Wrongful death' statutes are in place in most of the United States but their interpretation seems variable. In general, recovery will be limited to the death of a viable fetus. Non-viable fetuses are protected by statute in Georgia, Louisiana, Illinois, Missouri, West Virginia and South Dakota: see *Santana* v. *Zilog, Inc.* (1996) 95 F 3d 780.

[123] [1996] QB 581, [1996] 2 All ER 10, CA; [1998] AC 245, [1997] 3 All ER 936, HL. A similar case occurring in the United States would now be covered specifically by the Unborn Victims of Violence Act 2004.

[124] I have discussed the case briefly in J. K. Mason, 'A Lords' Eye View of Fetal Status' (1999) 3 *Edinburgh Law Review* 246–50. For discussion of the Court of Appeal decision, see Mary Seneviratne, 'Pre-natal Injury and Transferred Malice: The Invented Other' (1996) 59 *Modern Law Review* 884–92 and, for the House of Lords, Sara Fovargue and José Miola, 'Policing Pregnancy: Implications of the Attorney General's Reference (No. 3 of 1994)' (1998) 6 *Medical Law Review* 265–96.

the circumstances, it *was* possible to charge either murder or manslaughter. This decision was reached through a rather complex biphasic application of the doctrine of transferred malice which depended, in the first phase, on the understanding that the fetus was an integral part of the mother. As a consequence, serious injury to the fetus constituted a serious injury to the woman – just as, as the Lord Chief Justice put it, 'to injure her arm or her leg would be so viewed'.[125] In the second phase, the malice towards the mother could be, again, transferred to the fetus on its birth. As a result, the conditions for murder were established despite the fact that, at the time of the assault, the fetus was not a legal 'person'.

The result was widely interpreted as, at last, providing some protection for the fetus in the criminal law. If it did, it was a Pyrrhic victory as the protection offered depended upon denial of *any* autonomous fetal existence. Moreover, as was only to be expected, such advantage as was conferred, applied only to the neonate – the non-viable fetus in the womb could still be killed with impunity.[126]

The theory of a double transfer of malice was, in any event, too much for the House of Lords which rejected it out of hand and held, instead, that the relationship between mother and fetus was one of bonding rather than identity. Indeed, Lord Mustill, who wrote the most significant opinion, pointed out the obvious – that, at the very least, they have distinct genetic profiles. The mother and the fetus were distinct human beings – albeit that the latter did not have the attributes of a person. Then what was it? It was, said Lord Mustill, a unique organism and, 'to apply to such an organism the principles of a law evolved in relation to autonomous human beings is bound to mislead'.[127]

Looking back at the cases discussed in the last few pages, it is fascinating to see how this impasse of fetal identity can be manipulated according to need. The court in *Harrild* used the concept of bonding to establish a unity between mother and fetus; the House of Lords, on the contrary, saw a bonding relationship as negating one of common identity. The *Harrild* interpretation, albeit provided by the Chief Justice with obvious reluctance is, in my view, to be preferred insofar as it provides something of a

---

[125] [1996] 2 All ER 10 at 18. As has been noted, this view was rejected by the New Zealand Court of Appeal in *Harrild*, n. 120 above, where the concept of a 'union' between two saprophytic entities was preferred.

[126] A charge of malicious wounding would be competent in the event of neonatal survival: see Lord Mustill in *Attorney-General's Reference (No. 3 of 1994)*, n. 123 above, at AC 254, All ER 942. A civil action might also be available to the child building on *Burton* v. *Islington Health Authority, de Martell* v. *Merton and Sutton Health Authority* [1993] QB 204, [1992] 3 All ER 833.

[127] [1998] AC 245 at 256, [1997] 3 All ER 936 at 943.

template from which to work. The House of Lords, however, leaves the fetus in a legal limbo. It cannot be a person because it has no legal personality, nor can it be protected as being part of its mother – and we have no clues to the answer because the House singularly failed to elaborate on the status of this 'unique being'.[128] In fact, it may well be that the *only* way in which the fetus can be protected as things stand is to regard it as a unified part of the mother – and this, again, may account for the generalised preference for the approach of the Court of Appeal that is to be found in Commonwealth decisions.[129] In my view, the House of Lords 'decision' was, of necessity, based on legal precedents which most people would regard as being too old to be relevant today; in the end, the conclusion that the fetus has no rights remains grounded in rules established in the seventeenth century.[130] Moreover, as we have seen, it was not well accepted in other jurisdictions. A fresh consideration of the problem was needed, and an opportunity seemed to present in the most apposite forum when Mrs Vo took her case as far as the European Court of Human Rights.

The case of Vo v. France[131]

Mrs Vo was a Vietnamese woman living in France. She was some twenty weeks' pregnant when she went to hospital for a routine antenatal appointment. Following a truly remarkable series of mishaps, including mistaken identity, she was negligently treated for the removal of a non-existent contraceptive coil and, during the process, her membranes were ruptured.[132] A week later, it was decided that the pregnancy could no

---

[128] This is no place to discuss the intricacies of the criminal law but, for the record, the House refused to consider the question of murder although a conviction for manslaughter was possible.

[129] See, for example, *R v. King* [2003] NSWCCA 399: 'The purpose of the law is best served by acknowledging that, relevantly, the foetus is part of the mother', per Spigelman CJ at [97]. The position in Canada is similarly pragmatic: 'It would not have been illogical to find that bodily harm was done to [the mother] through the death of the foetus which was inside of and connected to her body and, at the same time, to find that the foetus was a person who could be the victim of criminal negligence causing death': *R v. Sullivan and Lemay* (1991) 1 SCR 489 per Lamer CJ at 506.

[130] Sir Edward Coke, *Institutes of the Law of England*. Pt. III, Chap. 7 at 50. It is, however, to be noted that the House was quite clear that this subsists: 'It is established beyond doubt for the criminal law as for the civil law that the child en ventre sa mère does not have a distinct human personality, whose extinguishment give rise to any penalties or liabilities at common law' (per Lord Mustill in *Attorney-General's Reference (No. 3 of 1994)*, n. 123 above, AC 245 at 261, 3 All ER 936 at 948).

[131] *Vo v. France (Application No. 53924/00)* (2004) 79 BMLR 71, (2005) 40 EHRR 12. The paragraph numbers are those in the original transcript.

[132] I have detailed the extraordinary story in J. K. Mason, 'What's in a Name? The Vagaries of *Vo v. France*' (2005) 17 *Child and Family Law Quarterly* 97–112.

longer continue and it was terminated.[133] Mrs Vo sued the hospital and the doctor in both the civil and criminal jurisdictions alleging the unintentional homicide of her child. The most important of the agreed findings at autopsy were: the age of the fetus was between 20 and 21 weeks; there were no indications of violence, there were no malformations nor any evidence that death was due to structural disease or damage to the organs; and, significantly, that the child had not breathed after delivery. Equally significantly, pathological investigation indicated that the fetal lungs were 20 to 24 weeks old; the fetus was, therefore, on the fringe of viability.

The case had a turbulent passage through the courts. One of its main interests lies in the various interpretations of fetal status that were made; it is worth repeating these in some detail.

The court of first instance[134] saw the issue as being that of whether or not a fetus[135] aged 20 to 21 weeks is a human person or 'another' within the meaning of the Criminal Code.[136] In reaching its conclusion, the court made a number of assumptions and assertions which provided the foundation of the arguments pursued throughout the jurisdictional hierarchy. The main points were:

- The underlying statutory provisions are that the law guarantees the respect of every human being from the beginning of its life;[137]
- There is no legal rule to determine the position of the fetus in law either when it is formed or during its development;
- It has been established that a fetus is viable at six months and on no account, on present knowledge, at 20 or 21 weeks;
- The court cannot create law on an issue which the legislators have not yet succeeded in defining;
- Accordingly, a 20 to 21 week-old fetus is not viable and is not a 'human person' or 'another' within the meaning of the Criminal Code.

As a result, it concluded that the offence of unintentional homicide or unintentionally taking the life of a 20 to 21 week-old fetus had not been

---

[133] On my reading of the case, the fetus could well have been dead at this time, making the operation one of evacuation of the uterus. It was, however, considered throughout to have been a therapeutic abortion. I have some, at least, tacit academic support: Katherine O'Donovan, 'Taking a Neutral Stance on the Legal Protection of the Fetus' (2006) 14 *Medical Law Review* 115–23.

[134] Lyons Criminal Court, 3 June 1996.

[135] The English translation of the judgment uses the spelling 'foetus'. However, to avoid confusion, I have used the preferred 'fetus' throughout.

[136] The French Criminal Code, Articles 221–6 defines the offence of unintentional homicide as 'causing the death of another' within the stated conditions.

[137] Article 16 of the Civil Code; Law of 17 January 1975 on the Voluntary Termination of Pregnancy.

made out since the fetus was not a 'human person' or 'another' – and the doctor was acquitted 'without penalty or costs'.

The applicant appealed and was supported by the public prosecutor for the following reasons:

By failing to carry out a clinical examination, the accused was guilty of negligence that caused the death of the fetus, which at the time of the offence was between 20 and 24 weeks old and following, normally and inexorably, the path of life on which it had embarked, there being no medical doubt over its future.

The Appeal was allowed[138] and the doctor was fined and given a suspended sentence of six months' imprisonment. The Court of Appeal did, however, in this writer's opinion, start to muddy the waters by attempting to harmonise the availability of voluntary termination of pregnancy in France before 10 weeks' gestation with the provisions of, say, Article 2 of the European Convention of Human Rights and Article 6 of the United Nations Convention on the Rights of the Child;[139] up to this point, abortion had not been mentioned. Even so, it became central to the discussion later. The views of the Court of Appeal on 'viability' are important in this context:

It follows that, subject to the provisions on the voluntary termination of pregnancies and therapeutic abortions, the right to respect for every human being from the beginning of life is guaranteed by law, *without any requirement* that the child is born as a viable human being, provided it was alive when the injury occurred [my emphasis] ... Indeed, viability is a scientifically indefinite and uncertain concept ... devoid of all legal effect as the law makes no distinction on that basis. (At [21].)

The Court concluded:

It is not yet known with precision when the zygote becomes an embryo and the embryo becomes a fetus, the only indisputable fact being that the life process begins with impregnation

and that, since a previous judgment[140] had decided that a non-fatal wound would have been classified as an offence of unintentionally causing injuries, a fortiori, 'an assault leading to a child's death must be classified as an unintentional homicide':

Thus, the strict application of the legal principles, established scientific fact and *elementary common sense* all dictate that a negligent act or omission causing the death of a 20 to 24-week-old fetus in perfect health should be classified as unintentional homicide. (At [21], emphasis added.)

---

[138] Lyons Court of Appeal, 13 March 1997.

[139] Signed in New York, 26 January 1990. It is to be noted that the former speaks of 'everyone's right to life' and the latter to 'a child's inherent right to life'.

[140] Uncited, Douai Court of Appeal, 2 June 1987.

The judgment of the trial court was, accordingly, overturned.

The case then went to the Court of Cassation where the findings of the Court of Appeal were summarily dismissed.[141] The provisions of the criminal law, it was said, must be strictly construed. The Court noted that a 20 to 21 week-old fetus was not viable and, accordingly, was not 'another person' within the meaning of the Criminal Code; the Code could not, therefore, be applied in the instant case.

Seldom can such a diversity of opinions have been expressed on a topic of major significance and Mrs Vo then proceeded to the European Court of Human Rights where it was hoped that such important issues might be resolved once and for all. Unfortunately we were to be sadly disappointed.

It is important to remember that the action was now concerned with a breach of human rights under the European Convention on Human Rights and, of the contraventions raised, it is that against Article 2 that is of main concern here. The following is the relevant extract:

1. Everyone's right to life shall be protected by law. No one shall be deprived of his life save in the execution of a sentence of a court . . . .

2. Deprivation of life shall not be regarded as inflicted in contravention of this Article when it results from the use which is no more than absolutely necessary:
   a) in defence of any person from unlawful violence; . . .[142]

In short, the case raised the acid test of fetal status – was fetal life protected by law?

The Court was, of course, in a difficult position which it explained at length,[143] Attention was drawn to the international European jurisprudence, quoting in particular, the Convention on Human Rights and Biomedicine[144] – in which the term 'everyone' is left undefined. It also emphasised the differences in opinion as to the moral status of the embryo and of the fetus that are held in Europe and it noted (at [41]) that the offence of unintentional fetal homicide is unknown in the majority of member states of the Council of Europe;[145] legislation protective of the fetus to some extent exists only in Italy, Spain and Turkey.

---

[141] On 30 June 1999, see n. 131 above, [22].

[142] For UK purposes, the Article is repeated in the Human Rights Act 1998, Schedule 1.

[143] The Court also quoted an analysis which indicated that 28 out of 34 published commentaries were critical of the Court of Cassation's rigid attitude: Jean Pradel, 'Violences involontaires sur femme enceinte et délit d'homicide involontaire' (2004) 7/7148 *Recueil Dalloz* 449–50.

[144] Opened for signature at Oviedo in 1997 and coming into force on 1 December 1999.

[145] For the United Kingdom, see the authoritative article by Adrian Whitfield, 'Common Law Duties to Unborn Children' (1993) 1 *Medical Law Review* 28–52. The early analysis by Jennifer Temkin, 'Pre-natal Injury, Homicide and the Draft Criminal Code' (1986) 45 *Cambridge Law Journal* 414–29 is remarkably prophetic.

The applicant's case was, therefore, wholly relevant to the nature of the discussion in this chapter. In essence, she contended that it was now 'scientifically proven' that all life begins at fertilisation; a child that had been conceived but was not yet born was neither a cluster of cells nor an object, but a person. The term 'everyone' in Article 2 was to be taken as referring to human beings rather than persons possessing legal personality and that, subject to exceptions provided in the law on abortion, French law guaranteed all human beings the right to life from conception; the availability of abortion did not exonerate the state from its duty to protect the unborn child under the terms of Article 2. She also contended that unintentional homicide of a fetus necessarily merited a criminal sanction because a civil remedy did not 'satisfy the requirement of expressing public disapproval of a serious offence, such as the taking of life' (at [47–49]).

The Court, however, pointed out that the still unsettled question of what constitutes the 'beginning' of 'everyone's right to life' in the context of Article 2 had, thus far, been raised within its jurisdiction only in connection with laws on abortion,[146] and it continued to look at Mrs Vo's case in this way even though it was of a quite separate nature. By tying the problem of fetal homicide to national abortion laws, the Court was able to say (at [82]) that the question of when the right to life begins comes within the margin of appreciation which it generally considers states should enjoy in this sphere – in essence, it was undesirable, and probably impossible, to answer in the abstract the question whether or not the unborn child is a person for the purposes of Article 2 of the Convention. Moreover, there was no call to decide whether or not 'the abrupt end to the applicant's pregnancy' fell within the scope of Article 2 insofar as there had been no failure in the particular case to comply with the national laws on abortion (at [85]). Thus, in the end, what had been hoped might become an 'evolutive interpretation' of a 'living

---

[146] It is, in fact, remarkable how few of the relevant applications have actually reached the court. In *X* v. *Austria* (Application no. 7045/75, Commission Decision of 10 December 1976) the Commission avoided the issue. The close relationship between the mother and her fetus was recognised in *Brüggemann and Scheuten* v. *Federal Republic of Germany* (Application no. 6959/75, of 12 July 1977; (1981) 3 EHRR 244) but the Commission did not find it 'necessary to decide . . . whether the unborn child could be considered as "life" in the context of Article 2 of the Convention'. Similarly, in *X* v. *United Kingdom* (Application no. 8416/79, Commission Decision of 13 May 1980) the Commission denied the fetus an absolute right to life in the face of fetal/maternal conflict but avoided a decision as to whether it was no rights or partial rights that were available. A further evasive opinion was given in *H* v. *Norway* (Application no. 17004/90, Commission Decision of 19 May 1992). See also *Boso* v. *Italy* no. 50490/99, ECHR 2002-VII, one case which went to the Court itself.

instrument'[147] petered out into a non-decision.[148] Due to a variety of circumstances, the unfortunate Mrs Vo left Strasbourg empty handed; she was even denied the opportunity to take action in the civil courts – though, even then, she might have had considerable difficulty.

Conclusion

In summarising our discussion, it is worth reconsidering what Mrs Vo was seeking. In the wide view, she was certainly hoping to establish a fetal right to recognition as a form of human life that was entitled to legal protection – a right that was at least that of a human entity, if not that of a human person. In the narrower, though perhaps the more easily appreciated, context, however, she was a woman seeking redress for the negligent loss of her child and, as such, she represented the, still, majority of pregnant women who want to carry their pregnancies to full term and parturition. I am, as a result, at a loss to understand how the European Court of Human Rights, while acknowledging that the case raised a new issue,[149] came to argue it on the basis of legislation that was designed for the benefit of those whose concern is diametrically opposed.[150]

I suspect that it stemmed from a fear that to address the question of fetal status head-on might involve reopening questions of conflicting maternal and fetal rights in pregnancy, which most would wish to be seen as being largely settled. In fact, of course, there was no need to run the risk. Insofar as there is a medico-legal definition, and absent disease in the mother, abortion is generally understood to mean the termination of a pregnancy that, for one reason or another, is unwanted. Thus, the major question that could have been addressed, even if not answered, is whether or not there is an offence of feticide that is independent of consensual termination of pregnancy. As the analytical paper that was so critical of the Court of Cassation judgment[151] put it – the freedom to procreate is

---

[147] As the Convention on Human Rights was described. See n. 131 above, at [82].

[148] It is only fair to say that this sense of disappointment was, in fact, shared by five of the seventeen-judge panel. In brief, Costa J and Traja J thought that the fact that there was a lack of uniformity among the legislatures of the member states provided no reason to stop the court defining the meaning of a person with a right to life. The most important aspect of their opinion for present purposes is that they considered the case to be clearly distinguishable from those dealing with termination of pregnancy at the request of the mother and could see no policy reason for not applying Article 2 in the circumstances. The most trenchant criticism, however, is to be found in the overtly dissenting opinions of Ress, Mularoni and Stráznická JJ who considered that Article 2 applied to the fetus.

[149] n. 131 above, at [81].

[150] It is to be noted that all the dissenting opinions held firmly that Mrs Vo's case was 'wholly unrelated to laws on the voluntary termination of pregnancy'.

[151] Pradel, n. 143 above.

less well protected than is the freedom to have an abortion, and this cannot, surely, be the right approach. Irrespective of any question of fetal rights, to deprive a woman of her future child cannot be seen as anything less than a gross insult to her bodily integrity. Looked at in this way, protection of the fetus in no way conflicts with women's rights – rather, it enhances their right to conceive and carry a child free from external interference.

That being the case, the problem of viability, which is so much a feature of the abortion debate at both moral and legal levels, loses its meaning The woman who loses her fetus involuntarily is losing her prospective child and the individual fetus is being deprived of his or her potential life. The existing legal protection of the viable fetus is inadequate and one can only question why the distinction should be made.[152] Intuition surely tells us that non-consensual feticide ought to be an offence rather than something on which the law turns its back.

Do we need an offence of feticide?

The offences under the Offences Against the Person Act 1861 are broadly related to procuring the miscarriage of a woman and there is no doubt that doing so will result in the death of the fetus she is carrying in the vast majority of cases. But this is not to say that the two are necessarily the same – rather, they can be distinguished on several grounds. Historically, the purpose of the original Offences Against the Person Act of 1837 was, probably, to protect the woman against the negligence of the professional abortionist rather than to secure the life of her fetus.[153] Secondly, the offences proscribed in the 1861 Act are offences of intent, and it is by no means always the case that an intent to procure a miscarriage is the same as an intent to destroy the fetus. And, finally, there are more ways of killing a fetus than through the medium of abortion. A very good case can be made out for seeking to fill what looks to be, at least, a lacuna in the criminal law.

Here, I suggest, the hiatus lies in the insistence that the fetus must have progressed to the status of the neonate before it can be said legally to have sustained injury, In the present context, the *reductio ad absurdum* lies in the judgment of the French Criminal Division of the Court of Cassation in a case heard on 25 June 2002.[154] Here, the negligence of the health

---

[152] As noted above, n. 20, Balcombe LJ in the Court of Appeal in *Re F (in utero)* [1988] Fam 122, [1988] 2 All ER 193, was unable to see any logical difference between the early and the viable fetus as regards a need for protection.

[153] See, for example, *R* v. *Tait* [1990] 1 QB 290.

[154] Case 2, [29] of the majority opinion in *Vo* v. *France*.

carers caused the death of a fetus that was not only full term but was actually overdue. The court overturned the Court of Appeal's verdict that the midwife was guilty of unintentional homicide, stating that the 'facts are not capable of coming within the definition of any criminal offence'.[155]

At the same time, it is almost impossible to suppose that a United Kingdom court could have upheld the criminal charges against Mrs Vo's doctor either, given the fact that the child was, I believe, stillborn – and this is clearly wrong. We tend to forget that the fetal ambience has changed dramatically in the last thirty years or so.[156] It is difficult, for example, to be able to return a fetus to the uterus for maturation after performing major surgery and still to maintain that it has no legal standing; common sense tells us that, if it merits individual medical treatment, it also merits legal recognition.[157] The conclusion that the legislators and the lawyers have been so immersed in the abortion debate and the associated problems of women's rights that they cannot disengage from them seems unavoidable. Remove the phrase 'termination of pregnancy' and substitute the word which describes what is in issue – 'feticide' – and most of the jurisprudential problems disappear. In addition, and as I have suggested previously,[158] there is very little reason why a crime of feticide could not be defined as being subject to the terms of the Abortion Act 1967.

The facts of *Vo* v. *France* should, surely, encourage the medico-legal forum to maintain its concern for fetal rights and, particularly, to consider how these should, and could, be accommodated within Article 2 of the European Convention on Human Rights. As to the former, it is suggested that some such legal intervention is becoming increasingly inevitable as the physical and social status of the fetus attracts new meanings and understanding. As to the latter, it has been argued – it is hoped,

---

[155] And see also the Canadian case of *R* v. *Sullivan*, n. 129 above.

[156] 'It no longer makes sense to retain the ['born alive'] rule where its application woud be perverse' per Major J in *Winnipeg Child and Family Services (Northwest Area)* v. *G(DF)* (1997) 152 DLR (4th) 193 (S Ct) at [110]. This was, admittedly, in a dissenting opinion in a maternal fetal abuse case but it illustrates that others hold this view.

[157] The majority in *Vo* reminded us that the French National Assembly voted to amend the law and to create an offence of involuntary termination of pregnancy – the so-called 'Garraud amendment'. This amendment was rejected by the Senate largely on the grounds that it 'caused more problems than it solved' (Assemblée Nationale, proposition du loi no. 837, 14 May 2003).

[158] For previous discussion, see Mason, n. 132 above. A recent paper precipitated by Mrs Vo's case accepts the need to apply Article 2 to the fetus but only when the 'bright dividing line' of viability has been passed – which is roughly the present position in England and Wales. See Aurora Plomer, 'A foetal right to life? The case of *Vo v France*' (2005) 5 *Human Rights Law Review* 311–36.

persuasively – that we have no need to interfere with the abortion laws on this score. In my view, the wholly negative approach of the European Court of Human Rights perpetuates the fallacy that there is a necessary connection between abortion and feticide and actually sets back any reconsideration of both maternal and fetal interests in this area. I conclude this chapter by suggesting that we should seriously reconsider the status of the fetus – not with the intention of restricting women's autonomous choices but, rather, in the interests of *all* pregnant women.

3   Antenatal care and the action for wrongful birth

Introduction

In the discussion of abortion that has gone before, I have deliberately avoided the fourth ground on which a legal termination can be founded. This is because the motivation of and the moral issues involved in that sub-section are of a very different type from those addressed in Chapter 2. The now relevant text of the 1967 Act, section 1(1), reads that a person shall not be guilty of an offence under the law relating to abortion if, again, two registered medical practitioners are of the opinion, formed in good faith:

(d) That there is a substantial risk that if the child were born it would suffer from such physical or mental abnormalities as to be seriously handicapped.

I have to admit that, at one time, I was prepared to suggest that, second only to the saving of the mother's life, this was the ground which was most likely to be widely acceptable. It will become clear in the following pages that I now consider that to have been an unjustifiable view.

As a start to the analysis, it is to be noted that no time limit is now imposed under the subsection.[1] The practical reason underlying this relaxation is that the diagnosis of genetic or chromosomal disease is time consuming; given that the test may also have failed at the first attempt, it was more than possible that the conditions justifying lawful termination would be discovered only after remedial action in the form of abortion was rendered potentially illegal by virtue of the Infant Life (Preservation) Act 1929, section 1. A classic case is that of Mrs Gregory[2] to which we will return later. The doctor who performs a termination within the terms of the 1967 Act is, however, now no longer subject to the 1929 Act[3] – and, because misfortunes comparable to that

---

[1] Consequent on amendments to the Abortion Act 1967 introduced by the Human Fertilisation and Embryology Act 1990, s.37(1). Note that discussion of cases under this heading is, therefore, of a different quality depending on whether or not the amendment was in force at the time of the hearing.
[2] *Gregory* v. *Pembrokeshire Health Authority* [1989] 1 Med LR 81.
[3] Human Fertilisation and Embryology Act 1990, s.37(4).

which befell Mrs Gregory were not uncommon,[4] many would regard this as an improvement on the original legislation. Nonetheless, the possibility of a termination being lawful up to full term raises ethical issues of considerable importance on its own account.

Late termination of pregnancy

First, it will be appreciated that the maternal environment has changed. Whereas the woman seeking a termination under section 1(1)(a) of the Act does not want a child, she who takes advice in respect of section 1(1)(d) wants a child – and, for reasons given above is likely to have been carrying her child for an appreciable time – but she does not want a disabled child. As a consequence, the ethical, emotional and legal considerations surrounding the process are, now, of a different dimension.

Second, the doctor performing the operation must also reappraise his motives, remembering that it was said in the debate preceding the 1990 amendment:

If the fetus is mature enough to have a reasonable chance of survival with intensive care, all possible steps are taken to optimise the recovery of both mother and fetus.[5]

Which is a lofty view, taken from an impeccable moral position – but is it meaningful in practice? The obstetrician has contracted to relieve the woman of a child who, at the time of the operation, was unwanted; he or she cannot personally guarantee a successful adoption[6] and it might be considered that, in achieving a live birth, the obstetrician is abrogating his duty of care to the pregnant woman. The legal and technical conditions are, in fact, such that a living *normal* abortus must be a very rare event.[7] The possibility of a live birth is far greater in the case of abortions

---

[4] The previous effect of the 1929 Act is very well demonstrated and widely discussed in *Rance* v. *Mid-Downs Health Authority* [1991] 1 QB 587, [1991] 1 All ER 801. However, not all such instances resulted from genetic investigation – *Rance* was a case of missed neural tube defect.

[5] Official Reports (Lords) vol. 522, col. 1043, 18 October 1990 per Lord Ennals at 1052.

[6] Though, given the present situation, a successful outcome might well be anticipated. It could, indeed, be suggested that, subject to the woman's right to choose, adoption of a viable fetus might well be the preferred objective in *any* abortion. See Sheila A. M. McLean, 'Abortion Law: Is Consensual Reform Possible?' (1990) 17 *Journal of Law and Society* 106–23.

[7] It could occur when the expectation as to the *risk* of abnormality proves unfounded. The mother might also have an unwarranted *fear* of a disabled child though, in such circumstances, the termination would probably be under s.1(1)(a) and subject to the 24-week restriction. Otherwise, the situation could arise from terminations under s.1(1)(b) and (c) – in which case a living child could be the desired outcome.

performed under section 1(1)(d) and it is likely to be harder – albeit, mercifully, not always impossible – to find adopting parents for a seriously handicapped child.[8]

The doctor's dilemma could, therefore, be acute[9] and, as a result, the current professional guidelines recommend that abortions performed after the twenty-second week of pregnancy should be preceded by feticide[10] – apparently a remarkable volte-face since the days of Lord Ennals. This is clearly a pragmatic approach but one that is virtually dictated by the uncertainty as to the doctor's duty of care. We have, moreover, to remember that the criminal law is also involved. The Abortion Act 1967, section 5(1)[11] protects the doctor from the charge of child destruction and domestic law as to death *in utero* has been reinforced by the European decision in *Vo* v. *France*.[12] No overt statutory protection is, however, offered once the child has been delivered and, since it can be forcefully argued that the doctor now has a duty of care to the neonate, charges of both manslaughter and murder could be brought against one who abandons a living abortus. Empirical reports indicate that the opportunity arises fairly often[13] yet, the fact that there is so little reported legal action[14] suggests that the authorities, in addition to displaying a clear reluctance to reopen the abortion debate at any time, appreciate that this is a medical problem that is best resolved by the medical profession – indeed, it is both a logical consequence of and a logical reason for the medicalisation of abortion.

All of which presupposes that the fetus *wants* to be born alive and, in practice, the dilemma is aggravated by the possibility of a neonatal action

---

[8] It is reported that there were 104 such live births in the West Midlands Region between 1995 and 2002 (which suggests that there could be some 130 cases annually on a national scale): Elizabeth Wicks, Michael Wyldes and Mark Kilby, 'Late Termination of Pregnancy for Fetal Abnormality: Medical and Legal Perspectives' (2004) 12 *Medical Law Review* 285–305. This is an outstanding review of the situation.

[9] 1,900 abortions (1 per cent of the total) were performed by reason of suspected neonatal handicap in England and Wales in 2004 (Abortion Statistics, England and Wales: 2004).

[10] Lois Rogers, 'Fifty Babies a Year are Alive after Abortion' (2005) *Sunday Times*, 27 November.

[11] As amended by the Human Fertilisation and Embryology Act 1990, s.37(4).

[12] (2004) 79 BMLR 71, ECtHR, discussed in detail at p. 44 above.

[13] For anecdotal evidence, which is probably all that can be obtained, see Sarah-Kate Templeton and Lois Rogers, 'Babies that Live after Abortion are Left to Die' (2004) *Sunday Times*, 20 June, p. 1.3.

[14] In over 20 years, I have still only uncovered one apposite case – *R* v. *Hamilton* (unreported) (1983) *The Times*, 16 September, p. 1 – where the magistrates decided there was no case to answer in a prosecution led by the DPP. There have been a number of coroners' decisions sporadically reported in the news media in which no action has been taken. These cases are discussed, inter alia, in J. K. Mason and G. T. Laurie, *Mason & McCall Smith's Law and Medical Ethics* (7th edn 2005), 5.99–100.

for 'wrongful life' – a concept that is discussed in detail in Chapter 6. The doctor terminating a late pregnancy is, therefore, in a most difficult situation whether measured on the practical or the moral plane. The latter is further complicated by consideration of the purpose behind section 1(1)(d) which is colloquially known as the 'fetal ground'. But is it? Many years ago, Glanville Williams wrote:

> The argument for abortion on the fetal indication relates to the welfare of the parents whose lives may well be blighted by having to rear a grossly defective child, and perhaps secondarily by consideration for the public purse ... The fetus is destroyed not necessarily in its own interest ... but in the interests either of the parents or of society at large, though of course only on the request of the mother[15]

and, to the best of my knowledge, this has remained the accepted legal interpretation of the subsection.

The ethical implications are considerable. The conclusion that the fetus is being destroyed simply because it is imperfect is hard to resist – as is the extrapolation that section 1(1)(d) is an invitation to discrimination on the basis of disability;[16] many who campaign for the rights of the disabled will, additionally, hold that the section strikes at the status of *all* disabled persons.[17] We must, at the same time, appreciate the uneasy position of the pregnant woman whose choice cannot be made in a vacuum. It has, for example, been stated that more than 10 per cent of obstetricians agree that:

> The state should not be expected to pay for the specialised care of a child with a severe handicap where the parents had declined the offer of prenatal diagnosis [and, presumably, the resulting abortion – Auth.].[18]

The profound dilemma for all concerned in a late termination, which can be legally performed under subsection 1(1)(d) up to full term, is

---

[15] Glanville Williams, *Textbook of Criminal Law* (London: Stevens & Sons, 2nd edn 1983) at 297.

[16] The moral position is explored in depth by Sally Sheldon and Stephen Wilkinson, 'Termination of Pregnancy for Reasons of Foetal Disability: Are There Grounds for a Special Exception in Law?' (2001) 9 *Medical Law Review* 85–109. After extensive argument, however, the authors conclude that the essential discrimination lies in not allowing women a choice of abortion whatever the circumstances.

[17] Lynn Gillam, 'Prenatal Diagnosis and Discrimination against the Disabled' (1999) 25 *Journal of Medical Ethics* 163–71. For rejection of this thesis, see Raanan Gillon, 'Is there a New Ethics of Abortion?' (2001) 27 *Journal of Medical Ethics* supp II: ii5–9. That author's argument, however, depends upon denying a full moral status to the fetus.

[18] J. M. Green, 'Obstetricians' Views on Prenatal Diagnosis and Termination of Pregnancy: 1980 compared with 1993' (1995) 102 *British Journal of Obstetrics and Gynaecology* 228–32. Quoted in a very sympathetic article by John Wyatt, 'Medical Paternalism and the Fetus' (2001) 27 *Journal of Medical Ethics* suppl II: ii15–20.

amplified by what I see as a third major moral consequence – that the distinction between feticide and neonaticide is irrevocably blurred, and this, of itself, provokes further theoretical and practical quandaries.

The background difficulties are several. First, a genetic history may alert us to the likelihood of a disabled fetus; it cannot tell us whether or not a genetic defect is present. Second, while numerous antenatal tests, involving both mother and child and of varying degrees of invasiveness, are available by which to identify the presence of abnormality, they tell us the *degree* of disablement with far less definition. And, finally, it is well-nigh impossible, in terms of the overall loss of human life, to distinguish between the killing of a fetus in the last week of pregnancy and ending the life of the same child in the first week of extra-uterine existence.[19] Why, then, do we accept feticide when we are in a state of uncertainty and prohibit neonaticide when the precise state of the infant can be assessed?[20]

It is difficult to find a satisfactory reply and we return to the subject in Chapter 7. Meantime, the honest, albeit philosophically unsatisfactory, conclusion is probably to be derived from the intuitive belief that, logic or no logic, neither the law, nor the profession nor public opinion would tolerate causing the deliberate death of a child unless it was achieved by way of omission and, by consensus, that it was in the child's best interests not to be sustained. Such is the attitude to disability engendered by section 1(1)(d), however, that one can only hope that it will be possible to say the same a decade from now.

The uncertainties of subsection 1(d)

As a coda to this discussion, it has to be noted that the subsection is singularly unhelpful in the resolution of these dilemmas. It speaks of a substantial 'risk' – and it means just that. The significance lies in the risk – not the fulfilment of that risk; it follows that a termination under this head can be lawful despite the fact that the fetus is normal. Moreover, 'substantial' is a subjective concept which is to be defined by those making the

---

[19] This, of course, would be accepted by those who follow the Tooley school of 'person-hood' – for which see p. 16 above. That construct is, however, of no significance in the present context as it holds that neither the fetus nor the neonate qualify as 'persons'.

[20] The case of Dr Arthur (*R* v. *Arthur* (1981) 12 BMLR 1), which is discussed in detail in Chapter 7, stands out in the memory as an exception. It is, however, now 25 years old and it is hard to believe that either the law or the medical profession would support Dr Arthur today.

choice – that is, the woman, assisted by her medical adviser.[21] The same criticisms apply to the interpretation of 'serious handicap' which, again, is a phrase which can be invoked according to choice. For example, Kleinfelter's syndrome (for which, see below at p. 61) is a genetic disorder which results in some feminisation of the physique and the probability of infertility in the male. The majority would probably place this very low in their classification of physical handicap; but the author has yet to find an obstetrician who would not certify a termination on the grounds that the fetus was so affected if asked to do so.

A recently publicised example arose in *Jepson* v. *Chief Constable of West Mercia*.[22] Here, a minister of religion was granted judicial review of the police decision not to prosecute doctors who performed a late termination on a fetus with a cleft palate – a condition that may or may not 'seriously handicap' a child depending on its severity and on the skill of the remedial surgeon. But, as has already been inferred, it is impossible to demonstrate 'bad faith' on the part of the professionals involved granted that the risk is there. The Crown Prosecution Service declined to prosecute – and the cynic might reasonably suggest that its hesitation was yet another example of the politico-legal determination to avoid reopening the abortion debate. As a result, the case stalled at the first hurdle and, even if it is reopened,[23] it is unlikely to recover – particularly as any argument based on fetal 'human rights' has been virtually eliminated by the decision in *Vo* v. *France*.[24] The fundamental question is, however, of a wider nature – is fetal abnormality too complex a subject to be governed by a section that is as loosely drafted as is section 1(1)(d) or is the section deliberately so phrased in order to preserve its subjectivity? One suspects that the latter represents the political view and the subsection is unlikely to be changed in the foreseeable future; nevertheless, a test prosecution could be helpful to all concerned and, for this reason at least, Ms Jepson's lack of success is to be regretted.

---

[21] In this connection, the Royal College of Obstetricians and Gynaecologists believed that, to be substantial, a risk should be recognisable as such by 'informed persons with no personal involvement in the pregnancy or its outcome': *Termination of Pregnancy for Fetal Abnormality in England, Wales and Scotland* (1996), para. 3.2.2. But, since only the antenatal care team can realistically assess the risk, this is doing little more than applying the *Bolam* test (see p. 10 above).

[22] [2003] EWHC 3318, (2003) WL 23145287.

[23] Press statement http://www.jjepson.org of 15 April 2005. My information is that Ms Jepson has, in fact, abandoned her action. Currently, the case has been reported only in the news media: Ruth Gledhill 'Curate loses legal challenge over 'cleft-palate' abortion' (2005) *The Times*, 17 March, p. 14.

[24] n. 12 above.

Antenatal care and fetal abnormality

Thus far, however, the road may have been difficult but it has been relatively even. A pregnant woman is aware that her fetus is less than perfect. She does not want such a child and she is aware that the law will support her rejection of it in the fetal stage of development. But how has this equilibrium been reached? Although she may be perfectly capable of reaching her own conclusion, a woman cannot be *expected* to make a reasoned decision as to the disposal of a fetus at risk of congenital abnormality unless she is supplied with adequate information. This is the function of the antenatal health carers and these comprise men and women of varying, yet integrated, expertise and of proximity to the pregnant woman. In order to appreciate this diversity of responsibility, it will be appropriate, at this point, to consider briefly those congenital abnormalities that are likely to give rise to an action for wrongful birth when they occur in a child.[25]

Congenital disease

Congenital disease – that is, disease in the fetus that is present at birth or for which the seeds are present at birth – can be looked on as being due either to:

- genetic and chromosomal abnormalities – which it is convenient, though, strictly speaking, incorrect, to combine;[26] or to
- environmental factors; or to
- a combination of the two.

Each of these can either cause or predispose to disease. Thus, as we have already observed, the mere discovery – or inference – of an abnormal gene in a fetus, or of a predisposing environment, does not necessarily inform as to either diagnosis or prognosis in the resulting child.

Genetic disease.[27] The reasons for these shortcomings in respect of genetic disease are several. As to the first, it is well-known that similar

---

[25] So-called late onset genetic disease – in which the condition may not be manifested until adult life – is a highly significant factor in genetic counselling but is unlikely to lead to an action for wrongful birth (see p. 60).

[26] The most important practical difference is that the former are hereditary conditions whereas the great majority of the latter arise spontaneously and are environmentally influenced.

[27] It is invidious to pick out any of the many authoritative texts on the subject, the majority of which are probably too detailed for the lawyer's purposes. This author happens to find Robert F. Mueller and Ian D. Young, *Emery's Elements of Medical Genetics* (Edinburgh: Churchill Livingstone, 11th edn 2001) a useful *vade mecum* – but there are many others.

genes are present in the cell nuclei in pairs or as *alleles*, one being derived from each parent. The gene responsible for an abnormal condition may be *dominant* over its normal counterpart – in which case it will always be free to express itself – or it may be *recessive*, in which case it will be active only when it is not suppressed by a normal partner – in other words, when *both* alleles are abnormal. The correlative importance is, of course, that, although he or she does not manifest the abnormality, the person with a single recessive gene becomes a *carrier* for the condition.

The second reason for the diversity of genetic disease is that the *penetrance* of a gene is determined to large extent by the company it keeps. In practice, almost all genetic disease is of this *multifactorial* type; even if the origin of the disease process can be traced to a single, identifiable genetic mutation, its *expression* will be influenced by other factors and these may be related not only to associated genes but may also be *environmental*.[28]

Two specific aspects of the transmission of genetic disorder must be remembered. First, we have the occurrence of X-linked (or sex-linked) disease in which the recessive mutation is carried on the X sex chromosome. The presence of a normal X chromosome in the XX female configuration means that, while the affected female remains a carrier, the abnormal gene can only express itself in the XY male situation. Second, we should note the condition of late-onset genetic disease. This is of practical importance in that it explains the persistence of severe disease caused by a dominant injurious gene. In the usual circumstance, such disease should be self-limiting in that those in the affected population will tend to die before the gene is passed on; if, however, the condition does not manifest itself until late in life, they may have procreated before the danger is appreciated. Huntington's disease is the well-known classic example which demonstrates some of the complexities added to reproductive counselling in this special situation. It is clear, for example, that termination of pregnancy because of the presence of the Huntington gene in the fetus poses an exception to the general rule, discussed above, that termination under subsection 1(d) is for the benefit of the mother; rather, it is designed to eradicate a deleterious gene which will express itself in the individual with uncertain severity and at an uncertain time if it does so at all.

---

[28] Recent work in so-called epigenetics suggests that current theories as to genetic expression are too simple and it may be that the whole nuclear mass is involved. A whole issue of *Science* (2001), vol. 293, pp. 1001–208 is devoted to the subject but the papers are extremely technical.

The dilemma for the mother of the affected fetus must be well-nigh unbearable.[29]

Chromosomal disorder. Chromosomal disorder is of a different nature and is, essentially, a matter of an excess of chromosomes due to the fact that the pair do not split properly on the formation of gametes; as a result, three chromosomes will be left at a given locus when the zygote is formed.[30] This is known as a trisomy of which there are many variants – including trisomies of the sex chromosomes such as Kleinfelter's syndrome (XXY) which has already been noted; however, trisomy-21 which results in Down's syndrome is by far the most important. As is well-known, this – and other trisomies – can result in a number of fairly specific anatomical abnormalities together with an unpredictable degree of learning disability.[31] The significant difference from genetic disorder is that, in general, trisomies arise spontaneously, the risk depending almost entirely on the environmental factor of the mother's age.[32] The socially, and legally, important exception to this generalisation lies in the so-called Robertsonian translocation abnormality in which part of one chromosome becomes attached to another. This occurs spontaneously and is of no consequence to the original individual but, once established, the abnormality can be passed on by way of standard genetic inheritance principles. The situation, then, is that the child of the carrier may have a normal number of chromosomes but an increased chromosomal mass, and this will result in Down's syndrome if the extra mass derives from chromosome 21.

[29] The problem of the late-onset genetic dsease is raised again in Chapter 6. There is an associated minor legal quibble in that s.1(1)(d) of the 1967 Act legalises abortion if there is a substantial risk that 'if the child were born it would suffer' from serious handicap. Whether this means at the time of birth has not been decided in the courts. That being the case, one would think that, as a matter of common sense, the additional words 'now or in the future' can be read into the Act. It is not, however, a very satisfactory assumption. I. Kennedy and A. Grubb in *Medical Law* (London: Butterworths, 2000) come to much the same conclusion at p. 1427. For the interpretation of parliamentary intention, see *R (on the application of Quintavalle)* v. *Secretary of State for Health* [2003] 2 AC 687, [2003] 2 All ER 113.

[30] Clearly, the alternative is that the zygote contains only one chromosome but this is virtually incompatible with life other than when it occurs in the sex chromosomes (Turner's syndrome, in which women have only one X chromosome, is a major example). It is to be remembered that chromosome abnormalities are common and probably are to be found in some 20 per cent of conceptions (Mueller and Young, n. 27 above at p. 215). The great majority of affected fetuses are, however, lost naturally so that the incidence at birth is less than 1 per cent.

[31] Note, however, that the Fragile-X syndrome, which is probably the commonest cause of such disorder, is an X-linked genetic condition.

[32] Mueller and Young quote an incidence of Down's syndrome of 1:1500 at the age of 20, through 1:400 at age 35 to 1:30 at age 45.

The chances of a carrier of such a translocation producing a child with Down's syndrome are about 10 per cent in the case of females and 4 per cent of males and this, of course, is independent of age. The case of *Al Hamwi* v. *Johnston*[33] is instructive and is discussed further at p. 77.

Environmental factors. Environmental factors may constitute the only cause of congenital disease. The extent of such disability will become apparent in the following pages. For the present, I suggest that *viral infection* in the mother is by far the most important of these as a source of actions in negligence. Rubella, or German measles, is the most common in this context – possibly because it can occur in such benign form that the diagnosis may well be missed. Other cases have been caused by varicella (chicken-pox) infection and there is no reason why viraemia of any type should not affect the fetus in some way.[34] The effects may be devastating and include blindness, deafness and severe neurological disorder.

Drug induced congenital disease is a further significant category and, if one includes the fetal alcohol syndrome and intrauterine opiate poisoning in the classification, it may be one of the commonest causes of neonatal morbidity.[35] We will see in Chapter 6, however, that fetal injury from prescription drugs raises particular jurisprudential issues and, although intense research on drugs prior to their release has now decreased the incidence of such injuries, the use of therapeutic drugs in pregnancy is still a matter of major importance.

Finally, *haemolytic disease of the newborn*, which is due to rhesus blood group incompatibility between mother and fetus, is often quoted as an example of pure environmental disease although, since it results from *genetic* incompatibility, that may be a semantic misallocation. Once again, the condition is now rare but it provides a good example of the distinctive pre-conception tort; we consider it further at p. 196.

Combined genetic and environmental factors. The purist might say, with some justification, that *all* disease is, ultimately, the result of such a combination. Be that as it may, the classic examples lie in the neural tube

---

[33] [2005] Lloyd's Rep Med 309, QBD. For an earlier presumed example, see *Gregory* v. *Pembrokeshire Health Authority*, n. 2 above. Interestingly, both cases failed for much the same reasons.

[34] I am not discussing transmitted HIV infection here. Not only has it widespread and irrelevant ramifications but actions for wrongful birth or wrongful life associated with the condition would, I think, be untenable.

[35] Again, neither is likely to precipitate actions of the type considered in this book but both illustrate the great difficulty in allocating fetal 'rights' which have been touched on in Chapter 2.

defects represented by anencephaly and spina bifida – there is a strong genetic susceptibility but also a strong association with folic acid deficiency in the maternal diet. Neural tube defects illustrate the importance of the underlying cause in the calculation of risk of a child being affected. In a pure single gene disorder the chances of the gene being transmitted can, at least in theory, be accurately determined with relative accuracy. But, because of the varying penetrance of genes and of the effect of the associated mutifactorial elements, the chances of the mutation expressing itself can, in the absence of total dominance, generally be predicted only on the basis of probability. The problem is amplified as the importance of environmental factors increases; in general, then, the counsellor can only base his or her opinion on an empirical analysis of the history of the family and of the population.

Investigations available in the face of potential fetal abnormality

Whether the antenatal care team can discharge its particular duty to the pregnant woman as to the condition of her fetus depends on the tests and techniques available for this purpose; whether or not they have satisfied their duty depends, to a large extent, on how they have used and interpreted those tests and, since the great majority of this chapter – and of Chapter 6 – is concerned with failure in this respect, a short aide memoire as to their availability must be included at this pont.

Antenatal investigations designed to ensure the normality of or, more importantly in the medico-legal context, to identify an abnormal fetus must start with a family history – while this is common to all medical diagnosis, it is, of course, particularly imperative when one is specifically seeking evidence of hereditary disease.[36] Beyond that, investigations may be maternal or fetal and, at the same time, relatively invasive or non-invasive. Invasive testing introduces the hazards of fetal injury or disimplantation and all scientific tests cost money. The primary concern is, therefore, whether or not the offer of a test is warranted, either in relation to the risk to the fetus or to resource allocation – is it, for example, effective to test women under thirty years old for the presence of a Down's syndrome fetus and, if it is not, at what age should we introduce such an investigation as a routine?

---

[36] Much is currently written about the ethics of genetic testing in general; it is often forgotten that taking a family history as an aid to diagnosis has been the norm since time immemorial – yet it is no more or less than a primitive form of 'genetic testing'. Moreover, given the uncertainties surrounding the accuracy of newer forms of genetic testing and screening, some commentators still view the family history as the most important indicator of disease.

Maternal testing

Maternal serum tests. The most common maternal tests involve estimates of various protein constituents of the blood that have been found to vary in the presence of a fetus suffering from Down's syndrome and also of one with an open neurological abnormality. The simplest, but now replaced, is to measure only the maternal serum levels of α fetoprotein and human chorionic gonadotrophin (HCG) but the best that this can do is to indicate the need for more specific – and invasive – investigations. It is now claimed that the addition of two further analyses together with repeated ultrasonography can provide a detection rate of 85 per cent with a false positive rate of only 1 per cent – which is virtually a diagnostic test.[37] It is noteworthy that the government at the time of writing is seeking to introduce routine testing for Down's syndrome in all pregnant women.[38] Insofar as Down's children, for practical purposes, make no contribution to the gene pool, that there is no treatment of the condition and that its gravity cannot be determined by diagnostic tests, the only significant effect of such a programme can be to encourage terminations on the grounds of disability.[39] Again, however, the ethics of screening programmes are beyond the remit of this book.

Ultrasonography. Within the parameters of antenatal counselling, the main function of fetal ultrasonography is to detect anatomical anomalies. The simplest will be manifest abnormalities of the limbs or other parts of the skeleton but the most important are those related to the central nervous system in the form of neural tube defects, of which the commonest is spina bifida. Anatomical abnormalities of the internal organs are increasingly open to discovery. Changes in the soft tissues of the neck – an increase in the zone of so-called nuchal translucency – is a useful indicator of Down's syndrome at ten to thirteen weeks' gestation, particularly when combined with serum testing as above.[40]

Invasion of the fetal environment. The primary purpose of non-invasive investigation is to estimate the risk of the fetus being abnormal and to provide firm ground on which to, either, reassure the pregnant

[37] N. J. Wald, H. C. Watt and A. K. Hackshaw, 'Integrated Screening for Down's Syndrome on the Basis of Tests Performed during the First and Second Trimesters' (1999) 341 *New England Journal of Medicine* 461–7.

[38] Department of Health *Our Inheritance, Our Future* (2003), Cm. 5791–II.

[39] We have raised this problem elsewhere: Sheila A. M. McLean and J. Kenyon Mason, 'Our Inheritance, Our Future: Their Rights?' (2005) 13 *International Journal of Children's Rights* 255–72.

[40] For a simple, up-to-date analysis, see Zarko Alfirevic and James P. Neilson, 'Antenatal Screening for Down's Syndrome' (2004) 329 *British Medical Journal* 811–12.

woman or to recommend a specifically diagnostic invasive test. Current practice is to recommend the latter when the risk is 1:250 or greater, but this is, of course, modified by numerous subjective features of the individual case. As it has been wisely put: 'any "one size fits all" policy sits uncomfortably with pregnant women and clinicians'.[41] Effectively, there are two major procedures available.[42]

Amniocentesis. In this process, a specimen of amniotic fluid is withdrawn under ultrasound observation. The fluid can be analysed biochemically, especially for the diagnosis of neural tube defects. The contained fetal cells can also be cultured for chromosome and DNA analysis and to demonstrate the presence of the rare, but important, inborn errors of metabolism. The difficulties are considerable. Most importantly, an induced miscarriage occurs in up to 1 per cent of investigations. Occasionally, no fluid is obtained or the culture fails. Amniocentesis is best performed at 16 weeks' gestation; satisfactory culture generally occupies a further two weeks. Given, also, that the progress of the investigation may not be ideal, it will be appreciated that a termination, if indicated, will certainly be late and, as we will see when considering the relevant cases, many women who would have accepted an early abortion will not do so in the second trimester and beyond.

Chorionic villus sampling. For these reasons, chorionic villus sampling, which is performed at 10 to 12 weeks' gestation, has obvious attractions. Here, cells of fetal origin are taken from the early placenta. Chromosomal analysis can be undertaken directly and the availability of large amounts of fetal DNA means that many single gene disorders can also be diagnosed without the need for culture. The main contraindications are that the technique is complicated; it is not everywhere available and it may be associated with later limb deformities. Most significantly, it carries a miscarriage rate of some 2 to 3% – at least twice that of amniocentesis. It may also harvest maternal rather than fetal cells – occasionally with disastrous results.[43]

---

[41] Alfirevic, n. 40 above. At the same time, failure to *offer* counselling and testing may well be regarded as a failure in the duty of care: *Enright* v. *Kwun* (2003) EWHC 1000 (QB), *The Times*, 20 May.

[42] Fetal or umbilical cord blood sampling, fetoscopy and fetal biopsy can be undertaken but their usefulness is very specific and, currently, they are out of favour, largely by reason of possible fetal loss.

[43] A remarkable example is provided in the US case *Schirmer* v. *Mt Auburn Obstetrics and Gynecologic Associates, Inc.* 802 NE 2d 723 (Ohio, 2003) in which maternal cells containing a balanced translocation trisomy were mistaken for fetal cells which, in fact, contained an unbalanced abnormality. For a very recent and significant UK case involving the β-thalassaemia gene, in which culture was needed, see *Farraj* v. *King's Healthcare NHS Trust* [2006] EWHC 1228, QB.

It is to be noted that, attractive though chromosomal and DNA analysis may be, it is not without its own ethical problems. It is emphasised once again that the mere discovery of the cause of an abnormality does not necessarily indicate how serious will be the result. Moreover, many discoverable single gene abnormalities do not indicate any more than the *propensity* to disease.[44] More important from the practical aspect is the number and choice of tests. The patient may seek advice on the likelihood of one particular abnormality being present. Yet routine testing may involve several conditions and the mere process of drawing the chromosomal map (or idiogram) dictates that *any* abnormality is likely to show up. Is it, then, ethical to load the woman with information she has not sought?[45] If not, then is it ethical to withhold information that may be of major importance to the woman herself and/or to the future child she is carrying? The dilemma is acute, and emphasises that antenatal care must be carefully predetermined – counselling begins before, not after, diagnostic tests have been performed.

The principles of antenatal care

In practice, the obstetrician has very little contact with the pregnant woman between diagnosis and delivery; antenatal care in the United Kingdom is the work of a team for which the relevant NHS Trust is vicariously responsible. The interpretation of the various tests performed, thus, devolves on a number of individuals.

Clearly there must be an overall coordinator, whether this be the obstetrician or a specialist employed for the task, who will be responsible, first, for taking a family history which is likely to indicate the scope of further investigations and, second, for integrating these into a composite of information that can be provided to the patient. From what has been said, it will be apparent that a number of professionals will contribute to information gathering – among which one might include the radiologist, the immunologist/microbiologist and the geneticist. Ultimately, however, one person will be responsible for distribution of that information which will enable the patient to decide on whether or not to continue with her pregnancy; it is convenient to refer to that person as the antenatal counsellor.[46]

---

[44] E.g. the breast cancer risk genes BRCA 1 and BRCA 2.

[45] For discussion of the role of ignorance in genetics in general, see Graeme T. Laurie, 'In Defence of Ignorance: Genetic Information and the Right not to Know' (1999) 6 *European Journal of Health Law* 119–32.

[46] The title of 'genetic counsellor' is often given but is a misnomer insofar as much of the data used is non-genetic.

Antenatal counselling

The theory and practice of antenatal counselling lies at the heart of this chapter yet it is almost impossible to provide an outline which will cover all individuals and all circumstances. At base, the extent and nature of the information provided must rest on the choice, or autonomy, of the recipient rather than on that of the provider and should, in theory, be non-directive. Yet, in satisfying the terms of the doctrine of 'informed consent',[47] the counsellor cannot help but indicate, at least, that there is some information to give – the neutrality of the ground is undermined from the start.

Once having started, the problems accumulate.[48] It is widely stated that antenatal counselling must be non-inductive – the parents should make up their own minds according to their circumstances. But, at the same time, one must ask whether this is ever possible – and, even, is it desirable?[49] To begin with, the answer is seldom clear cut and the counsellor is performing a mental balancing act ab initio. The parents cannot do this alone – they do not want a check list of facts, they want advice as to the interpretation of those facts. And, if the counsellor has come to a reasoned decision, is it ethically correct for him or her not to express that in positive terms? The duty of the counsellor is to give positive advice in an unprejudiced fashion and, at the same time, to explain the alternatives and why he or she is discarding them. This is not paternalism – the autonomy of the parents is preserved in that they can accept or refuse the advice.[50] The dark side of the equation is, of course, that we live in the age of blame and a wrong choice is likely to lead to recrimination. In order to avoid this, I suggest that, in summary, the counsellor's duty of care is satisfied if he or she:

- has ensured that such investigations and specific tests as would be appropriate in the circumstances have been carried out;

---

[47] Whether such a doctrine exists in English and Scots law, or whether it is a purely American construct, is a matter for discussion. Whatever the true answer, the phrase is now a matter of medico-legal lore even if not of medical law. The interested reader may like to compare Dunn LJ: 'The concept of informed consent forms no part of English law' in *Sidaway* v. *Board of Governors of the Bethlem Royal Hospital and the Maudsley Hospital* [1984] QB 493, CA at 517 with Lord Steyn in *Chester* v. *Afshar*, n. 63 below, at [16].

[48] As has been recognised from the outset: Nuffield Council on Bioethics *Genetic Screening: Ethical Issues* (1993).

[49] See Angus Clarke (ed.), *Genetic Counselling: Practice and Principles* (London, Routledge, 1994) and, the same author, 'Is Non-directive Genetic Counselling Possible?' (1991) 338 *Lancet* 998–1001.

[50] For a very good overview of antenatal counselling, albeit from a transatlantic aspect, see Sonia Mateu Suter, 'The Routinization of Prenatal Testing' (2002) 28 *American Journal of Law and Medicine* 233–70.

- has considered and interpreted the findings in a reasonable way;
- and, finally, has presented the facts in a balanced way such as to enable the parents to come to a reasoned decision.[51]

And therein lies the rub. No matter what tests have been done and have been interpreted in isolation, the end and the end-point of counselling lie in communication and it is failure in this respect that essentially deprives a woman carrying a disabled fetus of the opportunity to terminate her pregnancy. Inevitably, then, a high proportion of actions for wrongful birth will be based on what is known as 'information based negligence'. Equally inevitably, we must consider the principles underlying the 'duty to inform' before we can analyse the relevant cases – and, unfortunately, this cannot be done in a few lines.[52]

Information based negligence

The duty of care. The essential problem can, however, be distilled into a single question – is the provision of information to be regarded as an integral part of medical treatment or is it, rather, the foundation upon which the patient can build an autonomous therapeutic decision.

The former view, which expresses what is commonly called the professional standard, now closely resembles a reliquary tended by a rapidly diminishing number of medical and legal devotees who are confined to the United Kingdom. It probably reached its apogee in *Gold* v. *Haringey Area Health Authority*[53] in which the Court of Appeal held that the *Bolam*[54] test of the standard of care not only applied to the provision of therapeutic advice, but also when assessing the quality of non-therapeutic advice – in the instant case, to contraceptive technique. Lloyd LJ quoted Lord Diplock in the seminal case of *Sidaway*:

---

[51] In parentheses, I would not regard the offer of a test on condition that the counsellor's advice is followed as satisfying these conditions. See the House of Commons Science and Technology Committee *Human Genetics: The Science and its Consequences*, Third Report (1995), para. 90.

[52] Whole books – and large numbers of them – have been written on the subject. There are many more recent, but very few better, than the analysis by Sheila A. M. McLean, *A Patient's Right to Know: Information Disclosure, the Doctor and the Law* (Aldershot, Dartmouth, 1989). Professor McLean expresses her views more recently and succinctly in S. A. M. McLean and J. K. Mason, *Legal and Ethical Aspects of Healthcare* (Cambridge: Cambridge University Press, 2003), chapter 4. Some 200 pages are devoted to the subject in the major medico-legal work by Kennedy and Grubb, *Medical Law*, n. 29 above.

[53] [1988] QB 481, [1987] 2 All ER 888.

[54] *Bolam* v. *Friern Hospital Management Committee* [1957] 2 All ER 118, (1957) 1 BMLR 1. See Chapter 1 for explanation.

The general duty of a doctor [to improve the patient's health in any particular respect in which the patient has sought his aid] is not subject to dissection into a number of component parts to which different criteria of what satisfies the duty of care apply.[55]

The current general tenor in the English speaking world, however, is to see the adequacy of the information provided as a matter for the patient to decide – in other words to apply a patient orientated standard which can, itself, be broken down into, on the one hand, the objective, or reasonable, patient standard and, on the other, the subjective standard which measures what the *individual* patient would require to know. The subjective patient standard is, to some, the only logical response to the ideal of fully informed patient choice. Yet it is clearly open to abuse – a combination of hindsight and bitterness can, if allowed full rein, expose the doctor to unjustified accusations of information based negligence. Even today, it is doubtful if any jurisdictions demand such a test of liability save in the context of direct questioning; a false or evasive answer to a request for specific information would be most likely regarded as falling below the duty of care expected from a competent health carer.[56]

The construct of the objective patient standard is, however, now widely established. It was set in the United States in *Canterbury* v. *Spence*[57] and, in the Commonwealth, in the very persuasive case of *Reibl* v. *Hughes*[58] in which the concept of considering the importance of and the incidence of risks in relation to the expectation of being given information on the subject was developed. But by far the most trenchant rejection of the professional standard of information disclosure was provided in the Australian case of *Rogers* v. *Whitaker*, the gist of which is summed up:

There is a fundamental difference between, on the one hand, diagnosis and treatment and, on the other hand, the provision of advice or information to the patient ... Because the choice to be made calls for a decision by the patient on information known to the medical practitioner but not to the patient, it would be

---

[55] *Sidaway* v. *The Governors of the Bethlem Royal Hospital and the Maudsley Hospital* [1985] AC 871, [1985] 1 All ER 643, at AC 893.

[56] See Lord Bridge in *Sidaway*, n. 55 above, AC 871 at 898. It is possible, even in such an extreme situation, that the doctor could plead 'professional privilege' should he mislead on the grounds that to be truthful would damage the health of his or her patient – see the doubts expressed by Neill LJ in *Blyth* v. *Bloomsbury Health Authority* [1993] 4 Med LR 151, CA at 160 – but I am not convinced that such extenuation would be accepted more than a decade later.

[57] 464 F 2d 772 (DC, 1972). Needless to say, with a mix of 51 jurisdictions, there are differences and the professional standard is maintained, with diminishing authority, in a number of states.

[58] [1980] 2 SCR 880, (1980) 114 DLR (3rd) 1. Relevant UK cases refer repeatedly to *Reibl*.

illogical to hold that the amount of information to be provided by the medical practitioner can be determined from the perspective of the practitioner alone or, for that matter, of the medical profession.[59]

Meanwhile, as has already been intimated, the toehold that *Bolam* retains within the United Kingdom in respect of information disclosure is fast being loosened. In the House of Lords, *Sidaway* recognised its continuing application by a 4 to 1 majority, yet the speeches were scarcely enthusiastic, and all their Lordships, other than Lord Diplock, deviated from an unadulterated professional standard of disclosure to some extent. The most significant statement, in my opinion, came from Lord Templeman who said:

> If the doctor ... advises the patient to submit to [an] operation, the patient is entitled to reject that advice for reasons that are rational or irrational or for no reason. The duty of the doctor in these circumstances ... is to provide the patient with information which will enable the patient to make a balanced judgment if the patient chooses to make a balanced judgment.[60]

And that, I believe, still represents the law as it stands today. Moreover, it is important that the doctor not only provides the necessary information, but also that the information is provided in a format that is within the patient's understanding.[61]

Since then, the then Master of the Rolls, Lord Woolf, has very significantly introduced the concept of the reasonable patient to the Court of Appeal, where he said:

> It seems to me to be the law ... that if there is a significant risk which would affect the judgment of a reasonable patient, then in the normal course it is the responsibility of a doctor to inform the patient of that significant risk, if the information is needed so that the patient can determine for him or herself as to what course he or she should adopt.[62]

---

[59] (1992) 175 CLR 479 at 489, (1993) 16 BMLR 148 at 156 per the majority. Gudron J went so far as to suggest that a subjective patient test might be grafted on to the reasonable patient's expectations. For one of many useful reviews of *Rogers*, see Don Chalmers and Robert Schwartz, '*Rogers* v. *Whittaker* and Informed Consent in Australia: A Fair Dinkum Duty of Disclosure' (1993) 1 *Medical Law Review* 139–59. See also the South African acceptance of *Rogers* in *Castel* v. *De Greef* 1994 (4) SA 408.

[60] *Sidaway*, n. 55 above, at AC 904.

[61] *Lybert* v. *Warrington Health Authority* [1996] 7 Med LR 71, CA. See also *Al Hamwi* v. *Johnston*, n. 33 above discussed in detail at p. 77 below. It may be that the *Bolam* test is merely being modified as the threshold of the duty of the 'responsible doctor' changes. See Murray Earle, 'The Future of Informed Consent in British Common Law' (1999) 6 *European Journal of Health Law* 235–48.

[62] In *Pearce* v. *United Bristol Healthcare NHS Trust* (1999) 48 BMLR 118 at 124.

And, recently, the House of Lords, in *Chester* v. *Afshar*,[63] has virtually ignored *Bolam* and has accepted that the patient's expectations define the standard of information delivery.

Thus, the future may seem clear but, even so, the present is still cloudy. In *Pearce*, for example, although Lord Woolf spoke of the reasonable patient, he nevertheless reverted to *Bolam* in his analysis and, in a recent and most useful review of cases post-*Bolitho*,[64] Maclean concluded that *Bolam* was by no means dead.[65] Nonetheless, the overall, and strong, impression is that *Chester*, which is discussed further at p. 76 below, sends out an unmistakable message that *Bolam* will assume decreasing importance in future cases of information based negligence.

Causation. For an action in information based negligence to succeed, the complainant must prove that the failure in communication caused a recognisable injury. In the present context, this means that a woman would have made a different decision had she been better informed and this, in turn, in the context of the wrongful birth action, effectively means that she would have elected to terminate her pregnancy.

An analysis of the cases suggests that this is likely to be her stiffest obstacle – largely because she not only has to believe that she would have adopted a certain course but, so far as current cases of wrongful birth indicate, she also has to *prove* that she would have done so – and all this in face of the fact that the woman in the wrongful birth case was undeniably *seeking* motherhood. Hence, she not only has to be an effective witness but she also has to engage the sympathy of the judge in the face of a strong, corporate defence. Any assessment of the decision that an individual woman would have made in a hypothetical situation is bound to be subjective and this raises difficulties on both sides. In the first place, it is inherently unlikely that a woman who has been caused considerable distress as a result of a decision that was expected to result in much happiness is unlikely to believe that she would not have decided otherwise

---

[63] *Chester* v. *Afshar* [2005] 1 AC134, [2004] 4 All ER 587. I have discussed the case in Kenyon Mason and Douglas Brodie, 'Bolam, Bolam ... Wherefore Art Thou Bolam?' (2005) 9 *Edinburgh Law Review* 298–306. For a recent, in depth, analysis, see David Meyers, '*Chester* v. *Afshar*: Sayonara, Sub Silentio, *Sidaway*?' in Sheila A. M. McLean (ed.) *First Do No Harm* (Aldershot: Ashgate, 2006), chapter 16.

[64] *Bolitho* v. *City and Hackney Health Authority* [1998] AC 232, [1997] 4 All ER 771. *Bolitho* has been explored more fully in Chapter 1. For present purposes, it is important to remember that *Bolitho* was *not* concerned with information disclosure.

[65] Alasdair Maclean, 'Beyond *Bolam* and *Bolitho*' (2002) 5 *Medical Law International* 205–30.

had she received different professional advice.[66] Less commonly, the patient's state of mind may expose the doctor to her 'hindsight and bitterness'[67] and the judge may well have this at the back of his or her mind. Thus, on the other side of the bench, the subjective test depends not only on *the judicial* state of mind but also on the judge's assessment of the plaintiff's motivation and credibility – and these are matters of fact to be determined by the trial judge which the Court of Appeal cannot gainsay.[68]

Old though it is, the case of Mrs Gregory[69] still remains the exemplar. There was a history of Down's syndrome in Mrs Gregory's family, although she herself had already had a normal child, and, as a result, she was recommended an amniocentesis – although, since she was aged only 28, there was little enthusiasm behind the offer. She underwent the procedure but the specimen was unsatisfactory and, by the time this became apparent, she was 21 weeks' pregnant. Her medical advisers decided against a repeat test[70] – but, unfortunately, she was not informed of either the complication or the decision. On the birth of an affected child, she brought what was a relatively novel wrongful birth action against the Health Authority in which the facts were undisputed and negligence as to information disclosure was agreed. She failed, however, on the grounds that she had not shown that she would not have accepted advice against having a second diagnostic test nor that, as a consequence, she would have terminated the pregnancy. Rougier J took the view that:

[W]e can only conjecture as to what we would have done had matters turned out differently, and that conjecture is bound to be influenced, subconsciously, by

---

[66] Having said which, it is a source of comfort to recognise how often disabled infants rapidly become much loved members of the family. The basis for perhaps the majority of wrongful birth actions is no more than that to care for such a child often costs more than the parents can afford.

[67] A phrase used by Anonymous, 'Informed Consent: A Proposed Standard for Medical Disclosure' (1973) 48 *New York University Law Review* 548–63 at 550 which greatly influenced Laskin CJ and the Court in *Reibl* at 15.

[68] 'It is well-established that [the Court of Appeal] will not interfere with a finding of fact . . . if a judge has based, in part at any rate, his assessment on seeing and hearing the witness and on his view of him': Stuart Smith LJ in *Fallows* v. *Randle* [1997] 8 Med LR 160. Permission to appeal against the trial judge's decision that a woman *would* have had a termination if properly advised was, for example, refused in *Wyatt* v. *Curtis* [2003] EWCA Civ 1779 at [1]. Similar problems of causation were argued in this case which was eventually settled on grounds of liability.

[69] *Gregory* v. *Pembrokeshire Health Authority*, n. 2 above.

[70] On the grounds that she would have been 24½ weeks' pregnant by the time the result was available. The court accepted that, in 1979, 24 weeks represented the threshold for 'capable of being born alive' for the purposes of interpreting the Infant Life (Preservation) Act 1929, s.1(1). In fact, it played no part in the judgment but it would, very probably, have demonstrated a translocation defect (see p. 61).

what has happened to us in the meantime. It is not integrity which is in question but objectivity... This [evidence] provides an illustration of how the objectivity of an honest witness can fail in the circumstances of stress.[71]

The Court of Appeal unanimously upheld the judge's interpretation of the evidence. Nevertheless, *Gregory* is, I suggest, an unsatisfactory case – not least because what the trial judge considered to be 'well-nigh compelling' medical opinion was, at least, open to question.[72] Perhaps more importantly, one could ask if it is right that a major decision should turn on the interpretation of a woman's 'hypothetical response to hypothetical advice given at a hypothetical consultation'.[73] It seems to this writer that the effect of this approach to causation is to turn judges into psychologists rather than triers of fact and that this cannot be conducive to uniformity.

In the light of such subjectivity, there is, thus, much to be said for adopting the reasonable woman as the benchmark in addressing causation in this context – that is, to use an objective test. Insofar as reasonableness *can* be defined – and there are many who would reject the possibility as will-o'-the-wisp – it obviates many of the difficulties outlined above. At the same time, it is potentially unfair in that it prohibits the plea 'I am *not* a reasonable woman within your terms'. The issue is well-balanced and the arguments were particularly well exposed in the important Canadian case of *Arndt* v. *Smith* which, ultimately went to a nine-judge bench in the Supreme Court.[74]

Ms Arndt suffered from chicken pox during her pregnancy and was supplied with what was agreed to be inadequate information as to the possible effects on her fetus who was born with serious congenital disabilities that were attributable to the infection. The question of liability, thus, rested entirely on causation and this, in turn, was to be decided on the basis of the correct test to be applied in assessing Ms Arndt's likely reaction to abortion had she been properly advised. At first instance,[75] Hutchison J found that she would still have persisted with her pregnancy – this being based very much on evidence that the parents badly wanted a child and that Ms Arndt had refused an ultrasound scan.[76] In retrospect,

---

[71] *Gregory*, n. 2 above, at 86.

[72] The chances of a woman aged 28 having a Down's syndrome child were assessed as between 800:1 and 1000:1; whereas the chances in the case of a female carrier of the relevant translocation, which one may assume Mrs Gregory to have been, having such a child are about 10 per cent.

[73] The description is that of Nicholls LJ in the Court of Appeal, *Gregory*, n. 2 above, at 89.

[74] The case is also reported as far as the Court of Appeal in [1996] 7 Med LR 108.

[75] (1994) 93 BCLR (2d) 220.

[76] The Court of Appeal, however, considered that the evidence that Ms Arndt wanted a child and that she was suspicious of mainstream medicine was 'subjective' and inadmissible as to causation; *Arndt* v. *Smith* (1995) 126 DLR (4th) 705 at [86].

there is some doubt as to the test he applied and this is understandable in view of his remark:

If a physician fails to warn his or her patient of all material risks, the issue of whether that patient would have requested a therapeutic abortion had she been advised of those risks must be determined objectively by the trier of fact *after taking into account the patient and her particular circumstances*[77] (my emphasis)

which reads rather like a contradiction in terms.[78] Even so, the Court of Appeal[79] itself found very great difficulty in translating the test applied to the *duty of care* in respect of information disclosure that was elaborated in *Reibl* v. *Hughes*[80] to the issue of *causation*.[81] Lambert JA, for example, considered the position where *some* reasonable women would have adopted a different course from that taken by the plaintiff and concluded that, given that there is a fiduciary relationship between doctor and patient, which is an uneasy assumption, the court must find in favour of the plaintiff – a conclusion which seems to *assume* causation in any case of inadequate information disclosure.[82] Having set up this challenge, he then expressed the objective/subjective dilemma succinctly:

[T]he trial judge stated his conclusions in terms of what Ms Arndt herself would have done. This is not how I understand the modified objective test. It is not designed to determine what Ms Arndt would have done. It is designed to determine what a reasonable patient in Ms Arndt's objectively ascertainable circumstances would have done.[83]

Which, again, seems, at least to this author, to be a very slender distinction on which to judge the entitlement or non-entitlement of substantial damages. In the end, however, the court ordered a new trial on the more substantial grounds that the trial judge's rejection was wrongly based – perhaps, in so doing, providing an example of the 'subjective judge'.

---

[77] n. 75 above, at 222.
[78] But one can find the same confusion in the US courts: 'The objective standard affords the ease of applying a uniform standard while maintaining the flexibility of allowing the fact finder to make appropriate adjustments to accommodate the individual characteristics and idiosyncrasies of an individual patient': *Ashe* v. *Radiation Oncology Assocs.* 9 SW 3d 119 (Tenn., 1999) at 122.
[79] (1995) 126 DLR (4th) 705.   [80] (1980) 114 DLR (3rd) 1.
[81] Indeed, Wood JA went so far as to suggest that to do so was to invite a misappropriation of the evidence (see n. 79 above, at [92]).
[82] Or 'Once the Court has determined that the non-disclosed acts were material, speculation as to what course the constituent, on disclosure, would have taken is not relevant' quoted from *London Loan & Savings Co of Canada* v. *Brickenden* [1934] 3 DLR 465, PC per Lord Thankerton at 469: see n. 79 above, at [48].
[83] n. 79 above, at [61]. But, to complicate the issue still further, Hollinrake JA thought that a desire to have a child was evidence that was admissible under the 'reasonable patient' head.

And so the Supreme Court of Canada[84] where the question presented was seen as how to determine whether the patient would have actually chosen to decline surgery if he or she had been properly informed of the risks. Once again, the difficulties involved in answering the question correctly were rehearsed in the various opinions. Sopinka J and Iacobucci J believed that the trial judge had applied an objective test but had failed to consider Ms Arndt's testimony – in short he should have adopted the subjective approach. In contrast, McLachlin J interpreted Hutchison J as having taken the subjective path and it was, in her view, correct to have done so: 'The fundamental principles of negligence law suggest that the test is what the particular plaintiff before the court would have done' (at [40]).

The majority, however, held firmly that the correct approach was via the middle road – the court should adopt the modified objective test set out in *Reibl* v. *Hughes*, which relies on a combination of objective and subjective factors in order to determine whether the failure to disclose actually caused the harm of which the plaintiff complains. It requires that the court consider what the reasonable patient in the plaintiff's circumstances would have done if faced with the same situation. On the one hand, the 'reasonable person' who sets the standard for the objective test must be taken to possess the patient's reasonable beliefs, fears, desires and expectations; on the other, the trier of fact must take into consideration any 'particular concerns' of the patient and any 'special considerations affecting the particular patient'. The present author has always regarded the *Reibl* construct as providing the optimal solution to the problem of the duty of care as related to information disclosure – but this is largely because it represents a common sense approach which is probably taken, if only subconsciously, by most judges; there seems no reason why it should not be applied to causation.[85]

Be that as it may, appeals in 'wrongful birth' actions are so rare in the United Kingdom that it is difficult to assess with certainty what 'test' is in general use. Cory J, speaking for the majority in *Arndt*,[86] hinted that the subjective test may be the most logical and McLachlin J[87] said that it may be taken as settled that it applies in England. While this may well be so, there is no real evidence that it operates in favour of the hind-sighted patient as has been so widely feared – indeed, the opposing ill-effect may

---

[84] *Arndt* v. *Smith* [1997] 2 SCR 539.
[85] The English courts have had no difficulty in doing so in respect of the *Bolam* principle. See *Bolitho* v. *City and Hackney Health Authority* [1998] AC 232, [1997] 4 All ER 771.
[86] In *Arndt* v. *Smith*, n. 84 above at [17].   [87] ibid., at [46].

be operating[88] and there is a general impression that the courts may be anxious to achieve a fairer balance. For a look into the future, we can consider the apparently unrelated case of *Chester* v. *Afshar*.[89]

Chester v. *Afshar* was a classic case of information based negligence in which causation constituted the central question; the fact that it concerned failure to warn of the inherent risks in an orthopaedic operation does not foreclose discussion in the present context – deciding to have or not to have surgery on the basis of professional advice is on all fours with opting for or against a termination of pregnancy on similar grounds. In the instant case, Ms Chester was not informed of a 1 to 2 per cent risk of severe disability subsequent to the operation no matter how expertly it was performed; she underwent surgery, the risk materialised and she sued Mr Afshar in negligence. Mr Afshar's negligence in failing to warn her was not disputed. At the same time, however, it was agreed that, while Ms Chester, had she been warned, would not have had the operation at the time she did, she was unable to claim that she would never have done so – as a result her case would fail on grounds of causation if the conventional principles of tort law were applied. To an extent, then, she was a victim of her own honesty. This was considered when the case reached the House of Lords, where Lord Hope said:

> To leave the patient who would find the decision [whether to run a risk] difficult without a remedy, as the normal approach to causation would indicate, would render the duty [to inform] useless in the cases where it may be needed most. This would discriminate against those who cannot honestly say that they would have declined the operation once and for all if they had been warned.

And then, significantly:

> The function of the law is to enable rights to be vindicated and to provide remedies when duties have been breached. Unless this is done, the duty is a hollow one, stripped of all practical force and devoid of all content.[90]

And the resultant opinion of a 3 to 2 majority of the House is well-expressed in the words of Lord Steyn:

> I have come to the conclusion that, as a result of the surgeon's failure to warn the patient, she cannot be said to have given informed consent to the surgery in the

---

[88] There have been occasional cases of wrongful birth since *Gregory* in which negligence was accepted but the woman was unable to convince the judge as to causation – inter alia, *Deriche* v. *Ealing Hospital NHS Trust* [2003] EWHC 3104 (varicella syndrome). But the two elements of duty and causation are hard to separate – in *C* v. *Health Authority* [1999] CLY 4002, C would have terminated had she been given an additional scan; a conservative attitude to the use of scans was, however, considered justifiable in 1998.

[89] [2005] 1 AC 134, (2004) 81 BMLR 1.   [90] ibid., AC at [87].

full legal sense. Her right of autonomy and dignity can and ought to be vindicated by a narrow and modest departure from traditional causation principles.[91]

In summary, *Chester* appears, as we have seen, finally to reject the *Bolam* or professional standard of care as related to the provision of information and to replace it with, at least, that anticipated by the reasonable patient.[92] More importantly in the present context, in allowing full compensation for injury simply for denying the patient the right to choose or reject a treatment, the decision seems to be introducing a new tort based on breach of autonomy.[93] It will become apparent in the chapters which follow, that the sacrifice of legal principle in favour of a policy, no matter how well-intentioned, can result in, at least, a mixed blessing.[94] Nevertheless, the House of Lords has spoken and there is little reason why a similar policy should not be applied in future to actions for wrongful birth – and, possibly, for wrongful life[95] – in which case, the balance of success in such cases may alter markedly.

Epilogue – the case of Mrs Al Hamwi. As something of an epilogue to this lengthy review of antenatal care, it will, I think, be appropriate to visit the case of Mrs Al Hamwi[96] which gathers together many of the several threads we have drawn under that heading. Mrs Al Hamwi already had one normal child and was aged 29 at the time she sought a second. Four of her cousins, a niece, a nephew and a half sister all suffered from a rapidly fatal congenital condition which was considered to be Down's syndrome – and she informed the hospital of this.[97] At 11 weeks' gestation she was told by her general practitioner that it was 'too late to have genetic tests' – a rather strange comment that was not followed up in the judgment – and, owing to the doctor's failure to write an appointment letter, it was not until she was 17 weeks pregnant that she was referred for antenatal care at the hospital, where maternal serum tests were carried out and the question of amniocentesis was raised. From there on, the evidence of the claimant and the defendant, inevitably, differed. It is reasonably clear, however, that, while she originally wanted the invasive investigation, she had changed her mind at the end of an hour-long consultation.

---

[91] ibid., AC at [24].   [92] See Mason and Brodie; Meyers, n. 63 above.
[93] See also Sarah Devaney, 'Autonomy Rules OK' (2005) 13 *Medical Law Review* 102–7. A comparison with the case of *Rees* v. *Darlington Memorial NHS Trust* [2004] AC 309, discussed below in Chapter 5 is an interesting exercise.
[94] Lord Bingham, for example, pointed out that, if failure to warn was, of itself, sufficient to found a successful claim, the patient would succeed even if he or she would have opted for surgery in any event (see n. 90 above, AC at [9]).
[95] See Chapter 6 below.   [96] n. 33 above.
[97] In fact, it later turned out to be a much rarer, and unusual, translocation abnormality.

She had been provided with an amniocentesis information leaflet which stated that the risk of miscarriage following the procedure was 1:100; nonetheless, she believed adamantly that the risk was 75 per cent. She was also informed that her blood tests indicated the risk of her carrying a disabled child as being 1:8396 – though it has to be recognised that the hospital was working on the assumption that the family history was one of Down's syndrome, the true nature of the very unusual translocation having been discovered only in the postnatal follow-up. In addition, however, the case illustrates some of the general subjective difficulties in counselling – in this case, we have a devout Muslim[98] being counselled by an equally devout Christian who would no longer perform amniocenteses herself, having been once involved in the miscarriage of a normal fetus.[99]

Mrs Al Hamwi eventually refused amniocentesis and, in due course, gave birth to a child suffering from the familial condition. She sued the practitioner on account of the delay involved in referring her for antenatal screening and the hospital for misinforming her of the hazards of amniocentesis, the combined effect of which was to deny her proper diagnostic facilities and, hence, the opportunity to terminate her pregnancy which she would have done given the right information at the right time.

In the event, Simon J dismissed the case against the general practitioner on the factual evidence that the amniocentesis – or the alternative of chorionic villus sampling at another hospital – was not, in practice, delayed or voided by her admitted negligence; accordingly, the breach of duty had caused no damage. As to the hospital, he found that Mrs Al Hamwi had been given appropriate counselling by way of the information leaflet and, again factually, by what had been said during her interview with the obstetrician.[100] Even so, he conceded that she may have been confused – and it must be said that a full reading of the case indicates that all the elements of confusion were there in abundance. In this respect, the judge made some interesting observations. In answer to a specific comment by counsel, he took the view that to hold that it is the clinician's duty to ensure that the information given to the patient *is understood* is 'to place too onerous an obligation on the clinician'. He continued:

---

[98] The expert evidence was that the majority of Muslim jurists hold that ensoulment occurs 120 days after conception. Termination after this would be sinful but within the conscience of the woman who could, therefore, consent to a late termination if the fetus was known to be at risk of abnormality. The doctrine of 'darura' –'necessity permits prohibited things' – adds even more flexibility to the rule.

[99] The judge found no evidence of bias but such situations must often be difficult for both sides. In contrast, Morland J, in *Enright* v. *Kwun*, n. 41 above at [30], found that the defendant doctor's approach to counselling had been coloured by his religious beliefs.

[100] The Trust used a 'check-list' system by which to ensure that the patient was adequately informed.

Clinicians should take reasonable and appropriate steps to satisfy themselves that the patient has understood the information which has been provided; but the obligation does not extend to ensuring that the patient has understood.[101]

Which, when all is said and done, seems to move the goal-posts only marginally in favour of the patient and actually perpetuates the application of the *Bolam* test to the provision of information[102] – and the hospital's practice of suggesting that patients in Mrs Al Hamwi's position should go away and think about the decision with the aid of an information leaflet[103] survived peer review at the trial.

It may be that ensurance of success in achieving 'understanding consent' is an impossible goal in the circumstances. But one still wonders if Simon J's dictum is strictly in accord with modern medical practice – and the pursuit of that question is implicit in the remainder of the chapter.[104]

The development of the wrongful birth action

The application of the law of negligence to antenatal management is comparatively new. There can be no doubt that the doctor/patient relationship is one of proximity in which the former clearly owes the latter a duty of care. Thus, insofar as he or she is able, the obstetrician has a duty to ensure the successful birth of a healthy child to his or her pregnant patient. The obstetrician/patient relationship is, however, of a very special nature. As in any health caring situation, it is now, to a very large extent, governed at common law by the principle of patient autonomy. Moreover, as we have already seen, while the obstetrician certainly has a duty to the fetus, this duty is exercised *through*, and as an integral part of, his or her duty to the mother; given a conflict of interests, those of the mother must prevail – and, save in quite exceptional circumstances, the courts will support this principle.[105] Additionally, however, the

---

[101] n. 33 above, at [69].

[102] For explanation of the *Bolam* test, see Chapter 1. The propriety of applying it to information disclosure has been discussed already at p. 68.

[103] Paraphrased from n. 33 above, at [72].

[104] José Miola, 'Autonomy Rued OK?' (2006) 14 *Medical Law Review* 108–14 considered that, in giving preference to informing over understanding, Mrs Al Hamwi was denied an autonomous choice.

[105] This has been seen in the dramatic extinction of the enforced caesarean delivery – for which, see, for example, *Re S (adult: refusal of medical treatment)* [1992] 4 All ER 671, (1992) 9 BMLR 69 and *Tameside and Glossop Acute Services Trust* v. *CH (a patient)* [1996] 1 FLR 762, (1996) 31 BMLR 93 – by way of *Re MB (an adult: medical treatment)* [1997] 2 FLR 426, (1997) 38 BMLR 175 and *St George's Healthcare NHS Trust* v. *S* [1998] 3 All ER 673, (1998) 44 BMLR 160, CA.

relationship in the United Kingdom is bound not only by common law but also by statute in the form of the Abortion Act 1967 – indeed, it has been said that the mere existence of the Act establishes a *duty* to warn of possible fetal disability.[106]

On the face of things, it seems almost self-evident that a woman who did not want to rear a disabled child, who has sought help that was specifically designed to prevent that happening and, yet, has been placed unwittingly in that position, will have a sustainable case against the individual or health authority that was responsible for her predicament – or, in popular usage, can reasonably bring an action for 'wrongful birth'. The problem then lies in whether or not the courts will, in such circumstances, consider that the cost of raising an unhealthy child is a *compensatable* legal harm. Why should they not do so? There are at least two possible answers. First, given that the issue of life or death arises, the law will generally decide in favour of the preservation of life – and the only relief for the affected woman in the circumstances outlined lies in feticide.[107] Second, all the arguments surrounding discrimination against disability that have been aired in Chapter 2 now reappear in even starker form as we are dealing, here, not with a theoretical possibility but with the actual destruction of an individual, and possibly viable, fetus. As a result, actions for wrongful birth have had something of a turbulent history in the courts and, as so often happens when novel tort actions are involved, we must turn to the United States for a lead.

Early experience in the United States

The first recognisable US case is that of *Becker* v. *Schwartz*,[108] in which the New York Court of Appeals allowed the now almost standard parental claim for damages to offset the cost of the institutional care of a child suffering from Down's syndrome. 'Birth actions' are a matter of state law in the USA and it is unsurprising that the relevant jurisprudence has developed in different ways – indeed, such actions are statute barred in some states[109] where denial is presumably predicated on the assumption

---

[106] Per Newman J in *Rand* v. *East Dorset Health Authority* (2000) 56 BMLR 39 at 57; per Henriques J in *Hardman* v. *Amin* (2000) 59 BMLR 58 at 72.

[107] But this argument has been used in the main to counter claims for wrongful life which are discussed in Chapter 6.

[108] 386 NE 2d 807 (N.Y., 1978).

[109] As an example, the Utah Code Ann para. 78-11-24 provides: '[a] cause of action shall not arise, and damages shall not be awarded, on behalf of any person, based on a claim that but for the act or omission of another, a person would not have been permitted to have been born alive but would have been aborted'. Other states imposing some limitation

that abortion is to be discouraged.[110] Analysis of this and later cases is complicated by the fact that actions for wrongful birth, such as we discuss here, are often confused with those for wrongful pregnancy, which will be considered in Chapter 4.[111] In general, claims in the United States are based, first, on the emotional distress resulting from the birth of a disabled child and, second, on the actual or additional costs of rearing such a child. Emotional distress is a difficult concept which would almost cetainly have no place in United Kingdom jurisprudence;[112] we return to the question of compensation later in this chapter.

The general rule that has now emerged is that claims for wrongful birth will succeed.[113] There is, however, considerable opposition. It is hard to find two cases with such different results – despite occurring in the same relatively recent year – as, on the one hand, *Schirmer* v. *Mt. Auburn Obstetrics and Gynecologic Associates, Inc.*[114] in which it was held that 'a claim for wrongful birth remains, at its core, a medical negligence claim that is to be determined by application of common-law principles' and, on the other, *Grubbs* v. *Barbourville Family Health Center, PSC* where a wrongful birth action was described as:

include Idaho, Minnesota, Missouri, North Dakota, Pennsylvania, Kentucky and Georgia. For the constitutionality of such statutes, see *Hickman* v. *Group Health Plan, Inc.* 369 NW 2d 10 (Minn., 1986) and more recently *Wood* v. *University of Utah Med Ctr* 67 P 3d 436 (Utah, 2002). Maine appears unique in having legislated so as to ensure that the action is *available*.

[110] Thus, in *Molloy* v. *Meier* 679 NW 2d 711 (Minn., 2004), the statute was overruled because the claimant would not have *conceived* if her genetic disorder had been diagnosed.

[111] The same difficulty arises in a comprehensive review of the 'birth cases' by Dean Stretton, 'The Birth Torts: Damages for Wrongful Birth and Wrongful Life' (2005) 10 *Deakin Law Review* 310–64. My own classification, which follows that which is widely used, has been explained in J. K. Mason, 'Wrongful Pregnancy, Wrongful Birth and Wrongful Terminology' (2002) 6 *Edinburgh Law Review* 46–66. As has been discussed in Chapter 1, it is arguable that all are misnomers: 'Any "wrongfulness" lies not in the life, the birth, the conception, or the pregnancy but in the negligence of physician': *Viccaro* v. *Milunsky* 551 NE 2d 8 (Mass., 1990) at 9.

[112] Compensatable and non-compensatable actions are distributed about evenly across the United States.

[113] For a major list of the early cases, see *Siemieniec* v. *Lutheran General Hospital* 512 NE 2d 691 (Ill., 1987). These are discussed in Jeffrey R. Rotkin and Maxwell J. Mehlman, 'Wrongful Birth: Medical, Legal and Philosophical Issues' (1994) 22 *Journal of Law, Medicine and Ethics* 21–8 and, nearer to home, Patricia M. A. Beaumont, 'Wrongful Life and Wrongful Birth' in S. A. M. McLean (ed.), *Contemporary Issues in Law, Medicine and Ethics* (Aldershot, Dartmouth Publishing, 1996), chapter 6. Occasional cases, as will appear, deny liability on the grounds that the clinician has not caused the genetic defect: *Wilson* v. *Knezi* 751 SW 2d 741 (Mo., 1988) (for further discussion, see Chapter 6). This form of reasoning was specifically rejected in *McKenney ex rel McKenney* 771 A 2d 1153 (NJ., 2001) but it still persists.

[114] 802 NE 2d 723 (Ohio, 2003).

[A] tort without precedent, and at variance with existing precedents old and new. Indeed the [majority of the Supreme Court of Kentucky] are divided among themselves as to what principle of law requires the doctor to pay damages in this case.[115]

Thus it will be seen that the minority of American litigants are disadvantaged insofar as they may have no cognisable case should the court hold that the injury sustained lies in the existence of a living, but disabled, child; in such circumstances, the court may well maintain that the antenatal carers did not cause the defect and cannot, therefore be responsible for its existence.[116] The majority, however, are relatively well-placed in that the 'wrong' to be compensated will be seen as being deprived of a constitutional right to choose between termination and parturition. The advantage to the complainer is, then, that she has no need to face the second causation hurdle – that, given the necessary information, she *would* have elected for termination; and we have already seen how important this may be.

Developments in the Commonwealth

Claims for wrongful birth seem to have been accepted as actionable without major debate in Canada. Indeed, it has been authoritatively stated that: 'Although there may have been earlier claims for wrongful birth, it is *Arndt* v. *Smith* that established this claim in Canadian tort law'[117] – and *Arndt*, based at first instance on the US case of *Becker*,[118] was settled only in 1997. The decision in *Arndt*,[119] as we have seen, rested on the fulcrum of *Reibl* v. *Hughes*[120] and Zuber J continued: 'Thus, the claim for wrongful birth slipped quietly into Canadian tort law as a type of medical malpractice case without any fundamental analysis or delineation of such a claim.'[121]

One suspects that much the same could be said about other Commonwealth jurisdictions although, in fact, truly apposite cases are very hard to find in Australia. Costs for the rearing and support of a disabled child for 30 years were awarded in *Veivers* v. *Connolly*[122] in which there was a failure to identify a case of the congenital rubella syndrome.

---

[115] 120 SW 3d 682 (Ky., 2003) per Lambert CJ at 689. Other cases in which the claim has been rejected include: *Azzolino* v. *Dingfelder* 337 SE 2d 528 (N.C., 1985) and *Atlanta Obstetrics and Gynecology Group* v. *Abelson* 398 SE 2d 557 (Ga., 1990).

[116] The court may, however, be selective. In the early case of *Noccash* v. *Burger* 290 2d 825 (Va., 1982), for example, widely based damages were awarded for the birth of an infant with Tay-Sachs disease but costs concerned with the child's funeral were disallowed on the grounds that the fatality was the result of hereditary factors rather than of the defendant's negligence.

[117] In *Mickle* v. *Salvation Army Grace Hospital* (1998) 166 DLR 743 per Zuber J at 747.

[118] n. 108 above.   [119] n. 84 above.   [120] n. 58 above.   [121] n. 117 above, at 748.

[122] [1995] 2 Qd R 326.

By contrast, in *McMahon* v. *South Eastern Sydney Area Health Service*,[123] a couple whose child was found to be suffering from Down's syndrome were advised by the Legal Aid Board that 'there is no clear legal solution and any legal action is likely to be novel and fiercely contested'.[124] The case is still ongoing at the time of writing. Once again, part of the difficulty in case discovery may lie in the fact that wrongful birth and wrongful pregnancy actions are not distinguished in Australia.[125]

The development of 'wrongful birth' in the United Kingdom

In the absence of a constitutional background, the relevant law in the United Kingdom has also developed in a fairly straight line – indeed, as in the rest of the Commonwealth, there seems never to have been any doubt that inadequate antenatal care is to be dealt with within the tort of negligence. Occasional cases reported as news items are to be found before 1990 but the first case to reach the legal press appears to have been that of *Salih* v. *Enfield Health Authority*[126] in which, despite her obvious anxiety, the mother had been declared free from viral infection yet was delivered of a child suffering from the rubella syndrome. The words of Butler-Sloss LJ speak for themselves:

This is a sad case of an intelligent little boy, born into this world with major physical handicaps ... who would not have been born at all if the defendants had properly carried out their duty of care towards the plaintiffs [the parents of the child] ... It is difficult, and some might say invidious, to try to translate the consequences of the defendants' negligence into financial terms. But this is what the courts have to do and, in this type of case, with little assistance from earlier cases.[127]

And, later:

The child was born as a direct result of the lack of advice which, if given, would have resulted in a termination of pregnancy.

Thus, in the typical case, there is no doubt as to the fact of or the nature of a wrong, there is no doubt that the counsellors caused that wrong and, given the fact that the claim was made by the parents rather than by the child, the wrong was the imposition on their shoulders of a major burden of care for a disabled child which was not of their choosing – and this

---

[123] [2004] NSWSC 442.   [124] ibid., at [14].
[125] See Kirby J in *CES* v. *Superclinics (Australia) Pty Ltd* (1995) 38 NSWLR 47 at [106].
[126] [1990] 1 Med L R 333; on appeal (1991) 7 BMLR 1. The only cases referred to are essentially of 'wrongful pregnancy' type, for which see Chapter 4.
[127] ibid., at BMLR 1, 4.

assessment, including recognition of the difficulties of quantification of damages has governed the law in both England and Scotland ever since.[128] The question of compensation in such cases has, however, had to undergo radical rethinking following the very important decision in *McFarlane* v. *Tayside Health Board*[129] which is discussed in detail in Chapter 4.

Recompense for wrongful birth in the United Kingdom

McFarlane was concerned with the uncovenanted birth of a *normal* child as a result of faulty advice as to sterilisation; it, therefore, falls strictly within my definition of a case of wrongful pregnancy. We will see that it is a ground-breaking case which merits – and has received – extended analysis. For present purposes, however, it will be sufficient to state baldly that the House of Lords laid down a rigid rule that the birth of a child in such circumstances is not a compensatable harm – and this applies no matter what is the origin of the fault nor how the action for recovery is structured.[130] But, at the same time, the House left open the possibility of an exception in the event that the child resulting from a failed sterilisation procedure was disabled. The proposition was, however, couched in such indefinite terms that the extent of the exception – if one existed – was uncertain. Was it, for example, confined to the disabled child born *only* as a result of a negligently managed sterilisation or did it include – or exclude? – one born following negligent antenatal care?

Whether or not the House had both these possibilities in mind, I believe it is the former which most accurately reflects their Lordships' intentions and, in that case, as we will see, it can be cogently argued that the nature of the negligence that results in an uncovenanted child is the same irrespective of the health of that child. Why, then, should we differentiate in respect of liability according to the outcome? This very specific problem is addressed in depth in Chapter 5. As to the latter, we have already acknowledged the probable liability of the health carers given the application of the normal principles of tort law. At least a proportion of the

---

[128] For England and Wales and Northern Ireland, see *Gregory* v. *Pembrokeshire Health Authority* (1989) 1 Med LR 81 (chromosomal disorder), *Rance* v. *Mid-Downs Health Authority* [1991] 1 QB 587, [1991] 1 All ER 801 (neural tube defect). For Scotland *Anderson* v. *Forth Valley Health Board* (1998) 44 BMLR 108, 1998 SLT 588 (X-linked disorder), *McLelland* v. *Greater Glasgow Health Board* 1999 SC 305, on appeal 2001 SLT 446.

[129] [2000] 2 AC 59, 2000 SC 1.

[130] In *Richardson* v. *LRC Products Ltd* (2000) 59 BMLR 185, a case involving a burst condom was brought under the Consumer Protection Act 1987, s.3; the principle was said to apply equally whether the claim was laid in negligence or in breach of statutory duty.

purpose of antenatal care is, in modern terms, devoted to the prevention of the birth of a disabled neonate; the pregnant woman is aware of this and the mere offering of the service carries with it the acceptance of a duty of care. Failure in that duty constitutes a harm – and yet, the precise nature of that harm is not as certain as may appear at first sight. The pregnancy is voluntary; there should, therefore, be no compensation for the pain, suffering and inconvenience of childbirth per se. The woman *wanted* a child but she did *not* want a disabled child. Bearing in mind that strong policy arguments can be deployed against accepting the birth of a disabled child as something to be deprecated, can her distress as a result of giving birth to such a child be regarded as a compensatable injury? True, she may be prepared to love such child and to provide for its special needs, but love of this type costs money – money which she may not have or, at least, intended to spend in other ways. Can the upkeep of that child, then, be rightly regarded as the responsibility of another?

The legal situation post-*McFarlane* – which was, itself, a classic legal roller-coaster – was, therefore, not only unsettled but its resolution was urgent. As a consequence, a flurry of interrelated cases soon found their way to the courts.[131]

Wrongful birth during and after McFarlane

At this point, it will be useful to recapitulate the ways in which negligence could be claimed under the rubric of wrongful birth. Liability might be claimed in terms of failure to exercise a duty that arises from the mere existence of the Abortion Act.[132] Alternatively, it might be argued that responsibility arises under the rules of information disclosure which impose a duty on the health authority to inform a woman of a significant risk such as would affect the judgment of a reasonable patient.[133] The distinction is significant in that there are more justifications for termination of pregnancy than that of fetal disability. A woman who is unexpectedly pregnant following sterilisation almost certainly qualifies for termination under section 1(1)(a) of the 1967 Act – indeed, subject to the gestational time limits, it is difficult to see how one could be refused in the circumstances.[134] Such equiparation of the wrongful birth action with

---

[131] In discussion of these cases, I am drawing on my paper of 2002, n. 111 above.

[132] See n. 106 above.

[133] *Pearce* v. *United Bristol NHS Healthcare Trust* (1998) 48 BMLR 118 per Lord Woolf MR at 124.

[134] For reasons which we have discussed above in Chapter 2. I have enlarged on this in J. K. Mason, *Medico-Legal Aspects of Reproduction and Parenthood* (Aldershot: Ashgate, 2nd edn 1998).

the availability of lawful abortion as a whole may well seem to impose an unreasonably wide-ranging duty of care – indeed, it comes close to imposing an obligation to read its terms to a pregnant woman, something of a volte-face for a department of obstetrics. Perhaps more importantly in the present context, it also serves to explain the apparent anomaly of a potential action for wrongful birth in the face of a normal neonate.[135] In this author's view, the ratio of the wrongful birth action is summed up simply in the words of Toulson J:

> If the mother was entitled ... to have her pregnancy terminated, and if she would have exercised that right, but was deprived of the opportunity to do so as a result of clinical negligence, those facts should found a sufficient foundation for her claim.[136]

The basis for this approach is, perhaps, best appreciated through the Scots legal concept of *damnum* – that is, the deprivation of an interest that the law recognises as a legal interest. *Injuria* means the invasion of a legal right and a loss that attracts reparation arises when *injuria* and *damnum* coincide.[137] In present terms, the *injuria* is the failure to advise that the fetus is unhealthy and, by extension, to imply that termination is not indicated; the *damnum* lies in being deprived of a legal right – that is, a statutory opportunity for termination of a pregnancy. There is, currently, no English equivalent of this concept. Nevertheless, as already intimated, I have a strong impression that the English courts are moving towards a tort of interference with a woman's autonomy or her right to a choice of what is done to her body.[138] That being the case, the two jurisdictions are moving ever closer together and provide a suitable platform on which to found the action for wrongful birth. This comparative approach serves to provide an opportunity to consider the contribution of the Scottish juris- diction to the wrongful birth debate.

The Scottish cases. Strangely, actions for wrongful birth provide a relatively new experience for the Scottish courts. Indeed, the only nearly appropriate Scottish case cited in what I see as the index case of *Anderson v. Forth Valley Health Board*[139] was *Allan v. Greater Glasgow*

---

[135] A possibility discussed in Chapter 4 in relation to *Greenfield* v. *Irwin (a firm) and ors* [2001] 1 FLR. 899. It is also noteworthy that the important Australian case of *CES* v. *Superclinics*, n. 125 above, also involved the birth of a normal child following obstetric negligence. New South Wales has no Act comparable to the Abortion Act 1967. Kirby J's discussion of the interplay between negligence and legality makes interesting reading.

[136] In *Lee* v. *Taunton and Somerset NHS Trust* [2001] 1 FLR 419 at 431.

[137] Explained by Lord McCluskey in *McFarlane* v. *Tayside Health Board* 1998 SLT 307 at 313, (1998) 44 BMLR 140 at 152, IH.

[138] See, in particular, *Chester* v. *Afshar*, n. 63 above.

[139] 1998 SLT 588, (1997) 44 BMLR 108, OH.

Health Board[140] which was an instance of failed sterilisation or wrongful pregnancy to which we will return in Chapter 4. *Anderson* was decided between the Outer and Inner House hearings of *McFarlane* – i.e. when it had been heard at first instance only – and, as a result, Lord Nimmo Smith was governed by no compelling precedent.

Despite his Lordship's reluctance to distinguish between actions for wrongful conception (or pregnancy) and wrongful birth, *Anderson* remains one of the best analyses of the wrongful birth action as it was accepted in the United Kingdom at the time. The case concerned two children who, as they got older, were found to be suffering from muscular dystrophy – an X-linked genetic disease. A strong family history indicated that the mother should have been offered genetic counselling and had this been done, she would have terminated all male pregnancies or, at least, all male pregnancies once the diagnosis had been confirmed in her first son. The Lord Ordinary concluded that an action was available in the following terms:

While the [Abortion] Act does not expressly say so, it may, I think, be taken from its provisions that the birth of a child so handicapped may be regarded as a harmful event for those most immediately affected by his existence, who would in the ordinary course be his parents. That being so, I can see no reason why the course of action desiderated by the pursuers, which according to them would have resulted in the abortion of two foetuses, should not be regarded as having as its purpose, inter alia, the prevention of events harmful to the pursuers which were or ought to have been within the contemplation of the defenders . . .[141]

At the same time, he confirmed his belief that the parents had sustained personal injury[142] and, importantly, concluded that the 'fair, just and reasonable' test established in *Caparo*[143] was not compromised if the parents were recompensed. After deprecating the need to value a child in monetary terms, Lord Nimmo Smith concluded that a claim of this kind was governed by the straightforward Scots legal principles of delict

---

[140] 1998 SLT 580, (1993) 17 BMLR 135, OH. Possibly the nearest example is *Millar (P's Curator Bonis)* v. *Criminal Injuries Compensation Board* 1997 SLT 1180, (1996) 44 BMLR 70 – a case of incestuous rape though, if there is a parallel, it is more with wrongful life (see Chapter 6) and was argued as such. In fact, the question of termination does not seem to have arisen.

[141] n. 139 above, at BMLR 136–7.

[142] Following the Court of Appeal in *Walkin* v. *South Manchester Health Authority* [1995] 4 All ER 132, (1995) 25 BMLR 108. It will be seen later, however, that this is open to dispute.

[143] *Caparo Industries plc* v. *Dickman* [1990] 2 AC 605, [1990] 1 All ER 568. The significance of *Caparo* is addressed more fully in the chapter following. Essentially, it states that a tortfeasor will be held liable for damages only if it is 'fair, just and reasonable' to do so. The range of the test has been extended beyond its original application.

and conceded the pursuers' claim for the additional costs arising from the children's disabilities; these, he thought, arose from 'the natural bond between parent and child, an aspect of which is the parents' desire to care for the child'.[144]

The only other strictly relevant Scottish case is *McLelland*[145] which is also interesting in that its stages interweaved with those of *McFarlane*; in its way, it was, in my view, clearly seeking to maintain a Scottish dimension based on legal principle but was, ultimately, caught in the *McFarlane* net.

The case followed the familiar story of wrongful birth – the antenatal clinic failed to perform an amniocentesis and a child was born suffering from Down's syndrome.[146] In the Outer House, Lord Macfadyen awarded damages, inter alia, for *both* ordinary maintenance and for the costs of special care resulting from the disability. Interestingly, he also awarded *solatium* not only to Mrs McLelland but also to her husband, which, one feels can only be right – the husband's role and sensibilities as a parent are too often forgotten in the medico-legal ambience of reproduction. Beyond this, however, the Lord Ordinary was following the standard line established in *Anderson* and which was acceptable within the terms of the Inner House decision in *McFarlane*.[147]

By the time *McLelland* came to appeal, however, *McFarlane* had been debated in the House of Lords and the goal-posts had been shifted so far that the arguments were radically changed. The defenders (or reclaimers) could now maintain that, since the admitted negligence in both cases resulted in the birth of a child that would not have occurred in the absence of such negligence, there was no basis for saying that it was fair, just and reasonable to hold them liable for the costs of the ordinary maintenance of Gary McLelland when it was held not to be fair to do so in the case of Catherine McFarlane[148] – in short, as I have intimated above (at p. 84), that there was no distinction to be drawn between actions for wrongful pregnancy and wrongful birth. The pursuers, however, argued – as

---

[144] It is to be noted that the parents never claimed for expenses other than those arising from the extra costs involved in caring for two disabled children. Significantly, the judge decided that the recompense should be such as to allow for their care 'throughout the children's lives'.

[145] *McLelland* v. *Greater Glasgow Health Board* 1999 SLT 543, OH; 2001 SLT 446, IH.

[146] The negligence, which was admitted, was especially clear as it was yet another instance of a translocation chromosomal abnormality which is transmissible – and there was a positive family history.

[147] *McLelland* was contested in the Outer House largely on the 'offset' of the saving from not having another child which was allowed in *Salih* v. *Enfield Health Authority* [1991] 3 All ER 400. This line of argument was not pursued in the Inner House.

[148] *Caparo*, n. 143 above.

I would contend, rightly – that they were different. In particular, an action for wrongful pregnancy is, as we will see, essentially a matter of negligent family planning and, in those circumstances, the doctors concerned owe no more than a general duty of care to prevent future pregnancies; in a case based on wrongful birth, however, the medical team are under a specific responsibility to discover whether an unborn child is disabled and, in the case of Gary McLelland, they had the even more specific duty of excluding the possibility of Down's syndrome – indeed it was suggested that the conditions approximated to a contractual duty.

This was accepted in the leading speech by Lord Prosser, who was concerned to judge whether or not liability was fairly attributed according to what the doctors regarded as the extent of their duty. Here, he held that the responsibility of the doctors in *McLelland* was to avert the consequences of the child having Down's syndrome and this dictated liability in respect of the child's special needs.[149] Lord Prosser was not, however, prepared to go further. In fact, he found that, if anything, the 'possibility of an unwanted birth would be even less directly in [the McLellands' doctors'] contemplation [in a case of wrongful birth] than in a case like *McFarlane* [of wrongful pregnancy]'.[150] Accordingly, there was no proper basis for holding that it would be fair, just and reasonable for the defenders to be held liable in respect of the child's basic maintenance costs.

Lord Marnoch took his own path to a similar conclusion. His short speech implied that he was predominantly guided by the subjective reaction of the parents to the birth of an unexpected child.[151] The fact that the McLellands took pleasure in their child put them in the same position as the parents of a healthy child in respect of maintenance costs; accordingly, the claim for these was not made out.[152]

In a dissenting opinion, Lord Morison drew particular attention to the differences between actions for wrongful pregnancy and wrongful birth[153] and concluded that the former, as represented by *McFarlane*, had no direct application to *McLelland*. He rejected the 'moral' implications of the fair, just and reasonable test and argued that, if, as was agreed, the doctors were liable for the costs arising from the disabled state of

---

[149] 2001 SLT 446, at 454 F–G.   [150] 2001 SLT 446, at 454 L.

[151] In so saying, he relied on Lord Nimmo Smith in *Anderson* v. *Forth Valley Health Board* 1998 SLT 588, 605, which seems a doubtful interpretation as Lord Nimmo Smith's exact words were: [T]he fact that one set of parents reacts to a birth in a way in which others might not should not be determinative either way of an entitlement to damages.'

[152] Lord Prosser specifically rejected this approach at 2001 SLT 446, 455 C. Many years, and cases, earlier, Jupp J had pointed to the potential inequity of involving parental feelings in the decision-making process: *Udale* v. *Bloomsbury Area Health Authority* [1983] 2 All ER 522.

[153] For which, see also p. 85 above.

the child, it was illogical to hold that they were not also liable for his basic maintenance costs – the whole purpose of testing for Down's syndrome was to prevent the birth to a woman of a child suffering from the condition.

It will become clear in the next chapter that the present writer prefers the dissenting opinion in *McLelland*, and this is mainly because, in contrast to the majority, it appreciates the many differences between actions for wrongful pregnancy and wrongful birth. Nevertheless, the same error pervades the later English cases, the great majority of which were also argued in *McFarlane* terms.

The English cases after McFarlane. And this is the probable source of much unnecessary medico-legal argument in the reproductive field. We have seen above that, prior to 2000, United Kingdom medical jurisprudence accepted the action for wrongful birth virtually without demur – the only contentious elements concerned the scope and the basis for payment of compensation.[154] This relatively happy situation was seriously disturbed by concerns that it would be affected by the ruling in *McFarlane* which seem to the writer to have been founded upon a misconception. Given that wrongful pregnancy and wrongful birth are distinct legal entities, the jurisprudence of each should be allowed to develop independently. Conflating the two serves only to complicate the issues and to confuse the reader. Nonetheless, this was the path taken in a series of English cases which have some important inherent, as well as consequential, implications.

The first of these was *Rand* v. *East Dorset Health Authority*[155] which involved the negligent misreading of an untrasound scan which, in fact, indicated the presence of Down's syndrome in the fetus. The importance of *Rand* lies not in its facts – it was a fairly routine scenario. What made it different was that Newman J now thought it important to argue every aspect of the case through the medium of *McFarlane*, this being predicated on the belief that the two cases were on a par as to the claim for the costs of upbringing.

It is unnecessary at this point to consider Newman J's analysis of the *McFarlane* case in detail. It is sufficient to note that, at virtually every point, he was able to discern a reason for holding that the House of Lords'

---

[154] In *Salih* v. *Enfield Health Authority*, n. 126 above, legal principle dictated that damages for the basic upkeep of a disabled child were refused on the grounds that the parents had decided against having another child and were, accordingly, spared that expense. Small wonder that the reasoning was disapproved in *McLelland*, n. 145 above.

[155] (2000) 56 BMLR 39, [2000] Lloyd's Rep Med 181.

decision in what was a case of wrongful pregnancy was not binding in one of wrongful birth. In particular, he noted that a claim focused on the consequences of disability – as opposed to one focusing on the disability itself – requires a comparison between a normal healthy child and a disabled one which is something that everyone can understand and is, consequently, inoffensive. On much the same line, he found that costs, so far as they are consequent upon the disability, are recoverable as a head of economic loss[156] because such a calculation does not require assessing the benefits of having a child – in short, he circumvented his obvious reluctance to become involved in 'an invidious and morally offensive valuation' of an individual child's life by concentrating only on the costs derived from the degree of disability per se[157] and, accordingly, setting the pattern by awarding damages to cover the *extra* costs associated with the upkeep of a *disabled* child.

Perhaps of more significance to a medical observer, he further refined the distinction between wrongful pregnancy and wrongful birth actions in holding, as has already been noted, that the mere existence of the Abortion Act 1967 establishes a relationship between the medical advisers and the patient that is sufficient of itself to impose a liability for the financial consequences flowing from a negligent failure to warn of fetal disability. At the same time, he considered that the parents' means, rather than the needs of the child, determined the extent of the damages to be awarded – a somewhat surprising conclusion in that he had already observed that it was the actual disability that determined the result.[158]

The case of *Hardman* v. *Amin*,[159] this time an instance of the congenital rubella syndrome, was heard some eight months later. Liability for failure

---

[156] The significance of economic loss in the context of negligence cases was well explained by Toulson J in *Lee*, n. 176 below: '[E]conomic loss, unless consequent upon personal injury or damage to property … is normally regarded for the purposes of the law of negligence as an accident of life which must lie where it falls, regardless of the fact that some other human being has been the instrument of the misfortune … Every day countless people suffer economic loss of one kind or another through acts or omissions of others, and to seek to apportion blame and redistribute such losses would involve massively cumbersome and expensive legal machinery. However, the courts have departed from that general approach in certain cases where such a special relationship exists between the injured party and the party who has caused the injury … that to refuse recovery would seem a denial of justice' ([2001] 1 FLR 419 at 422).

[157] Newman J referred with marked approval to the suggestion made by Swinton Thomas J that the easiest way of dealing with the problem was 'to make an assessment of the difference between the cost and time and trouble expended on a normal child and [that] expended on the damaged child'; the learned judge had, however, been persuaded by counsel to adopt a different ratio: *Fish* v. *Wilcox and Gwent Health Authority* (1992, unreported), on appeal (1993) 13 BMLR 134.

[158] n. 155 above, at BMLR 52, Lloyd's Rep Med 194.

[159] [2000] Lloyd's Rep Med 498, (2000) 59 BMLR 58.

to undertake serological tests was admitted. Although the court recognised immediately that this was a case of wrongful birth, once again, the greater part of the argument was taken up with analyses of cases of wrongful pregnancy. Nonetheless, Henriques J's obvious concern was to decide whether the principles established in these could be extrapolated to the wrongful birth situation. He considered these under three main headings:

- were damages available for the pain and discomfort of pregnancy and childbirth;
- was this an action for damages for personal injuries; and
- were damages available for the cost of providing for the child's special needs?

and, in the event, the court delivered what, in this writer's view, is a model judgment.

It will be clear from what has already been said that the first of these questions is not easy to resolve. Certainly, the woman concerned has gone through the ordeal of pregnancy but, in contrast to the position in cases of wrongful pregnancy, she has chosen to do so willingly, and it is difficult to see how she has suffered damage as a result of the consequences of that choice. Nonetheless, it was held in *Hardman* that harm will derive from the realisation and continued knowledge that she has given birth to a disabled child – a concept that comes close to acknowledging a distinct injury due to 'nervous shock'. The difficulties in satisfactorily demonstrating the significance of this somewhat ephemeral condition are well known,[160] but the requirements of proximity as to cause and effect can hardly be denied and, given the occurrence of a 'recognised psychiatric illness', there seems little reason why damages should not be available.[161] While this wide view of pregnancy and its effects may be a little difficult to accept, it accords with the natural sympathy that women in such circumstances will evoke and, in fact, the parties in *Hardman* agreed to a modest recovery under this head.

Somewhat similar concerns surround the second issue insofar as it was agreed that such special damages were available only if the harm could be identified as a personal injury. Although, as we will see in the next chapter, it is possible to take the opposite view, few will doubt that

---

[160] See, for example, *Alcock* v. *Chief Constable of South Yorkshire Police* [1992] 1 AC 310, [1991] 4 All ER 907.

[161] For a good recent analysis in the present context, see *Farrell* v. *Merton, Sutton and Wandsworth Health Authority* (2001) 57 BMLR 158. The circumstances here, involving a negligently performed caesarean section, were rather more traumatic than in the standard wrongful birth case – being due to negligent operation rather than advice – but the underlying principles would be the same.

to inflict pregnancy and labour – or caesarean section – on a woman is to inflict a personal injury. This was accepted in the Court of Appeal in *Walkin* v. *South Manchester Health Authority*[162] and, of course, in *McFarlane* itself by way of what was known as the mother's claim. But these were, again, wrongful pregnancy cases in which the reasoning is easy to understand – the woman did not want the pregnancy but she was made pregnant and suffered as a result. On the other hand, it is, again, hard to dismiss an element of *volenti non fit injuria* as to the pain and discomfort of pregnancy involved in the wrongful birth situation. To circumvent this, the court in *Hardman* held that:

> It would be an anomaly for a wrongful conception claim to be an action for damages for personal injuries whilst a wrongful birth case was not.[163]

But is this so, given the arguments already outlined? Unfortunately, although the proposition was accepted by both counsel, the court's reasoning was not explained further. Most will applaud the sympathetic outcome but it will be seen, especially in the next chapter, that the question raises considerable jurisprudential debate. I think, therefore, that it merits a brief diversion from the main line of discussion – and it will be convenient to undertake this by way of the comparatively recent case of *Godfrey* v. *Gloucestershire Royal Infirmary NHS Trust*.[164]

Godfrey, which concerned the birth of a seriously disabled child following negligent ultrasonography and was, therefore, another classic example of a wrongful birth action, revisited the Limitation Act 1980, most famously first involved in *Walkin*.[165] The problem was the intensely practical one of deciding whether the claim for the cost of supporting the child was a pure economic loss (and, therefore, subject to a six-year time limit under s.2 of the 1980 Act) or was one for personal injury which carries an expiry time of three years (s.11).

Leveson J pointed to the fact that the possibility of separating a claim for wrongful pregnancy into, on the one hand, personal injury sustained 'in the period leading up to the delivery of the child', which is comparable to 'personal injuries resulting from the infliction of a traumatic injury' and, on the other, 'the totally different type of claim' for economic loss was first elaborated, at least in the United Kingdom, by Brooke J in *Allen* v. *Bloomsbury Health Authority*.[166] *Allen* was, however, followed by the very comparable case of *Walkin* in which the Court of Appeal rejected

---

[162] [1995] 4 All ER 132, [1995] 1 WLR 1543.
[163] n. 159 above, at BMLR 64, Lloyds Rep Med 501.   [164] [2003] Lloyd's Rep Med 398.
[165] n. 162 above.   [166] [1993] 1 All ER 651 at 658, (1993) 13 BMLR 47 at 54.

that argument, believing it to be unsupported by the authorities. Auld LJ went on to say:

> Post-natal economic loss may be unassociated with 'physical injury' in the sense that it stems from the cost of rearing a child rather than any disability in pregnancy or birth, but it is not unassociated with the cause of both, namely the unwanted pregnancy giving rise to the birth of a child.[167]

And he went on to say:

> Here, the question is ... whether ... the negligence causing the unwanted pregnancy gave rise to a claim for damages, in this instance, the costs of rearing the child. In my view, it clearly did.[168]

A problem arose in *Godfrey*, however, in that, meantime, *McFarlane* had been decided and, as we will see in the next chapter, the opinions were by no means uniform. Even within the individual speeches, one can pick out phrases to support one's case almost at will. In the result, however, it seems, at least to this writer, that the argument in *McFarlane* was not so much concerned with the distinction between personal injury and economic loss but, rather, that between pure and consequential economic loss – and this impression is supported by the conduct of later cases derived from *McFarlane*. Granted this distinction, there is no reason to insist that *McFarlane* overturns *Walkin*[169] and, consequently, Leveson J was able to consider the latter decision still binding and to apply it to *Godfrey*.[170]

We are left, then, in a very unsatisfactory situation. In the first place, *Walkin* remains the theoretical authority, while there is good reason to suppose that, in practice, it has been conveniently forgotten. Secondly, in allying his case with *Walkin*, Leveson J perpetuates the confusion of claims for wrongful pregnancy (*Walkin*) with those for wrongful birth (*Godfrey*)[171] and, as I argue at several points in this book, whereas the former actions are clearly being based on personal injury, the grounds for

---

[167] [1995] 4 All ER 132 at 139, [1995] 1 WLR 1543 at 1549.
[168] ibid., at All ER 141, WLR 1552. The Court relied heavily on the widely quoted American case of *Sherlock* v. *Stillwater Clinic* 260 NW 3d 169 (Min., 1977) and also on Kerr LJ in *Thake* v. *Maurice* [1986] 1 QB 644, [1986] 1 All ER 497 at 509.
[169] As suggested by Laws J in *Greenfield*, n. 135 above sub nom. *Greenfield* v. *Flather* [2001] Lloyd's Rep Med 143 at [53]. Laws LJ was, however, influenced by the fact that he thought the existence of a healthy child could never be regarded as a detriment. *Greenfield* is discussed in detail in the next chapter.
[170] For the benefit of the reader who is concerned for justice for Mrs Godfrey, the judge was able to apply s.33 of the 1980 Act which gives the court discretion to disallow the strictures imposed by s.11 if it causes injustice.
[171] See also *Anderson* v. *Greater Glasgow Health Board*, n. 139 above, discussed at p. 87.

so viewing the latter are, at best, tenuous. This seems to be an issue that is crying out for consideration at the highest level.

That diversion having been navigated, we can return to *Hardman* where the greater part of the judgment centred on the third question – that of the availability of damages for the child's upkeep. In much the same way as did Newman J in *Rand*, Henriques J reviewed the previous precedents in the United Kingdom[172] and found that the courts had had no difficulty in awarding special damages in cases of wrongful birth. The problem was to decide whether this still held following *McFarlane* and Henriques J detailed sixteen reasons why it did – including the fundamental observation that *McFarlane* was not concerned with a disabled child and had, in effect, dissociated itself from such considerations. He considered that the loss to the parents was pure economic loss but that, in view of the clear breach of duty to the mother and of the child's disabilities, it was, nevertheless, fair, just and reasonable to make an award both in *Caparo*[173] and distributive terms of justice. Having, as was done in *Rand*, established that the existence of the Abortion Act 1967 was sufficient to impose liability for the consequences of an omission to warn of the likelihood of fetal defect, the judge also followed Newman J in adopting a strictly practical attitude to the award of damages following the birth of a disabled child:

I do not consider it to be either invidious or morally offensive or impractical to draw a distinction between Daniel Hardman and a healthy child for the purposes of determining the present question. The task is merely to quantify the additional cost to the parents caused by the disabilities.[174]

Henriques J saw no difficulty in defining disability and he did not anticipate a growth of case law comparing disabilities. On both scores, he may or may not be right. The court did, however, depart from *Rand* in finding that any award made in respect of the child's special needs should be related to the degree of disability rather than to the parents' available resources. The latter scenario was considered 'deeply unattractive' – and few would regard this as a suitable area in which to introduce a means test.[175]

---

[172] Including *Emeh* v. *Kensington and Chelsea and Westminster AHA* [1985] QB 1012; *Salih*, n. 126 above; *Fish* v. *Wilcox*, n. 157 above; *Nunnerley* v *Warrington Health Authority* [2000] Lloyd's Rep Med 170; *Taylor* v. *Shropshire Health Authority* [2000] Lloyd's Rep Med 96; *Rand*, n. 155 above; *Anderson*, n. 139 above; *McLelland*, n. 145 above.

[173] *Caparo Industries plc* v. *Dickman* [1990] 2 AC 605.

[174] n. 159 above, at BMLR 72, Lloyd's Rep Med 506.

[175] Henriques J specifically discarded a notion of inconsistency in awarding damages to the parents when an action on behalf of the child was not available. The interplay of the wrongful birth and the wrongful life action is discussed in Chapter 6.

Having considered cases involving chromosome disorder and viral infection it is convenient to complete the picture and look at the last of the three main exemplar cases, *Lee* v. *Taunton and Somerset NHS Trust*,[176] in which the negligence lay in a failure to diagnose a neural tube defect in the fetus. Mrs Lee would have had a termination had she been appraised of the true situation.

The case was essentially concerned with the availability and the quantum of damages and, as a consequence, *Lee* is notable for its extensive review of the arguments deployed in *McFarlane* – to which we will revert in the next chapter. Stripped to the barest detail, Mrs Lee's case relied on the relatively simple proposition that, fundamentally, the claim for recovery in *McFarlane* failed because of the impossibility and offensiveness of attempting to balance the *benefits* of a *healthy* child against the *burdens* of a *healthy* child. The result was that *McFarlane* was irrelevant once the additional economic consequences of disability took on the role of the primary issue. Counsel for the defendants, by contrast, produced an impressive list of reasons why there was no distinction to be drawn between what were, essentially, cases of wrongful pregnancy and wrongful birth. These included the submissions that it was unreasonable to impose responsibility on the Taunton and Somerset Trust for the massive costs of caring for a disabled child when the Tayside Board was relieved of a far lesser responsibility for maintaining one that was healthy; that it was invidious to weigh in the balance the relative benefits and burdens of *any* child; and that it was neither just nor sensible to try to distinguish between a healthy and a disabled child when disability 'is a matter of infinitely variable degree'.

Toulson J found, it might be thought inevitably, that there was a special relationship between the plaintiff and the defendants and was unable to accept the proposition that the doctors concerned should not be held responsible for the economic losses sustained by the parents. The needs of a severely disabled child, he thought, would have been uppermost in everyone's thoughts when investigating the possibility of fetal abnormality and, in such circumstances, the Trust could find no refuge in *Caparo*. However, he was also closely concerned with the so-called 'blessings' of unwanted parenthood and, as a result, considered that *McFarlane* presented no obstacle to the claim in *Lee*. The thrust of the judgment lies in the words:

I do not believe that it would be right for the law to deem the birth of a disabled child to be a blessing in all circumstances and regardless of the extent of the child's disabilities.[177]

---

[176] [2001] 1 FLR 419, [2001] Fam Law 103.   [177] ibid., at FLR 430.

and, importantly, he could not see that the court was put in the invidious position of balancing the issues in the instant case.

In summary, Toulson J found that Mrs Lee should be entitled to substantial damages and that the law in such cases was unaffected by the decision in *McFarlane*. The question of a claim in respect of basic maintenance was not addressed in *Lee* but one suspects that the judge would have been sympathetic to full recovery. Finally, *Lee* followed *Hardman* rather than *Rand* in holding that the extent of the damages payable was governed by the infant's needs rather than by the parents' resources.

Conclusions

What, then, is to be concluded from these three linked cases? It must be, surely, that the viability of the wrongful birth action is confirmed and, in fact, reinforced. First and foremost, we must bear in mind the significance of the Abortion Act 1967. While the Act has, at most, a secondary role in the wrongful pregnancy case, it represents the crux of the action for wrongful birth – indeed, its very existence not only provides evidence of a woman's statutory right to avoid what is, in many cases, 'an unhappy and burdensome situation', but also indicates that Parliament must have considered it to be in the public good that she should be able to do so in such circumstances. The negligent antenatal adviser has, undeniably, deprived a woman of that right.

More specifically, it is possible to view the wrongful birth action from the strictly practical and economic aspects of parenting. There is nothing degrading or discriminatory in awarding damages. The parents wanted a child and were, therefore, accepting the anticipated costs of rearing that child. What they did not want were the extra costs and restrictions imposed by the needs of a disabled child. It follows that justice is done in awarding damages for those extra costs while denying them for the basic costs of maintenance and the courts are faced, not with an 'invidious' task of assessing the 'value' of a child, but with the everyday exercise of assessing the costs of disability – that is, the 'expense' of a disabled beyond that of a normal child. In doing so, there is no reflection on the 'quality' of the child – the damages are given so that the parents are provided with the materials and the opportunity to deliver the love and care which will restore the conditions, so far as is possible, of a normal family which have been compromised by negligent antenatal care. For this reason, it seems to me to be neither disproportionate in terms of the financing of the NHS, nor unfair in *Caparo* terms, to lay the consequences of failure on the responsible health carers. They had a specific job to do with readily foreseeable results in the event of incompetence, including those of economic loss. The conditions are close to those of a contractual relationship, and there can be no doubt as to the existence of a special relationship between patient and investigator; there is no need, in my view, to raise what is no more than the red herring of the infliction of the type of personal injury that is inherent in a case of wrongful pregnancy. The two actions are quite distinct and cannot be conflated – to quote Toulson J in a different context,[178] 'you can offset apples against apples, and pears against pears, but not apples against pears'.

One practical problem remains: that is, the time over which the damages are to be paid. It is arguable that the parents' legal duty to maintain a child normally ceases at the age of 18[179] and that, thereafter, such aid as they give is voluntary and beyond the responsibility of those who wrongly caused the child's existence. On the other hand, the disability will not go away at a designated moment in time and it is foreseeable that parental care will be needed – and will be morally, even if not legally, demanded – until the child's death. Moreover, the Children Act 1989 allows for unspecified 'special circumstances' that justify the provision of maintenance beyond the age of 18; do these include circumstances such as arise in wrongful birth? The problem is not new, nor is it confined to the United Kingdom jurisdiction, and it was specifically addressed quite recently in *Nunnerley* v. *Warrington Health Authority*[180] – this being a standard wrongful birth action, based on a failure to warn of the possible occurrence of genetically controlled tuberous sclerosis, in which the woman concerned claimed only in respect of economic loss.[181]

Morison J disposed of what, on the face of things, could be a very difficult question with relative ease. The normal principles of tort law apply – the claimants are entitled to be put into the position they would have been in but for the wrong done them:

And I can think of no principle which could apply so as to entitle them to compensation for the period up to 18 but deprive them of it for the period after he was 18. In each case the parents have suffered a loss they would not have incurred but for the tort.[182]

---

[178] In *Lee*, n. 176 above at FLR 429.   [179] Children Act 1989.
[180] [2000] Lloyd's Rep Med 170.
[181] The problems of 'personal injury' did not, therefore arise.
[182] n. 180 above, at 173. But not everyone will be so certain. See, for example, Hale LJ who said only: 'There is a great deal in family law to indicate that liabilities ... may indeed endure long beyond the age of 18' – *Gaynor* v. *Warrington Health Authority* (2000) unreported, CA, 9 March. The actual case, however, turned on previously agreed documents.

Nonetheless, there *are* other arguments which Morison J, admittedly did not deal with – such as the intervention of the local authority and the contribution of the National Health Service.[183] Thus, it seems that what *Nunnerley* does is to admit the possibility of damages being available 'until the earliest of the mother's or the child's death'; each case will, however, depend on its own facts.

The comment as to the mother's or the child's death depends, of course, on the action being brought by the mother; were the action to be brought by the child – and, therefore, represent a wrongful life action – the mother's death would be irrelevant. Morison J noted, however, that the child had no claim in law, since a person cannot bring an action in law alleging that he should not have been born.[184] We return to the reasons for this, and its significance, in Chapter 6.

---

[183] Quoting *Hunt* v. *Severs* [1994] 2 AC 350, [1994] 2 WLR 602.
[184] *McKay* v. *Essex Area Health Authority* [1982] QB 1166, [1982] 2 All ER 771.

4   Unsuccessful sterilisation

Introduction

A man or a woman who wishes to forgo parenthood may well opt for voluntary sterilisation. A number of prophylactic sterilisations are, however, performed in the case of those for whom pregnancy would be disastrous but who are, for reasons of mental incapacity, at the same time unable to consent to the operation. Such patients may be sterilised in their best interests – currently described as non-voluntary sterilisation – but to do so is considered such an affront to a woman's autonomy that it may only be done in the United Kingdom by way of a High Court declaration of lawfulness.[1] Such cases are of profound importance in family law but they are beyond the scope of this chapter which is concerned with the failure of sterilisation services rather than their provision.

Negligent sterilisation

Sterilisation in the context of family planning can, of course, be effected by surgery performed on either the male or the female within the partnership. Sterilisation of the male is generally achieved by way of division of the vas deferens on each side. Negligence in the actual operation is very uncommon but there are natural pitfalls. Amongst these are the residual presence of sperm in the distal genital tract – and hence the need for at least two sperm-free ejaculates before unprotected intercourse can be recommended[2] – and recanalisation of the vas, which may occur at any time after the operation due to the formation of granulomas or

---

[1] *Practice Note (Official Solicitor: Declaratory Proceedings: Medical and Welfare Provisions for Adults who Lack Capacity)* [2001] 2 FLR 158, (2002) 65 BMLR 72.

[2] Very occasionally, pregnancy can result even though the man is producing persistently negative specimens: *Stobie* v. *Central Birmingham Health Authority* (1994) 22 BMLR 135. The genuineness of the case was, in fact, proved by DNA testing. See J. C. Smith, D. Cranston, T. O'Brien et al. 'Fatherhood without Apparent Spermatozoa after Vasectomy' (1994) 344 *Lancet* 30.

inflammation tissue.[3] This is said to occur in some 1:2500 cases or fewer but, nevertheless, it accounts for a major proportion of the cases of wrongful pregnancy that come to court. The alternative procedure in the female is, generally, obstruction of the Fallopian tubes by either clipping or sectioning. The failure rate is said to be in the region of 1:600 but this is a relatively artificial figure as different estimates will be given depending to a large extent on how the procedure is carried out. It has to be said that, because of these variations, technical failure is rather more common in tubal occlusion than in the case of vasectomy. The argument in the event of litigation of such cases will almost certainly rest on whether a clip or ring was incorrectly placed or has slipped as a result of the vagaries of nature. As a consequence, much expert evidence will be involved and the *Bolam* test – see Chapter 1 – will be enlisted frequently. In just such a case, Stuart Smith LJ described the legal limitation of the test succinctly in saying:

[The *Bolam* principle] has no application when what the judge has to decide is, on balance, which of the explanations [of failure] is to be preferred. This is a question of fact which the judge has to decide on the ordinary basis of a balance of probability. It is not a question of saying whether there was a respectable body of opinion here which says that this can happen by chance without any negligence, it is a question for the judge to weigh up the evidence on both sides and he is … entitled, in a situation like this, to prefer the evidence of one expert witness to that of another.[4]

The problem of 'voluntary reversability' also arises because a large proportion of persons who elect for sterilisation are uncertain as to the future – and this applies particularly to women. Certainly, there are ways of performing tubal ligation that lend themselves to reversal should the need arise[5] and, indeed, in *Re P*,[6] it was averred that 'the situation today is that the operation is not irreversible'.[7] These cases admittedly

---

[3] A rather interesting recent Canadian case centred on the difference between the purpose of sperm tests in the two situations: *Bevilacqua* v. *Altenkirk* (2004) 242 DLR (4th) 338. The circumstances were, however, fairly unique.

[4] *Fallows* v. *Randle* [1997] 8 Med LR 160. In particular, explaining Lord Scarman in *Maynard* v. *West Midlands Regional Health Authority* [1985] 1 All ER 635, [1984] 1 WLR 634 at 639 – which was a matter of opinion rather than of fact. The reasoning in the Scottish case of *Allan* v. *Greater Glasgow Health Board* 1998 SLT 580, (1993) 17 BMLR 135, OH, should also be noted.

[5] In *Re M (a minor) (wardship: sterilisation)* [1988] 2 FLR 497, [1988] Fam Law 434, a case of non-voluntary sterilisation, the experts contended that the operation was reversible in some 75 per cent of cases and preferred to look on it as being contraceptive in nature.

[6] *Re P (a minor) (wardship: sterilisation)* [1989] 1 FLR 182, [1989] Fam Law 102, a very similar case to *Re M*, n. 5 above.

[7] Although, rather strangely and without further comment, Eastham J went on to say 'although it is the current *ethical* practice to tell the patients it is an irreversible operation', *Re P*, n. 6 above, at FLR 189 (my emphasis).

concerned non-voluntary sterilisation in which the doctors were concerned to obtain a declaration of lawfulness. Even so, one would imagine that, given an unexpected failure of a voluntary operation, the surgeon would be excused any suggestion of negligence had he or she been instructed to ensure reversibility.[8]

The situation as regards vasectomy is rather different. Men are probably less concerned as to their power to *reproduce* than are women and the operation in men is more destructive of tissue. While reversal *can* be achieved, the majority of surgeons will describe their efforts as 'irreversible'. I believe that the word means just what it says – the surgeon is merely stating that he or she cannot put back the clock if asked to do so. Yet it is surprising what a degree of medico-legal furore the word has caused. In the leading case of *Thake* v. *Maurice*,[9] the consent form relating to vasectomy read: 'I understand that the effect of the operation is irreversible' – and both Mr and Mrs Thake took this to mean that they could never have any more children. This was accepted by Peter Pain J at first instance who said: '[I am] driven to the conclusion that the contract was to make the male plaintiff irreversibly sterile'[10] – and, in this, he was joined by Kerr LJ in the Court of Appeal and, indeed, by the defendant himself, who acknowledged that the word 'irreversible' could, and probably would, be understood as meaning 'irreversible by God or man'. Notwithstanding this, however, both Neill and Nourse LJJ in the same court considered that a reasonable person would not have left the consulting room thinking that the defendant had given a guarantee of absolute sterility. Similarly, in the very comparable case of *Eyre* v. *Measday*,[11] which involved a failed sterilisation in a woman, Slade LJ had this to say:

I take the reference to irreversibility as simply meaning that *the operative procedure in question* is incapable of being reversed, that what is about to be done cannot be undone.[12] (my emphasis)

Despite this, however, Purchas LJ was happy to accept that 'misunderstanding relating to the word "irreversible"' had led the plaintiffs 'perfectly genuinely to believe that they were being given this guarantee [of 100 per cent sterility]'.[13] Both *Thake* and *Eyre* involved 'budget' operations performed privately and were, therefore, argued, additionally,

---

[8] The classic instance lying in the historic Canadian case of *Doiron* v. *Orr* (1978) 86 DLR (3d) 719 in which liability was not imposed following an operation modified at the patient's request.

[9] [1986] QB 644, QB & CA, [1986] 1 All ER 479, CA.   [10] ibid., at QB 658.

[11] [1986] 1 All ER 488, CA. This is not a very satisfactory case as it interwove through the courts with *Thake* v. *Maurice*, n. 9 above, and was consistently out of step.

[12] ibid., at 494.   [13] ibid., at 496.

under contract law. They are, therefore, very unlikely to recur – any later cases will almost certainly be taken in negligence.[14] However, at much the same time, a rather under-reported tubal occlusion case, involving failure to warn, occurred in which it was alleged that the words on the consent form: '... we understand that this means we can have no more children' constituted a misrepresentation in that they implied a guarantee of sterility.[15] The court held, and did not undertake the seemingly difficult task of justification, that the words implied no more than an *intention* that the couple should have no more children. At least it can be said that this rash of cases was sufficient to hasten the introduction of a new form of consent to sterilisation in the NHS which should lay the matter to rest.[16]

The duty of care

Quite clearly there can be no negligence in the absence of a duty of care. The question arises as to whether that duty extends to a spouse or partner when, as in a case of sterilisation, a failure of duty to one or other results in damage to both – and, so far as I know, this possibility has not been tested in the British courts. One's reaction would be to apply the wording of the Human Fertilisation and Embryology Act 1990 and speak in terms of a couple being 'treated together'. And this is not unreasonable in pragmatic terms; as we will see, the great majority of actions for wrongful pregnancy are couched in dual terms – the mother's claim and the parents' claim, and parents' is in the plural irrespective of which has been treated. But what if the other partner is not on the doctor's list? Or what of the casual partner? Does the fact that the standard consent form now has no 'spousal confirmatory clause' – such as was in evidence in *Thake* – indicate a change from the concept of a parental entity to one of the individual patient?

One suspects not – at least in respect of foreseeability of harm – but this may not be universally so. In a recent US case, a husband whose vasectomy failed was excluded from compensation on the grounds of his contributory negligence. His wife then brought an action on her own behalf which was refused insofar as the doctor performing a vasectomy

---

[14] No contract exists between doctor and patient within the National Health Service: *Pfizer Corporation* v. *Ministry of Health* [1965] AC 512.

[15] *Worster* v. *City and Hackney Health Authority* (1987) *The Times*, 2 June. The action was not taken in negligence because, as the court put it: 'an application of the *Bolam* test is conclusive against her'. It is almost incredible that a responsible body of medical opinion would not have warned of the risk less than 20 years ago.

[16] See Department of Health, *A Guide to Consent for Examination or Treatment* (HC (90) 22 amended by HSG (9) 32).

has no duty of care to the man's wife.[17] What has certainly been made clear is that the surgeon who operates owes no duty to potential future partners. In *Goodwill*,[18] a woman who entered a relationship with a man who had been advised three years earlier that he was sterile following vasectomy became pregnant and brought an action against the advisory service. The striking out of her action was confirmed on appeal on the grounds that there was none of the necessary proximity between her and the BPAS on which to found such an action – she was no more than one of many who might have had sexual intercourse with the man since his operation.

Breach of the duty. Whatever may be the extent of the duty, we can say that, as in the case of wrongful birth, it exists in dual form – there is a duty not only to operate with the skill of the competent practitioner but also to communicate with the patient in such a way that he or she has a reasonable understanding of the benefits, risks and limitations of the treatment proposed. The importance of the latter in the present context is clear. The patient without such knowledge cannot make the choice to which he or she is entitled – this time, whether to accept the risks or to continue with contraceptive methods. Considering that a major reason for seeking sterilisation will have been to avoid the consequences and inconveniences of contraception, the choice is stark and this is an area in which, as we have seen in *Thake* and *Eyre*, communication is all important.

Failure in these two duties coincides in the surprisingly common but distinct situation in which a woman who is already pregnant undergoes a sterilisation. Here, the doctor fails either to consider the possibility and, consequently, omits even a pregnancy test,[19] or he or she either fails to inform of the risk[20] or negligently performs a prophylactic uterine curettage.[21] The scenario is remarkably constant – the woman cannot believe she is pregnant, diagnosis is delayed and, by the time it is made, the woman is either unwilling to accept or is advised against termination.

---

[17] *Dehn* v. *Edgecombe* 865 A 2d 603 (Md., 2003).

[18] *Goodwill* v. *British Pregnancy Advisory Service* [1996] 2 All ER 161, [1996] 2 FLR 55, CA. And note, further, that Gibson LJ described the doctor's duty as extending to the man, his patient and *possibly* to that man's wife or partner if she receives intended advice from the doctor (my emphasis).

[19] *Groom* v. *Selby* (2002) 64 BMLR 47, [2002] Lloyd's Rep Med 1 is such an instance.

[20] *Crouchman* v. *Burke* (1997) 40 BMLR 163.

[21] In *Venner* v. *North East Essex Area Health Authority* (1987) *The Times*, 21 February, the gynaecologist accepted the patient's word that she was not pregnant and performed no curettage; negligence was excused on the *Bolam* grounds that others would have followed the same line. The more likely opposite result occurred in *Allen* v. *Bloomsbury Health Authority* [1993] 1 All ER 651, (1993) 13 BMLR 47, QB – a case of fetal survival following the curettage; only the quantum of damages was in issue.

Whatever the cause of the pregnancy, the nature of the claim is also double headed in this unique situation; this was well described by Brooke J in *Allen* which has become something of a leading case.[22] Following his analysis of previous decisions, he was able to identify two distinct foreseeable heads of loss. First, there is a claim for damages for personal injuries leading up to the birth of the child and, while we could see some doubt in a similar claim in cases of wrongful birth, the rationale in cases of wrongful pregnancy seems unassailable. The pregnancy is unintended and is accompanied not only by discomfort but also by considerable pain. So far as I can ascertain this head of claim, the so-called mother's claim, has been denied only once[23] – and this acceptance is very nearly on a universal scale. Second, there is the totally different type of claim for the economic loss occasioned by the loss of paid employment and by the obligations imposed by the upkeep and care of an unwanted child.[24] The viability of this second form of claim – the parents' claim – may be clear, but both the underlying ratio for and the extent of the liability it creates can be, and are, disputed. It is, indeed, the latter particularly that has provoked the massive legal debate which forms the basis for the majority of this chapter.

Liability and wrongful pregnancy

Disability in a newborn child can occur spontaneously, without premonition and in an environment of impeccable antenatal care. It follows that a pregnancy that occurs following a 'failed' sterilisation may result in either a healthy or an unexpectedly disabled child but, whatever the outcome, the underlying negligence has been the same – as has the result, the birth of an uncovenanted child.[25] Injury, either in the form of personal injury or economic loss or both, was foreseeable and, on the face of things, given that negligence has been demonstrated, the only variable should lie in the quantum of damages.[26] Yet, the question of whether damages should be available for the birth of a *healthy* child has plagued the courts ever since

---

[22] ibid.

[23] By Peter Pain J in the trial stage of *Thake* v. *Maurice*, n. 9 above, who attempted to offset this against the joy of parenthood. This may well be the common experience in normal circumstances; nonetheless, the proposition was overturned in the Court of Appeal.

[24] [1993] 1 All ER 651 at 658, 13 BMLR 47 at 54. Brooke J's unqualified use of the word 'unwanted' jars slightly and reminds one that a major reason for rejecting the claim lies in the unfortunate effect it may have on the child as it matures.

[25] As already noted in Chapter 1, n. 6 this term was introduced by Kennedy J in *Richardson* v. *LRC Products Ltd* (2001) 59 BMLR 185, [2000] Lloyd's Rep Med 280 in order to avoid the pejorative word 'unwanted'. In Scots law, it implies a happening which was not contemplated by the parties concerned.

[26] See Watkins J in *Scuriaga* v. *Powell* (1979) 123 Sol Jo 406.

an action for wrongful pregnancy was first brought. Clearly, there are factors involved other than those of strict legal principle. These are of a moral nature and, although others may be adduced and used on occasion, they can be summarised as follows:

- The birth of a healthy child should not be considered an injury on grounds of public policy;
- It is wrong that some persons should be compensated for an event that many other couples have been seeking unsuccessfully;
- It is undesirable that a child should grow up to discover that it was so unwanted that its parents did not pay for its upkeep.

These considerations were classically combined in the early Canadian case of *Doiron* v. *Orr*[27] in which a healthy child was born to a woman following a modified fallopian occlusion operation. As Garett J trenchantly put it (at 722):

I find this approach [to obtain compensation for upkeep] to a matter of this kind which deals with human life, the happiness of the child, the effect upon its thinking, upon its mind when it realised that there has been a case of this kind, that it is an unwanted mistake and that its rearing is being paid for by someone other than its parents, is just simply grotesque.

There are also practical antipathetic arguments, one being that the costs of rearing a healthy child are so speculative that they cannot be regarded as a satisfactory basis for compensation. Judicial disagreement and resistance on both an inter- and an intranational scale is, therefore, to be expected and is demonstrated most vividly in the United States whence much of the jurisprudence on the subject has arisen.

The transatlantic experience

The United States. Historically speaking, the first case appears to have been heard in 1934.[28] It is interesting in that it reminds us of how public attitudes to sexual activity and reproduction have changed over the decades. For example, it has to be remembered that, at that time, the question of the legality of voluntary sterilisation was being seriously considered by the courts;[29] moreover, the case – one of failed vasectomy – was taken as one of fraudulent misrepresentation rather than negligence. In the event, it set the pattern for refusing recompense for the immeasurable benefits of producing a healthy child, a pattern that seems to have

---

[27] n. 8 above.   [28] *Christensen* v. *Thornby* 255 NW 620 (Minn., 1934).
[29] And was still being questioned twenty years later in the United Kingdom: *Bravery* v. *Bravery* [1954] 3 All ER 59, [1954] 1 WLR 1169, CA.

remained undisturbed until the case of *Custodio* v. *Bauer*[30] in which the normal rules of tort were applied. Occasionally, maintenance costs have been awarded but have been offset to an extent by the advantages of having a new and healthy child – this is generally described as the 'benefits' rule.[31] It remains the case, however, that the majority of US courts will reject claims for the upkeep of a healthy child born as a result of negligent sterilisation – and any of the reasons outlined above can and have been used.[32] The situation in the United States is complicated, first, by the fact that several states prohibit actions for both wrongful pregnancy and wrongful birth by way of statute and, second, because many courts fail to distinguish between the two. Given these limitations, my assistants and I have, currently, identified some forty-two cases in which claims for upkeep of an uncovenanted healthy child were refused and thirteen in which they were accepted – albeit, some with a deduction for 'offset' of the benefits of parenthood.[33] Such actions being matters of state rather than federal law, the result, in my view, is that the US jurisprudence is of minimal value as a model for a parallel in the United Kingdom.

Canada. In fact, much the same problems have been considered in Canada. We have noted the early opinion in *Doiron* v. *Orr* above[34] and this has been generally followed.[35] The Canadian courts have, however, been prepared to consider maintenance damages with 'offset'; in the Quebec case of *Suite* v. *Cooke*,[36] the advantages and disadvantages of a new child were held to cancel each other out. Elsewhere, the financial *reasons* for avoiding parentage have been held to justify financial restitution[37] and a most interesting 'offset', because it is against mainstream thought, was allowed in *Keats* v. *Pearce*.[38] Here, refusal to undergo a termination was accepted, as it

---

[30] 251 Cal App 2d 303 (1962). And more recently *Zehr* v. *Haugen* 871 P 2d 1006 (Ore., 1994).

[31] The case of *Sherlock* v. *Stillwater Clinic* 260 NW 2d 169 (Minn., 1977) has been given great prominence in the UK courts. The whole matter is particularly well set out in *Burke* v. *Rivo* 551 NE 2d 1 (Mass., 1990) and, in what is this author's favourite by reason of the opinions given, *Ochs* v. *Borelli* 445 A 2d 883 (Conn., 1982): 'There can be no affront to public policy in the recognition of the costs of [raising a child from birth to maturity]' at 886.

[32] The classic case, perhaps, is *Terrell* v. *Garcia* 496 SW 2d 124 (Tx., 1973). See, more recently, *Johnson* v. *University Hospitals of Cleveland* 540 NE 2d 1370 (Ohio, 1989).

[33] There is very little point in recording them individually here. The situation in 1991 was summarised in *Girdley* v. *Coats* (1991) Mo. App. Lexis 1065 as: three states allow full recovery (New Mexico, Wisconsin and, now, Missouri), six adopt the 'benefit' rule (Arizona, California, Connecticut, Maryland, Massachusetts and Minnesota); and the majority insist on 'no recovery' for a healthy child.

[34] n. 8 above.

[35] For the most recent cases, see *Roe* v. *Dabbs* [2004] BCSC 957 and *Bevilacqua* v. *Altenkirk* [2004] BCSC 945.

[36] (1995) 58 ACWS (3d) 961.   [37] *Kealey* v. *Berezowski* (1996) 136 DLR (4th) 708.

[38] (1984) 48 Nfd & PEI R 102.

is almost universally, as being a reasonable action; failure to offer the child for adoption was, however, considered to be something which should be taken into account when assessing damages. These mixed results, however, again demonstrate no recognisable pattern and, within the Commonwealth, it is to Australia and, in particular, to the case of *Cattanach* v. *Melchior*, that we must look for the clearest exposition of the wrongful pregnancy action – and we will return to that case later in the chapter.

Historic wrongful pregnancy in the United Kingdom

By contrast, the jurisprudence associated with negligent contraceptive surgery in the United Kingdom followed a relatively easy path, albeit of up-and-down pattern, up to the turn of the century. *Udale* v. *Bloomsbury AHA*[39] is not, chronologically speaking, the first relevant British case but it provides a solid foundation on which to build an analysis.[40] In outlining the circumstances of the case, Jupp J said:

Fortunately or unfortunately, she gave birth to a normal healthy boy ... The phrase 'fortunately or unfortunately' encapsulates the most part of the legal argument which has surrounded the plaintiff's claim for damages.[41]

Thus, Jupp J grasped the nettle firmly at a very early stage in the development of the law in this area and *Udale* can be looked upon as the index case. The circumstances were relatively simple. Mrs Udale underwent a sterilising operation but, nonetheless, conceived a fifth child. There is no doubt that she had a difficult pregnancy but she came to terms with the situation and was delivered of a healthy boy who, as so often almost miraculously happens in these cases, was received into the family with love and affection. In due course, she sued the Area Health Authority under what we have seen to be the relatively standard headings – for the pain and suffering associated with pregnancy and childbirth, for associated loss of earnings and for the upkeep of the child until its majority, this last being the claim that is, for all practical purposes, the subject of this chapter.

In the event, Jupp J rejected all these except the first – on grounds which we have outlined above and which, singly or together, have formed the standard bases for argument worldwide.[42] These include the

[39] [1983] 2 All ER 522, [1983] 1 WLR 1098.
[40] I have analysed these cases previously in J. K. Mason,'Unwanted Pregnancy: A Case of Retroversion?' (2000) 4 *Edinburgh Law Review* 191–206 which provides the basis for this section.
[41] [1983] 2 All ER 522 at 523, [1983] 1 WLR 1098 at 1099.
[42] See the later article by Angus Stewart, 'Damages for the Birth of a Child' (1995) 40 *Journal of the Law Society of Scotland* 298–302.

disadvantage to the child who later found that he had been rejected; the fact that to offset the joys of parenthood against the economic damage sustained would mean that virtue went unrewarded while 'unnatural rejection of womanhood and motherhood would be generously compensated';[43] that doctors would be under pressure to arrange abortions; and, finally, having directed us to the Gospel of St John,[44] that:

> It has been the assumption of our culture from time immemorial that a child coming into the world, even if, as some say, 'the world is a vale of tears', is a blessing and a reason for rejoicing.[45]

Jupp J's decision was avowedly based on public policy and depended very much on the reasoning in the barely relevant 'wrongful life' case of *McKay*.[46] In the instant case, he concluded that: 'on the grounds of public policy, the plaintiff's claims ... in so far as they are based on negligence which allowed David Udale to come into this world alive, should not be allowed' (at 531). Even so, damages in respect of pain and suffering and of the necessary extensions to the plaintiffs' house were allowed – this being largely because doing so did not imply rejection of the child.

No matter how much one may agree or disagree with it, it is apparent that his opinion, like that of many of the courts that have followed this line, relies as much on moral values as on legal principles. As a result, Peter Pain J who, in his own words, firmly put sentiment on one side, was unable to see the logic of the *Udale* decision in the closely following case of *Thake* v. *Maurice*.[47] Coining the now famous phrase:

> [E]very baby has a belly to be filled and a body to be clothed.[48]

he proposed an award of damages not only for the pain and suffering attending an unexpected pregnancy and birth but also for the child's support. However, he conceded that there must be some offset as measured by the joy of having a healthy child and, to circumvent the injustice anticipated by Jupp J, he balanced this against the sorrows of pregnancy

---

[43] The contrary use of the same argument in *Ochs* v. *Borelli*, n. 31 above, is particularly apposite: 'The plaintiffs' .... love for Catherine should not become reason for denying them financial relief' at 886.

[44] John 16:21.

[45] n. 39 above, at All ER 531, WLR 1109. 'Blessing' is a word that has been widely used in the courts all over the world.

[46] *McKay* v. *Essex Area Health Authority* [1982] QB 1166, for which see Chapter 6.

[47] [1986] QB 644, [1986] 1 All ER 497 – already discussed in part at p. 102.

[48] ibid., at QB 666.

and child birth rather than against the economic costs of rearing the child. This approach was, however, rejected on appeal[49] with the result that damages under both these heads could be awarded without offset.

Meantime, *Emeh* v. *Kensington and Chelsea and Westminster Area Health Authority*[50] was progressing through the courts. The issues here were rather different and arose, primarily, from the fact that the trial judge regarded the refusal to abort a physically abnormal child as a *novus actus interveniens* – a possibility to which we will return below.[51] Even so, the Court of Appeal specifically rejected the concept of there being a public policy objection to the award of damages for the negligent conception and birth of a healthy, as opposed to a congenitally disabled, child.[52]

As Slade LJ put it

In these circumstances [a negligent operation], it seems to me clear that the loss suffered by the plaintiff as a result of the defendant's negligence would be any reasonably foreseeable financial loss directly caused by the unexpected pregnancy, and the subsequent birth of her child.

Or:

If a woman wants to be sterilised, I can see no reason why, under public policy, she should not recover such financial damage as she can prove she has sustained by the surgeon's negligent failure to perform the operation properly whether or not the child is healthy.[53]

The combined effect of *Thake* and *Emeh* was to overturn *Udale*, and *Emeh* was, at this point, regarded as representing the English law in this area.[54] But it is only fair to point out that it was, in many respects, a less than satisfactory case by which to do so. It was, for example, concerned with the birth of a congenitally disabled child and, while the arguments, as above, were extrapolated so as to include the birth of a normal child, there is no certainty that the result would have been the same had the case started from that premise. Moreover, it was later suggested that the

---

[49] Per Kerr LJ ibid., at 683, [1986] 1 All ER 497 at 509.

[50] (1983) *The Times*, 3 January, QBD; [1985] QB 1012, CA.

[51] For an early assessment of the relationship between abortion and wrongful pregnancy, see Kenneth McK. Norrie, 'Damages for the Birth of a Child' 1985 SLT 69–74 and Andrew Grubb, 'Damages for "Wrongful Conception"' (1985) 44 *Cambridge Law Journal* 30–2.

[52] Per Waller LJ, n. 50 above, at 1022.

[53] ibid., at 1025. The court also rejected the variation on 'offset' that, in the event of the child being handicapped, the damages awarded should be those for rearing that child less the costs of bringing up a normal child – a view that was to survive for some 15 years.

[54] 'It is the critical decision in the line of authority in England' per Lord Steyn in *McFarlane* v. *Tayside Health Board* [2000] 2 AC 59 at 79. See also E. J. Russell, 'Is Parenthood always an "Unblemished Blessing" in Every Case?' 1998 SLT 191.

authorities relied on in *Emeh* were of doubtful status, depending, as they did, on some uncertain US precedents.[55] Even so, *Emeh* founded the basis for later decisions in both England[56] and Scotland.[57]

As Butler-Sloss LJ intimated in the later English case of *Salih*,[58] these issues are often difficult to evaluate entirely unemotionally. For this reason, the present writer regards the case of *Walkin* v. *South Manchester Health Authority*[59] as being particularly important. Here the question, which arises surprisingly often, was couched simply in terms of the application of the Limitation Act 1980, section 11 – did the expense and tribulation of rearing the child constitute a personal injury[60] resulting from negligence giving rise to an unwanted pregnancy, or did they not? Auld LJ was in no doubt:

> In my view, it clearly did. It is true . . . that the claim depended on the birth of the child, but the birth was not an intervening act; it was caused by the personal injury, namely the unwanted pregnancy[61]

or, as summarised by Neill LJ: 'There is one cause of action which arises at the moment of conception.'[62]

It is concluded, therefore, that, until *McFarlane* had run its course, an award of damages for the upkeep of an unexpected – albeit not, eventually, unwanted – child was acceptable under both English and Scots

---

[55] Per Lord Hope in *McFarlane*, n. 54 above at AC 92. While I agree that the importance attached to *Sherlock* v. *Stillwater Clinic* (1977) 260 NW 2d 169 by several courts of the United Kingdom is disproportionate, it is to be noted that Purchas LJ quoted the case in *Emeh* only 'to identify the problem, not to solve it'. The same criticism as to 'uncertainty' might be levelled at the frequent reference to the 'purely personal' opinion of Ognall J in an unreported case (*Jones* v. *Berkshire Health Authority* (1986) quoted in *Gold* v. *Haringey Health Authority* [1986] 1 FLR 125; revsd [1988] QB 481).

[56] Including *Benarr* v. *Kettering Health Authority* [1988] NLJR 179 where the precedent was set for allowing expenses associated with private schooling.

[57] *Allan* v. *Greater Glasgow Health Board* (1993) 17 BMLR 135, 1998 SLT 580. Evidence that this was correct Scots law is to be found in two unreported cases: *Pollock* v. *Lanarkshire Health Board* (1987) *The Times*, 6 January; *Lindsay* v. *Greater Glasgow Health Board* (1990) *The Scotsman*, 14 March. Both were settled out of court and £50,000 was offered in compensation in the latter case.

[58] *Salih and another* v. *Enfield Health Authority* (1991) 7 BMLR 1 at 4.

[59] (1995) 1 WLR 1543.

[60] In which case, an action would be barred after 3 years. Whether or not a normal *unwanted* pregnancy can be regarded as an injury has been discussed in the preceding chapter, particularly in comparison with wrongful birth. Emotion cannot be ruled out, however, even in such a legal context. The judge frequently has to decide whether or not he or she can exercise discretion under s.33 to release the petitioner from the shackles of s.11. See, for example, *Das* v. *Ganju* (1998) 42 BMLR 28 (where, interestingly, it seems that the fetus, on birth, could be regarded as 'another person' for the purposes of s.11) or, more recently, *Godfrey* v. *Gloucestershire Royal Infirmary NHS Trust* [2003] EWHC 549, QB. Both these cases were, significantly, cases of wrongful birth and discretion was exercised in both.

[61] n. 59 above, at 1552.   [62] ibid., at 1556.

law. The picture was, however, to change dramatically when Mr and Mrs McFarlane brought their case to the Outer House of the Court of Session.

The case of Mr and Mrs McFarlane

McFarlane v. *Tayside Health Board*[63] arose from a vasectomy performed on Mr McFarlane in October 1989. In March 1990, having undergone the necessary tests, he was informed that his sperm count was negative and that he could safely resume sexual intercourse without contraceptive measures. Mrs McFarlane, who already had four children, became pregnant in September 1991 and was delivered of a healthy female child in May 1992. The child was subsequently admitted as a loved and integral member of the family.

An action in negligence was raised against the Health Board and was, as by now was standard practice, in two parts – the 'mother's claim' in respect of pain and suffering due to pregnancy and childbirth and the 'parents claim' for the upkeep of the child until the age of majority.

The Lord Ordinary, Lord Gill, rejected both claims in the Outer House. His reasons can be summarised in his own words:

> In my view, a pregnancy occurring in the circumstances of this case cannot be equiparated with a physical injury. Pregnancy and labour are natural processes resulting in a happy outcome ... Even if otherwise, I do not consider that it is an injury for which damages are recoverable. I cannot see how [the happiness Mrs McFarlane has and will have] can either be disregarded altogether or be held not to outweigh the natural pain and discomfort in the creation of life.
>
> I am of the opinion that this case should be decided on the principle that the privilege of being a parent is immeasurable in money terms; that the benefits of parenthood transcend patrimonial loss ... and that the parents in a case such as this cannot be said to be in a position of loss.[64]

The Inner House of the Court of Session then, unanimously allowed a reclaiming motion.[65] The reasons given by Lord Cullen LJ-C can be summarised: the defenders' contention that the costs of maintaining the child could not be due to their negligence was unsustainable; it was unwarrantable to assume that the birth of a child was a blessing in every case; the principle that the value of a child outweighed its costs was not one that was recognised in Scots law; and there were no overriding considerations of public policy that would be contravened by awarding damages to

---

[63] 1997 SLT 211, OH; 1998 SC 389, (1998) 44 BMLR 140, IH; [2000] AC 59, 2000 SC 1, HL.

[64] n. 63 above, SLT at 214, 216.

[65] Thus, negligence was neither admitted nor proved. The defender's duty of care to the pursuers was, however, admitted.

the pursuers. All three judges, as carefully explained by Lord McCluskey[66] agreed that the concurrence of *injuria* (in this case the provision of incorrect information) and *damnum* (prejudice to the McFarlanes' legitimate interests in not having any more children) derived from conception and pregnancy and provided grounds for an action for reparation – and the costs of rearing the child flowed directly from her conception.[67]

As we have already discussed, the vast majority of the courts that have considered the matter have no trouble with seeing unwanted pregnancy and labour as an injury to the mother. It also seems self-evident that, despite its being contrary to the majority of Commonwealth and American decisions, the Inner House decision as to the parents' claim was one that would be anticipated under the normal rules of delict. The McFarlanes wanted to avoid another child; they had another child due to the negligent advice provided by someone who clearly owed them a duty of care; their reasons for avoiding a further parentage were largely economic; and to return them to the position in which they would have been in the absence of negligence involved reparation of the costs of maintaining that child. To my mind, justice was done by way of established legal principle.

McFarlane *in the House of Lords*

Thus it seemed that peace and uniformity was restored. England had moved from the essentially moralistic position in *Udale* to the functional approach adopted in *Emeh*. The majority of those engaged in the study of medical jurisprudence would have regarded the decision of the Lord Ordinary in the Outer House[68] as a unique exception to the established precedents and now Scotland had taken the same journey. Lord Slynn was to say later:

Although these judgments refer to the law of Scotland . . . it is as I understand it accepted that the law of England and that of Scotland should be the same in respect of the matters which arise on this appeal. It would be strange, even absurd, if they were not.[69]

---

[66] n. 63 above at 1998 SC 400, BMLR 154.

[67] For the meaning of *injuria* and *damnum*, see Chapter 3 at p. 86. As noted there, there is no satisfactory English equivalent of the Scots concept of *damnum*; thus, while it is clearly correct to invoke *damnum* in the Scots law of delict, it does, at the same time, circumvent the difficulty elaborated in *Udale* of equating a natural process such as pregnancy with a 'personal injury'.

[68] *McFarlane* v. *Tayside Health Board* 1997 SLT 211. It is only fair to add that Lord Gill had powerful support: e.g. P. S. Atiyah, *The Damages Lottery* (Oxford, Hart Publishing, 1997) at 54.

[69] *McFarlane* v. *Tayside Health Board* [2000] 2 AC 59 at 68, 2000 SC 1 at 4.

And, in fact, they now were and, at the time, referral to the House of Lords was regarded by many as something of an obtrusion. On the other hand, no comparable English cases had been referred to the highest legal tribunal and an anxiety to ensure harmonisation of the law on such a contentious subject was understandable. The unexpected twist lay in the result. The House, by a majority, Lord Millett dissenting, held that a woman who had undergone an unexpected and unwanted pregnancy was entitled to damages for the pain, suffering and inconvenience of pregnancy and childbirth, but held unanimously that no recompense was available for the upkeep of the resulting, healthy child.

It might be convenient at this point to dispose of 'the mother's claim' and, at the same time, to consider the reasons for Lord Millett's minority view. Essentially, this depended on the application of logic. Few people can have qualms as to the relevance of the mother's claim for the suffering of pregnancy and childbirth once negligence has been demonstrated. Problems arise, however, when the two claims are taken as dependent upon each other, as, on one view, they must be. Rearing one's child without having survived pregnancy and child birth is, currently, an impossible concept and it can be seen as illogical to accept responsibility for the one without the other. This was the route taken by the Lord Ordinary in the Outer House and by Lord Millett in the House of Lords. Each then concluded that both claims should be denied if one is unacceptable – and this is where it is possible to part company with the learned judges. It is not easy to understand why, given the same circumstances, it is not equally logical to hold that both claims should be upheld if one is found acceptable – and it will be seen that this form of antithetic argument arises at several points in the assessment of the case. Irrespective of this particular point, however, those who would allow one claim and deny the other must produce some reason for rejection of what appears to be the evidence of nature. To do this, they must erect an artificial legalistic construct by way of what Hoyano[70] describes as a 'slicing up of the professional relationship' into several duties of care – thus separating the loss in the form of the mother's personal injury from the economic loss involved in maintenance – and we will see that, in one way or another, the remaining four Law Lords managed to achieve such a *modus vivendi*. Given that one can accommodate such a formula, the mother's claim can be regarded as unexceptional; accordingly, the remainder of this discussion is devoted solely to the joint claim for

---

[70] Laura C. H. Hoyano, 'Misconceptions and Wrongful Conceptions' (2002) 65 *Modern Law Review* 883–906 at 886.

recovery of the costs involved in maintaining an unexpected, albeit healthy, child during its minority.[71]

Given this limitation, then, all on the five Law Lords' bench reached the same conclusion but by very different routes and the House of Lords' decision in *McFarlane* is famous not only for its surprise result[72] but also for the manner in which it was reached. Indeed, the major problem for any later analyst, including a number of judges at first instance,[73] has been to find a consistent *ratio* – a fact which, ironically, has also served to ease the paths of those anxious to circumvent the decision. As a result, an understanding of *McFarlane* is impossible without a fairly extensive review of the speeches and we will consider these in turn.[74] Before doing so, however, it will be convenient to dispose of some matters which the House rejected as being significant to their conclusions.

Novus actus interveniens. Since the action for the upkeep of the unexpected child depends upon there being a child for whom the parents are responsible,[75] it must be open to the defenders to argue that they could have solved the problem either by lawful termination of pregnancy or by arranging for the neonate's adoption. This proposition was accepted at first instance in *Emeh* where Park J was of the opinion that the plaintiff's refusal to terminate the pregnancy was so unreasonable as to constitute a *novus actus interveniens.*[76] This was strongly rejected on appeal where Slade LJ considered that:

---

[71] The fact that Lord Steyn referred to the action as one for 'wrongful birth' (at AC 76, SC 11) can be ascribed to a *lapsus linguae*. Lord Clyde also referred to 'wrongful conception' (at AC 99, SC 31) and I have described in Chapter 1 why I prefer the term 'wrongful pregnancy'. I see the two as being synonymous, but see Bernard Dickens, 'Wrongful Birth and Life, Wrongful Death before Birth and Wrongful Law' in Sheila A. M. McLean (ed.), *Legal Issues in Human Reproduction* (Aldershot, Dartmouth, 1989), chapter 4 for further distinctions.

[72] 'I can think of few decisions that are . . . as odious, unsound and unsafe as this one': J. Ellis Cameron-Perry, 'Return of the Burden of the "Blessing"' (1999) 149 *New Law Journal* 1887–8. This is, obviously, an extreme view and certainly was not one that was universally held; nonetheless, it illustrates the intensity of the general reaction.

[73] In particular, and as discussed in the previous chapter, Newman J in *Rand* v. *East Dorset Health Authority* (2000) 56 BMLR 39, [2000] Lloyd's Rep Med 181; Henriques J in *Hardman* v. *Amin* [2000] 59 BMLR 58, [2000] Lloyd's Rep Med 498; Toulson J in *Lee* v. *Taunton and Somerset NHS Trust* [2001] 1 FLR 419, [2001] Fam Law 103.

[74] See Mason, n. 40 above. Also Hoyano, n. 70 above; Penny Booth, 'A Child is a Blessing – Heavily in Disguise, Right?' (2001) 151 *New Law Journal* 1738; Tony Weir, 'The Unwanted Child' (2000) 59 *Cambridge Law Journal* 238–41; Joe Thomson, 'Abandoning the Law of Delict?' 2000 SLT 43–5 and, particularly, the opinions in *Rand, Hardman* and *Lee*, Chapter 3 above.

[75] Children (Scotland) Act 1995, s.1; Family Law (Scotland) Act 1985, s. 1(1)(c).

[76] (1983) *The Times*, 3 January. As a consequence, damages were awarded only for the discomfort associated with the first four months of pregnancy.

The judge . . . was, I think, really saying that the defendants had the right to expect that, if they had not performed the operation properly, she would procure an abortion . . . I do not, for my part, think that the defendants had the right to expect any such thing. By their own negligence, they faced her with the very dilemma which she had sought to avoid by having herself sterilised.[77]

The approach taken by the Court of Appeal in *Emeh* was preceded, and has been followed, almost without exception in all jurisdictions – not least in *McFarlane* where Lord Steyn, for example, was unable to conceive of any circumstances in which the decision of the parents not to resort to even a lawful abortion could be questioned.[78] Yet their Lordships, as a whole, gave little reason for their unanimity on the question. Lord Hope was content to accept that they had no other choice;[79] Lord Clyde stated only that: 'the decision to keep the child, to accept into the family a baby who was originally unwanted, cannot rank as an acting on the part of the pursuers sufficient to break the causal chain'.[80] Lord Millett regarded the proposition that it is unreasonable for parents not to have an abortion or place a child for adoption as far more repugnant than the characterisation of the birth of a healthy and normal child as a detriment.[81] One feels that the majority would agree with those sentiments. The termination of pregnancy, and particularly a late pregnancy, represents a decision that is of profound moral and medical significance to the woman concerned and it must be within the anticipation of a tortfeasor that she will reject it.[82]

But one has to look to the position of the defendants and ask whether the concept is so unreasonable as to be dismissed out of hand. The House of Lords quoted widely from the Australian case *CES* v. *Superclinics (Australia) Pty Ltd* in which Priestly JA said:

The point in the present case is that the plaintiff chose to keep her child. The anguish of having to make the choice is part of the damage caused by the negligent breach of duty, but the fact remains, however compelling the psychological pressure on the plaintiff may have been to keep the child, the opportunity of choice was in my opinion real and the choice made was voluntary. It was this choice which was the cause, in my opinion, of the subsequent cost of rearing a child . . .

---

[77] n. 50 above, at QB 1024.
[78] n. 63 above, at AC 81, SC 15. This worrying aspect of 'wrongful pregnancy' is, however, of greater general interest rather than of importance to the *McFarlane* decision.
[79] ibid., at AC 97, SC 29.   [80] ibid., at AC 104, SC 36.   [81] ibid., at AC 113, SC 44.
[82] Mitigation of damages by way of abortion or adoption was seriously considered in the New Zealand case *Re Z* (1982) 3 NZAR 161. In the end, it was rejected as being 'inappropriate in the circumstances' (per Blair J at 163). This case is revisited briefly at n. 89 below.

The plaintiff having chosen to keep the child in the human way that ... I think most people in the community would approve of, is not entitled to damages for the financial consequences of having made that difficult but ordinary human choice.[83]

Lords Steyn and Millett were, in fact, the only Law Lords to discuss this aspect of causation in depth and the latter even offered grudging support for this view. We are, however, effectively left to fend for ourselves in establishing why it is unacceptable. The primary reason, it is suggested, is that to hold otherwise would be to imply that abortion is available on demand in the United Kingdom and, while I have argued that this is the situation de facto,[84] it certainly cannot be seen as that de jure.[85] Even so, some might wonder at the fairness of the win-win situation by which a woman can chose to terminate or retain her fetus at will and, yet, never lose her standing in the case. Secondly, as already noted, the moral implications in electing for abortion are of such intensity and variety that it could scarcely be right to lay down a rule as to the legal implications of the decision reached. And, finally – and, perhaps, most importantly – the majority would, one feels, agree with Lord Steyn that the law must and does respect these decisions of parents which are so closely tied to their basic freedoms and rights of personal autonomy.[86]

Perhaps the last word may be left to Lord Millett:

Catherine's conception and birth, and the restoration of the status quo by abortion or adoption, were the very things that the defenders were engaged to prevent ... The costs of bringing her up are no more remote than the costs of an abortion or adoption would have been. In each case the causal connection is strong, direct and foreseeable.[87]

'Public policy'. Much of the reasoning in *McFarlane* is devoted to considerations of 'public policy' – a life-line that, in the event, all were at pains to reject. The phrase 'public policy' is not all that easy to define. It was used first in the present context by Jupp J in *Udale*[88] where, indeed, it formed the basis of his decision. It might, therefore, be assumed that it is a

---

[83] (1995) 38 NSWLR 47 at 84–5. *CES* is certainly not on all fours with *McFarlane*. In the first place, it was an action for wrongful birth rather than wrongful pregnancy and, secondly, New South Wales has no statute comparable to the Abortion Act 1967, the law being currently based on *R* v. *Bourne* [1939] 1 KB 687. The case turned largely on whether an abortion would have been legal and, in the end, was something of a compromise decision.

[84] See Chapter 2 above.

[85] This may be the reason for Lord Hope saying that the parents had no other choice.

[86] It could be held that only the last consideration applies to adoption but, in essence, both abortion and adoption are matters within a woman's freedom of reproductive choice. I return to the problems of abortion, adoption and autonomy in Chapter 8.

[87] n. 63 above, at AC 113, SC 44.   [88] n. 39 above.

recognised feature of 'public policy' that damages should not be awarded for the birth of a healthy child – albeit one that is unintentionally conceived as a result of another's negligence. But, as Lord Clyde indicated, it is difficult to find any policy ground supporting one course of action in the resolution of wrongful birth (using his Lordship's terminology) without unearthing a countervailing consideration that points to the opposite conclusion. Moreover, there is no reason to suppose that a negative policy – that is, that there is no public policy contrary to a suggested solution – presupposes a positive policy to the effect that that solution should be adopted.[89]

In the event, the House unanimously excluded public policy as a basis for their reasoning – the issue was to be settled by recourse to principle. The difficulty, at least for this writer is, however, that, while the two are theoretically quite separate, they are in practice often difficult to distinguish. If, for example, as Lord Slynn proposed, the question of whether reparation for the expenses incurred in the upbringing of a loved child is resolved by way of legal principle, it is not easy to distinguish the result from a formulated policy. Or, where lies the difference between applying the principle of distributive justice and accepting that principle as a matter of policy? – a distinction which Lord Steyn managed to make with ease.[90] In fact, Lord Bingham was, later, to refer to the 'policy considerations' that underpinned the judgments of the House.[91] Among these was a concern that:

to award potentially very large sums of damages to the parents of a normal and healthy child against a National Health Service always in need of funds to meet pressing demands would rightly offend the community's sense of how public resources should be allocated.[92]

---

[89] The present writer is attracted by the down to earth approach in the New Zealand case *Re Z*, n. 82 above. In partially pre-empting the *McFarlane* decision, Judge Blair unhesitatingly relied on public policy as to the setting of limits to liability. The expenses relating to the birth of a child were allowed but it was held that the necessary 'intimate causal relation' between the medical error and the expenses involved disappeared as the child got older; a line had to be drawn between the direct and indirect causes of an 'accident'. The conditions were, however, peculiar to New Zealand in that the case concerned a claim under the Accident Compensation Act 1972 which imposes a 'stern test' as to the remoteness of damage.

[90] Hoyano, n. 70 above, at 889, also points to Lord Millett's unsolved conundrum: 'Legal policy is not the same as public policy, even though moral considerations may play a part in both' (n. 63 above, at AC 108, SC 39).

[91] In *Rees* v. *Darlington Memorial Hospital NHS Trust* [2004] AC 309, [2003] 4 All ER 987 at [6]. See also Lord Nicholls at [16].

[92] Which is coming close to involvement in rationing in the NHS, something that the courts have eschewed since *R* v. *Secretary of State for Social Services and ors, ex p Hincks* (1980) 1 BMLR 93, CA.

Indeed, one commentator has remarked that the House blocked the McFarlanes' claim:

for reasons of a 'legal policy' which, stripped of all linguistic embroidery, boils down to protecting the NHS ... from expensive claims when 'nothing worse happened than the birth of a healthy if unwanted child'.[93]

This may be a trifle hyperbolic and, perhaps, unjustified. Nevertheless, the 'policy' issue may be of considerable jurisprudential importance – Lord Clyde, for example, was wary lest the House should encroach on responsibilities which attach to the legislature rather than the courts. Lord Hope, for his part, believed the question for the court to be one of law, not of social policy and considered that the remedy lay in the hands of the legislature if the law was found to be unsatisfactory.[94] But the common law remains the common law no matter how it has been established and those involved in cases of wrongful pregnancy are now bound by the decision in *McFarlane* until it is superseded.

The disparate reasoning. So, what were the principles on which this dramatic sea-change was based? Each of the five judges involved gave individual reasons for allowing the defenders' appeal – and it has to be admitted that none appears wholly satisfactory to an observer who has no formal training in the law.[95]

Lord Slynn, pointing to the fact that the issue was one of the extent of the duty of care and of liability for economic loss,[96] simply applied the *Caparo* standard[97] and considered it neither fair, just or reasonable to impose on the doctor 'liability for the consequential responsibilities, imposed on or accepted by the parents to bring up a child'. A line is to be drawn before such losses are recoverable – but how fair, just or reasonable is it from the parents' point of view to do so? Lord Slynn did not comment on the question but it has been pointed out that this test, itself, allows for a different interpretation in the event of a child being

---

[93] A. Pedain, 'Unconventional Justice in the House of Lords' (2004) 63 CLJ 19.

[94] Hoyano, n. 70 above, at 890, points out that this is an interesting comment insofar as the court was changing case law that had gone unchallenged for 15 years. The strong reaction on the part of the Australian legislatures noted at n. 179 below is, however, to be remarked.

[95] It is interesting to note in another contemporaneous case that much the same arguments as were invoked can also be used to reach a different conclusion. See *Mukheiber* v. *Raath and Raath* (1999) http://www.uovs.ac.za/law/appeals/26297.htm (20 January 2000) – a case heard in the Supreme Court of Appeal of South Africa under the Roman-Dutch jurisprudence.

[96] Drawing very much on Stewart, n. 42 above.

[97] *Caparo Industries plc* v. *Dickman* [1990] 2 AC 605, [1990] 1 All ER 568.

born disabled.[98] He was, however, strongly supported by Lord Hope who also played the *Caparo* card and, in addition, stressed that, in the absence of a threshold, liability could be stretched almost indefinitely so as to include, for example, the costs of a private education for the resultant child.[99] Lord Hope's reasons for rejecting *any* restitution are, however, less easy to accommodate:

> It cannot be established that, overall and in the long run, these costs [of meeting the obligations to the child during her childhood] will exceed the value of the benefits. This is economic loss of a kind which must be held to fall outside the ambit of the duty of care which was owed … by the persons who carried out the procedures in the hospital and the laboratory.[100]

One wonders why this constitutes a sequitur – and Lord Hope's analysis is considered again below.

Reasonableness as to the extent of liability was also considered by Lord Clyde who believed that it includes an element of proportionality between the wrongdoing and the resulting loss suffered. Lord Clyde found it difficult to accept that, in a case such as *McFarlane*, there would be any reasonable relationship between the fault and the claim 'such as would accord with the idea of restitution' and he thought that the expense of child rearing could be wholly disproportionate to the doctor's culpability – a reason for limiting liability which was, incidentally, specifically rejected by Lord Millett. Once again, it is possible to argue from the other side – that the costs to the McFarlanes were wholly disproportionate to those anticipated when they acted on advice to resume non-contraceptive sexual intercourse.

Lord Millett's analysis of the principles involved was, possibly, the most comprehensive but is also the most difficult to interpret.[101] This is because, although he appeared to be the most anxious of the judges that the McFarlanes should 'not go away empty handed', he was, in the end, almost forced, by a process of elimination, to conclude that the reason why the costs of bringing up the child should not be recoverable lay in the fact that the law must take the birth of a normal, healthy baby to be a blessing, not a detriment – in other words, he joined hands with Jupp J in *Udale* and Lord Gill in the Outer House in *McFarlane* in making what can only be seen, *pace* Lord Gill, as a policy decision. Lord Millett concluded:

---

[98] See Newman J in *Rand*, n. 73 above, at BMLR 44, Lloyd's Rep Med 184.

[99] *Benarr* v. *Kettering Health Authority*, n. 56 above, has much to answer for as to its influence in *McFarlane*.

[100] n. 63 above, at AC 97, SC 29.

[101] Lord Millett's distinction between the recovery of costs for, on the one hand, acquiring and, on the other, replacing a high chair is an interesting detail.

It would be repugnant to [society's] own sense of values to do otherwise. It is morally offensive to regard a normal, healthy baby as more trouble and expense than it is worth.[102]

Lord Steyn almost hoed a row of his own in a direct appeal to distributive justice and, thereby, to the common man. It may, he said, become relevant to ask commuters on the Underground the following question:

Should the parents of an unwanted but healthy child be able to sue the doctor or the hospital for compensation equivalent to the cost of bringing up the child for the years of his or her minority – i.e. until about 18 years?[103]

and his view was that an overwhelming number of ordinary men and women would answer the question with an emphatic 'no'. Well – maybe; but very few of the commuters on the Underground are already striving to bring up four demanding children – and we will return to the commuter later on.[104]

There are a number of other difficulties in Lord Steyn's approach. In the first place, he did not explain how justice was to be distributed in the present case. If pressed, he said, he would say that the claim did not satisfy the requirement of being fair, just and reasonable – but this is no explanation and, as we have seen, fairness depends very much on the viewpoint; it is quite easy to visualise the *McFarlane* decision as an example of distributive *in*justice. Secondly, he relied on the twin cases of *Alcock* v. *Chief Constable of South Yorkshire Police*[105] and *Frost* v. *Chief Constable of South Yorkshire Police*.[106] Neither of these cases is particularly satisfying. One may have little sympathy for police officers who claim damages for carrying out duties for which they have been trained and paid; but to deny them compensation on the grounds that others were ineligible seems very like the fable of the 'sour grapes' – not, as Lord Steyn suggested, the language of distributive justice. Thirdly, in a search for coherence, Lord Steyn quoted the case, and deprecated the result, of *McKay* v. *Essex Area Health Authority*[107] in which an action for damages by a child born handicapped was rejected while the parallel action by her mother was allowed to proceed[108] – and this was regarded, rightly I believe, as incoherent. But, again, the two actions are, in fact, distinct entities. The former – for

---

[102] n. 63 above, at AC 114, SC 44.   [103] ibid., at AC 82, SC 16.
[104] In passing, the comments of Singer on a later, but closely allied case, deserve repetition here: 'It is not acceptable for our judiciary to make sweeping statements about society's sensibility without justifying it. It does not naturally follow that, because a baby is a blessing, parents should not be compensated for the ensuing financial loss when an unintended child is born due to the fault of another': – S. Singer, '*Rees* v. *Darlington Memorial Hospital NHS Trust* [2004] 1 AC 309' (2004) 26 *Journal of Social Welfare and Family Law* 403–15 at 409.
[105] [1992] 1 AC 310.   [106] [1998] QB 254.   [107] n. 46 above.
[108] Inferred from Stephenson LJ, ibid., at QB 1175.

'wrongful life' which we discuss in Chapter 6 – implies, *inter alia*, that the defective fetus has a right to be prevented from living, a proposition which has been rejected in the vast majority of jurisdictions.[109] The latter – for 'wrongful birth' – is one seeking compensation for the costs and anguish resulting from negligently depriving a woman of a choice available to her under the Abortion Act 1967, section 1(1)(d). The one does not depend upon the other although, as we will see later, the two actions are almost invariably taken in parallel and similar reasoning is applied in both. Even were it otherwise, to disallow the parental action simply because of the inadmissibility of the neonate's seems to be an example of equating two wrongs with a right. In the end, it is hard to identify any gain from applying the essentially moral doctrine of distributive justice to the solution of a wrongful pregnancy.

Thus, we are left wondering what is the true ratio of *McFarlane* and, more importantly, what it was that drove the House to make such a dramatic U-turn on such a united front. All the opinions contain at least a modicum of moral reasoning and my own view is that this centres on the problem of 'offset' where there is a clear clash of interests.

On the one hand, their Lordships were confronted by the established principle that some offset for the attending benefits must be included in the assessment of damages for another's negligence so long as the two are commensurate. But, in the present circumstances, this involves, firstly, the problem of comparing the emotional advantages of parenthood with its financial disadvantages and, as a consequence, of putting a monetary value on the life of a child. The combined difficulty was expressed by Lord Millett:

There is something distasteful, if not morally offensive, in treating the birth of a normal, healthy child as a matter for compensation. I cannot accept that the solution lies in requiring the costs of maintaining the child to be offset by the benefits derived from the child's existence ... The placing of a monetary value on the birth of a normal and healthy child ... provides no solution to the moral problem. The exercise must either be superfluous or produce the very result which is said to be repugnant.[110]

And he was fully supported by Lords Slynn and Steyn. Lord Hope expressed what seem to be the sentiments of the House in saying that

the value which is to be attached to these benefits [of rearing a child] is incalculable. The costs can be calculated but the benefits, which in fairness must be set

---

[109] See Amos Shapira, '"Wrongful life" Lawsuits for Faulty Genetic Counselling: Should the Impaired Newborn be Entitled to Sue?' (1998) 24 *Journal of Medical Ethics* 369–75.
[110] n. 63 above, at AC 111, SC 42.

against them, cannot. The logical conclusion, as a matter of law, is that the costs to the pursuers of meeting their obligations to the child … are not recoverable as damages.[111]

One must, of course, bow to his Lordship on a matter of law but it is difficult to see where the logic lies. The net costs to the parents of rearing the child are the gross costs less the beneficial 'offsets'. Admittedly, the latter cannot be assessed in the same terms as the former and the arithmetic is going to be difficult – but there is no logical basis for saying that, *because* of this, the costs have been wished out of existence. Lord Slynn, in particular, would not assume that the benefits of parenthood always outweighed their cost but, having described the many difficulties in estimating either, he concluded that the problems were of such gravity as to discourage the acceptance of the 'benefits' approach. On his own admission, however, it *could* be done, and the fact that a process is difficult seems a lame reason for discarding it absolutely – and, then, in favour of one which appears unfair to an aggrieved person.

I believe that the *moral* problems which have so beset their Lordships are, at least, minimised if one accepts that the McFarlanes' action is not about the resultant child but is simply a matter of *the costs of* the resultant child. This is not a wholly novel conclusion – the Australian A-CJ Kirby was widely quoted to the effect:

In most cases, it was not the child as revealed that was unwanted. Nor is the child's existence the *damage* in the action … It is the economic damage which is the principal unwanted element, rather than the birth or existence of the child as such.[112]

Once this is accepted, the moral opprobrium associated with apparent commodification of an infant is avoided. True, several difficulties remain but, at least, the consequences of whether the child is loved or unloved are eliminated. However, given that the unsought child *is* loved, it can still be argued that the parents who are compensated are, so to speak, 'getting something for nothing'. But this is nothing new – Lord McCluskey's quoted example of the miner who is compensated for injury sustained in the pits but who is not disadvantaged if he subsequently enjoys life in the open air[113] is a compelling analogy.

It leads, however, to the concept of a 'conventional child' which I have previously suggested as a possible construct for reconciling the opposing

---

[111] ibid., at AC 97, SC 29.
[112] *CES*, n. 83 above at 75. It will be remembered that this is also one reason why damages for wrongful birth are so much more acceptable to the courts – in the latter case, a direct comparison can be made between the costs of rearing a healthy child and those of caring for a disabled child. The value of a child *qua* child does not enter the equation.
[113] n. 63 above, at 1998 SC 403, 44 BMLR 156–7.

philosophies on the issue. Surely it is not beyond the wit of man to assess the damage done not on the basis of the actual circumstances but, rather, on the basis of the cost involved in the upkeep of the average child born to the average family. This is not a novel idea. To quote Lord Cameron:

> '[A]ccount [can] be taken of the parents' means in the sense that it will be unreasonable to compensate the well-to-do parents to any substantially greater level than the parents of more modest means. To take an example, the amount of the layette of which an allowance would be made should be set at a reasonable and not an extravagant level, albeit that the well-to-do may well have exceeded that level because they have the means to enable them to express their love and care for the child in a more expensive fashion. Equally the same principle of reasonableness should apply in relation to items as divergent as necessary accommodation and fees for schooling.[114]

Recourse to the 'conventional child' also eliminates the reverse of this – that is, the proposition that damages for upkeep of the child should be adjusted so as to accommodate the capacity of the family to withstand the costs[115] and, in so doing it provides a recognisable benchmark against which potential tortfeasors can know the extent of their liability. True, some would still come out comparatively worse or better than others. But, at least, it would maintain elements of fairness and consistency that are so essential to public acceptance of the legal process.

The difficulty in analysing their Lordships' principles is that each appears to have been seeking a legalistic escape from what is, essentially, a *moral* dilemma – and, indeed the House was later to admit the presence of those moral doubts was sufficient to deflect the normal rules of tort law.[116] We have not yet isolated a single, solid legal ratio that explains why responsibility for the economic loss sustained by the parents must be held to fall outside the ambit of the duty of care which was owed them by the health carers. Hoyano[117] concluded, simply, that the House decided, at least by a majority, that *no duty of care* was owed in respect of maintenance costs. This of itself, however, seems an inadequate explanation and I suggest, in addition, that the general tenor to emerge is that it was

---

[114] *Allan*, n. 57 above, at 585.

[115] It will be recalled that Newman J in *Rand* v. *East Dorset Health Authority* (2000) 56 BMLR 39, [2000] Lloyd's Rep Med 181 thought that it should be so; Henriques J in *Hardman* v. *Amin* (2000) 59 BMLR 58, [2000] Lloyd's Rep Med 498 and Toulson J in *Lee* v. *Taunton and Somerset NHS Trust* [2001] FLR 419, [2001] Fam Law 103 took the opposite view – to my mind, correctly.

[116] See discussion of *Rees* v. *Darlington Memorial Hospital NHS Trust* in Chapter 5.

[117] n. 70 above at 890, citing Lords Slynn, Hope and Steyn. She considered Lords Clyde and Millett to have adopted the ratio that there was no loss deriving from the pregnancy.

not fair, just and reasonable in *Caparo*[118] terms to attribute *liability*. My problem, and I suspect it is that of many, is to discover why it is not equally unreasonable to deny economic relief to couples who have been forced into economic loss through the admitted negligence of a person who was trusted to exercise a proper degree of professional skill. Returning to Lord Cameron, speaking before the *McFarlane* decision:

> The question must be asked whether there is any reason why the law ... should not recognise as elements sounding in damages, circumstances such as the additional financial hardships imposed on the parent or parents who require to take into the family the unexpected and unplanned child after birth, in accommodating and caring for that child thereafter and, particularly in the case of a handicapped child, in meeting the additional burdens arising from the distress occasioned by its handicap and the extra payments which they require to make to enable the child to live as near to a normal life as possible. Why, in the case of a handicapped child, for instance, should not a parent who requires to give up employment or the like to care for the child, sue for the loss so occasioned? I see nothing in principle to prevent this. If that be so, why should a healthy child be dealt with differently in regard to a similar loss?[119]

McFarlane was a dispute between two individual parties – can it be said that justice was seen to be done? As already remarked, we will have to turn to the Commonwealth in order to obtain a wider view of the debate.[120]

Wrongful pregnancy in Australia

One thing that is absolutely clear from *McFarlane* is that the precedent it set did not extend beyond the upkeep of a *healthy* child; the consequence,

---

[118] *Caparo* (n. 97 above) was concerned, in the main, with the duty of care *per se*. Lord Oliver, however, specifically associated this with liability (at AC 633, All ER 585). I have assumed that it would now be held as self-evident that the element of trust established in *Hedley Byrne & Co Ltd* v. *Heller & Partners Ltd* [1964] AC 465, [1963] 2 All ER 575 as being necessary before liability for economic loss can be entertained exists between the professionals and the patient in both wrongful pregnancy and wrongful birth scenarios: for discussion, see Toulson J in *Lee*, n. 73 above at FLR 423–4. In any event, as Lord Steyn said: 'it ought not to make any difference whether the claim is based on negligence simpliciter or on the extended *Hedley Byrne* principle' (at AC 83, SC 18).

[119] *Allan* v. *Greater Glasgow Health Board* n. 57 above, at 584.

[120] We have unearthed an interesting historic incident which may serve as a canapé to decisions from the major jurisdictions. In *Ho and another* v. *Chan and others* (1991) (Unreported, High Court of Hong Kong, HCA003490A/1986) a couple averred they had not been properly warned of a risk of failure of tubal ligation. The woman appears to have been almost pressurised into refusing a termination. At the end of a very thorough opinion, Liu J found that they had, in fact, had sufficient warning in accordance with Hong Kong medical practice in the 1980s. Nevertheless, had negligence been demonstrated, he would have awarded substantial damages including those for upkeep of a normal child. Interestingly, Liu J said there were 27 reported cases of conception 'even after hysterectomy'; unfortunately, he quoted no authority.

as we have seen from Chapter 3, was a rash of cases, each attempting, in its own way, to ensure that it remained that way. We have, however, also seen that almost all of these concerned instances of wrongful birth and, as such, were not strictly relevant to the wrongful pregnancy model of *McFarlane*. Nonetheless, they are of immediate interest in that none of the judges concerned showed any marked inclination to disturb the *basic* principle established in the House of Lords. Thus, such was the general mood of acquiescence to a unanimous decision in the highest forum, that the alternatives already expressed lay buried in the archives of the Court of Session and were scarcely discussed in the English courts. Instead, a steady tradition evolved of allowing the *additional* costs consequent upon the extra expenditure of child-rearing involved in the upkeep of a disabled minor; the plight of the reluctant parents of an additional healthy child was largely forgotten[121] – mainly due to the happy eventuality that the great majority of those who accepted their uncovenanted children did so in a loving and wholly admirable way.

But such a happy ending may not always arise, nor are we entitled to expect those whose lifestyle has been unwittingly disturbed to be content with their lot. It was fortunate, at least from the academic viewpoint, that a case of similar importance to *McFarlane* was litigated in Australia at the same time. An opportunity thus arose to extend the wrongful pregnancy debate into a comparative setting.

The case of Mrs Melchior

Mrs Melchior's case was first heard in the Supreme Court of Queensland[122] in 2000. Her obstetric history was interesting in that, at the age of 15, her right ovary had been removed on medical grounds. Nevertheless, she had had two children before she underwent an elective sterilisation at the age of 40. The right fallopian tube was not visualised and was assumed to have been removed with her ovary; consequently only the left tube was correctly clipped laparoscopically. Four years later, she became pregnant and was delivered of a healthy child. Further investigation revealed that the right tube was still present and patent and it was assumed that an egg from the left ovary had migrated across the pelvic cavity. Dr Cattanach was found to have been negligent but, however instructive the case may have been in physiological terms, we are concerned here only with the extent of the damages awarded.

---

[121] Until the case of *Parkinson*, which is considered in detail in Chapter 5.
[122] *Melchior v. Cattanach* [2000] QSC 285.

In the event, the standard claims were met by the particularly Australian variation on the defence of failure to mitigate – namely that any damages other than those allowed for pain and suffering should be curtailed by reference to the theoretical time at which the child could have been adopted.[123] Holmes J was guided, in the main, by the Australian NSW Court of Appeal decision in *CES* v. *Superclinics (Australia) Pty Ltd*[124] and by the House of Lords ruling in *McFarlane*. Having gone through the, by now, almost routine distillate of the five speeches in the latter, she had this to say:

> [W]ere there a single, distinct line of reasoning to be discerned from either [*McFarlane* or *CES*] I should follow it. However, given the divergence of approach, I can see no alternative but to distil from those decisions the reasoning which appeals to me as sound.[125]

She then went on, effectively – and, in this writer's opinion, with impeccable logic – to discard all the reasons given why recompense for maintenance should be withheld; innovatively, along the way, she regarded a failure to have the child adopted (and, by implication, to terminate the pregnancy) as being not so much an interruption in the chain of causation as, rather, a failure to interrupt it. She preferred the reasoning relevant to determining the existence and scope of a duty of care in cases of pure economic loss, as was expressed in the Australian case of *Perre* v. *Apand Pty Ltd*,[126] to that in *McFarlane* (at [61]). As a result, she awarded the, albeit comparatively modest, sum of A$105,249 for the costs of raising the child.

The case then went to appeal. This was dismissed by a majority but the report of the Supreme Court of Queensland, Appeals Division appears not to be available via database.[127] The nub of the case, however, lies in the subsequent appeal to the High Court of Australia[128] where the

---

[123] This may well be because there is no equivalent to the UK Abortion Act 1967 in either New South Wales or Queensland.

[124] (1995) 38 NSWLR 47– a case in the NSW Court of Appeal that was widely quoted in *McFarlane*; the case became procedurally confused and was settled before going to further appeal. Mention was also made of *Dahl* v. *Purnell* (1993) 15 QLR 33 in which damages for maintenance were allowed with a moderate 'offset' for the intangible benefits of a healthy child.

[125] n. 122 above, at [50].

[126] (1999) 73 ALJR 1190. In simplified form, the requirements for establishing a duty of care are knowledge that the vulnerable plaintiff belongs to an ascertainable class and that he or she relies on the specialised advice of the defender.

[127] *Melchior* v. *Cattanach* [2001] QCA 246. This is the citation quoted by the High Court of Australia. The Australasian Legal Information Institute website, however, reports only a procedural discussion under the heading.

[128] *Cattanach* v. *Melchior* (2003) 199 ALR 131. Hereafter referred to as *Cattanach*. My analysis of this case was published electronically as J. K. Mason, 'A Turn-up Down Under: *McFarlane* in the Light of *Cattanach*' (2004) 1 SCRIPT-ed, at http://www.law.ed. ac.uk/ahrb/script-ed/docs/mason.asp.

hearing was limited to the single issue: if, in consequence of medical negligence, a couple become the parents of an unintended child, can a court, in an award of damages, require the doctor to bear the cost of raising and maintaining the child?[129]

The reader may well think that I am making too much of *Cattanach*. It is, however, in my view, an exceptional case. It was the first in which the attribution of the responsibility for the costs of rearing an uncovenanted, healthy child, who is born as a result of medical negligence, was addressed by a panel of seven judges in the highest court of a Commonwealth country. It is also important in that, for the first time, a panel of judges at the highest level was divided on the issue; it therefore provides an opportunity to analyse discordant views that have been formed on the basis of precisely similar evidence. In the end, the High Court dismissed Dr Cattanach's appeal by a majority of 4 to 3. Thus, the result was close run by any standards and we must consider the conflicting arguments in some detail.

To an extent, the arguments for allowing the appeal were well rehearsed in *McFarlane* and are, therefore, of rather less interest in the present context than are those to the contrary. The opinions, however, convey a real sense of urgency which I hope to demonstrate; essentially, *Cattanach* represents a well-matched contest between moral and legal principle and both sides should be presented.

Gleeson CJ's minority opinion, although probing several avenues, can be summarised as adopting the 'public interest' route in support of the integrity of the family unit. He drew heavily on the social aspects of family life and on the obligations that are laid on parents both by statute and at common law which have always attached fundamental importance to human life. His approach is most vividly expressed at [6]:

[I]n this context, the concept of value is ethical not economic. It does not depend upon the benefits, tangible or intangible, that some children bestow upon their parents ... In the eyes of the law the life of a troublesome child is as valuable as that of any other ... The value of human life, which is universal and beyond measurement, is not to be confused with the joys of parenthood, which are distributed unevenly.

Nonetheless, he stressed that the ethical dimension could not foreclose the debate and that the problem to be addressed was legal in nature. Consequently, he declined to categorise the case as one of personal injury; were that the case, he pointed out, the child's father could be dismissed as a 'faintly embarrassing irrelevancy' whereas, in fact, his role

---

[129] Per Gleeson CJ, n. 128 above, at [1].

was one of the defining features of the joint claim by the parents (at [9]). The claim was, unarguably, one for pure economic loss. Indeed, the impression is left that at least a proportion of Gleeson CJ's antipathy to allowing the damages sought lay in the 'commercial' itemisation of the quantum of damages and the impossibility of defining or limiting these.[130]

The cornerstone of his argument was laid in paragraph [38] where he held that the case concerned the parent–child relationship and that to seek to assign an economic value to that relationship is neither reasonable nor possible. This, in turn depended on his understanding that actionable damage, if there was any, arose because of the creation of a parental relationship rather than as a result of conception; which, one feels, places the claimants in something of a Catch 22 situation. It appears to be saying that they have been forced into a position that involves economic loss; at the same time, however, it is a loss which, short of putting the child up for adoption, they cannot legally avoid; from which it follows that they cannot claim compensation.[131] Be that as it may, the Chief Justice covered his tracks by concluding that 'the law should develop novel categories of negligence incrementally and by analogy with established categories';[132] recognition of the present claim went beyond that and was, therefore, unwarranted (at [39]).

Hayne J began by acknowledging what most would see as the inexorable consequential cascade of a failed sterilisation – conception and pregnancy, childbirth, the financial consequences of these and the financial consequences of having a further child to maintain and nurture. Each was a foreseeable consequence of its predecessor, all the way back to the negligent advice, and he concluded that the relevant question was not why the mother should be held to be entitled to recover for them but, rather, why she should *not* be so entitled (at [192]). Hayne J also accepted that the consequentialist analysis pointed logically to the existence of a *single* cause of action rather than one split into the effects of pregnancy and economic loss – a conclusion which had previously led to Lord Millett's expression of dissent to the mother's claim in *McFarlane*.[133]

In the end result, however, Justice Hayne based his decision unequivocally on public policy.[134] His position was that the balance of benefit

---

[130] Thus following Lords Slynn and Hope in *McFarlane*.
[131] And see Hayne J, n. 128 above, at [244].
[132] Quoting Brennan J in *Sutherland Shire Council* v. *Heyman* (1985) 157 CLR 424 at 481.
[133] Hayne J also protested at categorising such actions as 'wrongful conceptions' or 'wrongful births' when the negligence lay in a failure to give proper advice.
[134] And, in so doing, gave a careful review of the historic relationship between the courts and the common law – quoting, in particular, *Egerton* v. *Brownlow* (1853) 4 HL Cas 1.

and disadvantage to be derived from motherhood cannot be assessed in monetary terms and, even if it could be so measured, 'the parent should not be permitted to attempt to demonstrate that the net worth of the consequences of being obliged to rear a healthy child is a financial detriment to him or her' (at [247]):

> If attention is to be paid to *all* of the consequences of the defendant's negligence, one of those consequences is that there is a new life in being . . . That life is not an article of commerce and to it no market value can be given.

He concluded that 'the common law should not permit recovery of damages for the ordinary costs of rearing a child'[135] and, quite simply, proposed the development of an inflexible rule in the common law – a rule which would preclude the parent from recovering damages in the circumstances envisaged:

> The parent would be denied treating the child as a commodity to be given a market value. The parent would be denied this . . . because the law should not permit the commodification of the child.[136]

In my view, however, it is Justice Heydon's opinion that provides the most comprehensive survey of the 'no recovery' position.[137] He began with the practicalities to be faced in the future should the appeal be dismissed. These include allowing for the expense of the child's schooling,[138] the duration of the upbringing, the importance to be attached to the diminished quality of life enjoyed by the parents with a new child to look after, and the difficulties of moderating the damages as related to the economic standing of the parents – the common law of Australia not permitting capping.[139] All of which looks very like the development of a 'floodgates' argument – 'it does indicate the nature of the litigation which will ensue if

---

[135] n. 128 above, at [255]. Hayne J would specifically allow the extra costs involved in the upbringing of a child with special needs (at [256] and [263]) thus coming into line with *Parkinson*, discussed in Chapter 5.

[136] ibid., at [261]. See also *Jaensch* v. *Coffey* (1984) 155 CLR 549 per Deane J at 583 quoted by Heydon J at [318]. The word 'commodification' was used on several occasions. It was left undefined which is a pity – there is no suggestion that the child would or could be used as a 'commodity'.

[137] Interestingly, Stretton, in an in-depth analysis of the case, considered Heydon J to have been the weakest of the *Cattanach* judgments: Dean Stretton, 'The Birth Torts: Damages for Wrongful Birth and Wrongful Life' (2005) 10 *Deakin Law Review* 310–64.

[138] Quoting, inevitably, *Benarr* v. *Kettering Health Authority* [1988] NLJR 179 and *Allen* v. *Bloomsbury Health Authority* [1993] 1 All ER 651.

[139] But see Kirby J, n. 128 above, at [162], n. 266. See also the conflict between *Rand* and *Hardman* at n. 115 above.

recovery is permitted'.[140] The uncertainty as to how the money would be spent was also considered.[141]

Heydon J then concentrated on the moral or public interest arguments that can be used to support a 'no recovery' rule and, in reviewing the existing published legal and academic comment, succinctly expressed (at [317]) the difficulties in making the case:

[I]t has been one thing to reach a conclusion after experiencing revulsion or feeling astonishment or observing a grotesque result. It has been another thing to formulate legal reasoning to support the conclusion reached.

And, therein, lies the weakness of the 'no recovery' school of thought for, despite the fact that Heydon J, for example, makes frequent appeals to legal principles embodied in both common and statutory family law,[142] these are often overshadowed by what appears to be emotive reasoning. This is not to decry the value and strength of such emotion – this writer and, one suspects, many readers, would agree with much of what is said. Moreover, to claim, with approval, that 'community views' as to the value of human life have been changed by the ready acceptance of contraception, sterilisation and abortion,[143] is not to say that change per se is necessarily a good thing – and, in fact, this is a criticism that can be rightly levelled against communitarian ethics in general. The problem is simply that to say that 'it is wrong to attempt to place a value on human life or a value on the expense of human life because human life is invaluable' and that 'the child itself is valuable ... because it is life'[144] does not answer the fundamental question – why should people like the Melchiors *not* be compensated for the financial loss imposed upon them by the negligence of another?

This is, of course, not the sum of Justice Haydon's case against recovery. He does, for example, make a specific issue of the potential damage to the child who has been the subject of litigation – a recurring theme which many might feel is better directed towards the use of adversarial

---

[140] Per Heydon J, n. 128 above, at [311].

[141] A factor that drove the French courts to the unusual conclusion of allowing an action for wrongful life brought on behalf of a disabled neonate: *X* v. *Mutuelle d'Assurance du Corps Sanitaire Français et al.* (2000) JCP 2293, for which see Chapter 6.

[142] See, for example, the importance in Australia of the Child Support (Assessment) Act (1989 (Cth), ss. 3, 4, 24.

[143] At [359] quoting McMurdo P and Davies JA in *Cattanach* v. *Melchior* [2001] QCA 246 at [51], [80]–[82] which I have been unable to access.

[144] Per Heydon J, n. 128 above, at [354]. A major conceptual difficulty for the courts in this situation is that they must accept this premise but, at the same time, admit that the parents have a free and legal choice of recourse to abortion – at least in the United Kingdom.

proceedings in the family court. Nonetheless, the whole tenor of his opinion is epitomised in his conclusion which can bear quotation in full:

> The various assumptions underlying the law relating to children and the duties on parents created by the law would be negated if parents could sue to recover the costs of rearing unplanned children. That possibility would tend to damage the natural love and mutual confidence which the law seeks to foster between parent and child. It would permit conduct inconsistent with a parental duty to treat the child with the utmost affection, with infinite tenderness, and with unstinting forgiveness in all circumstances because these goals are contradicted by legal proceedings based on the premise that the child's birth was a painful and a highly inconvenient mistake. It would permit conduct inconsistent with the duty to nurture children.[145]

And probably, at base, that sums up the case put by all three justices who were in favour of allowing the appeal – but one has to say that it rests on a tenuous base. The most that can be said is that their policy reflects 'an underlying value of society in relation to the value of human life'[146] – and the cynic will say that we have, here, the wish being father to the thought.

The counter-argument can be expressed in two ways. Either it can be postulated that the 'value' of human life and the costs of human existence are distinct and that to accept the significance of the latter is not necessarily to deny the importance of the former. Or, in a more down to earth way, it can be said that the rules of tort are well-established and they should not be displaced simply in order to accommodate the circumstances of the uncovenanted pregnancy.[147] Both these approaches were adopted by the majority in the High Court phase of *Cattanach*.[148]

Justices McHugh and Gummow quickly flew their colours in stating (at [57]):

> Merely to repeat those propositions on which the appellants rely does not explain why the law should shield or immunise the appellants from what otherwise is a head of damages recoverable in negligence under general and unchallenged principles.

Immunity in tort law implies protection against an action in respect of rights and duties for which the tortfeasor would be liable were it not for

---

[145] n. 128 above, at [404].   [146] ibid., per McHugh and Gummow JJ at [55].
[147] For discussion of this aspect of *McFarlane*, see J. Thomson, 'Abandoning the Law of Delict?' 2000 SLT 43.
[148] Since the House of Lords was unanimous in *McFarlane*, the only previous speeches in the higher Commonwealth courts which supported recovery are to be found in the appeal stage of *Cattanach* itself (n. 143 above) and in the Inner House of the Court of Session in *McFarlane* v. *Tayside Health Board* 1998 SC 389.

the circumstances being such that the public interest warrants his or her protection. But for immunity to be considered, there must be a duty to breach and the justices concluded that *Cattanach* was not a case in which 'immunity' would be appropriate in respect of family relationships. What was wrongful in the case, they said, was not the birth of a third child to the Melchiors but the admitted negligence of Dr Cattanach – a point that has been consistently argued by those who have found the decision in *McFarlane* to be unsatisfactory. They were emphatic that the damage suffered by the respondents was not the coming into being of the parent–child relationship:[149] 'The relevant damage suffered by the Melchiors is the expenditure that they have incurred or will incur in the future, not the creation or existence of the parent–child relationship' (at [67]), and this critical point was emphasised in paragraph [68]:

The unplanned child is not the harm for which recompense is sought in this action; it is the burden of the legal and moral responsibilities which arise by reason of the birth of the child that is in contention.[150]

Moreover, the Justices refuted the suggestion that the costs of rearing a child born as the result of negligence would constitute a novel head of damages:

[W]hen a plaintiff asserts that, but for the defendant's negligence, he or she would not have incurred a particular expense, questions of causation and reasonable foreseeability arise. Is the particular expense causally connected to the defendant's negligence? If so, ought the defendant to have reasonably foreseen that an expense of that kind might be incurred?[151]

The answer to both questions in respect of the award in issue, they said, should be affirmative.

Having addressed the problem positively, McHugh and Gummow JJ considered the negative approach of refuting the 'family unity' argument that underlies so much of the opposition to recovery for maintenance. Allowing that 'family values', in the wide sense, represented an element of corporate welfare, they could, nevertheless, perceive no general recognition that persons in the position of the Melchiors should be denied the full remedies of Australian common law. It was, they said (at [77]):

---

[149] See Gleeson CJ, n. 128 above, at [26].

[150] The Justices again disapproved the use of the term 'wrongful birth' in this context. I also believe that it is a misnomer (J. K. Mason, 'Wrongful Pregnancy, Wrongful Birth and Wrongful Terminology' (2002) 6 *Edinburgh Law Review* 46–66 at 49) and the criticism actually makes the distinction. The negligence of Dr Cattanach – i.e. the uncovenanted pregnancy – is wrongful, not the *birth* of the child.

[151] Quoting from *Nominal Defendant* v. *Gardikiotis* (1996) 186 CLR 49 per McHugh J at 54.

[A] beguiling but misleading simplicity to invoke the broad values which few would deny and then glide to the conclusion that they operate to shield the appellants from the full consequences in law of Dr Cattanach's negligence.

Although their argument here takes on the nature of some of the intuitive reasoning adopted by those of the opposing view, most would surely agree that the common law should not justify preclusion of recovery on the basis of speculation.[152]

I was very much drawn to Justice Callinan when he highlighted the sophistic approach taken by many of those who have been called upon to adjudicate in cases of wrongful pregnancy. 'I cannot help observing,' he said, 'that the repeated disavowal in the cases of recourse to public policy is not always convincing' (at [291]) and he followed with (at [292]):

In substance, almost all of the arguments that can be made against the awarding of damages for the costs of rearing a child consequent upon what [could be categorised][153] as a wrongful pregnancy case do involve emotional and moral values and perceptions of what public policy is or should be.

Even so, he was not without sympathy for the emotional track – but emotions, no matter how strong, must be subservient to legal principle.[154]

Justice Callinan's opinion can be summed up in two extracts (at [299], [301]) which are so definitive as to require no further comment:

The applicants were negligent. The respondents as a result have incurred and will continue to incur significant expense. That expense would not have been incurred had the first applicant not given negligent advice. All the various touchstones for, and none of the relevant disqualifying conditions against, an award of damages for economic loss are present here

and:

I accept the relevance in the debate of the existence of obligations imposed by the law relating to families ... as well as the sanctions of the criminal law, for a failure to maintain and support children. But the imposition of these legal obligations can no more absolve the negligent professional from his liability for damages than it can the negligent motorist from his obligation in tort to pay the increased cost of the care of a child he has negligently run over.

---

[152] n. 128 above, at [79]. The reference here was specifically to speculation as to the effect on the resultant child but it is clear that it could be applied generally.

[153] Quoting Lax J in the Canadian case *Kealey* v. *Berezowski* (1996) 136 DLR (4th) 708 at 723 as the authority. See also the Canadian academic Dickens, n. 71 above; Mason, n. 150 above.

[154] n. 128 above, at [296]. The quotation from *De Sales* v. *Ingrilli* (2002) 193 ALR 130 per Callinan J at [189] is particularly appropriate: 'That a judge might find a task distasteful is not a reason for the judge not to do it.'

Undoubtedly, however, it is the opinion of Kirby J that stands out as a strong and uncompromising contribution to the debate which, he held, had to be resolved by resort to the usual sources of the common law – that is through consideration of legal principle and of legal policy.

As to the first, he pointed to a significant and relevant difference between the common law of Australia and that of the United Kingdom. *McFarlane*, he suggested, was decided, at least in major part, on *Caparo* principles[155] – that to impose a duty of care in respect of economic loss depended, inter alia, on whether it was fair, just and reasonable to do so. *Caparo*, however, has not been followed in Australia;[156] accordingly, *McFarlane* provided no foundation of legal principle for guidance in *Cattanach*. Kirby J went on to deplore, in the strongest terms, how far from principle the later English decisions had drifted and to forewarn the Australian courts against following the same path.[157] Judges, he said (at [137]), should be willing to take responsibility for applying the established judicial controls over the expansion of tort liability[158] but they have no authority to adopt arbitrary departures from basic doctrine:

Least of all may they do so, in our secular society, on the footing of their personal religious beliefs or 'moral' assessments concealed in an inarticulate premise dressed up, and described, as legal principle or legal policy

– which is an unusually harsh criticism of some sincere judgments.

Kirby J's judgment was particularly helpful in setting out the various scenarios which may be played out when the courts are considering claims for the costs of rearing an unplanned child. These have, of course, been well aired both in the courts themselves and in the academic literature.[159] Nonetheless the possible options were so clearly defined by Kirby J that they can be extracted so as to provide a useful summary.

Option 1 – the child is born healthy and no damages of any kind are awarded (an option which, in the current series, only Lord Millett, in *McFarlane* had adopted). Kirby J traced this back to religious or social

---

[155] n. 97 above. This assessment was certainly accepted by Brooke LJ in *Parkinson*, discussed in Chapter 5 below.

[156] See, in particular, *Perre v. Amand Pty Ltd* (1999) 198 CLR 180; *Graham Barclay Oysters Pty Ltd v. Ryan* (2002) 194 ALR 337.

[157] n. 128 above, at [128], quoting Hoyano, n. 70 above. Although, as has already been noted, the cases referred to are not, in the main, direct comparators with *McFarlane*.

[158] For which, in England, see not only *Rees* in Chapter 5 below, but also the more recent cases of *Gregg v. Scott* [2005] 2 AC 176 and, more significantly, *Chester v. Afshar* [2005] 1 AC 134, [2004] 4 All ER 587 where the concept of 'fairness' was, at least partially, accepted. Neither of these last two was a pregnancy case.

[159] See, for example, Norrie, n. 51 above; Grubb, n. 51 above; Oliver Radley-Gardner, 'Wrongful Birth Revisited' (2002) 118 *Law Quarterly Review* 11–15; Stretton, n. 137 above.

views resting on the assumption that the birth of a child is an inalienable blessing;[160] to hold otherwise strikes at the foundations of family life and, hence, society. He dismissed the notion summarily in that to hold that the birth of a child is a 'blessing' in every case 'represents a fiction which the law should not apply to a particular case without objective evidence that bears it out' (at [148]) and (at [151]):

Neither the invocation of Scripture nor the invention of a fictitious oracle on the Underground[161] ... authorises a court of law to depart from the ordinary principles governing the recovery of damages for the tort of negligence.

And, in concert with McHugh and Gummow JJ: 'To deny such recovery is to provide a zone of legal immunity to medical practitioners ... that is unprincipled and inconsistent with established legal doctrine' (at [149]).

Option 2 – limiting compensation to the immediate damage resulting from pregnancy and childbirth – is what can be seen as the *McFarlane* solution, and, again, Justice Kirby did not mince his words. With reference to the lack of unanimity in the House of Lords' speeches, he said (at [158]):

[T]he diverse opinions illustrate what can happen when judges embark upon the 'quicksands' of public policy, at least when doing so leads them away from basic legal principle.

More specifically he pointed out, correctly, that severing the causal links between the various, and equally foreseeable, outcomes of pregnancy is incontestably arbitrary. Moreover: 'The propounded distinction between immediate and long-term costs of medical error is not drawn in other cases of medical negligence. It is arbitrary and unjust in this context' (at [162]). The former statement is certainly true; the latter epitomises the whole, lengthy, debate.

Option 3 – recovery is available for the extra costs of maintaining a disabled neonate (the *Parkinson* solution)[162] – would, now, seem to be the recognised United Kingdom policy within the appropriate scenario. Clearly, however, it introduces an element of arbitrariness – what constitutes *compensatable* disability? And does its recognition discriminate against the disabled? We will see later[163] how these questions exercised the minds of those establishing the *Parkinson* tradition and I fully

---

[160] See Jupp J in *Udale*, n. 39 above at 531. But, even here, Jupp J actually adopted Option 2, below.

[161] An allusion to 'the commuter on the London underground' – Lord Steyn's now legendary dispenser of distributive justice in *McFarlane*.

[162] *Parkinson* v. *St James and Seacroft University Hospital NHS Trust* [2002] QB 266, [2001] 3 All ER 97, CA.

[163] At p. 153.

appreciate the strength of the concerns. At the same time, I feel they are founded on a half-truth. It is perfectly possible to approve both the *McFarlane* approach and the *Parkinson* solution once one appreciates that the resultant distinction has nothing to do with either family values or disability discrimination but is simply a matter of imposed costs – and it is surely within the competence of the courts to assess those costs. The logic of what Justice Kirby called an 'unhappy differentiation' may be suspect,[164] but most people, one feels, would see it as making the best of a bad job – always assuming that *McFarlane*, in refusing to apply the same reasoning to the birth of a normal child, *is* a bad job.[165]

Option 4 offers the saving alternative of adhering to ordinary recovery principles but, at the same time, providing for the 'offset' of the joys of parenthood. A great deal of printers' ink has been expended on this question, especially in the United States where the principle has been both accepted and rejected.[166] It will be remembered that it was also rejected in *McFarlane*, largely because of the difficulty, not only of comparing like with unlike, but also because of that involved in assessing the 'benefits' – a difficulty which led Hale LJ to the useful, if fictitious, concept of a 'deemed equilibrium' of cost and benefit in *Parkinson*.[167]

Option 5 – compensation to include the foreseeable costs of child rearing, which could be described as the *Emeh* option[168] or the status quo ante *McFarlane*. This, of course, was the option accepted by the majority in the Court of Appeal in *Cattanach*. Effectively, failure to do so would be an arbitrary departure from the principle of corrective justice. 'Any such denial is the business, if of anyone, of Parliament not the courts.'[169] In a concession to the House of Lords, Justice Kirby acknowledged that concern to protect the economic viability of the National Health Service might help to explain its resort to 'distributive justice'; such concerns could not, however, be applied universally.

---

[164] The critical view being that you cannot calculate an 'added' expense without attaching a notional economic 'value' to the normal child.

[165] It is difficult to see how one can refute the reasoning of Lord Cameron in *Allan* v. *Greater Glasgow Health Board* 1998 SLT 580 at 584.

[166] The principles were also extensively analysed by McHugh and Gummow JJ at [90].

[167] See Chapter 5 below. Some, of course, might regard this as a fiction too far. See, for example, Robert Walker LJ in *Rees* v. *Darlington Memorial Hospital NHS Trust* [2003] QB 20, [2002] 65 BMLR 117, CA, at [35].

[168] *Emeh* v. *Kensington and Chelsea and Westminster Area Health Authority* [1985] QB 1012, CA. A relevant contribution from the United States makes a strong plea for recognition of this option in that country: Patricia Baugher, 'Fundamental Protection of a Fundamental Right: Recovery of Child-rearing Damages for Wrongful Pregnancy' (2000) 75 *Washington Law Review* 1205–36.

[169] Kirby J in *Cattanach*, n. 128 above, at [180].

Lessons from a legal 'test match'

It is impossible to say which side 'won' the *McFarlane* versus *Cattanach* contest in an intellectual sense. It is clear that the present writer firmly opposed the House of Lords decision in the former; he should, therefore, have welcomed that in the latter. In fact, the unexpected effect of *Cattanach* was to make one reconsider and, perhaps, modify one's original, relatively uncompromising, position. The reason for this is difficult to identify but, possibly, lies in the modes of the presentations in the two cases. It is, then, not out of place to reappraise these briefly.

It is highly simplistic to extract single ratios from the individual and complex speeches in *McFarlane*. With that limitation in mind, however, we can identify Lord Slynn as holding that it would not be fair, just or reasonable to impose on the doctor 'liability for the consequential responsibilities, imposed on or accepted by the parents to bring up a child' – and this is the theme which most commentators regard as the ratio of the case.[170] Lord Steyn depended on principles of distributive justice and, rather strangely, illustrated this by way of the reasonable man's likely reaction to an award; apart from the dubious use of public opinion as the architect of legal principle, it is, of course, difficult to decide who constitutes public opinion in a pluralistic society.[171] Lord Hope would not give any damages because the benefits of parenthood cannot be assessed in monetary terms and 'the logical conclusion, as a matter of law, is that the costs to the pursuers of meeting their obligations to the child ... are not recoverable as damages'. Lord Clyde considered that the damages available in a case such as *McFarlane* would be disproportionate to the doctor's culpability. But it was really left to Lord Millett to distinguish between Mr and Mrs McFarlane on the one hand and the public at large on the other. Lord Millett conceded and, indeed, elaborated on the real damage that had been done to them. They were, he reasoned, at least entitled to general damages[172] and it was illogical to approve these and deny the costs of upkeep – and we should note how close Lord Steyn and others were to acknowledging the validity of the parents' claim.

---

[170] Emily Jackson *Regulating Reproduction* (Oxford, Hart Publishing, 2001) concludes that, logically, this *must* be the ratio – at 33.

[171] Stretton, n. 137 above, quotes most aptly: 'Intuitive feelings for justice seem a poor substitute for a rule antecedently known, more particularly where all do not have the same intuitions'. From *National Insurance Co of New Zealand* v. *Espagne* (1961) 105 CLR 569, per Dixon CJ at 572.

[172] But, even then, damages which would amount only to a conventional sum – Lord Millett suggested a maximum of £5,000 which is hardly princely.

Why, then, is it possible to oppose the *McFarlane* decision and, yet, have qualms after reading the minority in *Cattanach*? The answer is elusive but, at root, it seems to me that their Lordships at Westminster were, each in his own way, seeking a route by which they could *avoid* giving maintenance damages to the pursuers. The minority in Canberra, by contrast, were providing *positive* reasons why such recompense should not be given – and, as a result, their opinions, although overtly emotional, were that much more compelling. In the event, however, soul-searching on the issue is relatively pointless – the reasoning of the *Cattanach* minority cannot really withstand dispassionate analysis, simply because there is no self-evident common law to support their case.

The fundamental difficulty with the wrongful pregnancy action as a whole is that, whether consciously or subconsciously, most judges who have decided against recovery for the upbringing of an uncovenanted child have done so because to do so is seen as placing a value on the child, whereas the true issue is that of the *costs* of maintaining a child. While we may call upon such of the civil and criminal law as governs family relationships to outline the ground rules for us, it is quite another matter to extrapolate these so as to create a moral Utopia in which families should live. Statute law deals with specific situations. Thus, when the law states that the interests of a child will be paramount, it refers to those circumstances in which there is a conflict of interests – it does not place a value on a child. Rather, given that the child's interests are paramount, any measure that will, in theory, improve that child's socio-economic ambience is serving the letter as well as the spirit of family law.

Probably, we would all want to live in Utopia but it is unlikely to be a low-cost area. Those who oppose restitution are forcing such an environment on uncommitted parents without, at the same time, appreciating that they may well not have a free choice – it may be, simply, that they cannot afford to live there. In short, they are expressing a moral paternalism without, themselves, having to undertake paternal responsibilities.[173] It is virtually impossible to see that recognition of reality is, in any way, striking at the roots of family life; in fact, the scene is set for precisely the opposite result, for an economically viable family is likely to be happier than one that is stretched financially. Followers of the *Cattanach* minority are, perhaps unwittingly, seeking not only the acceptance of their moral values but also of the economic consequences of so doing. And that is

---

[173] Or, of course, maternal. I express my admiration of Hale LJ's analysis of parenthood in *Parkinson* (n. 162 above, at [70]) in Chapter 5. What she says about a disabled child is immediately transferable to the healthy child.

what is wrong with the decision in *McFarlane* and right with that in *Cattanach*.

By contrast, the relatively uniform approach taken by the majority in *Cattanach* is extremely difficult to refute. All the ingredients and the consequences of the law of tort are present. The birth of a child is a foreseeable consequence of a negligent management of an operation designed to sterilise a patient and the consequent costs of maintaining that child are not only equally foreseeable but cannot be avoided by dint of statute law – and there is nothing novel in recompensing consequential damage. Moreover, since it is impermissible to balance the benefits to one legal interest against the loss occasioned to a separate legal interest,[174] the problem of offset can be avoided by recourse to principle.

The case made by Kirby J is particularly strong although, in places, it could have been phrased in more sympathetic terms. To dismiss a deeply considered opinion as relying on public policy 'with a passing nod towards the law's respect for the sanctity of life ... and occasional invocations of Scripture' smacks, once again, of hyperbole which some might find disturbing.[175] The opinion does, however, point us to two considerations that have, as yet, only been touched upon.

First, we are reminded of the decision in *CES*,[176] which might be regarded as opening up a theoretical 'Option 6' and which has not been fully considered. Here, it was accepted 'as the highest common denominator of the majority' that expenses for the upkeep of an uncovenanted child were recoverable up to the time when the parents could have opted for its adoption. Justice Kirby dissented from this 'solution' which was scarcely addressed in *McFarlane*.[177] Although, perhaps, representing a minority stance, I feel that the option should not be foreclosed – legal principle as to limitation of damage notwithstanding. The importance of a woman's autonomy is, of course, agreed. Nonetheless, it is at least arguable that the exercise of that autonomy involves acceptance of the consequences of that exercise. This is no place to open the subject in depth and I revert briefly to it in Chapter 8. Nevertheless, there must be

---

[174] Per McHugh and Gummow JJ at [90]. This, however, depends on the assumption that the benefits arising from the birth of a child are not legally relevant to the head of damage that compensates for the cost of maintaining the child – and the authorities, particularly in the USA, are by no means uniform on the point.

[175] n. 128 above, at [159]. See also [151]. One wonders, in passing, whether this might underlie the very cursory dismissal of the *Cattanach* decision which was evident in the later House of Lords opinion in *Rees* v. *Darlington Memorial Hospital NHS Trust* [2004] AC 309, [2003] 4 All ER 987.

[176] n. 124 above, at [113].

[177] Such discussion as there was concerned, mainly, abortion and abortion was the issue raised in *Emeh*, n. 50 above.

many who would still wonder whether the *CES* decision may not be the option which, all things considered, is the most fair, just and reasonable. Which brings us to the second reminder, which is that *Caparo*[178] is currently rejected as a precedent in Australia.[179] The importance of this is, of course, that as Justice Kirby pointed out (at [121]), *McFarlane* and *Cattanach* have been decided on different principles. As a result, the two opposing decisions may not be as incompatible as appears at first sight; it may be that two of the highest courts in the Commonwealth are not, as it might seem, at loggerheads.[180]

Even so, given the significance that *Caparo's* case has achieved throughout the field of negligence in the United Kingdom, we might suitably use it as a coda to this discussion and ask, as has already been suggested, if we could not use the test in reverse – is it fair, just and reasonable to *deny* restitution to those whose lives have been impaired? One senses a general feeling of doubt in the academic press not only as to the result in *McFarlane* but also as to how that result was achieved. I leave the last word to Weir,[181] who believed the *McFarlane* decision to have been correct but, at the same time, advised that we should not be surprised if the reasoning was uneasy:

[W]henever it enters the family home, the law of obligations – not just tort but contract and restitution as well – has a marked tendency to go pear-shaped.

McFarlane under fire

A unanimous decision in the House of Lords is a formidable barrier to those seeking the alternative outcome. Nonetheless, the significance of *McFarlane* is such that it is unsurprising that there were early attempts to breach the apparently impregnable doctrine of 'no restitution for the enforced upkeep of a normal child'. Two cases are relevant in this context. Neither is particularly significant of itself, but each demonstrates an

---

[178] n. 97 above.   [179] See n. 156 above.

[180] But the man on the Clapham omnibus in the form of the elected legislature probably has the last word. The New South Wales Civil Liability Act 2002, s.71(1) now states that the court cannot award damages for economic loss for the costs, or loss of earnings, associated with the birth of a child. S.71(2), however, does not preclude the recovery of additional costs arising from a child's disability. Statute law in the state thus corresponds to the current common law in England established in *Parkinson* v. *St James and Seacroft University Hospital NHS Trust* [2002] QB 266 – for which, see Chapter 5. See also the very similar Queensland Civil Liability Act 2003, s.49A which, while not including an exception for disability, nevertheless confines the prohibition to births following attempted sterilisation. South Australia's Civil Liabilities Act 1936, s.67 also includes actions for wrongful birth as defined in Chapter 3.

[181] Weir, n. 74 above.

understandable reluctance within the judiciary to be the first to charge into the breach.

The less proximate is *Richardson* v. *L.R.C. Products Ltd*[182] which was a claim for personal injuries suffered due to a pregnancy that, in essence, resulted from a burst condom. The case was raised under the Consumer Protection Act 1987, section 3 and not under common law alleging negligence. As a result, the greater part of the judgment is taken up with technical details including what, to most of us, must be the uncharted waters of the interaction between latex and ozone. There are, however, two aspects of the opinion that are of direct interest in the present context.

The claim failed on the technical evidence, but Kennedy J held that Mrs Richardson could not claim damages in any event as she could have taken steps to avoid pregnancy by way of post-coital contraception. An interesting collateral discussion might arise here by way of a comparison with Park J's discredited response to Mrs Emeh's refusal to terminate her pregnancy.[183] No-one would suggest that the practical aspects of taking a pill and undergoing an abortion are comparable. Nonetheless, it is possible to argue that, in terms of a woman exercising her reproductive choice, the difference is merely one of degree – and particularly so when one remembers that at least some women would regard the destruction of an embryo as being morally equivalent to the destruction of a fetus.[184] Moreover, we have seen, and will see, that, while many unexpectedly pregnant women would have terminated an early pregnancy, they have either refused or have been advised against a late abortion. It is therefore fair to ask at what stage a decision to continue with a 'wrongful' pregnancy becomes reasonable or, in the present circumstances, how early must such a choice have to be made in order to render it so unreasonable as to elide the responsibility of the person who caused the conception?[185] The problem may well be dismissed as being of no more than academic interest; nevertheless, it is sufficient to make one, yet again, wonder at the logic of accepting the current situation without question.

More significantly, and although the point was not argued in detail, Kennedy J took the opportunity to state his interpretation of the law and to cut the ground from under the feet of anyone attempting to circumvent *McFarlane* by way of restricting its terms to its specific facts. He said:

---

[182] n. 25 above.   [183] *Emeh* at first instance, n. 50 above.
[184] For discussion, see p. 16 above.
[185] Kennedy J quoted Hobhouse LJ: '[I]t is permissible and appropriate that damages should only be awarded to the plaintiff on the basis that he has discharged the duty which the law places upon him to act reasonably to mitigate his loss': *County Ltd* v. *Girozentrale Securities* [1996] 3 All ER 834 at 858. Which seems to be the basis for the Australian decision in *CES*, n. 124 above.

[T]o my mind, the law here was clear, as I believe it is. It is the policy of the law . . .
to exclude from a claimant's claim the costs of the upbringing of an uncovenanted
child. That is equally applicable whether the claim is laid in negligence or in a
breach of a statutory duty.[186]

The facts of the second case are very much closer to the current
discussion. In *Greenfield* v. *Irwin (a firm)*[187] a woman was undergoing a
course of contraceptive injections. The nurse responsible failed to note or
to test for the fact that she was already pregnant. As a result, the diagnosis
was delayed and, although she would have had a termination had she
been informed, she was unwilling to do so at a later date.[188] She was
delivered of a healthy child and sought recompense for a 'wrongful
pregnancy'. Thus far, then, Mrs Greenfield's case was fairly run of the
mill. However, rather than claim for the upkeep of the child, she based her
case on a loss of earnings due to her having to look after her child full time.
The judge of first instance refused this claim on *McFarlane* grounds and it
was this refusal that was the subject of appeal. In addition, at appeal, she
innovatively claimed an infringement of her rights to respect for her
private and family life under the European Convention on Human
Rights, Article 8.[189]

Buxton LJ conceded that the specific issue of the basis for the claim to
recompense had not been directly considered in *McFarlane*, effectively
because there was no need to address it. In any event, any effect of changing
from a claim for the upkeep of a child, which can be attributed to the *birth* of
that child, to one for loss of wages, which is due to the *presence* of the child,
will move the surgeon yet one more step further from responsibility for the
resulting economic loss and it is unsurprising that it was not relied on by
Mrs Greenfield. Rather, her counsel argued that, her action should be
characterised as one involving physical injury caused by omission in performance of a duty – in which case, all damage resulting from that injury
would be recoverable. Pared to the bone, the plea in *Greenfield* was an
attempt to extend acceptance of the 'mother's claim' for pregnancy and
birth into recognition of recompense for the 'parents' claim' for the burdens of childhood – and the Court of Appeal was unanimous in avoiding

---

[186] n. 25 above, at BMLR 195.
[187] [2001] 1 WLR 1292, [2001] 1 FLR 899; sub nom. *Greenfield* v. *Flather* (2001) 59
BMLR 43, CA.
[188] Interestingly, Buxton LJ is one of the rare judges who have considered the legality of
abortion in the circumstances. He assumed it would have been legal but did not pursue
the matter further.
[189] As incorporated in the Human Rights Act 1998, Sch. 1 which was not in force at the trial
stage of *Greenfield*.

this outcome.[190] Moreover, attractive as it seems, this approach is, to an extent, self-defeating in that, since the financial consequences of both maintenance and loss of earnings stem from the same root, *Greenfield* and *McFarlane* fall into perfect alignment. It also accords with my possibly naïve belief that the distinctions as to the categorisation of the nature of the damage, and particularly the nature of the economic loss, that were argued so heatedly in *McFarlane*, added an unnecessary gloss. We can look back to Lord Millett's observation on the point:

> I do not consider that the present question should depend on whether the economic loss is characterised as pure or consequential. The distinction is technical and artificial if not actually suspect in the circumstances of the present case … In principle any losses occasioned [by the defenders] are recoverable however they may be categorised.[191]

This seems eminently good sense – the claims may well be based on pure economic loss but it is difficult to see how the economic loss due to the presence of a child can be anything other than consequent on the birth of that child – the two are inseparable.[192]

Mrs Greenfield also contended that there was a fundamental difference between an 'advice' case – such as *McFarlane* was – and one based on faulty 'treatment' such as hers was. This argument was, in my view rightly, dismissed fairly tersely; it merely served to strengthen Buxton LJ's view that 'it is really quite impossible to distinguish between our case and *McFarlane* in any terms that protect this case from the broad view of liability and the broad view of the nature of the application of the law of tort that was adopted by all of the judges … in the *McFarlane* case' (at [28]). In short, it was *because* the cases are indistinguishable that Mrs Greenfield's appeal must fail.[193]

---

[190] E.g., Laws LJ: '[I]f this lady were to obtain the damages she seeks, she would happily be in a position whereby she would look after her much loved child at home, yet at the same time in effect would receive the income she would have earned had she stayed at work' (n. 187 above, at WLR [54]).

[191] n. 128 above, at AC 109, SC 40.

[192] I confess to having difficulty in understanding Buxton LJ's 'short point' that '[It is] simply not the case … that the cost of the existence of the child is *in law* caused by the pregnancy … It is caused by the existence of the child' (n. 187 above, at [29], emphasis added). Clearly the child's existence is due to the pregnancy; the difference in emphasis presumably lies in the difference between taking a legal or a physiological approach to reproduction. Even so, we have Lord Millett holding in *McFarlane* that: 'Normal pregnancy and delivery were as much an inescapable precondition of Catherine's birth as the expense of maintaining her afterwards was its inevitable consequence' (n. 128 above, at AC 114, SC 44).

[193] I am not pursuing discussion of the claim under Article 8 of the ECHR – suffice it to say that, although he was clearly breaking fresh ground, Buxton LJ held that the argument in which the claim was based was so wide that it would stand no prospect of surviving in the

It is, however, interesting to look at the Lord Justice's reason for so finding. In essence, this was because he considered that, far from being dismissed on narrow grounds, the claim in *McFarlane* was rejected by the House of Lords:

on grounds of very broad principle, broad principle reaching certainly beyond, in my judgement, the particular circumstances of an unwanted pregnancy.[194]

Thus, the significance of *Greenfield* seems to me to be that it puts *McFarlane* beyond the reach of any legalistic attack. We have already noted that the speeches in the House of Lords are so variant that we can extract any number of ratios on which to support the decision and the judgment is correspondingly difficult to undermine. *Greenfield*, in effect, takes us one stage further in that the 'breadth' of the *McFarlane* decision can be used to close any 'narrow' chink in its armour. In short, there are no openings other than that which the House of Lords knowingly left – the delivery of a disabled neonate.

A connecting case

It is to be remembered that there are two ways by which professional negligence can contribute to the birth of a disabled child. In the first place, we have the straightforward 'wrongful birth' which has been discussed in Chapter 3 and is characterised by the provision of negligent antenatal care either to a single woman or to a couple who are actively seeking parenthood. I do not believe that this was the situation envisaged by Lord Steyn when he conceded that the 'no recovery' rule might have to be different in the case of an '*unwanted* child who was born seriously disabled'.[195] Indeed, the lower courts have consistently accepted this exception and have gone unchallenged in so doing. Rather, the reference was surely to the alternative event – that is, the case of wrongful pregnancy that is *further complicated* by disability in the neonate.

Strasbourg jurisdiction were it taken there (n. 187 above, at [38]). In this, he relied in the main on the European Commission's observation that the right to respect for family life does not extend 'so far as to impose on States a general obligation to provide for financial assistance to individuals in order to enable one of two parents to stay at home to take care of children': *Andersson and Kullman* v. *Sweden* App. No 11776/85, 46 DR 251.

[194] n. 187 above, at [28].
[195] n. 128 above, at AC 84, SC 18. It is also to be noted that Lord Clyde referred to the possibility of a distinction between cases of *wrongful conception* according to whether or not the child was healthy (at AC 99, SC 31). Emphasis has been added in both quotations. The point that *a* child is *wanted* in the wrongful birth scenario has already been emphasised.

This possibility is considered further in the following chapter. Meantime, the opportunity is taken to remind the reader of the obvious – that few, if any, classifications within the 'troubled pregnancy' consist of watertight compartments; some overlap, or frank exception to the rule is inevitable. In a somewhat bizarre way, the case involving Ms Groom exemplifies both these caveats.

In *Groom* v. *Selby*,[196] Ms Groom had sought and obtained a sterilisation in October 1994 without a prior test for pregnancy. She complained of a vaginal discharge and abdominal pain in November having missed a period; no pregnancy test was undertaken and she was prescribed antibiotics. In December, she was diagnosed as being 15 weeks pregnant and, once again, while she would have undergone a termination had she been properly informed in November, she was unwilling to do so when her pregnancy was so far advanced. A daughter was born in May the following year and the report states that, following birth three weeks prematurely, '[The baby] was healthy at first.'[197]

Up to this point, then, the case was one of uncomplicated wrongful pregnancy and wholly comparable to *Greenfield*; it is noteworthy that Clark J specifically concluded that there was no congenital abnormality[198] – which I would take to mean there was no abnormality, whether or not it was detectable, *in utero*. However, at the age of some 3½ weeks, the infant contracted meningitis due to salmonella infection and was subsequently severely disabled. The unexpected twist to the case lies in the fact that the resultant action in damages for the upkeep of the child was directed against the general practitioner who admitted negligence in the management of the early pregnancy. *Groom*, thus, became something of a Janus case as to classification. On the one side, Dr Selby could be seen as doing no more than amplifying the wrongful pregnancy scenario that had been established by the surgeon. On the other, she could have, independently, arranged for a termination, which the patient would have accepted at the time; the fact that she did not do so, however, set up a wrongful birth case – albeit one that did not depend on the presence of a demonstrable fetal abnormality.[199]

Why do I see this as an 'unexpected twist'? Largely because, in order to accommodate the terms of the action for the expenses of a disabled and unsolicited child, Clark J had to resort to what I see as a contradiction in

---

[196] [2001] Lloyd's Rep Med 39, QBD; aff'd (2002) 64 BMLR 47, [2002] Lloyd's Rep Med 1, CA.
[197] ibid., QBD at 41, col 1.   [198] ibid., col 2.
[199] Although there was, in fact, such an extraordinary family history that an abortion under s.1(1)(d), although, in fact, ill-founded, could have passed the tests of 'risk' and 'good faith'.

terms – that is, having established that there was no congenital disorder, he concluded that: 'Megan is not and never has been a healthy child.'[200] His grounds for this were that: 'The infecting bacterium was sitting quietly on the surface of Megan's skin and/or gut' and 'it remained asymptomatic for about three and a half weeks'. As a result, 'Megan cannot, in my judgment, be treated as a healthy child.'[201] This is difficult to accept. The salmonellae were, presumably derived from the mother's birth canal rather than from a blood-borne intra-uterine invasion and opportunistic infection is common enough; we do not, for example, regard the person contaminated by a nasal carrier of a staphylococcus as being physically unhealthy before he or she becomes ill. Even if we ignore this, *Groom* must be exceptional in that it extends the concept of wrongful birth so as to include an unhealthy neonate who was a normal fetus – and this leads to the further question as to how long the intervening period may be before the link between conception and disability is severed?[202] Suppose, for example, the child contracted MRS infection while in hospital – is there any less of a direct link between the wrongful pregnancy and the disability? Indeed, Brooke LJ conceded that 'the longer the period before the disability is triggered off, the more difficult it may be to establish a right to recover compensation'.[203]

It will be apparent that I find *Groom* an unsatisfactory case. At first glance, it is difficult to see why the original surgeon was not a party to the action – he or she performed a negligent operation while, on the other side of the coin, many might think that a general practitioner whose patient has recently been sterilised in a specialist unit could be excused for failing to include pregnancy in her differential diagnosis.[204] Even if this is not conceded, would it not have been more appropriate to bring an action against the obstetric department on grounds of negligent hygienic practice? If, as was accepted, the risk of a birth canal being contaminated is foreseeable, does that not imply that the need for prophylactic measures is not equally foreseeable?

---

[200] ibid.   [201] ibid.

[202] This point was specifically taken up in *Parkinson*, n. 162 above, which is discussed in detail below. There, Hale LJ was of the opinion that the cut off point should be birth. It is arguable that, since the infection was contracted before the child was fully extruded from its mother, it was infected before it was legally born – but if one accepts that, one must also accept that injury due to birth trauma would be sufficient to found a similar claim. This problem was raised by counsel for Dr Selby at appeal (2002) 64 BMLR 47, [2002] Lloyd's Rep Med 1 ([23] and [26]) only to be summarily dismissed by the court. It is important to appreciate that the Court of Appeal heard *Parkinson* after the trial but before the appeal in *Groom*.

[203] ibid., at [26].   [204] Although, as already noted negligence in this respect was admitted.

Aside from these largely tactical considerations, the case as it stands does raise some additional and interesting considerations that have been explored only to a limited extent in other instances of wrongful pregnancy or birth. As already intimated, it was held that the fact of pregnancy itself was sufficient to render the birth of a disabled child a foreseeable possibility. Which cannot be denied – yet, intuitively one feels that, absent any indications to the contrary, the imbalance between the possibility of a normal and an abnormal neonate is too great for the latter to be regarded as being *reasonably* foreseeable.[205] This, in turn, leads to the question of causation. It is difficult to visualise a clear causative link between the actions of a general practitioner and negligent obstetric management. To surmount this hurdle, Clark J accepted the proposition that a distinction is to be made: 'between proximity in the relationship between the claimant and defendant, *which is required*, and causal proximity between the negligent act and the pure economic loss claimed, *which is not*'.[206] Clark J was able to establish proximity between the claimant and her general practitioner and concluded that, 'as a result, the claimant gave birth to an "unwanted" disabled child'.[207] With the greatest respect, I suggest that the only legitimate conclusion is that, as a result, the claimant gave birth to an unwanted child – which is by no means the same thing.

A further unsatisfactory element of *Groom* is that the trial was decided on the basis of agreed medical reports – there was no oral evidence by way of which some of these questions might have been resolved. It is unsurprising that the case went to appeal where, in my view, the situation was further complicated by semantics. Brooke LJ, for example, saw the case as clearly one of wrongful birth and then went on to attempt to equiparate this with the action for wrongful conception[208] – or, in my terms, wrongful pregnancy and which I think is the correct classification of this complex case. His resulting causative sequence from a failure to diagnose pregnancy to severe neonatal brain damage due to salmonella poisoning is persuasive but, in my view, crosses one bridge too far, particularly as to foreseeability which, as suggested above should be seen as, at best, a two-edged weapon.

---

[205] The incidence of congenital abnormalities depends to a large extent on how one defines abnormality. It was, however, held in *Emeh*, n. 50 above, that an incidence of between 1 in 200 and 1 in 400 was sufficient to make the risk clearly foreseeable. It is interesting to compare this with, say, *Sidaway* v. *Board of Governors of the Bethlem Royal Hospital and the Maudsley Hospital* [1985] AC 871 in which it was found acceptable medical practice not to warn of a risk of severe injury of the order of 1 in 100.

[206] n. 196 above, QBD at 45, col.1. My emphasis.   [207] ibid.

[208] n. 196 above, Lloyd's Rep Med at [20]. And see Hale LJ at [28] and [29].

One senses a practical significance here in that the multiple interventions involved in the case might have made it very difficult to apply liability to the surgeon.[209] Indeed, there is an impression that Brooke LJ, supported by Hale LJ, was *morally* anxious that Ms Groom should succeed, thus, again, reflecting the Court of Appeal's distrust of the decision in *McFarlane* which was so evident in *Parkinson* – to which we turn in the next chapter. This is expressed in the following rather long extract from the judgment of Brooke LJ:

> [Counsel] argued strenuously that if we did not fix the child's apparent state of health at birth as the cut-off point, we would be making the judges' tasks unnecessarily difficult when they are invited to try future cases on the borderline. I can see the force of that submission, but it appears to me that it should not stand in the way of our doing justice in a case like the present, in which a child's enduring handicaps, caused by the normal incidents of intra-uterine development and birth, were triggered off within the first month of her life.[210]

For a final comment on *Groom*, we can turn to Hale LJ who, while of necessity accepting that damages cannot, now, be awarded given the birth of an uncovenanted healthy child, went on to say:

> It is fair, just and reasonable that a doctor who has undertaken the task of protecting a patient from an unwanted pregnancy should bear the additional costs if that pregnancy results in a disabled child.[211]

The alternative view, which I support, is that, if it is fair that the doctor should be liable for the additional costs of maintaining a disabled child when, as in *Groom*, he or she had no responsibility for that disability, then it is fair that the doctor whose identical negligence resulted, by good chance alone, in the birth of a healthy child, should be liable for at least a proportion of the financial havoc he or she has wreaked on the parents. Be that as it may, *Groom* has provided an ideal link between the consequences of the inadvertent birth of a healthy child and those cases which involve disability – which we will now consider.

---

[209] See *Lord v. Pacific Steam Navigation, The Oropesa* [1943] P 32, [1943] 1 All ER per Lord Wright at All ER 215, cited at [20].
[210] n. 196 above, Lloyd's Rep Med at [26].   [211] ibid., at [31].

5 Uncovenanted pregnancy and disability

Introduction

We have seen how antagonistic the House of Lords has been to the grant of recompense for the upkeep of an originally unwanted but healthy child. There is no doubt that the tenor of the speeches was such as to raise doubts as to how, given the chance, they would approach a case of wrongful pregnancy resulting in a disabled child – remembering that they did, in fact, make no firm statements on the matter. Only two of their Lordships spoke to the point.

Lord Steyn had this to say:

> Counsel for the health authority was inclined to concede that in the case of an unwanted child, who was born seriously disabled, the rule may have to be different. There may be force in this concession but it does not arise in the present appeal and it ought to await decision where the focus is on such cases.

And Lord Clyde was equally indefinite:

> The present case relates to a conception which was followed by a successful birth of a healthy child. In the course of the argument this factor sometimes, but not at others, appeared to be of importance. If there is a distinction in cases of wrongful conception between those where the child is healthy and those where the child is unhealthy, or disabled or otherwise imperfect, it has to be noted that in the present case we are dealing with a normal birth and a healthy child.

Neither of these statements gives us any real idea of their Lordships' intentions nor, in truth, of their underlying philosophical approach to the possibility. It may, then, be helpful to reassess their speeches in an attempt to establish the answer.

Second-guessing the House of Lords

Lord Slynn, it will be remembered, crystallised the general feeling of the House in holding that it would not be '*Caparo*-fair' to impose liability for the responsibilities involved in rearing a child. His Lordship did not comment on fairness to the parents. Nevertheless, the extent of the doctor's responsibility would be the same irrespective of the health of the child but, insofar as the disabled child has special needs which must be paid for, his or her liability would be even greater in the latter case.[1] The implication is that Lord Slynn would still *deny* damages for the wrongful conception and birth of a disabled child – a conclusion that is reinforced by the fact that the sterilising surgeon cannot be responsible for the disability. For this reason alone, Lord Steyn, who depended on principles of distributive justice, would also have to deny damages on the grounds that the *basis* for the distribution of burdens throughout society remains the same irrespective of the state of the child. Lord Steyn's ordinary man on the London Underground would, however, have to be convinced of this and the ordinary woman on the Strathtay Omnibus even more so;[2] illogical though it may be, Lord Steyn would have to work harder to find support for his view – and the more disabled the child, the more difficult would be that task. Given that the guiding factor in cases of difficulty is what the judge 'reasonably believes that the ordinary citizen would regard as right',[3] Lord Steyn must, in my view, be registered as a 'don't know'. Lord Hope would, however, have to *deny* damages. He would not give any damages for maintenance of a healthy child because the benefits derived from the child's existence cannot be assessed in monetary terms and that, as a result, 'the logical conclusion, as a matter of law, is that that the costs to the pursuers of meeting their obligations to the child . . . are not recoverable as damages'. The benefits derived from a disabled child might or might not be so obvious but they would still be incalculable and, therefore, on the basis of what seems to be an unusual argument, unpayable. Lord Clyde considered that the damages available in a case such as *McFarlane* would be disproportionate to the doctor's culpability. The disproportion would be even greater in the event of the resultant child being disabled; so he, too, must then *deny* damages with even greater force. Lord Millett considered that: 'it would be repugnant to [society's] own sense of values to do otherwise . . . than take the birth of

[1] It was suggested that, in fact, Lord Slynn was the only member of the panel who firmly closed the door on recovery for the birth of *any* child. See Longmore J at first instance quoted, with some hesitation, in the Court of Appeal in *Parkinson* v. *St James and Seacroft University Hospital NHS Trust* [2002] QB 266, [2001] 3 All ER 97, CA, at [45].

[2] J. K. Mason, 'Unwanted Pregnancy: A Case of Retroversion?' (2000) 4 *Edinburgh Law Review* 191–206 at 205. The point made was that it is unreasonable to pick out one particular group as representing the whole population. Lord Steyn's supposition was no more than a supposition.

[3] *McFarlane* v. *Tayside Health Board* [2000] 2 AC 59, 2000 SC 1 at 17. For a generally similar analysis of the individual positions, see G. Hugh-Jones, 'Commentary on *Taylor* v. *Shropshire HA*' [2000] Lloyd's Rep Med 96 at 107–8.

a normal healthy baby as a blessing, not a detriment'. But that might well not be so in the case of a defective neonate and Lord Millett might, accordingly, *allow* damages – particularly as he was certainly sympathetic to the McFarlanes. Which leads us to the not wholly unsurprising conclusion that, given they maintained their position as stated, the House of Lords in *McFarlane* would probably have decided against recovery for the birth of a child who was disabled had the question arisen. Would there, then, have been any precedents to assist or to deter them?

The disabled neonate

The *pre*-McFarlane *position*

Truly appropriate cases are hard to find because the conditions for which we are searching are very precise. I have given reasons enough for explaining why the run of cases of wrongful birth that we have discussed in Chapter 3 are irrelevant as to wrongful pregnancy. The '*McFarlane*-exception' demands that there is a failed sterilisation (or similar error), that there is no fault in the antenatal care and that a disabled child is born. The exemplar of such a case occurring before the *McFarlane* decision is *Taylor* v. *Shropshire Health Authority*.[4]

Mrs Taylor had had four children and a termination before undergoing a sterilising operation at the end of 1987. She became pregnant the following year and was delivered of a seriously disabled child in 1989. The report does not tell us whether or not she was offered a second termination – certainly there were no obvious indications. Nor does it identify the precise abnormality suffered by the child, which seems to have been in the nature of mental disorder. Interestingly, her claim based on failure to warn of the possibility of failure was dismissed both in negligence – adequate warning being found to have been given – and in causation.[5] Liability was, however, imposed on the grounds of operator error.

As was to be expected at the time, Nicholl J followed *Emeh*[6] and Mrs Taylor was awarded the reasonable costs of caring for her son for the rest of their joint lives. Damages were assessed on the child's needs

---

[4] *Taylor* was a split trial and is recorded as [1998] Lloyd's Rep Med 395 (Popplewell J) and [2000] Lloyd's Rep Med 96 (Nicholl J).

[5] This being, to an extent, due to the fact the risks of pregnancy while on oral contraceptives – to which she would have been driven had she refused the operation – were considerably greater than those following properly performed tubal oblation.

[6] *Emeh* v. *Kensington and Chelsea and Westminster Area Health Authority* [1985] QB 1012, [1984] 3 All ER 1044.

independently of his mother's resources[7] and those based on loss of amenity were reduced by 'a modest amount' to represent what little joy and comfort could be derived from the child's existence – a form of 'offset' which would not now be applicable and is discussed further at p. 157. In addition, however, an award of £22,500 was made to reflect the stresses and responsibilities inherent in caring for a severely handicapped child.

In the end, *Taylor* teaches us very little save to demonstrate once again that, illogical though it may be following *McFarlane*,[8] the courts will strive, when they can, to provide support for those subject to the expense and hardship of caring for a disabled child as a result of negligence of no matter what type. *Taylor* was heard as *McFarlane* was on its way to the House of Lords and, in many ways, it is a pity it was not appealed as it seemed to be the ideal test of the *McFarlane* exception.[9] As a result it can be in no way precedental and, for this, we must look to the case of Mrs Parkinson.

Mrs Parkinson's case

On the face of things, *Parkinson v. St James and Seacroft University Hospital NHS Trust*[10] fulfils all the criteria one needs by which to analyse the '*McFarlane* exception'. Here, the claimant had undergone an admittedly negligent sterilisation by way of tubal occlusion. Some ten months later, she conceived a child and was warned that it might be disabled. There is some difficulty here in that the extent of the warning is unclear in the report; my own interpretation is that it was non-specific and, although it may appear to be an example of so-called defensive medicine, it did no more than refer to the fact that some 0.3 per cent of otherwise unremarkable pregnancies may result in a disabled child.[11]

---

[7] Thus pre-empting Henriques J in *Hardman* v. *Amin* for discussion of which, see Chapter 3.

[8] And, as we will see, was strenuously argued by the minority in *Parkinson* below.

[9] On reflection, I am not so sure of this as it is difficult to glean from the report when John Taylor's disability became apparent. I consider this problem further, below, when discussing *Parkinson*. The seldom discussed case of *Robinson* v. *Salford Health Authority* [1992] 3 Med LR 270 is comparable to both *Taylor* and *Parkinson* insofar as the costs of the child's upkeep were deemed recoverable, including those resulting from speech defects and behavioural problems which appeared some time after a premature birth. But beyond that, it is now an old case, the report is brief and I doubt if it adds anything significant to the jurisprudence.

[10] [2002] QB 266, [2001] 3 All ER 97. Once again, I have published my views on the case previously in J.K. Mason, 'Wrongful Pregnancy, Wrongful Birth and Wrongful Terminology' (2002) 6 *Edinburgh Law Review* 46–66.

[11] Certainly it was agreed that any disability from which the child suffered was not *caused* by any breach of duty on the defendant's part (*Parkinson*, n. 10 above, at QB [11], my emphasis).

This raises a parenthetic, albeit, in the context of this book, important question of the quantification of risk within the laws of tort. Waller LJ had this to say in *Emeh*:

[I]n my judgment, having regard to the fact that in a proportion of all births – (between one in two hundred and one in four hundred were the figures given at the trial) – congenital abnormalities might arise, makes the risk clearly one that is foreseeable, as the law of negligence understands it.[12]

From which one can surely extrapolate that civil law regards the *inherent* risk of having a disabled child as a material risk.

What, then, is the relationship between a risk that is clearly foreseeable under the law of negligence and one that is substantial in the criminal law of England or the common law of Scotland? In short, is it to be implied that a termination under the Abortion Act 1967, section 1(1)(d) – which, as we have seen, refers to lawful termination in the event of a substantial risk that the child will be born seriously handicapped – will always be lawful on the grounds of foreseeability? Or, to put it another way, is the *materiality* of risk to be equiparated with the *substantiality* of risk – at least for the purposes of abortion law? Probably, the introduction of the word 'seriously' is likely to distinguish the 1967 Act as Waller LJ's figures make no mention of the degree of *harm* involved. Nonetheless, his dictum raises once again, but in a different guise, the question which we have discussed at p. 28 of whether it is possible to perform an indefensible termination in Great Britain.[13]

In any event, that diversion aside, Mrs Parkinson chose not to have a termination. While this is immaterial to causation – insofar as we have seen consistently that, since *Emeh*,[14] a woman cannot be coerced in this way so as to absolve the wrongdoer of responsibility – the scenario as a whole indicates that *Parkinson* cannot be dismissed as an action for wrongful birth, a distinction that Brooke LJ also emphasised.[15] In the event, the judge at first instance awarded damages for the costs of providing for the child's special needs but not for the basic costs of his maintenance. The defendants appealed against the former decision and the plaintiff against the latter.

---

[12] [1985] 1 QB 1012 at 1019.

[13] One must also note that there is no certainty that Waller LJ would be followed. See the opinion of Lord Scott quoted at n. 79 below.

[14] n. 6 above.

[15] At [48]. Thereby agreeing with the present writer that cases such as *Rand*, *Hardman* and *Lee* (for which see pp. 90–7, above) are irrelevant in the context of the wrongful pregnancy debate.

On appeal, Brooke LJ undertook the by now almost mandatory analysis of the *McFarlane* case and, like so many before him, found that he had to pick out the several threads of argument and use them as best he might in the altered circumstances. He began by assuming the mantle of Waller LJ in *Emeh* in holding that the birth of a child *with congenital abnormalities* was a foreseeable consequence of a careless failure to clip the fallopian tubes. The italics are mine and I have used them merely to emphasise my strong doubts, as discussed above, as to the validity of that conclusion. Certainly it is foreseeable – indeed, it is incontrovertible – that a pregnancy *may* lead to a disabled child; but it is vastly more *probable* that it will lead to the birth of a normal child and it is this that must be uppermost in the mind of the surgeon.[16] Moreover, the surgeon is concerned with birth and the most that can be said in the case of Scott Parkinson is that, at that time, he suffered from no more than a latent disability.[17] Nonetheless, we must accept that this was the foundation stone of Lord Justice Brooke's argument which went on to find no difficulty in principle in accepting the proposition that the surgeon should be deemed to have assumed responsibility for the 'foreseeable and disastrous economic consequences' of his negligence; but he did not elaborate on this and, while one can equally happily accept the principle, it is not easy to see why one should do so in the case of a disabled child when Lords Slynn and Hope found it so hard to do so when the child was normal. Brooke LJ continued that the purpose of the operation was to prevent Mrs Parkinson from conceiving any more children, including children with congenital abnormalities, and the surgeon's duty of care was strictly related to the proper fulfilment of that purpose. Crunchingly, he pointed out that parents in a similar position had been able to recover damages during the 15 years between *Emeh* and *McFarlane* so that to accept the claim was not a step into the unknown – which leads one to wonder why, since those damages had included damages for the birth of a normal child, the House of Lords were so anxious to avoid the obvious. In Mrs Parkinson's case, the tests of foreseeability and proximity set out in *Caparo*[18] were satisfied. Accordingly, an award for looking after a child with serious disability which was limited to the special costs would be fair, just and reasonable – a conclusion which would be supported, if necessary, by an appeal to distributive justice as represented by ordinary people who would be

---

[16] It is interesting that Lord Scott in the House of Lords in *Rees* v. *Darlington Memorial Hospital NHS Trust*, n. 37 below, felt the same way and, in fact, used it as a main reason for considering *Parkinson* to have been wrongly decided: *Rees* at [147].

[17] There are many parallels between *Parkinson* and the hard to classify case of *Groom* v. *Selby* which has been discussed above at p. 146.

[18] *Caparo Industries plc* v. *Dickman* [1990] 2 AC 605, [1990] 1 All ER 568 per Lord Bridge.

satisfied if an award was limited to the extra expenses associated with the child's disability.[19]

In this writer's view, Lord Justice Brooke can be seen as steering his way between Scylla and Charybdis. To him, the course of action which he proposed was inevitable in terms of both logic and justice – and I certainly agree that, at least as to the latter, it is an advance on *McFarlane*. Significantly, in concentrating entirely on the disabled infant, its main effect, pragmatic though it may be, is to dissociate the reasoning in the event of the unwanted birth of a disabled child from that applied in *McFarlane*. Thus, as the Lord Justice himself pointed out, there is nothing in his decision that conflicts with that in the House of Lords[20] – effectively, he neither agrees nor disagrees with the latter, and the two cases are held as being quite distinct rather than as derivative.[21]

By contrast, the analyst is left in no doubt when we turn to the opinion of Hale LJ. In what might be termed flamboyant style – or, as characterised by Hoyano, a *tour de force*[22] – she introduced the very contemporary assumption that to cause a woman to become pregnant against her will is an invasion of her right to bodily integrity. It is an interesting observation that Lady Hale is, I believe, the only female judge, apart from Holmes J in the Supreme Court of Queensland,[23] to have been quoted thus far in this book which, throughout, is devoted to a condition that is almost entirely in the province of women – as Lady Hale pointed out in referring to child care: 'there are undoubted and inescapable differences between the sexes here'.[24] She then went on to drive home this point by listing some of the consequences of that condition which, because they should

---

[19] Although, rightly, holding that the United States decisions are of little use in the present context because of their variance, Brooke LJ called in aid the relatively recent decision in *Emerson* v. *Magendantz* 689 A 2d 409 (R. I., 1997) and its precursor from the opposite end of the country *Fassoulas* v. *Ramey* 450 So 2d 822 (Fla., 1984) both of which preempted the House of Lords as to refusal of maintenance for healthy children but allowed the special upbringing costs associated with disability. Indeed, he found these cases persuasive to the extent that he was anxious to arrive at the same answer (n. 10 above, at [50]).

[20] ibid., at [51].

[21] Almost as an aside, Brooke LJ opined that, in considering distributive justice, 'ordinary people' would approve an award that was limited to the extra expenses associated with significant disability in the child and, by implication, would not approve those associated with rearing a normal child (ibid., at [50]). The same comment was made picturesquely by Longmore J at first instance in *Parkinson*. This author still doubts the basis for this belief. For comment on the significance to the law of tort as a whole by one who was involved in the case, see Margaret Bickford-Smith, 'Failed Sterilisation Resulting in the Birth of a Disabled Child: The Issues' (2001) 4 *Journal of Personal Injury Law* 404–10.

[22] Laura C. H. Hoyano, 'Misconceptions and Wrongful Conceptions (2002) 65 *Modern Law Review* 883–906 at 897.

[23] *Melchior* v. *Cattanach* [2000] QSC 285.   [24] n. 10 above, at [63].

never have happened, remained invasive despite the fact that they derived from a natural process. The list is impressive and the opinion needs to be read in the original if one is to capture its emotional and emotive nature.[25] It includes the profound physiological and psychological changes that occur during pregnancy and for some time thereafter; these are accompanied by a severe curtailment of personal autonomy – 'one's life is no longer just one's own but also someone else's'. The mother can rid herself of that responsibility only by way of abortion or adoption – and it was the unanimous view of the House of Lords in *McFarlane* that the former, at least, was not a reasonable expectation.[26] The process of giving birth is 'rightly termed "labour"' and the hard work does not stop after pregnancy. Tellingly, Hale LJ recalled the requirements of the Children Act 1989 and reiterated that parental responsibility is not just a matter of financial responsibility – the primary responsibility is to care for the child and bringing up children is hard work:

> Here the care is provided by the very person who has been wronged and the legal obligation to provide it is the direct and foreseeable consequence of that wrong. It is, perhaps, an indication of the reluctance of the common law to recognise the cost of care to the carer that claims for wrongful conception and birth of healthy children have not previously been analysed in this way.... The law has found it much easier to focus on the associated financial costs ... [which] are not independent of the caring responsibility but part and parcel of it.

In short, all such consequences 'flow inexorably from ... the invasion of bodily integrity and personal autonomy involved in every pregnancy' and the mother's financial claim 'obviously represents the consequences of the fundamental invasion of her rights, which is the conception itself'.[27]

Thus, in following a clear consequentialist path, Hale LJ found that, once it was established that the pregnancy was caused wrongly, nothing unusual or contrary to legal principle was involved in awarding damages in a case such as Mrs Parkinson's. She clearly supported the Inner House decision in *McFarlane*[28] and pointed out that a majority of the House of Lords had accepted that, on normal principles, the McFarlanes' claim would have been allowable. The stumbling block rested on the 'feeling' that to compensate for the financial costs of bringing up a healthy child was a step too far – somehow room had to be made for the benefits to be derived from the presence of a new child; since these, in practice, were impossible to define, the solution was either to ignore the benefits

---

[25] ibid., at [63]–[71].
[26] ibid., at [66] quoting [2000] 2 AC 59 at 74, 81, 97, 105 and 113. See also [69].
[27] ibid., at [73].
[28] *McFarlane* v *Tayside Health Board* 1998 SLT 307, (1998) 44 BMLR 140.

altogether or to assume that they cancelled out the claim.[29] Insofar as majority support for this last contention is nowhere evident in the House of Lord's opinions, it is strange that Lady Hale held that the solution of the 'deemed equilibrium' was binding on the Court of Appeal.[30] Nonetheless, and although she thought it limited the damages that would otherwise have been recoverable on normal principles, it represented the cornerstone of her ultimate analysis. It accepted the limitation on damages imposed in *McFarlane* which catered for the ordinary costs of the ordinary child; there was, therefore, no need or reason to take that limitation any further. The principle of equilibrium applied to the disabled child 'treats a disabled child as having exactly the same worth as a non-disabled child ... It simply acknowledges that he costs more.'[31] In the event, both appeals were dismissed unanimously; permission to appeal to the House of Lords was refused and, significantly, that decision has not been challenged.

The sheer length of this 'précis' indicates the importance I attach to *Parkinson* which seems to be, in its own way, as significant a case as was *McFarlane*, despite the fact that it was decided in a lower court. This is for several reasons. Firstly, the two main speeches, argued as they were from very different angles, are complementary to one another and certainly fill the gap left in *McFarlane* in relation to the disabled child resulting from a wrongful pregnancy. In the light of the very powerful arguments expressed, it seems unlikely that the rule awarding special damages in such circumstances will be significantly disturbed – although its logic remains to be debated.[32] At the same time, *Parkinson* can be seen as a superior court's approval of – or, indeed, a form of de facto appeal in respect of – the several first instance decisions in cases of wrongful birth that we have discussed in the previous chapter.

Secondly, and with the greatest respect to Brooke LJ, the inherent importance of the report is enhanced by the speech of Hale LJ which, as has been noted above, is of special significance not only because it comes from a woman who has had and has brought up a child but more so

---

[29] n. 10 above, at [87], quoting Lord McCluskey in the Inner House at 1998 SLT 307, 317. Lord McCluskey went on to explain that, essentially, it depended on the financial status of the parents.

[30] ibid., at [90]. It was, of course, questioned by Robert Walker L J in the Court of Appeal stage of *Rees* v. *Darlington Memorial NHS Trust* [2003] QB 20.

[31] ibid., at [90].

[32] See p. 165 below. There are, however, some doubts as to the effect of the 'conventional award' proposed in *Rees* v. *Darlington Memorial NHS Trust* [2004] AC 309, for which, see p. 176 below.

because it is the *only* woman's opinion on the subject among the United Kingdom cases. To quote from her speech:

The studied calm of the Royal Courts of Justice, concentrating on one point at a time, is light years away from the circumstances prevailing in the average home [where] the mother is ... doing all the other things that the average mother has to cope with simultaneously, or in quick succession, in the normal household.[33]

In my opinion, the substitution of this vision of motherhood as a continuing process from conception to the moment when the chick flees the nest for the restricted concept of pregnancy forces us to look at wrongful pregnancy in a completely new light. The 'damage' lies in the uncovenanted invasion of and distortion of a woman's – and, perhaps, a family's – life over many years. I have said that I regard *Parkinson* as every bit as important as *McFarlane* and I still believe that one should have the former in one hand when reading the latter in the other.

At the same time, Lady Hale did consider the difficulties associated with the *Parkinson* decision; these included that of defining the degree of disability which separates the disabled from the healthy child and, secondly, that of agreeing a cut-off point in time beyond which the responsible surgeon can no longer be held liable. As to the former, she proposed adopting the language of the Children Act 1989, s.17(11) in which a disabled child is one:

[who is] blind, deaf or dumb or suffers from mental disorder of any kind or is substantially and permanently handicapped by illness, injury or congenital deformity or such other disability as may be prescribed.

For myself, I see this as doing no more than defining severe disability – it does not help in telling us the point at which we can identify a disabled child. To do that, we can, surely, use a more simplistic approach which says, in effect, that a disabled child is one who is agreed to be disabled either by the parties concerned or by the court. This would allow for acknowledgment of *any* genuine disability and would, at the same time, inhibit the frivolous claim in that, in the event of disagreement, the court could award either no damages or damages of such minimal value as to make the action economically unsound.

It will already be clear that I regard the cut-off factor as probably the weakest chink in the *Parkinson* armour. Hale LJ herself concluded that, of the two serious contenders for the end-point of professional liability, birth was to be preferred to the alternative of conception and that:

---

[33] n. 10 above, at [70] quoting *Surtees* v. *Kingston-upon-Thames Royal B.C.* [1991] 2 FLR 559 per Sir Nicholas Browne-Wilkinson V-C at 583.

[A]ny disability arising from genetic causes or foreseeable events during pregnancy (such as rubella, spina bifida, or oxygen deprivation during pregnancy of childbirth) up until the child is born alive, and which are not novus actus interveniens, will suffice to found a claim.[34]

This passage contains a number of conundra which merit consideration before returning to the main theme. In the first place, it seems to equate wrongful birth with the *McFarlane*-exception and, while it may be advantageous to confirm the validity of the currently unchallenged *Rand–Hardman–Lee* decisions, it is confusing to do so in this manner. Second, the dispenser of distributive justice would, one feels, rebel at the thought of the sterilising surgeon being held liable for the negligence of the obstetricians whose potential liability in cases of birth injury is already well-recognised. On this view, therefore, to base such disabilities on a claim under the *Parkinson* mantle is something of a tautology. The more complex problem raised, however, lies in what is to be excluded under the term *novus actus interveniens*. It is suggested that, given the context of the wrongful pregnancy action, and given the observations above, a relevant *novus actus* can *only* arise by way of negligence by those responsible for overseeing the pregnancy and labour. If, however, a court was to hold that their conduct at this stage was *not* negligent – but, nevertheless, the child was born disabled – then Hale LJ's dicta direct us backwards in time to the negligence of the sterilising surgeon. The implication, then, is that she is opening up an additional route to compensation for the uncovenanted birth of a disabled child.[35] Lady Hale gave no indication of her intentions. Those who feel that the 'victim' of the *McFarlane*-exception deserves recompense in any circumstances would, no doubt, welcome the latter interpretation. On the other hand, it is difficult to avoid the impression that to hold the surgeon responsible for others' obstetric practice would come close to offending all three limbs – foreseeability, proximity and fairness – of the *Caparo* test. I know of no apposite case but one is sure to come – when it will be interesting to see whether the courts will be prepared to allow the affected woman what is, effectively, a second bite of the cherry.

To return, however, to the most significant of the problems posed by Lady Hale – should we, and how are we to, limit the time beyond which the surgeon's liability ceases? This difficulty is built in to *Parkinson* itself

---

[34] ibid., at [92].
[35] There are, of course, very many hypoxic birth injury cases – including the truly seminal case of *Whitehouse* v. *Jordan* [1981] 1 All ER 267, [1981] 1 WLR 246, HL – where negligence has been rejected, often on *Bolam* grounds. I have in mind similar cases which involve an uncovenanted child.

insofar as, while it is true Scott Parkinson did not thrive from birth, his main disability was behavioural in nature; there seems little doubt that the diagnosis of autistic spectrum disorder was not made until he was some three years old. On the face of things, this seems to tear a hole in Lady Hale's 'cut-off at birth' proposition and the inconsistency was not addressed in the *Parkinson* speeches. No doubt the riposte to a questioner would be that the condition was one which was immanent from conception but this, apart from threatening a diversion into the interaction of genetic and environmental factors in the genesis of disease, forces us to think in terms of when the disability must manifest itself, rather than when it must arise, in order to impose liability. The stumbling-block, of course, is that the 'incubation' period is open ended depending upon how many conditions one includes – there is not, for example, an unbridgeable gap between, autism appearing in infancy, as affected Scott Parkinson, and psycopathy being evidenced in adolescence. And what, one might ask, of late onset genetic disease? The condition arises at conception but the thought of a surgeon finding him or her self liable for special damages decades after a negligent operation seems too bizarre to entertain – yet it is one that flows from the award to Mrs Parkinson. Moreover, a woman can choose whether or not to terminate her pregnancy on the grounds of possible latent Huntington's disease in the fetus;[36] to what extent, one may well ask, should this affect the surgeon's liability under the *Parkinson* ruling? I confess that I have no answer to the dilemmas posed and, in the absence of an appeal of *Parkinson*, we may have to await the deliberations of a court hearing a new case which raises these questions specifically in order to find the solution. The words of Waller LJ in the later case of *Rees*[37] are, in some ways, prophetic:

Once the court begins to disallow recovery, although normal principles would allow recovery, and once the court starts to consider the makings of exceptions to that decision – we are, as I see it, truly in the area of distributive justice.[38]

Perhaps, then, this is one problem that should be rightly answered by recourse to the traveller on the London Underground.

There is no doubt that, despite the facts that *McFarlane* was strictly concerned with the birth of a healthy child and that *Parkinson* dealt with the exception left open by its predecessor – and that, on the surface,

---

[36] Insofar as s.1(1)(d) of the Abortion Act covers only the situation where the *child* may be disabled, this is an assumption; nonetheless, there have been no prosecutions for undertaking what is undoubtedly a frequent occurrence.

[37] *Rees* v. *Darlington Memorial Hospital NHS Trust* [2003] QB 20, (2002) 65 BMLR 117, CA. The case is discussed in detail at p. 163.

[38] ibid., at QB [45].

Parkinson 'does no violence to the reasoning' of the House of Lords[39] – there is no doubt that an antipathy to *McFarlane* can be discerned in the speeches of both Brooke and Hale LJJ. The following extract from the transcript of Proceedings in *Cattanach v. Melchior* is hard to resist:

GUMMOW J: But there are signs of subsequent rebellion in the Court of Appeal, are there not, in England?
KIRBY J: There is rebellion there.
GUMMOW J: *Parkinson* is one example, to put it mildly.[40]

And, as we will see later in this chapter, *Parkinson* stands as the last remaining potential port of entry into fortress *McFarlane*. Leaving aside the residual problems as to the duration of liability left by Lady Hale, the speeches are persuasive and resistant to counter-attack. Why, then, are there still grounds for concern over the case?

The problem lies in the apparent paradox in that virtually everything said by Hale LJ and much of Brooke LJ's reasoning can be applied almost verbatim to the wrongful pregnancy terminating in a normal child.[41] The basic obligations of parenthood are the same irrespective of the health status of the child. The simple fact is that, the more disabled is the child, the more difficult and costly it is to fulfil those obligations – but the additional costs will be always relative, never nil. Henriques J, referring to the child in *Hardman*, said:

However, he is disabled and, but for the negligence, the claimant would not have spent any money bringing up a disabled child.[42]

Hale LJ makes it quite clear that one could equally say: 'Catherine was not disabled yet, but for the negligence, Mr McFarlane would not have spent any money bringing up a child that he may not have been able to afford'.

If, then, the effects of unexpected and negligently enforced parenthood are similar, differing only in degree irrespective of the health of the child, the logical conclusion is that they should be treated similarly and produce the same results. In other words, the non-violent parallel relationship between *McFarlane* and *Parkinson* identified by Lady Hale[43] is a fiction and the two cases are, in fact, in direct conflict. This may be due to the

---

[39] See Hale LJ, ibid., at [20].
[40] *Cattanach v. Melchior*, High Court of Australia, Transcript of Proceedings, 11 February 2003. The High Court report is at (2003) 199 ALR 131.
[41] And see confirmation of this by Waller LJ in *Rees*, n. 37 above, at [44].
[42] *Hardman v. Amin* [2000] Lloyd's Rep Med 498 at 506, (2000) 59 BMLR 58 at 73.
[43] n. 39 above.

fact that 'the court in *McFarlane* apparently did not see *Parkinson* coming'[44] but, whatever the underlying cause, it means that either *McFarlane* or *Parkinson* is wrong – and we are left wondering which it is to be.

It will have been clear for some time that I am among those who disapprove *McFarlane*. To quote Robert Walker LJ,[45] 'there is a strong moral element in the basis of the decision' and a majority of the Law Lords in *McFarlane* – and, as we will see, all in *Rees*[46] – concurred in admitting that the decision would have been different had the normal rules of tort law been applied. Without wishing or intending in any way to denigrate the 'moral stance', it simply seems to me that the tenuous and adventitious prospects of a 'blessing' from the birth of an unsought child are insufficient grounds on which to overturn well-established and, generally, successful legal principles; the strength of the reasoning of the majority in *Cattanach* seems overwhelming. Nonetheless, *McFarlane*, being a House of Lords' decision, clearly held poll position and was unlikely to be overtaken except in unusual circumstances. Almost fortuitously, such circumstances arose following the authoritative Australian decision in *Cattanach* which we have considered and, more importantly, with the simultaneous appearance on the scene of Ms Rees, to whose case we can now turn.

The disabled mother

McFarlane was concerned with the single issue of whether damages were payable in respect of the maintenance of an uncovenanted healthy child born as a result of professional negligence; it left open, as we have seen, the possibility that the decision might be different in the event of the child being disabled. *Parkinson* also raised only a single issue – that is, the validity of what I have called the *McFarlane* exception. Thus, although the two cases were clearly interrelated, they were not interdependent; the decision in *Parkinson* could have gone either way without appearing to challenge *McFarlane* – the issues were distinct. Ms Rees' case was, however, a different matter. Her history was the familiar one of a wrongful pregnancy resulting in the birth of a healthy baby, comparable in every way save one to that of Mrs McFarlane. The exception was that, while Mrs McFarlane was healthy, Ms Rees was severely disabled due to partial blindness. Thus, Ms Rees, rather than exploring a lacuna knowingly left in *McFarlane*, was seeking to impose a *new* exception while, at the same time, preserving the essential element of the case – that is, a healthy baby.

---

[44] Peter Cane, 'Another Failed Sterilisation' (2004) 120 *Law Quarterly Review* 189–93.
[45] In *Rees*, n. 37 above, at [29].   [46] For which see p. 166 below.

Ms Rees, thus threatened to undermine *McFarlane* at its roots. Moreover, were she to be successful at appeal, she would force the House of Lords to review its controversial decision in *McFarlane*. The result of her case was, therefore, of fundamental importance.

Ms Rees's case

Rees v. Darlington Memorial NHS Trust,[47] as already explained, concerned a woman who was severely visually handicapped. On being referred to a consultant surgeon, she was adamant that she would never want a child because of the difficulties she would have in caring for it; she also had problems with contraception. Accordingly, she underwent tubal clipping in the course of which one tube was inadequately occluded. She gave birth to a healthy boy some 21 months later.[48] Ms Rees then sued for the full cost of maintenance of her child. The court of first instance, which is unreported, found, however, that *McFarlane* had already been sufficiently tested in the 'wrongful birth' cases[49] and held that no recovery was available given that the negligence resulted in a healthy child.

The ball was then firmly in the Court of Appeal where, after some initial confusion, it was agreed that the action was effectively limited to the recovery of special expenses resulting from Ms Rees' disability – how might or might not these be different from those incurred by *any* parent faced with rearing an unintended child? Put another way, did *McFarlane* mean that none of these costs could ever be claimed in any circumstances in the case of a healthy child or can that ruling, by analogy with *Parkinson*, be modified in the light of the particular circumstances of the individual case? In the event, the Court was prepared to see the circumstances of Ms Rees' case as representing a legitimate extension of the ruling in *Parkinson*[50] and Lady Hale, who was, again, a member of the panel, showed no disinclination to renew her challenge.

In many ways, the circumstances in *Rees* were a gift to Lady Hale who, as we have seen above, predicated her case on the concept and responsibilities of motherhood. If disability in the child is likely to complicate the mother/child relationship in both physical and economic terms, disability in the mother is likely to do so to an equal or even greater extent – and particularly, perhaps, as to the former. Thus, the pure economist is likely to say that the costs, both emotional and financial, of rearing a healthy

---

[47] [2003] QB 20, (2002) 65 BMLR 117, CA. For an outstanding review of the Court of Appeal decision, see, again, Hoyano, n. 22 above.

[48] There is no comment as to the offer or refusal of a termination in the case.

[49] For which, see Chapter 3.   [50] n. 37 above, per Robert Walker LJ at [41].

child are the same irrespective of the mother's ability to meet them and there is no need to single out physical disability as one extenuating circumstance; Lady Hale, however, is able to say that it is a precise reason why an unwilling mother deserves special consideration. It is worth setting out her actual words at length rather than attempting to paraphrase:

[A]ble bodied parents are both of them able to look after and bring up their child. No doubt they would both benefit from a nanny or other help in doing so. But they do not need it in order to be able to discharge the basic parental responsibility of looking after the child properly and safely, performing those myriad essential but mundane tasks such as feeding, bathing, clothing, training, supervising, playing with, reading to and taking to school which every child needs. They do not need it in order to avoid the risk that the child may have to be taken away to be looked after by the local social services authority or others, to the detriment of the child as well as the parent. That is the distinction between an able-bodied parent and a disabled parent who needs help if she is to be able to discharge the most ordinary tasks involved in the parental responsibility which has been placed upon her as a result of the defendant's negligence.[51]

Hale LJ recognised the difficulty imposed by having to accept that the parental benefit of having a child must negative the ordinary costs of bringing up that child – an aspect of 'deemed equilibrium' that is, from this author's standpoint, far easier to accept in the case of a healthy child than in that of one born into the *Parkinson* scenario; at the same time, however, she believed that the disabled mother was not being over-compensated by being recompensed for the exceptional costs involved – she was merely being put into the same position as her able-bodied fellows.[52]

Finally, Lady Hale referred to the problem of the doctor's assumption of responsibility and concluded, as this writer has always considered to be the case, that it is impossible to separate responsibility for the pregnancy from responsibility for preventing parenthood and the parental responsibility that brings – 'the two go hand in hand just as pregnancy and childbirth go hand in hand'.[53] I have to say that I regard this as an important indicator of the relationship between *McFarlane, Parkinson* and *Rees*. Firstly, if it applies to *Rees*, it should, in logic, apply to the birth of a healthy child irrespective of the health of the mother – and, by implication, it should also involve responsibility for the ordinary costs; while

---

[51] ibid., at [22]. Rather surprisingly, Hoyano, n. 22 above, finds this passage unacceptable insofar as it forces the parents of healthy children born following a failed sterilisation to depict themselves as inadequate parents incapable of ensuring the child is looked after properly if they are to win exemption from the *McFarlane* rule. For my part, it seems to do no more than recognise the de facto situation.

[52] ibid., at [23].   [53] ibid., at [24].

admitting that it probably represents no more than a lost cause, I will return to this briefly when discussing *Rees* in the House of Lords. More importantly, I see it as providing a significant distinction between *Parkinson* and *Rees*. In the latter case, the surgeon *knows* he or she is treating a disabled mother; in doing so, he or she is clearly accepting a special responsibility. By contrast, there is no way by which a sterilising surgeon can *know* that his or her negligence will lead to the birth of a disabled child – and, as has been argued above at p. 155, it is difficult to accept that such an outcome must even be anticipated. For this reason alone – and there are others – it is illogical to regard *Rees* as no more than a gloss on – or a legitimate extension of[54] – *Parkinson*; the conditions in each are different and the cases are different. There is no reason to assume that special damages should be available in one *simply because* compensation has been admitted in the other. On the other hand, once one accepts this view of the doctor's responsibilities, there is little reason to cavil at Robert Walker LJ's support for Hale LJ on the grounds that there is 'nothing unfair, unjust, unreasonable, unacceptable or morally repugnant in permitting recovery of compensation for a limited range of expenses which . . . have a very close connection with the mother's visual impairment'.[55]

Waller LJ's dissent was, however, powerfully argued and was widely quoted later in the House of Lords. He emphasised the dangers of undermining the *McFarlane* rule concerning a healthy child and gave a number of reasons why it might be unfair to the healthy mother whose social wellbeing might be equally affected by unwanted parenthood.[56] Even so, the Court of Appeal held, by a majority, that Ms Rees was entitled to recover the extra costs in bringing up a child that were imposed by her condition.[57] The Health Trust appealed the decision and, thereby, introduced a direct attack on the *McFarlane* decision; the stage was, thus, set for a major confrontation in the House of Lords.

Rees *in the House of Lords*

It was always apparent that *Rees* v. *Darlington Memorial Hospital NHS Trust*[58] was likely to be argued as something of a hybrid case. Looked at

---

[54] As per Robert Walker LJ, ibid., at [41].   [55] ibid., at [37].

[56] ibid., at [55]. To which Robert Walker LJ replied that these provided no reason for not making the attempt to assess the individual case.

[57] But it is to be noted that the nature of the excess costs was never properly explored.

[58] [2004] AC 309, [2003] 4 All ER 987. Again, I have written previously at some length on this case in J. K. Mason, 'From Dundee to Darlington: An End to the *McFarlane* Line?' [2004] *Juridical Review* 365–386 and this forms the basis for the discussion that follows.

from one angle, it was a straightforward appeal from the decision of the Court of Appeal. At the same time, the confrontational nature of the case and the composition of the Committee as a seven-judge bench particularly invited the House to step back and reconsider its own decision in *McFarlane*. The decision rested on a bare 4 to 3 majority and, as might be expected, the reasons underlying the opinions again varied markedly and the case opened up a number of innovative variations on tort law. In its way, the whole legal panorama of 'the troubled pregnancy' supports the recent *cri de coeur* from Australia: 'The time may have come when the traditional individuality of the English (and Australian) final–appellate judge should give way to a more collegial style of opinion-writing deigned to produce an agreed majority position on the main points in a case.'[59] Meantime, faced with seven disparate opinions, we must settle into the role of Snow White as best we can.

The scope of the appeal. The fundamental issue before the House appears in full in Lord Steyn's speech at [26]:

In the light of the decision of the House of Lords in *McFarlane* v. *Tayside Health Board* [2000] AC 59, where a person who suffers from a physical disability undergoes a negligently performed sterilisation operation, conceives, gives birth to a healthy child and, as a consequence of the birth of the child incurs:
(a) costs of bringing up the healthy child which would be incurred by a healthy parent; and
(b) additional costs of bringing up the healthy child which would not be incurred by a healthy parent and which are incurred because of the particular parent's disability;
which of those costs of bringing up the healthy child (if any) may be recovered by the parent in an action in negligence brought against the person responsible for the performance of the sterilisation.

On this basis, the main concern of the House was to ratify, or reverse, the findings of the Court of Appeal in *Rees*[60] and this was to be done while bearing the *McFarlane* decision in mind. The formulation contains no inherent threat to *McFarlane* – rather, the conditions of that case are impliedly accepted. The answer to a relatively straightforward question does not, however, justify a seven-judge bench and the Presiding Judge, Lord Bingham, summarised the practical situation as:

The appellant NHS trust now challenges that decision [in the Court of Appeal] as inconsistent with *McFarlane*. The claimant seeks to uphold the decision, but also

---

[59] Cane, n. 44 above.   [60] n. 47 above.

claims the whole cost of bringing up the child, inviting the House to reconsider its decision in *McFarlane*.[61]

Thus, on both counts, the emphasis has shifted and the case has, simultaneously, become an appeal to and about *McFarlane*. Even so, in the event, the claimants opted to revert to the *fons et origo* of the problem and to base their case on a challenge to the decision in *McFarlane* itself.

Should McFarlane *be reconsidered?* It is a consistent feature of the appeal that, despite being equipped, able[62] and invited to do so, the House effectively refused to reappraise their decision in *McFarlane*. The leading statement is that of Lord Bingham who said (at [7]):

> I am of the clear opinion . . . that it would be wholly contrary to the practice of the House to disturb its unanimous decision in *McFarlane* given as recently as 4 years ago, even if a differently constituted committee were to conclude that a different solution should have been adopted. It would reflect no credit on the administration of the law if a line of English authority were to be disapproved in 1999 and reinstated in 2003 with no reason for the change beyond a change in the balance of judicial opinion.

Lord Millett[63] quoted Lord Wilberforce, with approval, as having said: 'it requires much more than doubts as to the correctness of the previous decision to justify departing from it'[64] and he considered that the established criteria for so doing were nowhere near satisfied in *McFarlane*.

Among the ultimate minority, Lord Steyn, while accepting that it could be done, quoted similarly powerful authority to the effect that it would be highly undesirable if litigants could return to the House 'in the hope that a differently constituted committee might be persuaded to take the view which its predecessors rejected'.[65] Thus, the facts that the decision was controversial and that the individual decisions in *McFarlane* were based on different premises are immaterial.

An interesting feature of the discussion is that the precedents quoted[66] involved intervals of eleven years – in effect, *McFarlane*, covering a matter of four years, never stood a chance and one can easily empathise with their Lordships' anxiety not to indulge in see-saw lawmaking. At the same

---

[61] n. 58 above, at AC [1]. This seems to have changed at some point in the proceedings as Lord Steyn remarks that the case for the claimant at the hearing was restricted to seeking to recover the extra costs resulting from Ms Rees' disability (at [26]).

[62] *Practice Statement (Judicial Precedent)* [1966] 1 WLR 1234. And see *R* v. *Shivpuri* [1986] 2 WLR 988.

[63] n. 58 above, at AC [102].

[64] In *Fitzleet Estates Ltd* v. *Cherry* [1997] 3 All ER 996 at 999, [1977] 1 WLR 1345 at 1349.

[65] n. 58 above, at AC [32].

[66] Including *R* v. *Knuller (Publishing, Printing and Promotions) Ltd* [1973] AC 435.

time, the man in the street might well think that, if something is wrong, the sooner it is put right, the better. No-one could, or should, legitimately attempt to tell the House of Lords how to run its business but one can still wonder about it – and, like it or not, there *is* a whiff of obduracy in some of the statements. 'The most that can be said', said Lord Millett, 'is that the decision was controversial', which is not a very satisfactory reason for avoiding further controversy. And if 'a change in the balance of judicial opinion' is an insufficient ground on which to alter judge-made law, then, again, the supposed arbiter of distributive justice is entitled to ask what *is* sufficient? Supposing, then, that the precedental hurdles had not been insurmountable,[67] what might have been the result? For once, the House of Lords left us in no doubt – at least six of the seven judges confirmed their agreement with the *McFarlane* decision as it stands.

Lord Bingham (at [7]) would not be persuaded that the policy considerations which he thought drove the decision had lost their potency. Lord Nicholls (at [16]) had heard nothing in the submissions advanced to persuade him that *McFarlane* was wrong. Lord Steyn (at [33]), while accepting that the decision represented a least bad choice, thought it to be sound. Lord Scott (at [143]) posited, with good reason, that the majority in the Court of Appeal in *Rees* thought that the decision in *McFarlane* was wrong but, nevertheless, thought, himself, that that case was correctly decided. Lord Hope (at [50]), while agreeing that the House should not depart from that decision, added: 'even if some of your Lordships had been persuaded that they would have decided the case differently'. Neither Lord Hutton (at [86]) nor Lord Millett (at [103]) would have departed from the unanimous decision of the House in *McFarlane* even if, after further reflection, they had thought it was wrong.

Thus, the greater part of the claimants' case in *Rees* – that is, the challenge to the *McFarlane* decision – was stillborn. We need, therefore, only consider the alternative question – is the Court of Appeal decision in *Rees* compatible with that of the House of Lords in *McFarlane*?

McFarlane, Parkinson *and* Rees *in perspective*

The agreed remit in *Rees*, as we have seen, made no reference to *Parkinson*.[68] Yet it is clear that that case could not be avoided. As Lord Steyn emphasised (at [27]), *Parkinson*, in deciding that a case involving

---

[67] And Lord Steyn quoted *Miliangos* v. *George Frank (Textiles) Ltd* [1976] AC 443 as admitting the possibility.

[68] Indeed, both Lord Millett (at [112]) and Lord Scott (at [145]) specifically noted that *Parkinson* is not involved in the Appeal. Lord Millett 'would wish to keep the point open'.

the birth of a disabled child falls outside the principle laid down in *McFarlane*, has some bearing on the ultimate decision in *Rees* even if it is relevant only by way of analogy.

Lord Millett (at [101]) posed the question even more clearly: are the conditions surrounding *Rees* to be seen as a legitimate and natural extension of *Parkinson* or is *Rees* governed by the overriding principle established in *McFarlane*? We cannot know the answer to this without looking back and asking whether the division of wrongful pregnancy cases on the grounds of neonatal disability that was envisaged by Lords Steyn and Clyde in *McFarlane* was theoretical or real. Unfortunately, since *Parkinson*, which alone poses that basic question in relatively uncomplicated fashion, has not been argued in the House of Lords, we can only theorise as to the answer.

Any analysis of the relationship must begin with the cornerstone fact that *McFarlane* dealt with a wrongful pregnancy resulting in the birth of a healthy child; although the question was not considered, the coincidence of healthy parents must either be assumed or regarded as irrelevant to the ultimate decision. *Parkinson*, in being concerned with a disabled child, deals with an alternative scenario that is quite distinct from that surrounding *McFarlane*. In genealogical terms, it is a sibling of *McFarlane* rather than a descendant – and, this being so, it is perfectly appropriate to accept the two decisions as being compatible. *Rees*, however, is a new variant which was not envisaged in *McFarlane*. Thus, its place in the hierarchy remains to be determined.

The view of the Court of Appeal, typified in the judgment of Robert Walker LJ,[69] appears, by analogy, to be that *Rees* and *Parkinson* both accept that disability on either side of the parent/child relationship distinguishes them from *McFarlane* to an equal extent. To accept one is to accept the other – if *Parkinson* was right, then the same principles apply to *Rees*.[70] The alternative view was, however, well expressed by Lord Millett in the House of Lords. He identified the central issue as being the health of the child – in which case, *McFarlane* and *Rees*, as has been suggested above, are on a par. As he put it: 'the decision of the Court of Appeal in the present case is not a legitimate extension of *Parkinson*, but an illegitimate gloss on *McFarlane*' (at [113]). In other words, the Court of Appeal ruling in *Rees* is, prima facie, incompatible with *McFarlane* and, so long as

---

[69] n. 47 above, at [41].

[70] This reaches the same conclusion but is based on a slightly different premise from that of Hale LJ who depended on her 'deemed equilibrium' between the advantages and disadvantages of 'normal' parenthood – anything that upsets that equilibrium represents a deviation from *McFarlane* (see *Rees*, n. 37 above, at [23]).

the latter cannot be overturned, the appeal to the Lords in *Rees* must succeed.

Speaking from the minority in the House of Lords, Lord Steyn also accepted that the health of the child is central to *McFarlane* and, accordingly, distinguished *Parkinson* as standing alone. When it came to *Rees*, however, he conceded that holding the health of the mother to be a significant factor in the award of damages creates serious difficulties – in particular, that of arbitrariness. It was, said His Lordship, 'unrealistic to say that there is only one right answer' to *Rees* and, at the same time, it was 'logically not straightforward to treat *Rees* as simply an extension of *Parkinson*' (at [39]) – a view with which, as has become apparent, this writer is in entire agreement. His alternative reason for following the Court of Appeal is, however, less satisfying. To say: 'I am persuaded that the injustice of denying to such a seriously disabled mother the limited remedy of the extra costs caused by her disability outweighs the considerations emphasised by Waller LJ' seems a rather negative way of making a positive decision.[71] In offering specific approval to Robert Walker LJ,[72] he may well be introducing a new head of argument – that is, the importance of the developing law on disability and the need to ensure compatibility between the statutory and judicial approaches in this field. This aspect of the case was particularly emphasised by Lord Hope (at [63]–[69]) who pointed out that the aim of anti-discrimination law was to provide 'civil rights for disabled people whose impairment affects their ability to carry out normal day-to-day activities'. This might provide a wholly different route by which to distinguish *Rees* as a distinct, free-standing entity and is one which has much to commend it.[73] Even so, it is not easy to see why the particular tortfeasor under consideration should be held liable to implement government policy; for this, Lord Hope's reference to the surgeon's prior knowledge (at [63]), and which has been discussed already at p. 166 above, is greatly to be preferred.

Lord Hutton (at [98]), however, again speaking from the minority, approached the problem from the opposing viewpoint. He recognised that, as agreed by all members of the Committee, Mrs McFarlane would have been entitled to damages under the normal rules of tort law; *McFarlane* was, therefore, the exception and, in his view, it was possible to say that the exception would not apply when either the mother or the

---

[71] It does, of course, crystallise the reason why I, with all due deference, am at loggerheads with their Lordships in general. At the risk of being repetitive, I see the *basic* injustice, from which all the later problems spring, as being the denial of maintenance costs to Mr and Mrs McFarlane.

[72] n. 47 above, at [41].   [73] Despite Hoyano's very firm rejection noted in n. 51 above.

child was disabled. This is a neat debating point but it does little to *justify* the Court of Appeal in either *Parkinson* or *Rees*. Effectively, it seems to be saying no more than that, if *McFarlane* is immutable, then let us isolate it in whatever way we can so that its wayward effect on the law of tort can be limited. *McFarlane* would, then, exonerate the negligent practitioner only on its own strict terms and, that being the case, his or her responsibility for reparation is restored when those terms are varied – in the present context, either, and equally, on the physical or mental state of the mother or those of the neonate.[74]

The differences of opinion expressed have significant repercussions in respect of liability and it is important to bear in mind that both *McFarlane* and *Parkinson* are cases of wrongful pregnancy. For all practical purposes, there was no reason to suppose that Mrs Parkinson's baby would be disabled – the matter, it seems, was discussed only in general terms. It follows that the professional responsibility in terms of outcome is the same in each case. Ms Rees was, however, known to be disabled and it is suggested that, because of this, the duty of care is that much more compelling in her case than in that of either Mrs McFarlane or Mrs Parkinson.[75] It could, of course, be said that the duty to accomplish a sterilisation with due care is the same in any event[76] and, to that extent, the discussion may be considered sterile – it certainly does little to lessen the jurisprudential confusion which is the legacy of *Rees*.[77]

One positive result of the decision in *Rees*, however, is to clarify the distinction between the wrongful pregnancy case resulting in a disabled neonate and the wrongful birth action which has the same result. As Lord Bingham pointed out (at [9(1)]), the doctor did not *cause* the disability in either Ms Rees' or Mrs Parkinson's case;[78] it is, therefore, anomalous that he or she should be responsible for the rearing costs in excess of those

---

[74] I have to admit that this assessment probably exceeds Lord Hutton's true intentions.

[75] Lord Hope (n. 58 above, at AC [63]) thought, on balance, that the fact that the parent was seriously disabled provided grounds for distinguishing *McFarlane* and that it would be right to hold that 'such extra costs as can be attributed to the disability are within the tortfeasor's duty of care and are recoverable'. Cf. Lord Millett (ibid., at [120]) – the mother's disability is not the responsibility of the defendants at all.

[76] See, for example, Nicky Priaulx, 'Parental Disability and Wrongful Conception' [2003] *Family Law* 117–20.

[77] Lord Millett (n. 58 above at AC [116]) points to a somewhat contrary circumstance – that, while the disadvantages of a child's disability persist throughout childhood, the disadvantages of a healthy child to a disabled mother diminish as the child matures. This view was challenged in a review of the case by S. Singer, '*Rees* v. *Darlington Memorial Hospital NHS Trust* [2004] 1 AC 309' [2004] 26 *Journal of Social Welfare and Family Law* 403–15.

[78] An idea of the complex interplay of the three cases is given by Lord Bingham's reference to *Parkinson* at this point.

available in the case of a healthy child. Or, to quote from Lord Scott in similar vein:

In a case where the parents have had no particular reason to fear that, if a child is born to them, it will suffer from a disability, I do not think there is any sufficient basis for treating the expenses occasioned by the disability as falling outside the principles underlying *McFarlane*.[79]

The same does not apply in the wrongful birth case where the negligent genetic counsellor, using the term in its widest sense, is directly responsible for the existence of a *disabled* child. It follows that the decisions in cases such as those of *Rand* and *Hardman*[80] are unaffected by *Rees*.

In summarising this section, it is fair to say that, closely related though they are both conceptually and temporally, there is no logical continuum to be discerned between *McFarlane*, *Parkinson* and *Rees*.[81] In the end, the conclusion is forced that the three cases are close but distinct, despite sharing a common origin – that is, the union of a sterilisation operation and professional negligence. The concept of a *McFarlane* line, such as I have tried to develop, is illusory and the ultimate decision in *Rees*, as expressed both by the majority and minority, supports this view.[82]

Deconstructing the decision in Rees

The definitive decision of the House of Lords in *Rees*, taken by a majority of 4 to 3, was to allow the appeal of the NHS Trust against the award of expenses to a disabled mother over and above those which would be incurred by a healthy mother for the upkeep of a child born as the result of a negligent sterilisation operation. The ramifications of the appeal were, however, widespread and it is unsurprising that the greater part of the opinions was directed to the collateral issues which have been discussed above. When it came to the basic question, however, the speeches were quite succinct – despite being, inevitably, open to argument.

The majority opinion. Lord Bingham (at [9]) gave three reasons for allowing the appeal. First, the rule established in the Court of Appeal

---

[79] n. 58 above, at AC [145].   [80] For which, see Chapter 3.

[81] Ben Golder, 'From *McFarlane* to *Melchior* and beyond: Love, Sex, Money and Commodification in the Anglo-Australian Law of Torts' (2004) 12 *Torts Law Journal* 128 found a tenuous progression and, as a result, categorised the UK jurisprudence on the subject as revealing 'both a doctrinal incertitude and a political vacillation' (at 139).

[82] As Lord Steyn put it (n. 58 above, at AC [37]), an award of damages in *Rees* is only possible if an exception to *McFarlane* is created – 'it is logically not straightforward to treat [*Rees*] as simply an extension of *Parkinson*'s case' (ibid., at [39]).

would lead to anomalies such as were highlighted by Waller LJ in his dissenting opinion and, in this, Lord Bingham was supported by Lord Nicholls (at [18]). But, as Lord Hutton said (at [96]), such difficulties should not deter the Court from coming to a decision. Second, it is undesirable that parents, in order to recover compensation, should be encouraged to portray either their children or themselves as disabled – but this cannot be avoided when the description is a matter of obvious fact. And, third, the quantification of additional costs attributable to disability is a task of acute difficulty in a state with a strong social services tradition – but, again, that is scarcely a satisfying reason for not trying.[83]

Lord Millett also emphasised the difficulty of assessing the costs of bringing up a child but recalled that they were not recoverable on *McFarlane* principles even though they were reasonably attributable. In principle, he held, the same must be true of the disabled parent (at [114]) – the distinction of what costs are reasonable 'cannot be drawn on the line which distinguishes the disabled parent from the normal, healthy one' (at [115]). Lord Scott also reverted to *McFarlane* – all the features in that case that justified creating an exception from the normal principles of tort law were present in *Rees* (at [142]). To follow the Court of Appeal was to accept an exception to *McFarlane* and 'an exception to an exception is apt to produce messy jurisprudence' (at [143]). Such views are hard to refute once it is accepted that it is the presence of a normal baby – and *only* the presence of a normal baby – that defines what is an unreasonable head of damages on which to found a claim for wrongful pregnancy.

The minority case. Lord Steyn, who also specifically approved the *Parkinson* decision on the grounds of corrective justice,[84] dismissed the appeal but he seemed unhappy with the evidence on which he had to base his decision. Ultimately (at [39]), his case rested on the *injustice* of denying a limited remedy to a seriously disabled mother rather than on the *justice* of providing a remedy for the victim of medical negligence – and this is probably the only line available once *McFarlane* is regarded as written in stone.

Lord Hope, having agreed with *Parkinson* on the grounds that the extra costs involved in the rearing of a disabled child were recoverable as a matter of legal policy, concluded, on balance, that the fact that a child's

---

[83] 'Viewing the decision of the two House of Lords cases from the perspective of the law on child maintenance reinforces the conclusion . . . that assessing the cost of having children and dividing the cost of upbringing from financial provision can be a normal uncontroversial legal exercise': Singer, n. 77 above.

[84] But this depended upon the case being recognisably distinct from *McFarlane* – i.e. that the exception dictated by a healthy child did not apply.

parent is seriously disabled also provides a ground for distinguishing *McFarlane* and that it is fair, just and reasonable to hold that such extra costs are within the scope of the tortfeasor's liability (at [63]). Lord Hope admitted his difficulty in reaching this conclusion. He explained, however, that it was the inescapable fact of her disability which distinguished the seriously disabled parent from those who were disadvantaged by way of lifestyle or to other social conditions which were beyond their control. He also argued, convincingly, that, by allowing the seriously disabled parent to recover the extra costs of child rearing which were due to her disability, the law would be doing its best to enable her to undertake the task on equal terms with those who were not affected by impairment – that is, it would be actively supporting an anti-discrimination policy (at [68]). Lord Hutton followed almost identical reasoning and, having agreed that *Parkinson* was correctly decided on the basis of the *Caparo* test, had no difficulty in transferring this reasoning to *Rees*. As has been already remarked, he concluded that the exception to the normal rules of tort law created by *McFarlane* does not apply when *either* the child *or* its mother is disabled (at [98]).

The approaches of both the majority and minority in *Rees* give rise to some dissatisfaction insofar as, at base, they are founded on negative approaches. The former are concerned to say why Ms Rees should *not* succeed; the main thrust of the minority lies in showing that *McFarlane* is *not* undermined. I suggest that part of the difficulty lies in the judicial concentration on the *costs* involved in both cases. The woman concerned in all the relevant cases has, however, already been awarded damages related to the *pain, suffering and discomfort* associated with pregnancy and childbirth. Could this not be extended in the case of the disabled mother to include the added suffering associated with childcare that is imposed *by reason of* her disability? Taking this route absolves us from quantifying the value of a child and focuses *positively* on the one factor that distinguishes Ms Rees from Mrs McFarlane. The latter is subjected to the trials of normal motherhood; the former carries out her duties in conditions of added discomfort and, perhaps, pain – moreover, as already intimated, it is additional discomfort and pain that is *clearly foreseeable* by he or she who is responsible for the pregnancy. This approach does not seem to have been considered in any of the arguments advanced but it is not so far fetched as might appear. It is not difficult to combine the views of Hale LJ in the Court of Appeal[85] with those of Lord Hope in the House of Lords[86] and to conclude that both appear to be at least toying with the concept of

---

[85] n. 47 above, at QB [22].   [86] n. 58 above, at AC [65].

injury to the mother. It seems a pity that that route – which, by concentrating on the mother, loosens the straitjacketing circumstance of the normal child[87] – was not explored further.

The conscience of the Lords

Lord Millett's original and lone plea that Mr and Mrs McFarlane should not be sent away empty-handed[88] received scant notice when he proposed it. There is little doubt, however, that, by the time *Rees* was heard, the mood of the House had changed and the tone of the opinions delivered on both sides in the latter case strongly suggests that their Lordships nurtured a general concern that justice was, at least, not being seen to be done under the pure *McFarlane* rule. This was epitomised by Lord Nicholls (at [17]):

An award of some amount should be made to recognise that in respect of the birth of the child the parent has suffered a legal wrong, a legal wrong having a far-reaching effect on the lives of the parent and any family she may already have.

And the answer lay with Lord Bingham who, in the leading speech for the majority, proposed that: 'in all cases such as these there be a conventional award to mark the injury and loss'.

This 'conventional award' provides possibly the most complex and controversial aspect of the *Rees* judgment – indeed, it is hard to find a commentator who does not, at this point, start to scratch his or her head. This is not because of any disapproval of some form of recompense for a woman who has been wronged – far from it, although we will return to the particular position of Mrs Parkinson below. The interest lies, rather, in the manner of its bestowal and its consequent effects on the existing – and future[89] – jurisprudence. The award was approved by four of their Lordships but Lord Bingham's opinion provides us with the reasoning that justifies it.

Lord Bingham very clearly had doubts as to the fairness of a rule which denies the victim of a wrongful pregnancy any recompense at all beyond that designed to compensate for the immediate effects of pregnancy and

---

[87] And also avoids perpetuating 'pathologising assumptions about the effects of parental disability on children' – Nicky Priaulx, 'That's One Heck of an "Unruly Horse"! Riding Roughshod over Autonomy in Wrongful Conception' (2004) 12 *Feminist Legal Studies* 317–31. See also the objections of Hayano, n. 51 above.

[88] *McFarlane* v. *Tayside Health Board* [2000] 2 AC 59 at 114, 2000 SC 1 at 44.

[89] Singer, n. 77 above, remarks: '*Rees* has provided an interesting precedent for judges to avoid the strict application of the principles they expound by creating novel remedies to detract attention from obvious injustices' (at 414).

birth – that part of the claim identified as 'the mother's claim' in
McFarlane.[90] Accordingly, he proposed an award of £15,000 to all
women who are the victims of a wrongful pregnancy irrespective of
whether the parent or the child is healthy or unhealthy or claims to be
unhealthy; he would award this over and above that authorised in settle-
ment of the 'mother's claim' (at [8]).[91] Two conjoined questions arise –
what were his reasons for such a surprise recommendation and what did
he intend it to achieve? As Cane has said, its adoption by the House could,
not unreasonably, be seen as a result of no more than 'a change in the
balance of judicial opinion'.[92]

There are, indeed, some aspects of his Lordship's speech which give
rise to more that a little analytical concern. The proposal was justified, for
example, on the grounds that:

The members of the House who gave judgment in *McFarlane* recognised [that
wrong had been done] by holding, in each case, that some awards should be made
to Mrs McFarlane (although Lord Millett based this on a ground which differed
from that of the other members and he would have made a joint award to Mr and
Mrs McFarlane).

This is difficult to reconcile with what was actually said in *McFarlane*
where the House agreed[93] that only 'the mother's claim' for the pain and
suffering of pregnancy and childbirth should succeed. Lord Millett's
proposal for an award of £5,000 was made independently and was contingent upon there being no other recognition of the wrong done to the
claimants.[94] Lord Bingham's proposal, being additional to the mother's
claim, is, therefore, distinct from that originally outlined by Lord Millett;
as a result, and as it is to be allowed across the whole spectrum of wrongful
pregnancy cases, it appears to modify the *McFarlane* ruling significantly –
as Priaulx puts it: 'Quite simply, *McFarlane* no longer stands as good law
in the light of *Rees*.'[95]

There is considerable force behind this comment. Lords Bingham and
Nicholls spoke of it being a gloss on the ruling, but surely it is more than

---

[90] Which does, of course, mirror the feelings of all those who disagreed with the *McFarlane*
decision – including, it has to be said, the majority in the High Court of Australia in
Cattanach, discussed in detail in the preceding chapter.

[91] Cane, n. 44 above, regarded it as 'most unfortunate' that Lord Bingham did not define
'all cases such as these' (at 190).

[92] n. 44 above at 190 quoting Lord Bingham himself at [7].

[93] n. 88 above, Lord Millett dissenting on logical grounds at AC 114, SC 44.

[94] ibid., at AC 114, SC 45.

[95] n. 87 above at 327. It is to be noted that Priaulx, and feminist writers in general, find little
or no satisfaction in the award as recognition of the interference with the woman's
autonomy – largely on the grounds that it generalises a situation that is intensely personal.

that? At the very least, it looks like silver-plating; to quote Lord Steyn, 'it is a radical and most important development which should only be embarked on after rigorous examination of competing arguments'.[96] What, then, were their Lordships' individual justifications of and objections to the award?

Lord Bingham (at [8]) spoke of a *recognition* of harm done but defined that in negative terms. 'The conventional award would not be compensatory', he said. 'It would not be the product of calculation. But it would not be a nominal, let alone a derisory award.' It affords 'a more ample measure of justice than the pure *McFarlane* rule' – and, significantly, the implication is that Lord Bingham would make the award to the mother rather than to the parents, thus, perhaps, supporting the concept of continuing personal injury that I have suggested at p. 175. Lord Nicholls (at [18]) regarded it as a way of avoiding a means-tested analysis of the injury done – and, thereby, impliedly, accepted it as a form of compensation. Lord Millett (at [123]) followed much the same line in awarding the parents 'a modest conventional sum by way of general damages'. He reminded us that his original proposal in *McFarlane* was not conceived as an alternative to the mother's claim – he would have made his award to both parents; and, insofar as the matter was not discussed in the course of *McFarlane*, he believed that this could still be done without prejudice to that decision. Lord Scott (at [148]) went the furthest of the majority and regarded the award as compensation for lack of due care in performing the operation; it was open to the court to put a monetary value on the deprivation of a benefit the woman expected – that is, her sterility.

In the light of all of which, one cannot but help feel that Lord Hope (at [74]) was justified in being disturbed at 'the lack of any consistent or coherent ratio in support of the proposition'. Lord Hope also pursued the negative line in pointing out that the award is in no sense punitive and, at this point, it seems that we are running out of possible purposive options. An immediate emotional reaction is to see the award as a form of conscience money or as a charity designed to offset the sense of injustice left by the original *McFarlane* decision. To do this, however, is to risk relegating the decision to what Lord Steyn suggested might be 'a backdoor evasion of the legal policy enunciated in *McFarlane*' (at [46]) without adequate consideration of what was the form of the wrong that Lord Bingham recognised as needing to be righted.

---

[96] See also Lord Hope (n. 58 above, at AC [74]).

Lord Bingham, himself, saw the mother as having been denied, through the negligence of another, the opportunity to live her life in the way that 'she had wished and planned'.[97] This implies a long-term 'detriment' and one is reminded of Hale LJ's vivid description of motherhood in *Parkinson*.[98] Lord Millett, by contrast, saw the wrong as a denial of the parents' right to limit the size of their family (at [123]) but, since he then went on to concur with Lord Bingham, any distinction that is made between the two approaches may be one without a practical difference.[99]

Not unexpectedly, the validity of the award was directly questioned, especially by Lord Steyn (at [45]) who felt strongly that there is no United Kingdom authority that provides the courts with power to make such an award; he went so far as to suggest that, to do so, is to stray into forbidden territory – territory that is strictly within the fiefdom of Parliament. At the same time, none of the Law Lords in *Rees* opposed the understanding that, given an orthodox application of the law of tort, persons in the position of Mrs McFarlane or Ms Rees would be allowed full damages against the tortfeasor for the cost of rearing the unsolicited child. However one likes to look at it, in the end, the *McFarlane* decision removes this right on the grounds of legal policy. Any conflict between a legal right and legal policy is normally settled at the stage of recognition of that right. In *McFarlane*, it is being resolved at the stage of quantification of compensation for breach of a right – which is a new departure. The majority of the House, however, then decided that the fact that Ms Rees was disabled could not, of itself, justify making an exception to *McFarlane* in hers and similar cases. They were, thus, on the horns of a self-made dilemma – and this must be the anomaly that the House was anxious to set aside.

Consequently, by far the most important feature of *Rees* lies in the introduction of the concept of a wrong comprised of an affront to autonomy – whether this be that of one or both of the principals.[100] This derives from insult to that element of personal autonomy which is vested in freedom of choice. We can, then, revert to Lord Bingham and view the award as no more than a form of recognition of a wrong having been done for which there is no other appropriate form of reparation.[101]

---

[97] It is to be remembered that the claimant in this case was a single mother. It is not absolutely clear whether, in other circumstances, the award would go the parents.

[98] n. 10 above at [63]–[71]. This raises some misgivings as to whether £15,000 constitutes a suitable recognition.

[99] Priaulx, n. 87 above, at 326 is particularly critical of Lord Millett's attempt to dissociate the effects of the birth of a child from the right to limit one's family.

[100] It was also introduced by Hale LJ, n. 10 above, at [66].

[101] The House of Lords is clearly moving towards this line of reasoning. A similar 'autonomy' position was adopted in *Chester* v. *Afshar* [2005] 1 AC 134, [2004] 4 All

But one still as to ask if this goes sufficiently far to lead to the conclusion that justice has been done. Granted that a wrong has been done, surely there *ought* to be a remedy and, indeed, Lord Millett believed that, whether one regards the opportunity to exercise one's autonomy as a right or as a freedom, its loss *is* a proper subject for compensation by way of damages (at [123]). In this writer's view, the scene would be transformed were such a new head of damages to be admitted. It would allow us to visualise the award in terms of compensation;[102] should it be necessary, we could return to *McFarlane* freed of any 'sense of distaste or moral repugnance';[103] and, because the basis of any such action would be the same, the courts would be able to treat every variation on the wrongful pregnancy theme on its factual merits.[104]

Whether a fixed sum in the form of a 'conventional award' represents an adequate way of compensating for a variable injury is, however, still open to doubt.[105] Lord Millett might be right in saying that a modest award would adequately compensate for the injury to the parents' autonomy but he might not be. A figure of £15,000 was, at best, one which Lord Bingham 'had in mind' and it is more than likely that most people would share Lord Hope's doubts (at [77]) as to its universal application.[106] Lord Bingham leaves some other questions hanging in the air. For example, does the quantum attract the semi-permanency of other House of Lords' decisions? Can it be index-linked? In any event, is there any viable alternative or modification available?

An interesting consequence of recognising infringement of autonomy is that the House of Lords, at least as represented by Lords Bingham, Nicholls and Millett, is coming very close to the Scottish concept of *damnum* which we have already considered in Chapter 3. The *injuria* in

---

ER 587 which has been discussed in Chapter 3: 'Her right of autonomy and dignity can and ought to be vindicated by a narrow and modest departure from traditional causation principles' (per Lord Steyn, ibid., at AC [24]).

[102] Which is where Lord Scott, at least, thought it rightly lay (n. 58 above, at AC [148]).

[103] The words of Lord Millett (ibid., at [125]).

[104] For further discussion of autonomy – and on many aspects of 'the troubled pregnancy' see Stephen Todd, 'Wrongful Conception, Wrongful Birth and Wrongful Life' (2005) 27 *Sydney Law Review* 525–42.

[105] 'The conventional approach not only risks "pleasing no one", but if applied across the board to include cases of disabled children, will only further entrench the manifest unfairness that results from it's application': Nicolette M. Priaulx, 'Damages for the "Unwanted" Child: Time for a Rethink?' (2005) 73 *Medico-Legal Journal* 152–63. Priaulx also draws attention to the gender discriminatory attitude to reproductive autonomy that is inherent in the House of Lords' decisions. See also Golder, n. 81 above, for exposition of the feminist criticism.

[106] I fancy that a majority would agree with Singer, n. 77 above: 'At best, the figure of £15,000 for loss of reproductive and personal autonomy is nominal and, at worst, it is an affront to the female role of child-bearing.'

a case of wrongful pregnancy is either the negligent performance of the operation or the negligent provision of information; the concurrence of this with *damnum* – that is, the prejudice to the parents' interest in being able to choose whether or not to have any more children – then provides grounds for reparation. This principle was unanimously accepted in the Inner House hearing of *McFarlane* but, as Lord McCluskey pointed out, there is no satisfactory English word by which to express this construct.[107]

Although the concept of a conventional award has no place in Scots law, I believe that the way it was used in *Rees* brings the House of Lords and the Inner House so close in principle as to be separated by little more than semantics. Lord Slynn said: 'it is, as I understand it, accepted that the law of England and that of Scotland should be the same in respect of matters which arise [from *McFarlane*]'[108] – and there are good reasons why this should apply to principles as well as to actuality. By concentrating on an award for breach of autonomy – and by leaving open the door for true compensation to be paid – *Rees* may have furthered this aim and, indeed, may also have, in principle, bridged the seemingly unbridgeable gap between *McFarlane* and *Cattanach*.

Could this be applied in practice? Suppose we reconsider the wrongful pregnancy case and invoke the loss of a legal interest – or *damnum* – as a head of damage as *Rees* now allows us to do. Lord Hope (at [75]) drew attention to the near impossibility of assessing the appropriate conventional level of an award in such circumstances and it is certainly true that any standardised figure must involve a compromise. One way of achieving such a compromise and, hopefully, going some way to satisfying those supporting both sides of the argument, might be to assess the actual costs of the unexpected child and assign a proportion of this to 'injury to autonomy' such that, while the *full* costs of rearing a child were not provided, an amount of compensation that was neither excessive nor derisory was made available. In doing so, we would probably not offend the commuter on the London Underground and, thereby, we might satisfy the claims of distributive justice; at the same time, we could scarcely be said to have offended the spirit of *Caparo*; we would provide genuinely recognisable reparation for the affected parents and we have not over-stretched the resources of the National Health Service.[109] In short, we have established an ambience of fairness which all those involved in this difficult area have so earnestly sought and, perhaps

---

[107] *McFarlane* v. *Tayside Health Board* 1998 SLT 307 at 313.
[108] n. 88 above, at AC 68, SC 4. Despite being heard in the same House, *McFarlane* was, of course, still a Scottish case while *Rees* was English.
[109] See Lord Bingham, n. 58 above, at AC [6].

above all, we have eliminated the intense emotions which Kirby J found to provide such a poor basis for law making.[110] Given the premise that the proposal is based on a wholly different head of damages, there is no conflict with *McFarlane* and the House of Lords could rest easy and with a clear conscience.[111]

All of which seems neat and tidy – but it still carries a taint of sophistry Would it not have been better had the House taken the bull by the horns and, having carved an acceptable escape from the strict *McFarlane* rule, had allowed room for realistic compensation – including, perhaps, compensation that was variable on the facts of the case ? As things stand, the law on wrongful pregnancy is all but settled for the foreseeable future, yet it still remains an area in which uncertainty as to equity persists. It places the principals in *McFarlane* and *Rees* on a par – an end-point which the largest possible minority of the House regarded as unsatisfactory. And it leaves the *Parkinson* dilemma – the one specific problem left open in *McFarlane* – unresolved.

Mrs Parkinson's case revisited. Theoretically, Lord Bingham's juxtaposition of cases involving healthy and unhealthy mothers and children would include the *Parkinson* scenario within the ambit of the 'conventional award'. But, as Lords Millett and Scott reminded us (at [112] and [145]), *Parkinson* was not under consideration in *Rees*; Lord Bingham's observation is, therefore, obiter. On the other hand, although their reasons were not argued in depth, the three dissenting Law Lords in *Rees* specifically approved the Court of Appeal decision in *Parkinson*.[112] I confess to being in some difficulty here. One cannot fail intuitively to agree, say, with Lord Hutton that it may be fair, just and reasonable that a woman left with an uncovenanted and disabled baby should be entitled to an award of damages for the extra costs imposed by that disability. But it is extremely difficult to see that the doctor's *responsibility* is different in *McFarlane* and *Parkinson* – given that the disability in the latter was a matter of chance occurrence.[113] But, then, I have already flown my colours as to believing that, if one decision is wrong, it is *McFarlane*, not *Parkinson*.

---

[110] In *Cattanach*, n. 40 above, at [151].

[111] The further possibility that £50,000 could be regarded as a variable benchmark subject to the specific conditions of the case is left open. The possible difficulties expressed by Walker LJ, n. 56 above, at [52]–[55] are appreciated although they can be overcome – see Lord Hope in *Rees*, n. 58 above, at AC [76].

[112] ibid., Lord Steyn at [35]; Lord Hope at [57]; Lord Hutton at [91].

[113] Which is, of course, precisely the opposite argument to that used by Brooke LJ in *Parkinson* at [50] – and see Lord Scott, n. 58 above, at AC [147].

The fact that *Parkinson* is unresolved at the highest level could, of course, turn out to be an advantage or a disadvantage depending on one's viewpoint. A future Mrs Parkinson might well be disadvantaged by comparison with her prototype were her case to be subsumed under Lord Bingham's umbrella conventional award – for it is clear that her recompense under an unmodified *Parkinson* assessment might be considerably more than £15,000.[114] On the other hand, the higher court reviewing her case might find the means to alter the quantity of, if not the reason for, that award and, thus, improve the lot of the 'victims' of wrongful pregnancy as a whole. In any event, it seems that this is another lacuna that needs to be filled before the saga of the wrongful pregnancy case can be said to be completed.[115]

The proximity test

Rightly or wrongly, the *Caparo* test has been taken to represent the ratio of the decision in *McFarlane* and this has spilled over into the subsequent allied cases. The emphasis has, however, been very much on the 'fair, just and reasonable' containment of the extent to which liability for the economic losses resulting from negligence can be attributed. The remaining limbs of the test – those of foreseeability and proximity – have tended to get lost along the way.

Perhaps this is to be expected in respect of the former insofar as there is no question but that economic loss is a foreseeable outcome of the birth of a child, and this is irrespective of the health of that child or of its parents. Proximity is, however, a more variable consideration as opinions will differ as to the strength of the bond between the tortfeasor and his or her victim – we will, for example, see in Chapter 6 how arguable is the relationship between the negligent health carer and the fetus or child arising from that negligence. For the present, we can round off the discussion of maintenance costs that has occupied the last three chapters with a brief look at two cases which illustrate how the liability of these can be affected by the concept of proximity.

The first of these, *R* v. *Croydon Health Authority*,[116] considers the status of the incidental tortfeasor. Mrs R was seeking employment with the

---

[114] And this seems to be the message delivered by Lord Bingham (at [9]) and Lord Nicholls (at [19]).

[115] Clare Dixon, 'An Unconventional Gloss on Unintended Children' (2003) 153 *New Law Journal* 1732–3 pointed out that, while the conventional award would be additional to 'the mother's claim', it is still uncertain whether it will be added to any special damages available under the *Parkinson* decision. She thought it should be.

[116] (1998) 40 BMLR 40, [1998] Lloyd's Rep Med 4.

health authority and underwent a pre-employment chest X-ray. The radiologist failed to note a significant abnormality which should have been diagnostic of a condition known as primary pulmonary hypertension (PPH). This is an untreatable disease which significantly reduces life expectation and which, most importantly in the present context, is exacerbated by pregnancy. Soon after commencing employment, Mrs R became pregnant and was delivered of a healthy daughter. The diagnosis was established while she was on maternity leave, when she was informed of her poor prognosis and declared unfit for her demanding job. As a result, she developed reactive depression and retired on the grounds of ill-health.

Mrs R brought an action against the Authority the terms of which will be apparent from the findings of the trial judge who held:

- that the pregnancy itself was a foreseeable consequence of the failure to diagnose PPH;
- that pregnancy was so likely to have devastating consequences for a woman with PPH that it 'should have been in the forefront of the mind of a competent radiologist';
- that, if there had been no breach of duty, Mrs R would have been told of the dangers of pregnancy 'not only because of the threat to her life . . . but also because she would be giving birth to a child . . . to whom she would be unable to act as a normal mother';
- that, therefore, pregnancy and its consequences are the kind of damage from which the health authority must take care to save a plaintiff;[117]
- that Mrs R is, therefore, entitled to the reasonable costs of raising her child.

I have set these findings out in full because they demonstrate the profound sea change that *McFarlane* has forced upon judicial thinking. Even so, the scope of Astill J's attribution of liability was too much for the Court of Appeal even in 1997.

The major circumstance distinguishing Mrs R's case from any other reported case of wrongful pregnancy was that she wanted both a pregnancy and a healthy child – and she had both. There was, as Kennedy LJ put it, simply no loss which could give rise to a claim for damages in respect of either the normal expenses and trauma of pregnancy or the costs of bringing up the child – and, subject to Chadwick LJ's analysis of

---

[117] Kennedy LJ in the Court of Appeal at BMLR 45 pointed out that the judge concluded that there was no difference in principle between this case and other cases of 'unwanted births' arising out of failed sterilisation. It is clear that I would regard Mrs R's case as being one of 'unwanted pregnancy' and the Court in *R* v. *Croydon* consistently failed to make the distinction.

the chain of causation, to which we return below, it is almost impossible to argue to the contrary.[118] The Lord Justice did, however, concede that the radiologist's breach of duty deprived her of the opportunity to evaluate properly the arguments for and against pregnancy – and this brings us very close to the concept of an affront to autonomy which we have discussed in respect of Ms Rees's case. Would Mrs R have been entitled to an 'award' of £15,000 had it been available at the time? I believe she should have been, assuming that that is, in fact, the correct interpretation of the ratio of the award; whether she would have been is one of those matters that are left unsettled by Lord Bingham's relatively brief explanation of his reasoning.[119]

In point of fact, on the assumption that Mrs R would not have become pregnant had she been informed of the diagnosis when the evidence was available, Chadwick LJ was able to trace an unbroken chain of causation from the radiologist's failure to identify and report the pulmonary abnormality to the birth of her child; the only question for him was whether liability for her consequent distress and expenses lay within the vicarious duty owed her by the health authority. This question of proximity, which is the main, albeit not the only, interest of *R* v. *Croydon* in the present context,[120] was addressed in detail by Kennedy LJ who concluded that, even if the plaintiff's pregnancy could be regarded as an injury, that damage was too remote from the beach of duty to establish liability. On the one hand, the chain of events had too many links. On the other, a professional's duty, when undertaking an examination to assess a person's fitness for employment, is limited to observing and reporting on the abnormalities found and their relevance to the purpose of the examination.[121] The express obligations assumed by the radiologist did not, in Lord Justice Kennedy's opinion, extend to the plaintiff's private life. Mrs R's claim for damages for personal injures failed and was restricted to general damages for pain and suffering limited to those due to the complications of pregnancy attributable to PPH and to those later complications which would have been avoided had the diagnosis been made at the right time – and one cannot help feeling that even the most determined critic of the *McFarlane* decision would be forced to agree.

---

[118] In fact, the Authority, in somewhat ambiguous terms, admitted liability for the 'injury sustained during pregnancy' and Chadwick LJ was undecided as to what would have happened had that admission not been made (at BMLR 51).
[119] *Rees*, n. 58 above, at [8].
[120] Chadwick LJ was able also to call upon the fairness test elaborated in *Caparo*, n. 18 above.
[121] See also the almost contemporaneous employment case of *Kapfunde* v. *Abbey National plc and Daniel* (1998) 46 BMLR 176.

The second case, *AD* v. *East Kent Community NHS Trust*,[122] takes us into the realm of the proximity of the injured party and can be seen as little more than a variation on *Rees*: indeed, the Court of Appeal considered that, had Ms A been able to bring up her own child, they would have had to apply *Rees*.[123] Ms A's case was unlike any of those we have discussed thus far in that there was no negligent sterilisation and the antenatal care provided was faultless. Rather, the claimant was an intellectually disabled woman who was compulsorily detained under the Mental Health Act 1983. She became pregnant, and gave birth to a healthy daughter, having been housed in a mixed psychiatric ward. Effectively, she sued the responsible authority for the costs of maintaining her child who, it was contended, was the result of a 'wrongful pregnancy' consequent upon negligent supervision of the ward. The really significant deviation from *Rees* lay, however, in the fact that Ms A was incapable of looking after the child who was, in lieu, being cared for by Ms A's mother; Ms A contended that her birth was not a benefit and that the costs of maintenance were an additional burden that was being carried by the child's grandmother.[124]

The judge at first instance applied the jurisprudence developed in *McFarlane*, *Parkinson* and *Rees* and dismissed the claim. On appeal, Judge LJ, speaking for the court, started with *McFarlane* and concluded that, as a result of that decision, Ms A's claim for maintenance would have been unsustainable had she been able to bring up the child herself (at [12]). Attention was, however, focused on *Rees* which could, nonetheless, be distinguished on the basis that, whereas that case was decided by way of the *additional* costs imposed by the mother's disability, Ms A was claiming the full costs of upkeep – largely because there *were* no additional costs. It followed that the costs, which were being claimed on behalf of another person, were the same costs as had been disallowed since *McFarlane* was decided.

In a trenchant observation, Judge LJ drew an 'illuminating' comparison between the woman who loses earnings in order to look after a negligently injured child[125] and one who, similarly, loses earnings in order to be at home to care for a healthy child born as a result of negligent health

---

[122] [2003] 3 All ER 1167, (2003) 70 BMLR 230.

[123] ibid., at [15]. It has to be remembered, however, that *Rees* had not been heard in the House of Lords at the time *AD* was considered in the Court of Appeal.

[124] The action was brought by Ms A because a person providing voluntary services to a relative has no cause of action in his or her own right: *Hunt* v. *Severs* [1994] 2 AC 350, [1994] 2 All ER 385.

[125] Drawing on *Donnelly* v. *Joyce* [1974] QB 454, [1973] 3 All ER 475.

care.[126] 'No one doubts', he said, 'that the tortious defendant would be liable to pay damages to the injured child [in the former case]. Nevertheless, as we have already seen in *Greenfield*, losses sustained on the same basis (loss of earnings to be at home to care for a healthy child) were not recoverable by the mother who had been the victim of negligence by a hospital authority.'[127] Tellingly, he continued:

The difference is not accidental: it reflects the principle that even if the birth of the child resulted from medical negligence, damages are not recoverable to compensate for the cost of rearing a healthy child, notwithstanding that that identifiable expense can be established,

thus pre-empting the House of Lords' universal admission that *McFarlane* represents an exception to normal legal principle.

We can, then, take leave of this chapter in the realisation that judges may not always like the decisions that circumstances force them to take. In dismissing the appeal in *AD*, the Court of Appeal expressed great sympathy with and admiration for Mrs A. And that, surely, provides us with a fitting epitaph to the *McFarlane* case and its aftermath – the victims of wrongful pregnancy deserve more than tea and sympathy.

---

[126] Quoting *Greenfield* v. *Irwin (a firm)* [2001] 1 WLR 1279, (2001) 59 BMLR 43, see. p. 143 above.

[127] See n. 122 above, at [19].

6 Wrongful neonatal life

Introduction

Thus far, we have been dealing exclusively with the effects of the birth of an unwanted or unexpected child on its parents. But what of the child itself? We have seen throughout that public policy – whether expressed by the voice of the public itself or through the medium of the courts – strives to ensure that such a child is not made aware of the unusual circumstances of its conception and birth. We have also seen that, such is the nature of humanity, most children born as a result of negligence by third parties are accepted into the family as much loved additional members – and this includes many who are disabled.[1]

Thus, the healthy child, at least, is unlikely to resent his or her existence. There may, however, be circumstances in which a newborn child is so badly disabled that it may be inferred that he or she would rather not be alive. As Templeman LJ put it in the ground-breaking case of *Re B (a minor)*:

There may be cases of severe proved damage where the future is so certain and where the life of the child is so bound to be full of pain and suffering that the court *might* be driven to a different conclusion [than that the child must live] (emphasis added).[2]

But the doubts expressed by the Lord Justice serve to underline that we are, here, in uncharted waters for we cannot *know* what are the intentions and aspirations of a neonate who has never known an alternative

---

[1] This book is not, of course, concerned with the far greater number of children who are not actively sought but whose existence owes nothing to failure on the part of outside agencies. The fact that they exist in happy families must, however, be evidence that non-planning is not a frequent cause of psychological conflict between parents and children.

[2] *Re B (a minor) (wardship: medical treatment)* [1990] 3 All ER 927 at 929, [1981] 1 WLR 1421 at 1424. I believe this still represents the common law and do not accept the very limited meaning described by Ackner LJ in *McKay* v. *Essex Area Health Authority* [1982] QB 1166 at 1188. We will return to *Re B* in the next chapter.

situation. An action brought by a neonate against someone believed to be responsible for his or her 'wrongful life' is one brought on an assumption – and it cannot be denied that it is, in practice, activated by others who, in the modern jargon, often have their own agenda.

The wrongful life action in history

The essential feature of the wrongful life action is that it is brought by a disabled neonate. The fact that it is almost always accompanied by a complementary action on the part of the child's parents leads to confusion but is otherwise immaterial – the two will run independently of each other. At the same time, it is difficult to decide where and when the phrase 'wrongful life' originated – if it ever did as such. Capron suggested that the term 'wrongful life' was 'a play on the statutory tort of "wrongful death"' which, he said, had inspired judges in subsequent opinions to coin a number of related phrases.[3] Whoever is responsible, he or she certainly did the later plaintiffs no service as the implication that 'life' can, of itself, be wrongful, or a type of harm, has always been something that the courts – and perhaps even the general public – have found hard to accept. What the infant plaintiff finds 'wrong' is not that he or she is alive but, rather, that he or she is *alive and suffering* as a result of another's negligence and it is a widespread failure to appreciate this unity that has led to much of the confusion.[4]

The introduction of the concept of negligent *injury*, however, itself raises problems of definition. The umbrella of wrongful life does not include life with injuries of a type which could be prosecuted under the criminal law; furthermore, no-one is denying the *fundamental* right of a neonate to sue for physical injuries sustained *in utero*[5] as a result of civil negligence. Rather, in searching for a positive definition, we are considering the existence of a disabled child which, but for the negligence of

---

[3] Alexander Morgan Capron, 'Tort Liability in Genetic Counselling' (1979) 79 *Columbia Law Review* 618–84. In other words, the conventional categories of pre-natal torts, like Topsy, 'just growed'. The Court in the relatively recent US case of *Kassama* v. *Magat* 792 A 2d 1102 (Md., 2002), see n. 14 below, drew attention to the classification of troubled pregnancies provided in *Walker by Pizano* v. *Mart* 790 P 2d 735 (Ariz., 1990) but, although that court recognised the 'confusion as to the proper denomination of these prenatal torts' (at 737), no origin was suggested.

[4] Put another way, it is 'precisely by focusing on the plaintiff's *life* (as a whole), rather than negligent causation of physical damage, that courts have been led to misapply ordinary principles and thus deny recovery': Dean Stretton, 'The Birth Torts: Damages for Wrongful Birth and Wrongful Life' (2005) 10 *Deakin Law Review* 310–64.

[5] At least since *Burton* v. *Islington Health Authority, de Martell* v. *Merton and Sutton Health Authority* [1993] QB 204, [1992] 3 All ER 833, CA. We revisit the subject at p. 210.

the health carers, could have been averted if the parents, *acting as the guardians of the potential neonate*, had been advised of the opportunity to terminate the pregnancy.[6] There are, then, two main ways in which such a cause may arise. Most commonly, and typically, an event injurious to the fetus arises during pregnancy and is either misdiagnosed or ignored – the same conditions as will set the scene for an action for wrongful birth. Alternatively, a negligent action or negligent advice will have set up the conditions that predispose a woman to carry a disabled child in the future; such a situation may give rise to what is known as a pre-conception tort in respect of the fetus. Both may open the way for an action by the resulting neonate in respect of wrongful life but one raised in the latter circumstance is, in my view, atypical in that the choice denied the woman is whether or not to conceive rather than whether to terminate a pregnancy. The choices are not of precisely the same order and we will return to the distinctions below at p. 196.

It is remarkable that, wherever one looks in the several Commonwealth jurisdictions, cases involving an action for wrongful life in the last decades of the twentieth century are spoken of in terms of a 'novel cause of action'. There is virtually no development of a jurisprudence, and the great majority of cases have fallen at the first hurdle; the jurisdiction simply does not recognise so-called wrongful life as actionable and, indeed, much of the courts' time has been taken up with adjudging whether the claim should be struck out as disclosing no cause of action. It might, then, be said that the issue is dead and does not merit examination after exhumation. Yet it is precisely because of this remarkable stay of evolution that interest in the subject has recently revived. A quarter of a century or thereabouts is a long time between comparative cases. Community attitudes change and the common law allows for this by continued review of the various situations it covers. A precedent that is not reconsidered in due time may become dangerously out of step with related law and this may be particularly true of attitudes to wrongful life which have remained static while those on abortion, which are integral to the concept, have altered dramatically. Some of the comments

---

[6] Several courts and commentators would include children born under social disability within this definition. The old US case of *Zepeda* v. *Zepeda* 190 NE 2d 849 (Ill., 1963), in which a child pled 'wrongful life' because of being born illegitimate, is an archetypal case. It was rejected, not because there was no tortious element involved, but because of the extended jurisprudential issues involved. Such actions are unlikely to recur and are peripheral to the current discussion. In any event, my definition involves the availability of legal termination of pregnancy – it is at least arguable that it would not be in such cases in the UK despite the virtual *carte blanche* provided by the Abortion Act 1967, s.1(1)(a) (for which, see p. 28).

quoted from the cases which follow would be, at least, surprising if they were made today.[7]

The fact that wrongful life actions are not entirely dormant may be due to their close association with those for wrongful birth – if only as a matter of form[8] – and there is a recognisable trend to this effect in many of the judicial opinions given in the more recent cases wherever they have been heard. Moreover, we will see that this has spilled over into actual acceptance of the claim in Europe, a matter that may become of more than passing interest to the courts of the United Kingdom. It is, therefore, not entirely otiose to consider the subject from a historical perspective and, in view of the generally negative approach of the Commonwealth courts, we must, almost inevitably, turn for this to the United States.

Wrongful life in the United States

The judicial discussions in *McFarlane* v. *Tayside Health Board*[9] have shown us how difficult it can be to establish distinct precedents by way of the jurisdictions of the United States and, as has been noted, this is unsurprising in view of the varying cultures and the large number of individual legal systems involved. In fact, this difficulty hardly arises in respect of wrongful life. The number of courts that have accepted such an action is very small and while, paradoxically, those that have done so have attracted particular analytic consideration, it could be that this virtual unanimity has been so striking as to be highly influential in shaping the pattern in other Anglophone countries.

The scene was set by *Gleitman* v. *Cosgrove*[10] in which a woman who sustained German measles in pregnancy was assured there was no likelihood of resulting abnormality in her fetus. The child, who was seriously afflicted, sued on the grounds that, but for the negligent advice given, his mother would have terminated the pregnancy and he would not be

---

[7] 'This is an evolving area of the law . . . It is only recently that the parents' wrongful birth claim has been recognized by a Canadian court . . . More generally, the legal regime relating to abortion has undergone significant change resulting in an expanded scope for parental choice.' Per Sharpe J in the Canadian case *Sharma* v. *Mergelas, Nowaczyk* v. *Majewski* (unreported, 1997), quoted by Epstein J in *Petkovic* v. *Olupona* [2002] O.J. no. 3411.

[8] 'In the circumstances of this case, it would not be an efficient use of resources to carve out the wrongful birth part of the claim to proceed through the appeal route bare of the facts while the rest of the action proceeds to trial.' Per Epstein J in *Petkovic* v. *Olupona*, n. 7 above at [27].

[9] See, in particular, p. 107 above.   [10] 227 A 2d 689 (N.J., 1967).

living in a disabled condition.[11] The court rejected the claim on three grounds:

- Damages in tort are measured by comparing the condition the plaintiff would have been in if the defendants had not been negligent with his or her condition that resulted from the negligence; it is impossible to make such a determination when the difference is between an impaired existence and 'the utter void of non-existence';
- In view of the fact that the law places a very high value on human life, the birth of a defective child could not be regarded as an injury to the child;
- Given the opportunity, the child, himself, would probably have chosen life. This was expressed in the now famous extract:

It is basic to the human condition to seek life and hold on to it however heavily burdened. If Jeffrey [the child] could have been asked as to whether his life should be snuffed out before his full term of gestation could run its course, our felt intuition of human nature tells us he would almost surely choose life with defects as against no life at all.[12]

In the equally well-known case of *Becker* v. *Schwartz*,[13] a wrongful life action that was raised by a child with Down's syndrome whose 37-year old mother had not been offered amniocentesis, was denied – largely on the grounds that the child did not suffer any cognizable injury and, second, that the action demanded:

A calculation of damages dependent upon a comparison between the Hobson's choice of life in an impaired state and non-existence,

a task which the court considered it was not equipped to undertake.

Thus, we can see that, *ab initio*, the American courts have resisted the wrongful life action but for a variety of well-rehearsed reasons. A case by case analysis of these would be interesting to the medical historian but, once the principles have been established, I doubt if it would be of great significance in the present context. We should, however, have some idea as to the extent of diversity of early opinion and, to this end, I will lean gratefully on the listings provided in two recent US cases:

---

[11] It is to be noted that *Gleitman* was decided before the seminal decision in *Roe* v. *Wade* 410 US 113, 93 S Ct 705 (1973) (see p. 19 above). The court, however, assumed that a termination would have been lawful given the predictability of birth defects.

[12] n. 10 above, at 693. The problems of 'substituted judgment' are discussed in greater depth in the next chapter. For the moment, it only needs to be remarked that this is a very subjective assessment which, again, raises the question of whether judges should be swayed by their own morality when fashioning the law.

[13] 386 NE 2d 807 (N.Y., 1978).

Kassama v. *Magat*[14] and *Willis* v. *Wu.*[15] The latter's assessment is likely to be particularly authoritative as it was the first case to be heard in South Carolina which, at the time, remained among twenty-one states in which it was believed that the issue of 'wrongful life' had not been previously addressed. The indications were that twenty-seven states had expressly refused or limited a wrongful life action either by way of judicial opinion, statute or both, while three, to which we will return, had allowed the cause of action.

In general, we can isolate two main reasons that are fundamental to the rejection of the wrongful life action in the United States, the first – and most common – being, as in *Becker,* that there was no cognizable injury in being born and that it was impossible to compare the effects of being born disabled with not being born.[16] The second lies in the obvious problem that the health carers concerned in the management of the pregnancy did not *cause* the children's disabilities when they were, in fact, due, for example, to a chromosomal abnormality; no *person* could be blamed and, without physical causation, there can be no legal causation and, hence, no negligence. Other, more individualised, reasons include a distinction between the physician's duty to inform the parents and the absence of a similar duty to the fetus.[17] However, in the majority of instances, multiple reasons have been given and, lurking in the background of judicial opinion, there is always the problem of quantifying the value of non-life in comparative terms. It has become almost customary for judges to avoid this issue by recourse to pseudo-theology; this is generally unhelpful and I will turn to alternative approaches in the conclusion to this chapter. Meantime, it is noteworthy that a number of state legislatures have appreciated the severity of the judicial dilemma and

---

[14] 792 A 2d 1102 (Md., 2002).   [15] 607 SE 2d 63 (S.C., 2004).
[16] The following is the illustrative list provided in *Willis: Elliott* v. *Brown* 361 So 2d 546 (Ala., 1978), *Walker* v. *Mart* 790 P 2d 735 (Ariz., 1990), *Lininger* v. *Eisenbaum* 764 P 2d 1202 (Colo., 1988), *Garrison* v. *Medical Center of Delaware, Inc.* 581 A 2d 288 (Del., 1990), *Kush* v. *Lloyd* 616 So 2d 415 (Fla., 1992), *Blake* v. *Cruz* 698 P 2d 315 (Idaho, 1984), *Siemieniec* v. *Lutheran General Hospital* 512 NE 2d 691 (Ill., 1987), *Cowe* v. *Forum Group, Inc.* 575 NE 2d 630 (Ind., 1991), *Bruggeman* v. *Schimke* 718 P 2d 635 (Kan. 1986), *Grubbs* v. *Barbourville Family Health Center* 120 SW 3d 682 (Ky., 2003), *Kassama* v. *Magat* 792 A 2d 1102 (Md., 2002), *Wilson* v. *Kuenzi* 751 SW 2d 741 (Mo., 1988), *Greco* v. *United States* 893 P 2d 345 (Nev., 1995), *Smith* v. *Cote* 513 A 2d 341 (N.H., 1986), *Azzolino* v. *Dingfelder* 337 SE 2d 528 (N.C., 1985), *Nelson* v. *Krusen* 678 SW 2d 918 (Tex., 1984). The Court in *Kassama* suggests that we should add: *Strohmaier* v. *Associates in Obstetrics and Gynecology* 332 NW 2d 432 (Mich., 1982), *Berman* v. *Allan* 404 A 2d 8 (N.J., 1979), *Flanagan* v. *Williams* 623 NE 2d 185 (Ohio, 1993), *Ellis* v. *Sherman* 515 A 2d 1327 (Pa., 1986), *Dumer* v. *St. Michael's Hospital* 233 NW 2d 372 (Wis., 1975). We also have *Hester* v. *Dwivedi* 733 NE 2d 1161 (Ohio, 2000) continuing the trend.
[17] *James G* v. *Caserta* 332 SE 2d 872 (W.Va., 1985).

have solved it by outlawing – or, at least, limiting – the wrongful life action by way of statute.[18] The most common ground for so doing appears to be a rejection of any action that depends on a finding that, in the absence of negligence, a 'person' would have been aborted – thus, tacitly undermining the state's basic interest in the preservation of human life.[19] As a result, there is a considerable collateral antipathy to actions for wrongful birth which we have discussed in detail in Chapter 3.

Wrongful life accepted in the USA. Only three US jurisdictions have accepted an action for wrongful life and in none of these could supporters of the suit be said to have gained an outright victory. This, coupled with the exceptional nature of the cases, dictates the need for their study in rather greater depth than has been given to the norm. The starting point is *Curlender v. Bio-Science Laboratories* – a case in which the parents of the plaintiff child were given incorrect information as to the likelihood of their being carriers of the gene for Tay-Sachs disease.[20] As a result, Shauna was born with severe disabilities.

The *Curlender* court was markedly influenced by the dissenting opinions in *Gleitman*[21] and in *Berman v. Allan.*[22] In the former, the failure to redress a wrong – and the consequent indemnity of the wrongdoer – was given as a strong reason against disallowing a wrongful life action and, in the latter, it was said:

An adequate comprehension of the infant's claims under these circumstances starts with the realization that the infant has come into this world and is here, encumbered by an injury attributable to the malpractice of the doctors,[23]

---

[18]   These include Idaho, Indiana, Maine, Michigan, Minnesota, Missouri, North Dakota, Pennsylvania, South Dakota and Utah – and in many there is both judicial and statutory disapproval.

[19]   It is important to remember that, at least in a high proportion of cases, the fetus will be comparatively well-developed by the time intervention to avoid wrongful birth or wrongful life is indicated. The 'three trimester' rule developed in *Roe v. Wade* (see Chapter 2 at p. 19) can, therefore, be invoked in such cases, thus avoiding a clash with the woman's constitutional right to control her own early pregnancy.

[20]   (1980) 165 Cal Rptr 477, CA. There is some confusion in this case insofar as the court was uncertain as to whether the negligence occurred before or after conception. It could well be that, were the former true, the case might be one of 'preconception tort' and, accordingly, less than strictly relevant in the present context. See discussion of *Turpin v. Sortini*, n. 26 below.

[21]   n. 10 above.

[22]   404 A 2d 8 (N.J., 1979). A case of a Down's syndrome birth to an elderly mother who had not been offered amniocentesis. The court allowed damages for emotional distress but refused to award lifetime support for the child. At the same time, it rejected the child's action for wrongful life.

[23]   ibid., at 404 A 19.

an observation with which, surely, few would disagree – that is, so long as one accepts that the 'wrong' lies in a failure to *advise the parents*. The nub of the dilemma is, of course, that, as we have already noted, no-one could accuse the health care team of having *caused* the child's genetic defect – and it was this difficulty that the *Curlender* court was mainly concerned to circumvent.

In a somewhat subjective analysis of a surprisingly large number of cases, the court identified a measure of progression in the law – particularly by way of a retreat from the 'impossibility of measuring damages', the acceptance of a changing 'public policy' and the persistent pursuit of such actions despite their general judicial disapproval – that being, perhaps, based on 'the understanding that the law reflects, perhaps later than sooner, basic changes in the way society views such matters'.[24] The reality of the 'wrongful life' concept, it was held, is that the infant plaintiff both *exists* and *suffers* due to the negligence of others – effectively other considerations were of secondary significance only. The court concluded that it was clearly consistent with the applicable principles of tort law to recognise the cause of action by the child. It is of more than passing interest that a refusal to terminate a pregnancy in the face of good advice would, in the opinion of the court, have provided an intervening act such as to preclude liability insofar as defendants other than the parents were concerned. The court went even further and could see no sound public policy which would protect the parents from being answerable for the 'pain, suffering and misery' of their offspring.[25]

Although the *Curlender* decision is, at least in the writer's opinion, to be applauded on the grounds of equity, it is difficult to avoid the conclusion that it was based to a large extent on pragmatism. Indeed, there is much in it to criticise – in particular, its failure to consider the relationship between the wrongful birth and the wrongful life action. As a result, it is unsurprising that it had a relatively short life, even within the confines of California, where the problem was next considered in *Turpin* v. *Sortini*.[26]

Turpin is, however, yet another case which demonstrates the extraordinary difficulties in the way of achieving clear definitions within the parameters of the troubled pregnancy. The Turpins had a daughter who, it transpired, suffered from congenital deafness. The condition was, however, not diagnosed at the time and, consequently the parents were not

---

[24] Per Jefferson J, n. 20 above, at Cal Reptr 477,
[25] Such an action, which one can hardly see as being compatible with public policy, is now statute barred in California: Cal. Civ. Code §43.6.
[26] (1982) 31 Cal. 3d 220.

warned of a possible hereditary, genetically determined cause.[27] The parents maintained that they would not have conceived another child had they been properly counselled; in the event, however, they proceeded to a second pregnancy which resulted in a child, Joy, who was similarly afflicted. There is, thus, no doubt that, as was a possibility in *Curlender*, *Turpin* is fundamentally classifiable as a preconception tort and, as such, sits uneasily in a discussion of the wrongful life action in the United States. It follows, therefore, that, before addressing the case in detail, we should first take a diversion by which to assess the relationship between the two actions and, thus, to establish the true significance of *Turpin* within the wrongful life scenario.

Wrongful life and the preconception tort. Actions resulting from 'wrongful' – or, far better, 'diminished' or 'disabled' – life that are due, on the one hand, to preconception and, on the other, to postconception negligence have much in common. Both may depend upon information based negligence – or defective counselling – and, in such circumstances, the parallel claim for wrongful birth that is commonly raised on behalf of the parents has never been denied in recent tort law. Similarly, the child, in both cases, is effectively saying that he or she has been deprived of the opportunity to decide, by proxy, whether or not it should exist in a disabled state. There is, however, a major distinction to be made as to the purpose of the advice that is sought, insofar as the vexed question of *encouraging* abortion has no place in the preconception case; thus, a major policy argument against allowing a wrongful life action is eliminated. Moreover, in the majority of – though not, as we will see, in all – preconception torts, a responsible tortfeasor will be recognisable. The clear inference is that the child's action is more acceptable in the preconception case than it is in the event of postconception negligence.[28]

There is, however, a conflicting distinction to be made as to the extent of the duty of care – and, hence, liability – in the two cases. We have seen that it is, at least, arguable – and is, in my view correct – that the physician attending a pregnant woman also owes a recognisable duty of care to her fetus; this has, indeed, been a mainstay of many wrongful life actions of

---

[27] Some 50 per cent of cases of congenital deafness are of genetic origin – at least in the United Kingdom. We have discussed the significance of this in the modern context of genetic testing and screening in Sheila A. M. McLean and J. Kenyon Mason 'Our Inheritance, Our Future: Their Rights?' (2005) 13 *International Journal of Children's Rights* 255–72.

[28] This discussion is, of course, based on common law principles. We return to the statutory situation at p. 210.

the postconception type.[29] The distinction is, essentially, one of proximity. Thus, while a significant relationship between the fetus and its mother's physician may yet be regarded as uncertain, it will certainly be far more difficult to establish a proximate relationship giving rise to a duty of care between the health carer and a non-existent being – which describes the status of the principals at the time of the preconception negligence. One cannot help feeling that the class of 'potential child' should be regarded as being too wide and too remote a basis on which to found such a legal duty on the individual physician; it might just be possible to classify 'the next affected child, or any other child, that Mr and Mrs X may have' as an identifiable person, but it would surely be difficult to do so.[30] In such an instance, it might also be asked whether it is fair or just to leave an admittedly negligent health carer in doubt as to his or her liability for an eventuality that may or may not arise at some time in the future depending on conditions that are outside his or her control.[31]

This argument was well developed in the comparatively recent Californian case of *Hegyes* v. *Unjian Enterprises, Inc.*[32] in which a child claimed that injuries sustained by her mother in a vehicular accident were responsible for disabilities due to her premature birth some two years after the incident. The trial court having rejected the claim, the appeal depended entirely on the question of whether or not a negligent motorist owed a legal duty of care to the subsequently conceived child of a woman who was injured as a result of the negligence. Although it may be unusual to call upon a road traffic accident as a precedent for clinical medical negligence, *Hegyes* is, in the writer's opinion, highly significant in the present context in that it crystallises the question that is intrinsic to the preconception tort – that is, whether *causation* (which will scarcely be in doubt in the majority of cases) is the essential element in establishing negligence or whether it must always take second place to the existence

---

[29] I. Kennedy and A. Grubb *Medical Law* (London: Butterworths, 3rd edn 2000) cite *Poynter* v. *Hillingdon Health Authority* (1997) 37 BMLR 192, QBD and *Thomson* v. *James* (1997) 41 BMLR 144, CA as analogous precedents in this connection – duty to inform parents on behalf of their child.

[30] It seems to me that the principles evolved in, say *Palmer* v. *Tees Health Authority* [1999] Lloyd's Rep Med 351 (Authority has no duty of care to *potential* but unidentifiable victims of a psychopath) or *Goodwill* v. *British Pregnancy Advisory Service* [1996] 2 All ER 161, [1996] 31 BMLR 83 (no duty of care to *potential* sexual partners) would apply.

[31] For arguments as to the indeterminate time over which such an action could be brought, see *Albala* v. *City of New York* 420 NE 2d 786 (1981, N.Y.). See also the dissent in *Renslow* v. *Mennonite Hospital* 367 NE 2d 1250 (Ill., 1977) where the effect of allowing such actions was described as 'emasculating the principles of duty and foreseeability [in cases of negligence] whenever causation can be shown', per Ryan J at 1262.

[32] (1991) 234 Cal App 3d 1103. The tortfeasor in this case was a driver rather than a health carer. Nonetheless, the court considered that this did not alter the principles involved.

of a *duty of care* and its breach – which most commentators would see as the essence of the negligence action.[33] The majority opinion in *Hegyes* is worth quoting *in extenso* if for no reason other than to emphasise its uncompromising terms:

The tort rationale for imposing liability on a defendant for preconception negligence is grounded on duty, and not just causation analysis. While causation is an indispensable element of negligence liability, it is neither the only element, nor a substitute for 'duty' ... The determination that a duty of care exists is an essential prerequisite to liability founded in negligence ... There must be a legal duty owed to the person injured to exercise care under the circumstances, and a breach of that duty must be the proximate cause of the resulting injury.[34]

And more specifically as to the preconception tort:

It has been aptly observed, however, that causation cannot be the answer; in a very real sense the consequences of an act go forward to eternity, and back to the beginning of the world. Any attempt to impose responsibility on such a basis would result in infinite liability for all wrongful acts, which would 'set society on edge and fill the courts with endless litigation'.[35]

Even giving full allowance to the fact that the defendant in *Hegyes* was a driver and not a health carer, extrapolation of this view to the latter's responsibility seems to be such a logical step as to be virtually incontestable. Nonetheless, the analysis is certainly contrary to the mainstream United Kingdom view.[36] The arguments that I have developed above were, for example, also well aired in the Australian case of *X and Y* v. *Pal*[37] from which it is clear that, given the right circumstances, the courts are happy to accept that the special relationship that is needed so as to avoid reliance on a simple causation/liability formula can be constructed:

Although factors such as the passage of time or the intervention of other medical practitioners might serve to deny the existence of a causal connection ... I see no reason why ordinarily the doctor should not be regarded as having been in a

---

[33] I.e. there is no cause of action in the absence of a duty, thus rendering *causation* irrelevant.
[34] n. 32 above, per Woods J at 1134.
[35] Per Woods J quoting from *Renslow* v. *Mennonite Hospital*, n. 31 above, at 1254. A good example is to be found in *Estate of Amos* v. *Vanderbilt University* 62 SW 3d 133 (Tenn., 2001), in which a later husband successfully claimed damages for infection with HIV from a hospital that failed to warn a woman she might have been given a contaminated transfusion; the hospital owed no duty to the potential husband but, nonetheless, it was foreseeable that the patient would one day marry and have a family.
[36] See the important article by Adrian Whitfield, 'Common Law Duties to Unborn Children' (1993) 1 *Medical Law Review* 28–52.
[37] (1991) 23 NSWLR 26, [1992] 3 Med LR 195. Here, the doctor failed to diagnose syphilis in a pregnant woman and a later sibling also suffered from undiagnosed congenital syphilis. The case is complicated by the fact that the index child was disabled due to a combination of pre- and post-conception negligence.

relationship of proximity with a category of persons including the patient and children later born to her.[38]

Simplistically, therefore, it seems that liability for a preconception tort resulting in disability can be imposed – but only if the tortfeasor was, at the time, in a *professional* relationship with the mother of the damaged child; and, while it may be hard to apply the principles of justice and reasonableness even in such limited conditions, many would see it as a pragmatically acceptable solution to a problem that defies logic.[39]

We are, however, still not out of the jurisprudential wood as there are subtle variations in the tort itself which can, once again, result from negligent clinical practice or faulty communication. The classic instance of the former is to be found in *Renslow* v. *Mennonite Hospital*[40] in which the doctors transfused Rh-positive blood into an Rh-negative woman who, consequently, developed anti-Rh antibodies; they were found liable for the disabilities sustained by a later child who developed haemolytic disease of the newborn. As to the latter, there is little doubt that *Turpin* stands out as the best argued example from the US jurisdiction. As we have already noted, however, the difficulty lies in the anomaly that, while *Turpin* is unarguably an instance of preconception tort, it is widely quoted as the US case which has come closest to accepting a plea of wrongful life. One can, therefore, reasonably ask if there is any practical purpose in separating the two actions.

To an extent, and given the specifics of Californian law, the problem is already solved – Californian law distinguishes only two torts in respect of the troubled pregnancy:

Some authorities have broken the categories down further, but in this opinion we will follow the general usage: 'wrongful life' for all actions brought by children and 'wrongful birth' for all actions brought by parents.[41]

Thus, the argument is sterile in respect of the state of California although it is doubtful if the same can be said on a global basis. The great majority of preconception torts, as already noted, are fought on the basis of negligence simpliciter; there is little of the deeper philosophical or moral argument that surrounds the action for what is generally known

---

[38] Per Clarke JA at (1992) 3 Med LR 206.

[39] For some additional difficulties imposed by the time relationship see *Enright* v. *Eli Lilly & Co* 570 NE 2d 198 (N.Y., 1991) where an attempt to attribute liability for third generation disability was dismissed as an unreasonable extension of tort law.

[40] n. 31 above. Later similar cases include *Lazevnick* v. *General Hospital of Munro County, Inc.* 499 F Supp 146 (Md., 1980) and *Yeager* v. *Bloomington Obstetrics and Gynecology, Inc.* 585 NE 2d 696 (Ind., 1992).

[41] *Turpin* v. *Sortini* (1982) 31 Cal 3d 220 at 225, n. 4.

as 'wrongful life'.[42] Indeed, we will see that these differences may form
the basis for preferring to follow the former course of action rather than
the latter.[43] It is doubtful if everyone would dismiss the difference
between the two actions as depending only on the damages sought.[44]
Enough has, however, been said to justify the inclusion of *Turpin* v. *Sortini*
as a major contribution to the wrongful life debate.

Turpin *and its siblings revisited.* The history of *Turpin* has been
outlined above at p. 195, from which it will be seen that the case fits easily
within the matrix of the action for wrongful life based on failure of
communication. Its main jurisprudential importance, however, lies in
its having imposed an early halt to the development of the wrongful life
action along the lines that were initiated in *Curlender* – the whole purpose
of the Californian Supreme Court hearing of the case was to resolve
the conflict raised by the dismissal of Joy Turpin's action in the Court
of Appeal in the face of the contrary decision by a different panel of the
Court in *Curlender.*

Turpin, however, followed the now familiar pattern in, firstly, accepting
the fact that compensation for negligent antenatal injury was widely
acceptable and available to the neonate throughout the common law
jurisdictions but, secondly, appreciating that actions for wrongful life
constitute an exception to the rule insofar as a child has sustained 'no
legally cognisable injury' through having been born. Even so, the Court
found a public policy that dictates that 'life of whatever type is preferable
to non-life' to be inadequate grounds for rejecting the child's claim for
wrongful life. Amongst other arguments, the court noted that adult
patients have an absolute right to control their own therapeutic destiny
and that this right is generally extended to parents when the interests

---

[42]   The availability of the preconception tort is established in the United Kingdom by way of
the Congenital Disabilities (Civil Liability) Act 1976. S.1(1) holds that:

If a child is born as the result of such an occurrence before birth as is mentioned in
subsection (2) below, and a person (other than the child's own mother) is under the
section answerable to the child in respect of the occurrence, the child's disabilities are to
be regarded as damage resulting from the wrongful act of that person and actionable
accordingly at the suit of the child.

The relevant part of subsection (2) defines an occurrence to which section 1 applies as
one which:
(a) affected either parent of the child in his or her ability to have a normal, healthy child.
The conditions for the preconception tort are, thus, established precisely.

[43]   See, in particular, *Cherry* v. *Borsman* (1992) 94 DLR (4th) 668 discussed in detail here
at p. 228.

[44]   See Woods J in *Hegyes,* n. 32 above, at 1112.

concerned are those of their children – the wrongful birth action can, therefore, be seen as being brought as much in the defective child's interests as in those of its parents. True, Joy Turpin's only disability was deafness but it is hard to disagree with the *Turpin* court that there will be times when the disability is such that it would be impossible to assert with confidence that the resultant life was preferable to no life at all.

The court was, however, still not persuaded by its own powerful argument and preferred to revert to the practical impossibilities of determining whether the child has, in fact, suffered an injury in being born and, even if that were to be shown, in assessing the general damages – or, indeed, the benefit offset available to a much-loved child – in any fair way.[45] Even so, the *Turpin* court offered a significant olive branch to the supporters of the wrongful life claim in holding that Joy was entitled to claim for the 'extraordinary expenses for specialised teaching, training and hearing equipment' that she would incur during her lifetime. The importance of this decision lies in the award of special damages to the plaintiff child and, accordingly, the withdrawal of such damages under the parents' action for wrongful birth. The reason given by the court depended on the principle that the child's own medical care should be available to the child directly and should not be subject to the inherent vagaries of an indirect award. We will see later that this very sensible interpretation of the law of compensation has found its way into the European jurisprudence.[46] Nonetheless, it is arguably inconsistent to allow special damages but deny general damages for what is, in effect, the same tort.[47]

In the following year, the Supreme Court of the State of Washington considered the issues in *Harbeson* v. *Parke-Davis, Inc.*[48] and, in a single decision, affirmed the availability of actions for preconception tort, wrongful birth and wrongful life within that jurisdiction. We are, here, most obviously concerned with the last of these, as to which, the Court agreed with its opposite number in California that the child's need for medical care 'will not miraculously disappear when the child attains his majority'. Rather than leave the future to something of a lottery decision, the court preferred to place the burden of all such costs on the

---

[45] 'When a jury considers the claim of a once-healthy plaintiff that a defendant's negligence harmed him – for example, by breaking his arm – the jury's ability to say that the plaintiff has been "injured" is manifest, for the value of a healthy existence over an impaired existence is within the experience [or] imagination of most people. The value of non-existence – its very nature – however, is not.' Quoting from *Speck* v. *Finegold* 408 A 2d 496 (Pa., 1979) per Spaeth J at 512.

[46] See p. 233.   [47] See the dissenting opinion of Mosk J.

[48] 656 P 2d 483 (Wash., 1983).

negligent medical advisers – thus, effectively, again underlining the logical superiority of the wrongful life action over that for wrongful birth once the breach of a common duty of care has been established.

So much, then, for the West Coast. We must, however, look at one further case if only to show that acceptance of the wrongful life action is not simply a matter of a cultural divide between the eastern and western states of the USA. *Procanik* v. *Cillo*[49] is, in fact, interesting for its own sake in that the New Jersey court overturned its own ruling in *Gleitman* v. *Cosgrove*[50] – a case which, as we have already seen, had hitherto provided the main foundation for the general rejection of the wrongful life suit. *Procanik* is, at the same time, an unsatisfactory case insofar as the parents' parallel action for wrongful birth, a suit which had already been accepted in New Jersey,[51] was time-expired – leading the Court to muse:

Law is more than an exercise in logic, and logical analysis … should not become an instrument of injustice. Whatever logic inheres in permitting parents to recover for the cost of extraordinary medical care incurred by a birth-defective child, but in denying the child's own right to recover those expenses, must yield to the injustice of that result. The right to recover the often crushing burden of extraordinary expenses visited by an act of medical malpractice should not depend on the 'wholly fortuitous circumstance of whether the parents are available to sue'.[52]

As a result, *Procanik* has been described as 'the paradigm of hard cases making bad law'.[53] Which, of course, depends on your interpretation of 'bad law' – it is clear that, despite its vagary, this writer, for one, sees it as a preferable conclusion to outright rejection irrespective of the legally suspect means adopted in reaching it.[54] The story of *Procanik* is the now familiar one of the child born with the congenital rubella syndrome as a result of the physician's failure to recognise infection in his mother. The court accepted the opportunity to review and revise two previous significant decisions which we have already noted. In *Gleitman* v. *Cosgrove*,[55] the court, as we have seen, had retreated into the 'impossible comparison' position – as between impaired and non-existence – inherent in the wrongful life action and, accordingly, had rejected the child's claim. At the same time, however, it had also rejected the parents' claim for

---

[49]   478 A 2d 755 (N.J., 1984).   [50]   n. 10 above.
[51]   *Berman* v. *Allan* 404 A 2d 8 (N.J., 1979).
[52]   Per Pollock J at 762. Quoting from *Turpin*, n. 26 above, at 965.
[53]   *Schloss* v. *The Miriam Hospital* 1999 R.I. Super LEXIS 116 per Israel J at 15. *Procanik* also resulted in an unsuccessful action for legal negligence: *Procanik* v. *Cillo* 543 A 2d 985 (N.J., 1988).
[54]   *Procanik* has, in fact, stood the test of time, at least in New Jersey: *Michelman* v. *Ehrlich* 709 A 2d 281 (N.J., 1998).
[55]   n. 10 above.

wrongful birth – on the dual grounds of the impossibility of assessing the damage sustained and of the importance of sustaining life however heavily burdened it might be. This decision had been substantially modified in *Berman* v. *Allan*[56] – a 'missed' Down's syndrome case – in which the change in public attitudes to termination of pregnancy during the intervening seventeen years[57] was accepted as was the feasibility of assessing the parents' emotional suffering in monetary terms. Thus, the *Berman* court allowed a wrongful birth action. At the same time, it still rejected the parents' claim for expenses in rearing a disabled child and it declined to recognise a wrongful life action on behalf of the child – not only had the child 'not suffered any damage cognizable at law by being brought into existence' but 'such an award would be disproportionate to the negligence of the defendants and would constitute a windfall to the parents'.

The *Procanik* court, however, went one, albeit tentative, step further forward in recognising that the trend of the decisions to date indicated 'an awareness that damages would be appropriate if they were measurable by acceptable standards'.[58] To this end, they elaborated the interesting proposition that injury to one member of the family results in financial impact upon the family as a whole.[59] Extraordinary expenses incurred by parents on behalf of a birth defective child were predictable and certain; moreover, recovery of such expenses by either the parents or the child, but not both, was compatible with such a holistic view of a family tort. Accordingly, the court held that this was applicable in the present and similar cases – and it followed *Harbeson* even to the extent that the child could recover during his majority. All of which is to be applauded in the interests of justice but which, at the same time, fails to explain under which particular head the extraordinary expenses were allowed – a lacuna which, it is suggested, was inevitable once the parents' wrongful birth action was barred by statute.[60] Be that as it may, that represented the limit to which the court was prepared to go; 'sound reasons', and, in particular,

---

[56] n. 51 above.

[57] Heavily influenced, of course, by the Supreme Court decision in *Roe* v. *Wade* 93 S Ct 705 (1973) for which see Chapter 2.

[58] n. 49 above, at 478 A 761.

[59] Relying on the uncompleted case of *Schroeder* v. *Perkel* 87 N.J. 53 (1981) in which the parents' claim was allowed but that of the child deferred. But how far does the definition of 'family' go? The difficulties are examined, and the extended family rejected, in *Michelman* v. *Ehrlich* 709 A 2d 281 (N.J., 1998) (grandfather claiming for wrongful birth): *Moscatello* v. *University of Medicine and Dentistry of New Jersey* 776 A 2d 847 (N.J., 2001) (claim by siblings).

[60] It is interesting that the two dissenting opinions were diametrically opposed – the one maintaining that the award of extraordinary expenses goes too far, the other that it is inadequate.

the impossibility of comparing non-existence with an impaired existence, prohibited the recognition of a claim for general damages.

So where does this rather extensive analysis of the American cases leave us? It is clear that the wrongful life action remains difficult to uphold so long as it is argued from the metaphysical or quasi-theological stance and, whether it be on these or on other more practical grounds, the over-whelming majority of courts in the United States have refused – and continue to refuse – to acknowledge such an action. But, at the same time, we can identify an increasing unease among the American judiciary that this involves injustice.[61] It is an unfortunate, but very real, fact that current attitudes which increasingly see abortion in terms of family plan-ning provide little support for counter-arguments based on the affront to the sanctity of life 'doctrine' posed by accepting the wrongful life action. To admit this attitude to abortion is by no means to approve it – only to accept that it is now ingrained, at least within the Anglo-Saxon culture.[62] A review of the cases shows, increasingly, that negligent deprivation of the right to terminate a pregnancy involving a disabled child is tortious and the only question remaining lies in who is to be recompensed, bearing in mind that the wrongful birth action is about emotions and financial loss while the wrongful life action concerns pain and suffering. *Procanik*, in particular, indicates, even if only by force of circumstances, that this interrelated approach is open and leaves us wondering if 'wrongful life' is anything more than a rose by any other name. We can now go on to consider whether developments in other jurisdictions will support this view.

The perspective in the United Kingdom and the Commonwealth

For reasons that are by no means clear, wrongful life actions have never been a prominent feature of United Kingdom medical jurisprudence[63] – in fact, so far as I am aware, there never has been an apposite case reported in Scotland. There are at least two possible answers. In the first place, the relatively long history of wrongful life cases in the United States was marked by their unremitting failure; as we have seen, it was not until

---

[61] But see B. Kennedy, 'The Trend toward Judicial Recognition of Wrongful Life: A Dissenting View' (1983) *UCLA Law Review* 473–501. Kennedy was concerned lest the wrongful life action led, logically, to the acceptance of neonaticide; the same applies, however – and even more forcefully – to the acceptance of abortion on fetal grounds.

[62] Although, as we have seen in Chapter 2, a remarkable swing of the pendulum may be emerging in the United States instigated by the South Dakota legislature.

[63] Interestingly, we will see that the same applied throughout the Commonwealth. See n. 139 below.

1983 that a glimmer of light appeared in that jurisdiction. Secondly, the first English case, heard in the Court of Appeal in 1982, arose at much the same time as the legal approaches to the far more common problems of wrongful pregnancy and wrongful birth were being developed and one fancies that the courts were disinclined to advance further than need be into what was already an area of doubtful public morality. By the time Mary McKay brought her hitherto unprecedented action, her mother was virtually assured of a successful action for her 'wrongful' birth. Moreover, it was believed that Parliament had already sealed the fate of a wrongful life action by passing the Congenital Disabilities (Civil Liability) Act 1976 – a point to which we will return later. Mary's cause of action, however, preceded the passing of the Act and the Court of Appeal was, in fact, being asked to resolve what could have been a difficult jurisprudential conflict. It did so with such determination that, Act or no Act of Parliament, no similar case has since been allowed to proceed. It might have been supposed, then, that wrongful life was, indeed, a problem of the past that was scarcely worth reopening. We will see, however, that it has acquired a new lease of life in the courts of the European Union.[64] Despite its comparative antiquity and its currently unchallenged position, *McKay* v. *Essex Area Health Authority*[65] may yet return as an important precedential authority. Moreover, since most of the basic aspects of the action were well covered, *McKay* provides a relatively easy 'Guide to Wrongful Life'. We ought, therefore, to consider it in some detail.

The case of Mary McKay

Although it was described as a novel cause of action 'for or against which there is no authority in any reported case in the courts of the United Kingdom or the Commonwealth',[66] *McKay* v. *Essex Area Health Authority* occupied the centre of the medico-legal stage of the United Kingdom for a surprisingly short time. To an extent, this may have been due to the way in which the case was conducted.

It was not contested that Mary was severely disabled as a result of the Health Authority's failure in their vicarious duty to interpret correctly a blood sample taken from her mother for the presence of rubella infection and to treat and advise her accordingly – and her mother brought a separate action for wrongful birth.[67] Mary, however, brought her own

---

[64] For which see p. 232 below.   [65] [1982] QB 1166, [1982] 2 All ER 771, CA.
[66] ibid., per Stephenson LJ at QB 1177, All ER 778.
[67] The validity of this claim was not contested and, in the absence of any further report, it is assumed it was settled in her favour.

action which, following the American example, was, essentially, in two parts. First, she claimed that, as a result of the combined negligence of the Health Authority and her general practitioner, she was 'burdened with injuries';[68] second, and more importantly in the present context, she claimed that she had suffered 'entry into a life in which her injuries are highly debilitating'.[69] These claims were originally struck out by the Master as disclosing no reasonable cause of action.[70] Lawson J at first instance, however, thought that Mary had a 'highly reasonable and arguable cause of action' and overruled the Master – largely on the grounds that her real complaint was not that she was born 'at all' but, rather, that she was 'born with deformities', and we will see that other jurisdictions have, since, adopted this position. Thus, the Court of Appeal's discussion of the actual case may be said to have been distorted in that it was directed to determining a relatively narrow point of proce-dure.[71] Nonetheless, their Lordships' reasons for allowing the appeal, and, at the same time, refusing leave for a further appeal, were clearly displayed and are typical of such jurisprudence as existed at the time.

This is expressed in Stephenson LJ's introduction to his analysis of Mary's claim:

I have come, at the end of two days' argument, to the same answer as I felt inclined to give the question before I heard argument, namely that plainly and obviously the claims disclose no reasonable cause of action.[72]

Seldom can a judicial opinion have been given more clearly and suc-cinctly – so much so that one feels the answer must be so obvious that the reasons behind it are not worth pursuing further. However, although arriving at the same conclusion, neither Ackner nor Griffiths LJJ spoke with anything like the same certainty and we will see later that times have changed; we must, therefore, consider the arguments more closely. At the same time, while Stephenson LJ's speech provides the most exhaus-tive opinion – and is the most widely quoted – we must bear in mind the possibility that it may not be typical of the mind-set of the court as a whole. Given that proviso, it will be convenient to take the relevant points in the order that the Lord Justice made them.

---

[68]   Statement of claim, para. 14. A claim against the general practitioner on the grounds that Mary's injuries resulted from her mother not being treated with anti-viral globulins was not struck out but is not pursued any further here. Globulin treatment could not reverse any damage that had already occurred; nonetheless, Ackner LJ, at least, considered that such an action might well succeed (n. 65 above, at QB 1185, All ER 784).

[69]   Statement of claim, para. 16(b).   [70]   Under R.S.C., Order 18, r.19(1).

[71]   That is, the conditions in which it is right and proper to strike out a claim – an argument that is not followed up here.

[72]   n. 65 above, at QB 1177, All ER 779.

First, he considered the nature of the health carers' duty to the fetus and concluded that there was a duty not to injure it – the corollary being that damages for injury sustained while in the womb were recoverable when such injury manifested itself after birth.[73] It is, then, of course, central to the argument against allowing an action for wrongful life that the health carers have not failed in that duty. Mary's injuries, like those of any fetus in a similar situation, were caused by the rubella virus; save in the unlikely event of a mother being negligently advised as to the dangers of her *exposing* herself to the virus, a fetus's right not to be injured before birth by the carelessness of others will not have been infringed in this way. In short, the action against the health carers fails simply on the grounds of causation and this is probably the most difficult of the many hurdles one has to cross on the way to justifying an action for wrongful life.[74]

Stephenson LJ's second argument derives from the first, that is that the only[75] right the disabled child can claim from his or her carers is a right not to be born disabled – and this means a right to be aborted or killed or, as he preferred to put it 'being deprived of the opportunity to live after being delivered from the body of [his or] her mother'.[76] This, in turn, he considered led inexorably to the question – how can there be a duty to take away life? – and it is here that the Lord Justice seems, at least to this writer, to lose some coherence, in particular by confusing a *duty* to take life with a *legal opportunity* to do so.

To some extent, this confusion is of his own making. The text of the Abortion Act 1967, section 1(1)(b)[77] at the time legalised the termination of a pregnancy of less than 28 weeks' duration if there was 'a substantial risk that if the child were born it would suffer from such physical or mental abnormalities as to be seriously handicapped'. As we have discussed in Chapter 3, this subsection has been generally interpreted as being drawn

---

[73] ibid., at QB 1178, All ER 779. In fact, the Lord Justice was foreseeing future developments in which such a cause was argued and sustained. See *Burton* v. *Islington Health Authority, De Martell* v. *Merton and Sutton Health Authority* [1993] QB 204, [1992] 3 All ER 833 or, in Scotland, *Hamilton* v. *Fife Health Board* 1993 SLT 624.

[74] Much of this chapter is derived from J. K. Mason, 'Wrongful Life: The Problem of Causation' (2004) 6 *Medical Law International* 149–61 where an attempt is made to overcome the difficulty.

[75] This can hardly be taken literally; intuition, if nothing else, tells us that the doctor, be he or she physician or obstetrician, owes a duty of care to the pregnant woman as a whole – and this must involve care of her fetus, including protection of that fetus's interests. The negligent doctor cannot escape liability to the neonate simply on the grounds of an absence of duty to the fetus. Fortin has argued strongly, inter alia, that the common law lays a duty on the doctor to advise the fetus, albeit through his or her mother, of the risks in being exposed to infection: Jane E. S. Fortin, 'Is the "Wrongful Life" Action Really Dead?' [1987] *Journal of Social Welfare Law* 306–13.

[76] n. 65 above, at QB 1178, All ER 779.   [77] Now s.1(1)(d).

in the interests of the fetus's mother.[78] Stephenson LJ, however, stated that he 'would prefer to believe that its main purpose, if not its sole purpose, was to benefit the unborn child'.[79] He continued:

[I]f and in so far as that was the intention of the legislature, the legislature did make a notable inroad on the sanctity of human life by recognising that it would be better for a child, born to suffer from such abnormalities as to be seriously handicapped, not to have been born at all.

In so saying, he admits to the health carers' duty to inform the fetus, albeit by proxy, of the available options and, thus, acknowledges the fetus's right to choose not to accept his or her abnormalities – in other words, as I will argue later, he has made the case for a fetal action for wrongful life. To avoid this trap, the Lord Justice pointed out that the doctor is under no obligation, or duty, to terminate the fetus's life – or that the fetus has a legal right to die – simply because he *can* do to a fetus what he cannot do to a person who has been born. No-one would deny this – but the more correct approach is, surely, to ask whether he should accept the *opportunity* to accede to the fetal best interests and whether, in failing to consider that opportunity, he becomes liable to the resulting neonate. Stephenson LJ's riposte is now so well-known as scarcely to bear repetition:

To impose such a duty towards the child would, in my opinion, make a further inroad on the sanctity of human life which would be contrary to public policy. It would mean regarding the life of a handicapped child as not only less valuable than the life of a normal child, but so much less valuable that it was not worth preserving.[80]

Which is a sentiment that, as we have already discussed, many would endorse. But, taken in conjunction with the Abortion Act 1967, does it make for good law?

Stephenson LJ's final reason for rejection of Mary's claim rested on the far more pragmatic analysis of the nature of the injury and the damage she had suffered. Having rejected the proposition that the health carers were, in fact, liable to her in respect of her injuries, he concluded that the only loss for which they could be held responsible was the difference between her disabled condition and non-existence. Since we can know nothing of the latter, the conclusion was that such an assessment was impossible.

---

[78] The major authority for this seems to be Glanville Williams, *Textbook of Criminal Law* (2nd edn, 1983) but it is accepted without comment by Kennedy and Grubb *Medical Law*, n. 29 above, at 1425.
[79] n. 65 above, at QB 1179, All ER 780.   [80] ibid., at QB 1180, All ER 781.

Nonetheless, the Lord Justice was clearly not entirely happy with his conclusions and, again, it is instructive to quote him in full:

The defendants must be assumed to have been careless. The child suffers from serious disabilities. If the defendants had not been careless, the child would not be suffering now because it would not be alive. Why should the defendants not pay the child for its suffering? The answer lies in the implications and consequences of holding that they should. If public policy favoured the introduction of this novel cause of action, I would not let the strict application of logic or the absence of precedent defeat it. But as it would be, in my judgment, against public policy for the courts to entertain claims like those which are the subject of this appeal, I would for this reason, and for the other reasons which I have given, allow the appeal.[81]

And one cannot avoid the uncomfortable feeling that this may be yet another example of how judicial morality has been allowed to cloud judicial principle across the whole field of the troubled pregnancy.

Even so, Stephenson LJ was fully supported by his fellow judges, in particular Ackner LJ who, again, could not accept that, absent specific legislation on the point, the common law would ever include an obligation to terminate the life of a person within the envelope of a duty of care to that person, whether or not *in utero*: 'Such a proposition runs wholly contrary to the concept of the sanctity of human life.'[82] The difficulty here, of course, is that the same could be said of the Abortion Act 1967 in general while, in particular, it involves an interpretation of section 1(1)(b) – as it then was – that is diametrically opposed to that of Stephenson LJ. Moreover, although it was not so stated at the time, it is clear that any such argument must also apply to the mother's claim for wrongful birth and I will consider this again at the end of the chapter. Ackner LJ was, therefore, almost obliged to seek an alternative 'root of the whole cause of action' and he found it in the impossibility of comparing the value of non-existence with that of existence in a disabled state. No comparison was possible and therefore no damage could be established which a court could recognise.[83] He was supported in his selection of this as the most compelling reason to reject the action by Griffiths LJ – 'the common law does not have the tools to fashion a remedy in these cases', a line of thought that is strangely pre-emptive of much of the reasoning in the

---

[81] ibid., at QB 1184, All ER 784.
[82] Ackner LJ specifically rejected Templeman LJ in *Re B*, n. 2 above, as authority to the contrary and was surely right in so doing. The words of Lord Donaldson MR may be recalled: 'I have to cavil at the use of such an expression as "condemned to die" and "the child must live" in Templeman LJ's judgment', in *Re J (a minor)(wardship: medical treatment)* [1991] Fam 33, [1990] 3 All ER 930.
[83] n. 65 above, at QB 1189, All ER 787.

wrongful pregnancy case of *McFarlane* that we have discussed at length in Chapter 4.

Given such specificity, however, we must assume that the 'impossible assessment' factor provides the ratio of *McKay* and, because of its negative nature, this is unfortunate. While many problems may be difficult or very difficult to solve, very few solutions are irrevocably beyond the capacity of human ingenuity – in short, we cannot, or ought not to, deny the existence of a cause of action because we find it hard to redress. Meantime, as something of an envoi, I return to Stephenson LJ to quote what may, in the end, constitute the most significant aspect of his opinion:

> though the judge was right in saying that the child's complaint is that she was born with deformities, without which she would have suffered no damage and have no complaint, her claim against the defendants is that they were negligent in allowing her, injured as she was, in the womb, to be born at all, a claim for 'wrongful entry into life' or 'wrongful life',[84]

a statement that must, once again, leave us wondering – as we were following the review of the American cases[85] – if the whole discussion of wrongful life is anything much more than a war of words, or a simple problem of semantics. An obvious inference to be derived from Lord Justice Stephenson is that the stumbling block to the action lies in the concept of the wrongfulness of being *alive*. Most of our conceptual and practical difficulties fade away if we concentrate on the wrongfulness of being *injured* and, again, I will explore this avenue later in the chapter.

The Congenital Disabilities (Civil Liability) Act 1976

We must also consider the significance of the wrongful life action in relation to statute law. Largely as a result of the unsatisfactory outcome of the litigation following the thalidomide disaster,[86] the status of the tort related to pre-natal injury had already been examined in depth by the time *McKay* came to be tried[87] but no definitive action had been taken. This had to await the passing of the Congenital Disabilities (Civil Liability) Act 1976 the terms of which, of course, largely depended on the Law Commission's Report. Mary McKay's birth preceded the Act

---

[84] ibid., at QB 1179, All ER 780.   [85] At p. 204 above.

[86] *S* v. *Distillers Co. (Biochemicals) Ltd* [1969] 3 All ER 1142, [1970] 1 WLR 114. As is probably well-enough known, a number of pregnant women treated with thalidomide for the relief of 'morning sickness' gave birth to children with severe limb deformities. The action resulted in an agreed compromise payment in which allegations of negligence were withdrawn.

[87] Law Commission *Report on Injuries to Unborn Children* (1974, Law Com. No. 60) (Cmd. 5709).

which was, however, passed before her action was heard. If, then, the Act excluded the wrongful life action, *McKay* was a nine-days wonder which, in the absence of further legislation, would never be repeated. Put another way, the foregoing discussion has been a waste of everyone's time – and this may, indeed, have been in the minds of the Lords Justices at the hearing and may, at the same time, account for their evident intention to dispose of the case with decent haste. In point of fact, I do not think we have to reach such a depressing conclusion. In the first place, many, including myself, would hold that the fetus ought to have such an action available – even though establishing its base may involve a degree of philosophical and legal legerdemain. Second, we will see that the courts of some jurisdictions are now prepared to allow the action. And, third, it is at least arguable that the 1976 Act does not, truly, dispose of the matter.

It is true that the Law Commission's inclinations were clear. Paragraph 89 of the Report says:

We do not think that, in the strict sense of the term, an action for 'wrongful life' should lie ... To justify an action in logic, therefore, it is necessary to argue that the child would have been better off had he never existed. Nor would it be easy to assess his damages on any logical basis for it would be difficult to establish a norm with which the plaintiff in his disabled state could be compared ... We have given this problem the most careful consideration and have not, we think, been unduly influenced by these considerations. Law is an artefact and, if social justice requires that there should be a remedy given for a wrong, then logic should not stand in the way. A measure of damages could be artificially constructed ... [W]e are clear in our opinion that no cause of action should lie [which arises out of medical advice]. Such a cause of action, if it existed, would place an almost intolerable burden on medical advisers in their socially and morally exacting role. The dangers that doctors would be under subconscious pressure to advise abortions in doubtful cases through fear of an action for damages is, we think, a real one.

In many ways, there is a sense of *fin de siècle* about this statement. With abortions in England and Wales now running at some 180,000 per year it is difficult to think of advising in favour of termination of pregnancy as imposing an intolerable moral burden on doctors. Moreover, it is unreal to use the abortion argument against a wrongful life action without, at the same time admitting that it is also central to the wrongful birth action – which is, itself, acceptable. For present purposes, however, the most important phrase in the above quotation lies in the words 'in the strict sense of the term' which, again, implies that the distinction to be made between the possible actions in negligence depends on the wording of the plea. The problem here is that we are faced with two hard and contra-dictory choices. On the one hand, we can attempt to find a place for direct negligence in fetal care within the standard scenario of a wrongful life action and, although, as we will see, it is not impossible to do so, this is a difficult task. The alternative is to define and isolate the wrongful life action as being one in which damage has occurred for which no-one is liable – and we are left wondering which of these scenarios identifies the 'strict sense' of the term.

Section 1(2)(b) of the 1976 Act defines an antenatal occurrence for which the doctor may be answerable to the resultant child as one that, inter alia:

affected the mother during her pregnancy, or affected her or the child in the course of its birth, so that the child is born with disabilities which would not otherwise have been present.

Ackner LJ stated without qualification:

Subsection (2)(b) is so worded as to import the assumption that, but for the occurrence giving rise to a disabled birth, the child would have been born normal and healthy – not that it would not have been born at all. Thus, the object of the Law Commission that the child should have no right of action for 'wrongful life' is achieved.[88]

In view of the fact that his fellow judges agreed with him,[89] it is clearly treading dangerous ground to question their reasoning. Nonetheless, try as I will, I cannot see it as being anything other than a *non sequitur*. Section 1(1) of the 1976 Act refers to a person (other than the child's mother) who, under the section, is answerable to the child in respect of the occurrence and we have seen how difficult it will be to attribute causation to the health carers in wrongful life cases – indeed, it is a major part of the argument against wrongful life that it cannot be done. Subsection (2)(b) is concerned only with recognisable injury to the fetus by a responsible person and simply has no place in the melodrama if there is no villain. In short, the 1976 Act is irrelevant to the wrongful life action *as it is commonly understood*. Fortin[90] has suggested that, in interpreting the Act, the Court of Appeal in *McKay* was unduly influenced by the Law Commission's expressed *intentions* and she goes on to argue that section 4(5), which states that the Act replaces any law in place before its passing, would not necessarily prohibit bringing a case of wrongful life under the common law.[91]

---

[88] n. 65 above, at QB 1186–7, All ER 786.

[89] ibid., Stephenson LJ at QB 1178, All ER 779, Griffiths LJ at QB 1191, All ER 789.

[90] n. 75 above. I should point out that she reaches the same conclusion as I have done as to the significance of the 1976 Act. Similar doubts have been expressed more recently: Anne Morris and Severine Saintier, 'To Be or Not to Be: Is That the Question? Wrongful Life and Misconceptions' (2003) 11 *Medical Law Review* 167–93.

[91] It is to be noted that the 1976 Act does not run to Scotland where a neonatal right to sue for injuries sustained *in utero* has always been accepted.

It is also difficult not to see the creation of section 1A within the 1976 Act by way of the Human Fertilisation and Embryology Act 1990, section 44, which establishes a neonatal right to sue in the event of injury resulting from negligent acts or omissions, including embryonic selection, during the course of assisted reproduction, as going very close to acknowledging a wrongful life action – at least in a specific situation.[92] Such arguments, however, do little save add confusion to an already confused concept. In my view, the 1976 Act is concerned to establish a tort of negligence affecting the unborn child – something that was essential in view of the doubt imposed by the legal rejection of a fetal persona as discussed in Chapter 2. As it stands, it is not there to rule out an action for wrongful life and attempts to read it as such are no more than extrapolations. There may still be a need for such an action and, if the provision of a remedy requires an 'artificial construct' in the form of identifying a form of negligence, then so be it.[93]

Wrongful life in Australasia

As is so often found in the field of medical jurisprudence, some of the most helpful discussions of the issues stem from the Antipodes and this is, perhaps, most evident in the field of reproductive medicine. While some judicial decisions may appear to many to be unfeeling – and the decision in *Cattanach* v. *Melchior*,[94] which we have discussed in Chapter 4, may be cited as one which attracted maximum opposition on this score – others will see the Australian and New Zealand courts as dragging the relevant jurisprudence into the twenty-first century. Perhaps the most interesting characteristic of the Australasian decisions is the degree of polarisation of the opposing judicial opinions such as we have seen in *Cattanach* v. *Melchior*. Much the same is to be found in the important case of *Harriton* v. *Stephens*[95] which provides the most recent, and possibly the most exhaustive, review of wrongful life actions throughout the Commonwealth jurisdictions. The life of an author in the field of medical law is, indeed, a hard one for, once again, we have a case in which the picture has completely changed since the relevant chapter was first flagged as completed. Thus, when heard in the Court of Appeal of New South Wales, *Harriton* appeared

---

[92] Indeed, it has been said that, in doing so, Parliament has clearly recognised a 'wrongful life' claim. Kennedy and Grubb, *Medical Law*, n. 29 above, at 1552. We return to the 1976 Act with reference to the Australian case of *Waller* at p. 222 below.

[93] The 1976 Act clearly operates once negligence by an individual is established. See n. 42 above.

[94] (2003) 199 ALR 131.

[95] *Harriton* v. *Stephens; Waller* v. *James; Waller* v. *Hoolahan* [2004] NSWCA 93.

to bring the wrongful life action a considerable step nearer to acceptance. By the time the case had gone through the High Court of Australia, however, it represented its death-knell – at least in Australia. Nevertheless, the case is so important to this chapter that, before moving on to the definitive judgment, it will still be helpful to consider the Court of Appeal stage of *Harriton* – even if for no other reason than to introduce the dissenting opinion.

On the face of things, the facts of the conjoined cases of *Harriton* and *Waller* are fairly standard, although we will see later that there were significant differences that require us to reconsider *Waller* as a distinct entity. Alexia Harriton and Keeden Waller were both born with severe disabilities – the former resulting from the maternal rubella syndrome and the latter from paternally transmitted anti-thrombin 3 (AT3) deficiency. Each asserted that their suffering and consequent financial liability would not have occurred absent a failure to provide their mothers with sufficient information on which to found a choice that ensured they would not have been born. The judge at first instance held that the health carers owed no such duty to their mothers and that, consequently, the children could have no cause of action against them.[96] The children then lost their appeal – but only by a 2 to 1 majority with the President of the Family Division, Justice Mason, taking the dissenting view.

The majority opinion was based on an interesting mix of both well rehearsed and novel arguments. Amongst the former were recourse to the compensatory principle which, essentially, states that the objective of the successful action in tort is to restore the pursuer to the same position as he or she would have occupied had not the wrong been sustained; this, of course, must, in the context of personal injury, be qualified by some such phrase as 'insofar as money can do so'. Ipp JA discussed the history of this principle and its application to the wrongful life action in great depth and he quoted many of the many authorities to which attention has already been drawn. In the final analysis, he concluded that:

[W]ithout recourse to considerations of policy that compel a departure from both the compensatory principle and the principle that damage is the gist of the cause of action in negligence, the appellants' arguments must fail.[97]

This, in turn, depended on the widely held belief that it is impossible to use non-existence as a comparator with disabled existence:

---

[96] For an admirable review of the topic in the light of the first instance decision in *Harriton* and related cases heard by the same judge, see Penelope Watson, 'Wrongful Life Actions in Australia' (2002) 26 *Melbourne University Law Review* 736–49.

[97] n. 95 above, at [279].

No amount of imagination and broad-axe wielding can conjure up a basis for assessment when no such basis exists or is known to human ken.[98]

Basic to the compensatory principle, however, are, first, the identification of the loss which has been suffered and, second, a decision as to whether a duty was owed by the defender in respect of that kind of loss. As to the former, the court agreed with the trial judge – and much of the previous international jurisprudence – that, given it was impossible to say that non-existence was preferable to a life with disabilities, there was no identifiable damage sustained *by the children*.[99] Some of the reasoning of the majority as to the latter is, however, novel and is interesting in that, once again, it demonstrates the recourse to moralism which has been, perhaps unsurprisingly, such a feature of the judicial approach to all those aspects of the 'troubled pregnancy' which we have discussed thus far. Many of the relevant dicta of Spigelman CJ have their origin in the distant past,[100] and I have extracted some of those that appear significant in the present context:

The delineation of legal duties has never been derived from an exclusively legal analysis (at [18]) ... Decades of decision making which employed only legal concepts has created a situation in which there is a false appearance of intellectual autonomy (at [19]) ... The most important aspect of the ethical basis for legal duties that have been recognised by the law of negligence is that a duty must reflect values generally ... held in the community ... These values change and the courts must adapt to new community standards (at [20]).

So far, so good, but the Chief Justice went on to say (at [21]) that:

In my opinion, the duty asserted by the Appellants should not be accepted as it does not reflect values generally, or even widely, held in the community.

It is, here, that one begins to wonder whether the judge may not be passing off his own morality as a legal fact. How, one wonders, can he possibly know that this is true? – we will return to this aspect of this case later in the chapter.[101]

---

[98] ibid., at [269].

[99] See Spigelman CJ, ibid., at [43]. The emphasis in the original was intended to emphasise that the problem did not arise in the case of an action by the parents. There was, therefore, no inconsistency between success of a parental claim and failure of one on behalf of the child (see [44]).

[100] One is reminded of Lord Coleridge LCJ in *R* v. *Instan* [1893] 1 QB 450: 'It would not be correct to say that every moral obligation involves a legal duty, but every legal duty is founded on a moral obligation' (at 453).

[101] There are echoes here of Lord Steyn's commuter on the London underground in *McFarlane* (see p. 121 above) who, the commentators generally agreed, may not be the best lawmaker.

This is but one aspect of the majority decision that might be considered unhelpfully negative in character. The Chief Justice, however, then went on to say (at [24]) of the action by the child:

The assertion by the child that it would be preferable if he or she had not been born raises ethical issues of the same character as those involved in the debate over euthanasia ... [T]he issues are highly contestable and are strongly contested. There is no widely accepted ethical principle. The law of negligence should not, therefore, recognise a legal duty to the child.

It may well be said that the court is, here, moving into the sphere of political decision-making which is the remit of Parliament. Nevertheless, it is difficult to see why the *absence* of consensus on the matter should *prohibit* the court from seeking an answer. Moreover, this didactic conclusion closes the door on the alternative approach that the patient is entitled, even in surrogate fashion, to refuse any form of medical management – a matter which is discussed further in the next chapter.[102] And as a final example of negative decision making, both the majority opinions contended that it never has been the law that a person who suffers foreseeable harm attributable to the negligence of another should always receive compensation[103] – an attitude that seems to lead to the circular conclusion that there has been no negligence if a loss is declared to be irrecoverable.[104]

Insofar as an action for wrongful birth is accepted almost universally and one for wrongful life is virtually always refused, it is integral to the decision in *Harriton*, and to those in all other cases which have followed the same line, that the conditions in the two actions are different both as to the duty of care – as between duty to the fetus and its mother – and as to responsibility for the damage done.[105] This is one reason why the dissenting opinion of Mason P was so important to what was, in effect, a precedental case in Australia.

---

[102] Admittedly, this was taken up by Ipp JA (n. 95 above, at [313] et seq.) and was discounted on the grounds that the interest in a wrongful life case 'does not concern the issue whether life should be preserved; the contrary is the case'. Note that it is part of the judge's argument that it is the *mother's* interest that is served by termination ([296]). But before extrapolating this to UK cases, one must note that, in the absence of an Abortion Act, the law in New South Wales restricts lawful abortion to the grounds of maternal well-being ([312]).

[103] See, in particular, Ipp JA at [248].

[104] And Ipp JA, himself (at [250]), drew attention to the consequent difficulties of reconciling the decisions in *McFarlane* and *Cattanach* which we have discussed in Chapter 4.

[105] As put by Stretton, n. 4 above: '[L]iability in wrongful life depends crucially on whether the doctor's conduct can cause physical damage to the plaintiff.' The difficulties imposed by the uncertainty on this point are well illustrated in the Canadian case of *McDonald-Wright* v. *O'Herlihy* [2005] OJ No.1636 (see n. 115 below).

Justice Mason started from the premise that the perceived dichotomy of interests between mother and fetus is a false one. The negligence of the health carers lay in their failure to give the mothers advice with which they would have agreed to terminate the pregnancies. To do so would have been in their best interests and in the best interests of the children – this being made inherently clear by their bringing the action.[106]

Mason P emphasised the central importance of this causal connection by decrying the tendency to describe the child's claim as asserting a 'right to be killed'. This, he considered, was getting 'the real issues off to a false start'[107] – in particular, by raising the spectre of having to compare the value of non-existence with that of existence in a disabled state, an issue that he considered to be one of the two main arguments used against recovery in 'wrongful life' claims.[108]

The first of these he identified as the assertion that life, itself, cannot be a legal injury[109] and it is noteworthy – and perhaps inevitable – that he drew the main support for this contention from the highly emotive dissenting speeches in *Cattanach*.[110] Justice Mason, however, held that there was no conceptual difference between the actions for wrongful pregnancy, wrongful birth and wrongful life; all were triggered by the same mechanism – that is, the *creation* of life. It was irrational to recognise the second and to refuse the third; indeed, if any distinction was to be made, the child's claim should be regarded as superior to that of the parents. As to the second argument, the near impossible task of comparing non-life with a disabled condition had, as we have already noted, been cited by many judges as being one that was beyond the remit of the law. Mason P, however, considered this to be looking at the problem from the wrong aspect. Assuming that the children could express their complaint, they would, he thought, do so not in a comparative sense but, rather, with direct reference to their current and future suffering and the needs thus

---

[106] Which seems to put paid to the commonly voiced argument that wrongful life actions should not be accepted because of a potential conflict between maternal and fetal interests.

[107] Quoting, in support, the early and important paper by Harvey Teff, 'The action for "wrongful life" in England and the United States' (1985) 34 *International and Comparative Law Quarterly* 423–41.

[108] Following, to a large extent, the opinion in the very significant US case of *Becker* v. *Schwartz* 386 NE 2d 807 (N.Y., 1978).

[109] Interestingly, Mason P attributed this 'question-begging conclusion' to a failure to distinguish between the early US cases brought for having been born into socially disadvantaged conditions (for which, see *Zepeda* v. *Zepeda* 190 NE 2d 849 (Ill., 1963), n. 6 above) and those concerned with genetic disease. The former, he thought, should be reclassified as 'dissatisfied life' claims and should be seen as quite separate from the latter which involve medical negligence.

[110] *Cattanach* v. *Melchior* (2003) 199 ALR 131 discussed at p. 126.

created.[111] Moreover, Mason P pointed out that we have no problem with comparing life with non-life when adjudicating futility of treatment of the disabled, insentient neonate.[112]

What is to my mind the President's crucial conclusion lies in his analysis of the duty of care to the fetus that is undertaken by the doctor and, hence, his or her liability for the neonatal disabilities. There is no better approach than to quote him verbatim (at [116]):

> [T]here is no reason in principle why the medical practitioners' negligence in the advice and treatment they gave the mothers cannot sound in damages being awarded to the appellants [i.e. to the children]. The appellants were born alive and their disabilities were in one sense caused by the negligence of the respective doctors, who omitted to give advice and treatment to the mothers that would have prevented the suffering presently endured by the appellants.[113]

This reasoning is very comparable to that adopted by the French and Dutch courts which, as we will see, have, possibly, set a trend for the acceptance of the wrongful life action. Even so, it is interesting to note that, despite the power of each of the arguments that I have selected above by way of illustration, Mason P summarised his dissent as resting mainly on the consistency that he saw between the parents' admitted cause of action and the children's putative cause of action [166].[114] We may, here, usfully revert to Stephenson LJ in *McKay* who regarded the importance of

---

[111] I have to admit my fancy for the parallel with the prophet Job (Job 3:3). 'Like Job, [the children] might curse the day they were born or conceived, but that would really be a poetic exclamation about their present plight' (n. 95 above, at [156]). Justice Mason's argument, here, is very comparable to my plea for an action for 'diminished life' to which I refer at p. 237.

[112] Discussed in detail in Chapter 7. For the present, I need only say that, in common with Justice Mason, I have long posited that to deny the fetus a preference for non-existence is to deny him or her a right to choice, albeit a surrogate choice, that is recognised as being available to a similarly affected neonate – e.g. J. K. Mason, *Medico-Legal Aspects of Reproduction and Parenthood* (Aldershot: Ashgate, 2nd edn 1998) at 164.

[113] The case law quoted by which to infer that a plaintiff need not to have been in existence as a legal personality at the time of an 'injury' in order to bring an action included *Watt* v. *Rama* [1972] VR 353, *X and Y (by her tutor X)* v. *Pal* (1991) 23 NSWLR 26 and the UK case *Burton* v. *Islington Health Authority* [1993] QB 204 and we will see at the end of this chapter that there are other important Scots cases in point. To use them as precedents in the present context, however, means that one must accept that birth itself *can* be an injury.

[114] See, also, n. 8 above. In passing, it should be noted that the overlap and duplication between the two actions pose more than academic problems. The very practical question of the distribution of damages must also be considered insofar as, in the absence of special considerations, damages that are available to the parents alone will generally cease to be payable when the child reaches majority; damages payable to the child by way of a wrongful life action will, however, be payable so long as his or her disabilities persist – which, in the most likely scenario, means until his or her death.

the wrongful life action as being 'somewhat reduced' by the existence of the mother's claim which, if successful, would give the child some compensation in money or in care. The implication must be that the Lord Justice saw the two actions as being, at least, complementary and certainly directed to a common end.

Indeed, as has been apparent throughout, there is a nagging impression that the distinction between the wrongful birth and wrongful life action is an artificial construct. Each action has the same ultimate objective – that is, recompense for a wrong done – and the wrong in each case lies in a similar failure to advise the pregnant woman and her fetus of their available choices. The interweave of the principles involved is such that, when Lax J began her hearing of the, then, novel Canadian trial of *McDonald-Wright* v. *O'Herlihy*,[115] she announced that she was doing so on the understanding 'that the underlying legal issues of "wrongful birth" and "wrongful life" were relevant to damages, and only to damages'. Effectively, she decided that no different considerations applied as to the duty of care in the two causes of action – 'it is difficult even to conceptualize the existence of two separate duties owed by a radiologist or an ultrasound technologist to a mother and her fetus'.[116]

In general, Justice Mason's opinion in *Harriton* was so robustly expressed and so grounded in principled law that it seemed very likely that the majority decision to the contrary would be overturned if it was further appealed. Such prescience was, however, again wide of the mark for, in the event, a seven-judge bench dismissed the appeal in the High Court of Australia by a majority of 6 to 1.[117]

Although the approach of the two courts differed,[118] the New South Wales Court of Appeal being concerned mainly with the basic question of whether the damage as alleged was capable of being recognised for the purposes of judicial proceedings, the High Court did not – and, in truth, probably could not – say much that was entirely original. The truly significant features were, first, the relative exclusion of emotive language and, second, the clarity with which the opposing arguments were presented. For these reasons, coupled with the fact that most of the discussion as to the general concept has already been detailed, it is proposed merely to outline the opposing views and, thereby, provide something of a summary of the wrongful life debate.

---

[115] [2005] O.J. no. 1636.
[116] n. 115 above, at 29. The case was one of neural tube defect of the 'missed ultrasound' class at 22 weeks' gestation.
[117] *Harriton* v. *Stephens* [2006] HCA 15.
[118] It is to be remembered that there was no trial, as such, of the case.

Crennan J made the following points, among others, for the majority:[119]

- The ultimate conclusion is that the nature of the damage alleged in a wrongful life case is not such as to be legally cognisable in the sense required to found a duty of care. That conclusion, in fact, makes it unnecessary to address any other aspects of the suit (at [243]);
- The damage alleged will be contingent on the free will, free choice and autonomy of the mother (at [248]); the woman cannot be required or compelled to have an abortion;
- The possibility of the child suing its mother for the fact of its existence is to be avoided (at [250]);
- A comparison between a life with disabilities and non-existence for the purposes of proving actual damage is impossible (at [252]);
- A duty of care cannot be stated in respect of damage which cannot be proved and which cannot be apprehended or evaluated by a court (at [254]);
- To allow a disabled person to claim his or her own existence as actionable damage is not only inconsistent with statutes preventing differential treatment of the disabled but it is also incompatible with the law's sanction of those who wrongfully take a life (at [263]);
- To posit that the real test is to compare an actual life with disabilities with a notional life without disabilities – or a 'fictional healthy person' – depends on a legal fiction; life without special pain and disabilities was never possible for the appellants (at [266] and [270]);[120]
- A need for corrective justice – if such is relevant when no-one is found responsible – cannot be determinative of a novel claim in negligence (at [275]).

In short: 'Life with disabilities', said Crennan J, 'like life, is not actionable'.

Against this, we have the very powerful argument put by Kirby J in the minority. The opinion, well-structured as it is, ultimately does little more than replicate that of Mason P in the court below – and, in doing so, confirms most of the points I have been trying to establish in the course of this chapter. Nevertheless – and, again, at the major risk of being repetitious – I think it is only fair to treat his speech in the same way as that of Crennan J so that we can have a wide picture of the debate as it

---

[119] In the event, three of the concurring judges made no independent speeches but expressly concurred with Crennan J.

[120] This 'fiction' (already raised by Mason P – see n. 112 above) also provided the rationale for recognising a legal basis for damages in the ground-breaking Israeli case of *Zeitzoff* v. *Katz* [1986] 40(2) PD 85. See Amos Shapira, '"Wrongful Life" Lawsuits for Faulty Genetic Counselling: Should the Impaired Newborn be Entitled to Sue?' (1998) 24 *Journal of Medical Ethics* 369–75.

stands in its most recent exposition. Thus, Kirby J's counter argument runs along these lines:

- As to causation in general, the child would not have been born had it not been for the respondent's negligence; consequently, the suffering, expense and losses of which she now complains would have been avoided. 'True, the respondent did not give rise to, or increase, the risk that the appellant would contract rubella. However, he did, through his carelessness, cause the appellant to suffer, as she still does, the consequences of that infection.'[121]
- The duty owed by the health carers to take reasonable care to avoid causing pre-natal injury to a fetus is sufficiently broad to impose a duty of care on the respondent in this case (at[71]);
- To deny the existence of a duty of care amounts, in effect, to the provision of an exceptional immunity to a tortfeasor – the common law resists such an immunity (at [72]);
- A mere potential for a conflict of maternal/fetal duties will not prevent a duty of care arising (at [74]);
- The respondent owed the appellant a relevant duty of care (at [77]);
- As to the 'unquantifiable' nature of the damage, the courts have had no difficulty in assessing these in relation to the parallel parental claims,[122] nor as to special damages – and, as a result, the 'impossible comparison' argument also falls away (at [87]);[123]
- It is wrong to deny compensation where resulting damage has occurred 'merely because logical problems purportedly render that damage insusceptible to precise or easy quantification';[124]
- Both 'general damages for proved pain and suffering and special damages for the needs created by the negligence of the medical practitioner in respect of a foetus in utero are recoverable in an action brought by or for that child' (at [109]).

---

[121] n. 117 above, at [39]. Kirby J also drew attention to the earlier article by Anthony Jackson, 'Wrongful Life and Wrongful Birth. The English Conception' (1996) 17 *Journal of Legal Medicine* 349–81.

[122] ibid., at [80], quoting J. G. Fleming, *The Law of Torts* (London: LBC Information Services, 9th edn 1998) at 184.

[123] To quote Kirby J in full: 'It follows that, by ordinary principles, at least special damages are recoverable in a case such as the present. There is no difficulty in the computation of such damage. In my view, this application of basic principles of law discloses starkly that the impediment to recovery is founded in policy considerations, not law.' (at [93]).

[124] Referring to Pollock J in *Procanik*, see p. 202 above. See also the recent English case *Chester* v. *Afshar* [2005] 1 AC 134, [2004] 4 All ER 587, referred to again below at n. 192. As was said in a paper published while this book was in press: 'Logic may have demanded the outcome reached by the High Court in *Harriton*, but fairness demands another': Alice Grey, '*Harriton* v. *Stephens*: Life, Logic and Legal Fictions' (2006) 28 *Sydney Law Review* 545–60 at 560.

Kirby J also summarily – and, to my mind, successfully – disposed of many of the supposed policy arguments against recovery for 'wrongful life'. Of these, I would highlight, particularly, his contention that it is absurd to suggest that the action implies a duty to kill the fetus – which would, in any event, be incompatible with a woman's right to decline a termination. The duty is no more than to detect, and warn of, the foreseeable risks to the fetus and to provide advice and guidance to the mother.[125] And, as a corollary of paramount importance:

This argument against allowing actions for wrongful life [that 'life' cannot be a legal injury] depends upon a false categorisation of such actions. It is not life, as such, which a plaintiff in a wrongful life action claims is wrongful. It is his or her present suffering as a life in being.[126]

I admit that, as with the opinion of Mason P in the New South Wales court, I find Kirby J's arguments so persuasive that it is difficult to understand how it is that they stand alone in the Commonwealth jurisdictions. I conclude that, as Kirby J himself suggested, the words 'wrongful life' implicitly denigrate the value of human existence and that, as a result, that label has made judges reluctant to afford remedies in such cases.[127]

Be that as it may, the most novel and, to my mind, most interesting features of the High Court hearing result from the fact that an appeal in *Waller* v. *James*[128] was heard consecutively to that of *Harriton*. The arguments deployed were repetitious and the appeal was, again, dismissed by a majority of 6 to 1. But were the acts so similar as to justify what was close to a conjoined hearing?

First, there were two main respondents[129] in *Waller* who stood in distinct relationships to the appellants – Dr James who was a specialist in the management of infertility and Dr Hoolahan who was the obstetrician responsible for Mrs Waller's prenatal care. The Wallers' general practitioner referred the family to the former doctor, remarking at the time that Mr Waller suffered from the dominant genetic abnormality known as anti-thrombin 3 deficiency – a condition which predisposes to intravascular clotting. Mr Waller was not tested for this condition although he was investigated to determine whether there was a genetic

---

[125] n. 117 above, at [112]. See also confirmation in *McKay* v. *Essex AHA*, n. 65 above per Griffiths LJ at QB 1192, All ER 790.
[126] n. 117 above, at [118].   [127] ibid., at [13].
[128] *Waller* v. *James*; *Waller* v. *Hoolahan* [2006] HCA 16.
[129] In fact, there were three – Dr James was working in conjunction with Sydney IVF Pty Ltd. In addition to the action for 'wrongful life', Dr Hoolahan was sued in respect of his management of the pregnancy which was a distinct issue and is of no concern for present purposes.

reason for his spermatic abnormality and Mrs Waller was later screened for the carriage of a Down's syndrome child. In the end, Mrs Waller was impregnated with an embryo formed in vitro by way of intra-cytoplasmic sperm injection of her own eggs. Thus, it was agreed in the statement of facts that, if the couple had been properly advised, they could have deferred the IVF procedure until pre-implantation genetic tests for AT3 deficiency were available or they could have opted for donor insemination – this being, essentially, the basis for the case against Dr James. In any event, given the way that the child, Keeden, had been conceived, there was a 50 per cent chance that he would be affected; thus, Mrs Waller could have arranged for a lawful termination of pregnancy had she been informed of the risk – and this founded part of the case against Dr Hoolahan.[130] The problems as to whether or not a duty of care was owed to the child have already been discussed in sufficient depth both in relation to *Harriton* and to other relevant cases.[131] The main concern at this point, however, is with causation.

Crennan J who, again, gave the major speech for the majority, considered that the decision in *Harriton* settled the case against Dr Hoolahan and there can be few who would doubt that this is the necessary conclusion. However, she also considered that it disposed of the case against Dr James and Sydney IVF and, while the judge herself clearly recognised the differences between the two,[132] this conclusion is far less clear. As Kirby J said in his minority opinion: 'Indeed, the evidence pointing towards the existence of the requisite causal relationship is arguably stronger in this case than in *Harriton* in relation to [Dr James and Sydney IVF].'[133]

And this must, surely, be so. Nobody can say that Dr Stephens was responsible for Alexia's infection with rubella; equally, of course, it cannot be said that Dr James was responsible for Keeden's genetic mutation However, Sydney IVF *were* responsible for choosing to use Mr Waller's sperm. Admittedly, they could not, at the time distinguish between normal and abnormal spermatozoa for this particular mutation[134] but

---

[130] n. 128 above, at [76].

[131] It is true that there was a significant difference in that Keenan's parents were bringing their own case whereas the Harritons were time barred. To that extent, therefore Keeden Waller was supported by Mason J's main argument; Alexia Harriton, by contrast, was fighting a lone battle.

[132] n. 128 above, at [84].   [133] ibid., at [38].

[134] Spigelman CJ was concerned as to the relation between public policy and the practice of eugenics (*Waller* v. *James* (2004) 59 NSWLR 694 at [30]). Pre-implantation genetic diagnosis is, however, being increasingly accepted and authorised in the United Kingdom – for a recent update, see Clare Dyer, 'HFEA Widens its Criteria for Pre-implantation Genetic Diagnosis' (2006) 332 *British Medical Journal* 1174.

they *could* have recognised the potential advantages of using donor sperm – and they were surely at fault in not putting the proposition to the Wallers. In short, it seems to me that the case against Dr James and Sydney IVF rests on the concept of a pre-conception tort[135] similar to those we have discussed above at p. 196. As such, it is clearly to be distinguished from the case brought against Dr Stephens by Alexia Harriton.[136]

Moreover, it might well succeed.[137] In this respect, *Waller* is of considerable interest to the United Kingdom jurisprudence where, as we have mentioned above at p. 213, the Congenital Disabilities (Civil Liability) Act 1976, section 1A holds that, in any case where:

b) the disability [in a child born disabled following assisted reproduction] results from an act or omission in the course of selection . . . of the embryo carried by her or of the gametes used to bring about the creation of that embryo, and

c) a person is under this section answerable to the child in respect of the act or omission, the child's disabilities are to be regarded as damage resulting from the wrongful act of that person and actionable accordingly at the suit of the child.

It seems to me, therefore, to be, at least, arguable that Keeden Waller would have won his case in England[138] and this, in turn, leads, again and particularly starkly, to the question of whether the soubriquet of 'wrongful life' does not act to the detriment of the pursuer. Would the results be different were the actions to be brought in negligence *per se* or would the hurdle of legally cognisable damage still persist? The point arose, perhaps most emphatically, in the leading Canadian case on the subject – to which jurisdiction we now turn.

A Canadian anomaly

Canada is yet another Commonwealth country where the wrongful life action appeared relatively late. As recently as 2005, Lax J considered that

---

[135] This was recognised in the Australian courts but was not argued at length. See, for example, Ipp JA in *Harriton* in the Court of Appeal, n. 95 above, at paras [206] – [208].

[136] This argument is, I think, different from the suggestion that *Waller* was a 'stronger' case than *Harriton* because the respondents in the former were more 'actively involved' in the 'transmission' of the fault than the respondent in the latter – which was implicitly rejected by Crennan J, n. 117 above, at [84].

[137] In Australia, see *X and Y* v. *Pal*, n. 37 above. The arguments raised at p. 198 against the imposition of indeterminate liability would not apply in relation to a *specific* pregnancy.

[138] And, thus, unless *Waller* v. *James* is incorrectly labelled, enabling a wrongful life action in England.

the 'existence of a cause for wrongful life remains unsettled in Canadian jurisprudence[139] and has never been settled in Ontario'.[140]

In fact, the more one looks at the relevant Canadian cases, the more one gains the impression that the Provincial courts are unwilling to set the pattern for the country as a whole and it may be that this accounts for several apposite cases being unreported and others being struck out at an early stage in the proceedings. The first case[141] to go to appeal appears to have been *Lacroix v. Dominique*[142] – a Manitoba case involving teratogenic treatment during pregnancy. Here, both the trial judge and the Court of Appeal relied heavily on *McKay v. Essex Area Health Authority*[143] and found the reasoning in that case to be too compelling to allow for such an action to be recognised in Canada – 'and I am unaware of any Canadian circumstances which would cause judges here to think differently' said Twaddle JA.[144]

Lacroix, however, raises an important general point in respect of causation which we have not yet addressed. *McKay* was an example of viral infection during pregnancy; *Lacroix* was a matter of medication. The health carers were ostensibly negligent in both cases – in the former by failing to identify the infection, in the latter by prescribing a drug with a known potential for harming an immature fetus. As we have already seen, no-one could accuse the staff of *causing* Mrs McKay's infection; Mrs Lacroix' physician *had*, however, prescribed the offending drug – one's instinct, then, is to say that the hurdle of causation no longer stands in the way of her child's action. In response, Twaddle JA held that the doctor was under no duty of care to the child – to hold otherwise, he thought, would create an irreconcilable conflict between his or her duties

---

[139] This, however, is uncertain. In a Manitoba case occurring at much the same time, it was said that the law in Canada does not recognise the neonate's right to bring such a claim: *Bosard v. Davey* (2005) CarswellMan 92, QB.

[140] In *McDonald-Wright*, n. 115 above at 4. Once again, the wrongful birth action is well recognised (see *Arndt v. Smith* (1997) 148 DLR (4th) 48 discussed in Chapter 3); the parallel action for wrongful life in this case was abandoned: ([1994] 8 WWR 568) and was not contested in *McDonald-Wright* save as to the 'time-frame'. In the end, the relevance of a wrongful life action was not decided in *McDonald-Wright*, it being thought that the question was best left to the Court of Appeal. (At the time of writing it is uncertain whether or not the case will proceed).

[141] This depends on whether or not you regard *Cherry v. Borsman*, n. 153 below, as one of 'wrongful life'. In my view it should be so classified – and as an important one at that. But it is hard to maintain this in view of the Court of Appeal's statement: 'The first thing that must be said here is that in our opinion this is not a "wrongful life" case' – (1992) 94 DLR (4th) 487 at 503.

[142] (2001) 202 DLR (4th) 121.   [143] n. 65 above.

[144] n. 142 above, at [43]. The main reason extracted from *McKay* was the impossibility of assessing the damages to be awarded – which, in passing, seems to the writer to be the least acceptable of the many reasons adduced for denying the claim.

to both mother and child. On the other hand, the court had to face the fact that a previous judgment in the Manitoba Court of Appeal had found a physician negligent in respect of a child's disabilities for having *continued* to prescribe teratogenic drugs to its mother before taking specialist advice[145] and this would seem to fit more comfortably with the strong intuition that we have already expressed to the effect that the pregnant woman's attending physician owes a duty of care to both her and her fetus.[146] The 'drug cases' do not materially alter the fact that the majority of wrongful life cases are, essentially, instances of communication based negligence – the pregnant woman has a right to choose or reject treatment in the light of the *information provided*, even though it may appear irresponsible of her to do so.[147] The clinical, jurisprudential and, not least, semantic problems arising from the drug related action are particularly formidable – so much so that they, perhaps, merit independent categorisation.

In passing, *Lacroix* provides one last note of comparative interest in that the parental action for wrongful birth was time expired; it, thus, invites comparison with the New Jersey case of *Procanik* v. *Cillo*[148] which we have discussed earlier in this chapter. *Procanik* may, as has been suggested, be 'bad law' but it does indicate that, given the urge to do so, the courts can fashion a reasonable case for accepting the wrongful life action.

The question still remains, do the Canadian courts want to join the hawks or the doves? One might have thought that *Lacroix* was sufficient to settle the issue but, of course, Canada is a multi-jurisdictional state and what happens in one province may well not be replicated in another. The situation was confused by a number of cases heard at first instance in Ontario which have been well summarised in *Petkovic* v. *Olupona*.[149] Here, Epstein J attempted to resolve the conflict that had developed in Ontario where, on the one hand, Jennings J struck out a claim for wrongful life on the grounds that it:

---

[145] *Webster* v. *Chapman* [1998] 4 WWR 335. I am unconvinced by the Court's distinction between the cases on the grounds that Mrs Lacroix would have elected to remain on medication while avoiding intentional pregnancy.

[146] The prospect of conflicting loyalties has, of course, been aired at Court of Appeal level in the United Kingdom in *Re F (in utero)* [1988] Fam 122, [1988] 2 All ER 193. The problem, that of wardship of an unborn child, was, however, more akin to administrative law than to medical law. See also the Canadian case *Winnipeg Child and Family Services (Northwest Area)* v. *G(DF)* [1997] 2 SCR 925. Yet, on the face of things, *Lacroix* is at odds with the earlier Canadian case of *Cherry* v. *Borsman* (n. 153 below) and it is surprising this was not brought up in argument.

[147] *Re MB (an adult: medical treatment)* (1997) 38 BMLR 175, CA per Butler-Sloss LJ at BMLR 186.

[148] n. 49 above.   [149] [2002] O.J. no. 3411.

was plain and obvious that the common law that will be applied in Ontario knows no action for 'wrongful life'[150]

but, on the other, Sharpe J held:

This is an evolving area of the law. The issue has not been considered in depth by Canadian courts ... More generally, the legal regime relating to abortion has undergone significant change resulting in an expanded scope for parental choice.[151]

This later view was backed in the trial stage of *Petkovic* by Gans J who specifically disapproved Jennings J's view as to the certainty of the current law. In the end, Epstein J agreed that the matter was not settled in Canada and refused to overturn the trial judge's discretionary decision to allow Trajan Petkovic's action to proceed to trial. It is important to remember, however, that these arguments have arisen and the decisions have been taken mainly within the ambience of court procedure and administration and, indeed, have been influenced by the fact that a trial of the parents' claim was inevitable; accordingly, there was no economic advantage in refusing to hear the wrongful life action – and, once again, one is tempted to question the logic of separating the two. Nonetheless, it does seem that *Petkovic* has, at least, chipped the well-nigh impervious wall of resistance to such a suit that appears to have been built up in Canada;[152] we will have to wait and see if the chip becomes a breach.

There are, however, many defences that have yet to be tested. The problem of causation, for example, has scarcely been considered – yet, we have noted that, elsewhere, causation consistently presents a main difficulty in establishing an action for wrongful life. Indeed, as we will see, it is possible to define, or distinguish, the wrongful life action as a distinct jurisprudential entity on the grounds that no person has *directly caused* the injuries of which the neonate complains – from which it follows in logic that there can be no issue of culpability once an action is so framed. Carrying this one stage further, we can reach the anomalous situation whereby, such is the general antipathy to the suit, it would be to the tactical advantage of the tortfeasor to be sued for wrongful life of the neonate even when a causative link between wrong-doing and injury was accepted. Relevant instances must, a priori, be very rare but such an argument was, in fact, pursued in the extraordinary British Columbian

---

[150] *Mickle* v. *Salvation Army Grace Hospital* (1995, unreported).
[151] *Sharma* v. *Mergelas, Nowaczyk* v. *Majewski* (1997, unreported).
[152] Though one must be careful using such a generalisation. In view of the very few reports available, the most that should be said is that there is no evidence to suggest otherwise; indeed, the topic may not even have been addressed as such outside Ontario and Manitoba.

case of *Cherry* v. *Borsman*[153] which might have provided a perfect illustration had it not been for the court's obvious reluctance to run it as such – possibly because of the danger of distorting case law in the process.

> *The case of Mrs Cherry.* Mrs Cherry underwent an abortion on what would correspond to the 'social grounds' in the UK Abortion Act 1967, section 1(1)(a). The obstetrician misinterpreted the gestational age of the fetus – possibly because of a failure in communication – and, as a result, he failed to terminate the pregnancy.[154] As so often happens when an error occurs, things went from bad to worse. She was re-examined by Dr Borsman a month later and, despite an expressed suspicion on the part of her general practitioner to the contrary, she was declared not to be pregnant – although her pregnancy test was not repeated. Two months later she was diagnosed by another obstetrician as being between 19.3 and 23.5 weeks pregnant which made her beyond the time at which a termination could be legally performed in Canada. Nonetheless, Dr Borsman assured her that there was little, if any, chance of the fetus having been damaged and, in all the circumstances, she was resigned to continuing her pregnancy – and was even anxious to do so. The saga of complications continued and, after a stormy gestation, she was delivered of a 31-week-old baby by caesarian section. The baby, Elizabeth, was markedly deformed, the abnormalities being, in general, compatible with prolonged intrauterine compression due to a deficiency of amniotic fluid – the so-called oligohydramnios syndrome. As if this was not enough, she sustained severe necrosis of the bowel with accompanying organic brain damage; she was severely disabled both physically and mentally and required constant nursing. Her condition as described by the judge of the British Columbia Supreme Court

was such as, in my view, to place her clearly within the ambience of an 'intolerable existence' foreshadowed by Templeman LJ in *Re B*.[155]

Mrs Cherry's case, therefore, provides us with yet another problem of classification. During the course of the trial it was held that Dr Borsman

---

[153] (1990) 75 DLR (4th) 668, BCSC; (1992) 94 DLR (4th) 487, BCCA.

[154] Mrs Cherry had a retroverted uterus. Skipp J noted that some 49 per cent of women in whom a termination fails have this condition; he considered that this laid a duty on the doctor to be especially vigilant (at 75 DLR 671). The case also raises, once again, the question of the pathologist's role – and the interpretation of the pathologist's report – in such cases.

[155] n. 2 above. For examination of the meaning of 'intolerable', see the relatively recent, albeit unrelated, cases of *W Healthcare NHS Trust* v. *H* [2005] 1 WLR 834, CA and *R (on the application of Burke)* v. *General Medical Council* (2005) 85 BMLR 1, CA – and, even more recently, *An NHS Trust* v. *MB and others* [2006] EWHC 507, [2006] 2 FLR 319.

was at fault in the post-operative care he gave and that, had he, at an early stage, determined that Mrs Cherry was still pregnant – as he should have done – she would have had a second abortion and the infant plaintiff would never have been born. Moreover, intuition, if nothing else, tells us that there is a possibility of damage to a fetus that has survived an attempted abortion; no matter how well the contrary could be argued, the possibility is surely such as is sufficient to justify an appropriate warning to the patient.[156] The potential child was already disabled when the opportunity to give such a warning was rejected and the child was born disabled. To my mind, the scene was set for a wrongful life action and, moreover, an action from which the stumbling block of lack of causation had been removed – as the trial judge helpfully acknowledged 'the admissions almost encourage such an action'.[157]

The unique, if not bizarre, aspect of *Cherry* is that it was the defendant who described it as a case of wrongful life and it is not difficult to see the reason. Dr Borsman's duty of care to his adult patient – and, hence, the availability of a wrongful birth action – was never in doubt. The interest of the case lies in the additional concept of a duty of care to the fetus which is inherent to the wrongful life action. Given that it was classified as such, there was a very good chance that it would be held that there was no such cause in British Columbia;[158] the court in *Cherry* was palpably anxious to avoid such a result and adopted the alternative view that the plaintiff's claim could be determined on ordinary negligence principles.

We have argued at several points in this book that, with the possible exception of therapy designed for her benefit, a pregnant woman's medical attendant owes a simultaneous duty of care to the woman herself and to her fetus. Consequently, a fetus that is harmed *in utero* has a right of action against the tortfeasor once he or she is born. In the current case, Skipp J held that Dr Borsman owed a duty to Elizabeth not to injure her and, here, we come up against what the writer, at least, sees as a major conceptual problem. Certainly, the doctor/patient relationship imposes a duty on the former not to harm the latter. At the same time, the law, and, to an extent, common sense, tell us that to kill another being is to inflict the maximum harm on that being. It is a strange interpretation of a duty

---

[156] As Skipp J at first instance said: 'It is clearly foreseeable that a negligently performed abortion *may* affect a fetus' (at 75 DLR 676, emphasis added).

[157] ibid., at 679.

[158] The Supreme Court quoted no British Columbia precedents other than *Fredette* v. *Wiebe* (1986) 29 DLR (4th) 534. But the question of wrongful life did not arise in that case of failed abortion. Similarly, a number of Canadian and English cases cited under 'Wrongful Life' (at 685 et seq.) were, in fact cases of wrongful pregnancy brought by the mother – for which, see Chapter 4.

of care to say: 'I am going to kill you and promise not to injure you' – it is a sobering thought that, transferring this to capital punishment, the condemned man might well have settled even for tetraplegia rather than death. The abortionist may have a duty of feticide – and even this may be limited[159] – but, again, he or she owes this to the mother. To extend this to a duty of *care* to the condemned fetus is grossly to overstretch the meaning of the words. Mrs Cherry's case, in fact, raises a whole host of medical ethical issues including doubts as to whether a woman's obstetrician should also be her abortionist. Does the conflict of interests inherent within the combined role render it unacceptable practice?[160] But such concerns can only lead us back to the Hippocratic Oath and to follow that path is, as Chapter 2 has shown, little better than to divert into a moral cul-de-sac.

Rather, we can more usefully follow the paralogic of Skipp J who held quite clearly that, insofar as it is foreseeable that a negligently performed abortion may cause injury to a fetus, the doctor has a corresponding duty to prevent this foreseeable harm.[161] There are several difficulties here. The first, as has already been intimated, is the conceptual one of visualising injury as being more damaging than death but this is an inevitable consequence of denying the fetus personality until it is born – it has long been recognised in law that it is safer to kill a fetus than to scratch it.[162] This hurdle was recognised by Skipp J, but he did not believe that he was, thereby, conferring legal personhood on the fetus; rights accrued only to the neonate who could claim compensation for injuries sustained *in utero*.[163] As a result, the claim for injury could be settled on ordinary negligence principles and both the adult *and* the infant were entitled to recover for their pain and suffering.

---

[159] We are concerned here only with the early termination of pregnancy. It is arguable that the abortion of a 'normal' and *viable* fetus involves a collateral moral duty to preserve its life.

[160] The defendant in *Cherry* in fact based his case very largely on the question: 'How can the surgeon have a duty to the mother to destroy the foetus and at the same time have a duty to protect the foetus?' – going on to say that the duty to the mother negatives any duty of care to the foetus. The Court of Appeal however held that the abortionist 'owes a duty of care to the mother to perform his task properly but at the same time owes a duty of care to the foetus not to harm it if he should fail in the duty of care he owes to the mother' ((1992) 94 DLR (4th) 487 at 504). All of which seems very like expecting the horse to be in its stable after it has bolted and is not very helpful. In this respect, it is interesting to compare the reasoning in the later case of *Lacroix* (n. 142 above) with that in *Cherry*.

[161] n. 153 above, at 75 DLR 676.

[162] *Amadio* v. *Leven* 501 A 2d 1085 (Pa., 1985). See also P. J. Pace, 'Civil Liability for Prenatal Injury' (1977) 40 *Modern Law Review* 141–58 at 148.

[163] And this, as we have seen, represents the law in the vast majority of jurisdictions.

Nevertheless, the judge was ambivalent to the extent of admitting that the claim contained the elements of a wrongful life action as well, thus entitling the claimants to be compensated on either basis and, while the Court of Appeal dismissed the appeal in respect of liability,[164] it appeared equally anxious to dispose of this doubt once and for all – and it did so very shortly:

> The first thing that must be said here is that in our opinion this is not a 'wrongful life' case as asserted by the defendant ... This is not a case where the plaintiffs assert a legal obligation to the foetus to terminate its life as was the position in *McKay* v. *Essex Area Health Authority*.[165]

And, again:

> It is significant that the infant plaintiff relies on the injuries she alleges she sustained in the [first] operation. No reliance is placed by the infant plaintiff on the defendant's failure to realize the abortion had failed. The duty of care in that respect, say the plaintiffs, is a duty to the mother and the mother only. That, say the plaintiffs, is why this is not a wrongful life case. We agree with that analysis.[166]

So, is the generally unsatisfactory nature of *Cherry* down to no more than the nature of the pleadings? That may be so, but for an alternative, and more positive, view, we must return to Skipp J:

> The admissions by the defendant doctor ... do set up a wrongful life action ... But they constitute only a part of the plaintiff's allegations. It is the additional allegation that the defendant caused the infant plaintiff's injuries that sets this action apart from wrongful life actions.[167]

If this be so, apart from indicating that Canada is unlikely to adopt such an action, *Cherry* leads us to a remarkable circular conclusion which we have already mooted. A wrongful life action brought against a health carer will almost certainly fail on a number of grounds – one of which is the major difficulty of attributing causation to that health carer. If, however, causation can be shown, the case ceases to be one of wrongful life and remains one of negligence simpliciter. We have, therefore, unearthed another reason why the wrongful life action can be seen as little more

---

[164] *Cherry* v. *Borsman* (1992) 94 DLR (4th) 487.   [165] ibid., at 503.   [166] ibid., at 506.

[167] n. 153 above, at 75 DLR 679. It seems, however, that *Cherry* is not unique in a global sense. The circumstances appear to have been very similar in a French case which I have not been able to check personally. An abortion was carried out ineffectually and damages were awarded to the neonate by way of the doctor's negligence in failing to check whether or not the abortion was successful: CE. 27 December 1989, D.1991. J.80, cited by Tony Weir, 'The Unwanted Child' (2002) 6 *Edinburgh Law Review* 244–53. Weir points out, however, that the Conseil d'État subsequently withdrew the damages to the child but substituted an award to the parents for the upkeep of the child for life.

than duplicative. Yet both the French and the Dutch courts have found a need for the suit and have found their own ways round allowing it. How has this come about?

Wrongful life in Europe

In France, *l'arrêt Perruche*[168] caused a major political crisis and it certainly had its own problems during the course of the litigation.

The circumstances of the case were fairly standard and very comparable to those in *McKay* in that the fact that Mme Perruche suffered from rubella during her early pregnancy was ignored by her health carers; as a result, her child was born with severe disabilities. In brief, the court of first instance held that both the physician in charge and the laboratory were negligent in their interpretation of her antenatal condition and awarded damages not only to the woman herself but also to her son in recompense for the loss caused by his resulting handicap. On appeal to the court in Paris, the mother's claim was upheld but that of the handicapped child was denied on grounds that were, in general, similar to those given in *McKay*. Following the rather complex French judicial system involving parallel paths to recompense for negligence, the case was, then, re-appealed and cross appealed, to the Cour d'Appel in Orleans where it was agreed that the child did not suffer any compensable harm resulting from the negligence in question – the reason being on the standard grounds that his affliction resulted not from such negligence but solely from his mother's having German measles.

The case then went to the highest court. The definitive findings of the Assemblée Plénière are brief[169] and can be quoted verbatim:

[C]onsidering that the negligence of the doctor and the laboratory in the performance of their contracts with Mme [Perruche] prevented her exercising

---

[168] *X* v. *Mutuelle d'Assurance du Corps Sanitaire Français* (2000) JCP 2293. French courts do not issue lengthy and explanatory judgments. The opinions of the Avocat Général Sainte-Rose and of the Conseiller-Rapporteur to the court, P. Sargos, are, however, available in full and are widely quoted in the relevant literature. The opinion of the latter is especially valuable as a contribution to the general debate: J.C.P. G 2000, II-10438.

[169] The translation used is that provided by Weir, n. 167 above. The court decision is further disapproved in Thérèse Callus, '"Wrongful Life" à la Francaise' (2001) 5 *Medical Law International* 117–26. For a wide-ranging, and particularly helpful, review of the Anglo-French position, see Anne Morris and Severine Saintier, 'To Be or Not to Be: Is That the Question? Wrongful Life and Misconceptions' (2003) 11 *Medical Law Review* 167–93. An analysis in depth and a particularly useful review of the French literature on the case are provided by Penney Lewis, 'The Necessary Implications of Wrongful Life Claims: Lessons from France' (2005) 12 *European Journal of Health Law* 135–53.

her freedom to proceed to a termination of the pregnancy in order to avoid the birth of a handicapped child, the harm resulting to the child from such handicap was caused by that negligence and he can claim compensation for it.[170]

This judicially binding decision caused widespread and professional consternation.[171] The opposition came from such apparently disparate groups as the anti-abortionists, campaigners on behalf of the disabled and the medical profession backed by its insurers – and the French Parliament rapidly made it impossible for a later court to follow that precedent.[172] The effect is that not only wrongful life is now not actionable in France but, also, a wrongful birth action is available only in strictly limited circumstances. The economic shortfall for the injured parents is to be made up from the state social security services. One of the main factors taken into account by the Cour de Cassation was that damages awarded to the parents might not be applied where they were needed – that is, to the care of the disabled infant or, in more practically important terms, to the care of the disabled young adult.[173] Many on this side of the English Channel might wonder if the social services would provide an even less certain altruistic source of

---

[170] Morris and Saintier, n. 169 above, point out that it is a well-accepted principle in French law that a third party who suffers damage because of a breach of contract can use the contract against that party in order to claim damages (at 179, n. 58).

[171] It has to be said that the flames of public dissatisfaction at the *Perruche* decision were almost certainly fanned by those in two comparable cases – though, this time, of Down's syndrome – which arose at much the same time and which were settled in the same way: Alexander Dorozynski, 'Highest French Court Awards Compensation for "Being Born"' (2001) 323 *British Medical Journal* 1384. The case of *Child L* is discussed by M. Spriggs and J. Savulescu, 'The Perruche Judgment and the "Right Not to be Born"' (2002) 28 *Journal of Medical Ethics* 63–4. See also A. M. Duguet, 'Wrongful Life: The Recent French Cour de Cassation Decisions' (2002) 9 *European Journal of Health Law* 139–63. I have always contented that attitudes to physical and mental disablement should be distinct. See Mason 'Wrongful Life', n. 74 above, at 158.

[172] The relevant sections of the provisional law adopted by the French Senate, and subsequently embodied in Loi no. 2002–303 of 4 March 2002, run:

One cannot treat the mere fact of being born as constituting damage. A child born with a handicap which is due to medical malpractice may claim compensation if the faulty conduct directly caused the handicap, aggravated it or prevented the adoption of measures which could have alleviated it. The parents of a child born with a handicap which remained undiagnosed during pregnancy owing to serious fault on the part of a professional or health establishment may claim compensation only for the harm suffered by them personally, not including any special costs attributable to the child's being handicapped, for which compensation will be provided through national solidarity.

[173] 'The defence of his interests, such as the expression of dignity in the conditions of his future life, seem to be better assured by the provision of an indemnity which is his very own', Le texte de l'arrêt Perruche, *Le Monde*, 10 January 2002 (author's translation).

funding;[174] but, then, the welfare state is an integral component of the French culture.

The difficulties experienced by the French were not, however, to deter the Dutch from following the same path in the case of Kelly Molenaar.[175] In *Molenaar*, the midwife managing the pregnancy failed to heed a strong indication of the need for amniocentesis and the child was born with a severe chromosomal defect. The nature of this is uncertain but it is clear that she was in very considerable pain due to extensive physical and mental disabilities. The case first came to international notice in the Court of Appeal in The Hague where compensation was awarded, not only to the parents, but also to the child in respect of non-pecuniary damage.[176] As to the first, the Court followed the relatively standard approach to claims for wrongful birth – the mother's legal right to opt for termination of the pregnancy had been infringed as a result of the hospital's negligence. Interestingly, despite the latter's contention that it had not been demonstrated that Mrs Molenaar would have elected for abortion had she been properly informed, the court held that, given the circumstances, it could be reasonably assumed that she would have done so. It was, thus, prepared to adopt an objective test of causation in the wrongful birth action.[177]

The court's reasoning in respect of the child's action was, at first glance, a trifle convoluted and took two lines. First, it was proposed that the midwife had a contractual obligation to the pregnant woman and that the unborn child could be considered to be party to that contract.[178] The logic underlying this appears to the present writer to look very much like a civil variation on the criminal concept of transferred malice. The latter has been criticised in the United Kingdom[179] and it is, at best, uncertain whether such an extended interpretation would be accepted here.[180] The Hague court was, itself, clearly hesitant on the point and opined that, in the alternative, the health authority was under a

---

[174] Indeed, Morris and Saintier, n. 169 above, criticise the resulting law as being without teeth and arguably providing, in the end, 'the greatest affront to personal dignity' (at 191). For earlier discussion, see Shapira, n. 120 above.

[175] *X* v. *Y*, The Hague, Court of Appeals, 26 March 2003.

[176] I am indebted to personal communication with Professor Nys and Dr Derckx and to H. F. L. Nys and J. C. J. Dute, 'A Wrongful Existence in the Netherlands' (2004) 30 *Journal of Medical Ethics* 393–4.

[177] Compare the strongly subjective approach adopted in the United Kingdom: e.g. *Gregory* v. *Pembrokeshire Health Authority* [1989] 1 Med LR 81 (see Chapter 3).

[178] As had previously been accepted in the unreported 'Baby Joost' case of 8 September 2000.

[179] *Attorney-General's Reference (No.3 of 1994)* [1998] AC 245, HL.

[180] It would, in any event, be complicated by the fact that there is no contract between patient and medical attendant within the National Health Service – *Pfizer Corporation* v.

legal obligation to look after the interests of the fetus as an independent entity – and it is to be noted that this has been argued as an evident duty, albeit partially confined, throughout this chapter. As might be expected in that jurisdiction, however, the Dutch Court of Appeal relied to an extent on the *nasciturus* principle – that is, that a child *in utero* can be regarded as being alive if it is in his or her interests to do so.[181] The element of causation necessary for a successful action in negligence was supplied by the fact that the birth of the child could have been prevented; the damage from which the child suffered was, as a result, a direct consequence of a negligent medical error.

To accept the principles of the *Molenaar* judgment involves accepting a number of conclusions with which many other jurisdictions have been unable to come to terms. Firstly, one has to accept not only that, despite the court's protestations to the contrary, it implies that to be born with physical disability represents a compensable harm. As is attributed to the Professor of Health Law at the Free University of Amsterdam:

> To recognise a disabled life as a source of financial damages gives the wrong signal to society. Disabled people should be fellow citizens not someone who should have been aborted.[182]

With which we would all, surely, agree but to which one can reply – as I see it, rightly[183] – that it is not the *child* that is being valued but, rather, the cost of *caring* for that child's needs. This paraphrase of Pierre Sargos, Rapporteur to the *Perruche* court,[184] is particularly telling:

> Refusing to compensate the [disabled] child is equally contrary to human dignity [as it is to place a negative value on his life]. Compensation gives him the means to protect his dignity, and enhances that dignity by giving him, personally, the right to claim.[185]

But the more practical problem raised by the European decisions lies in the considerable semantic juggling that they demand in surmounting the apparently insurmountable hurdle of causation – and this may not always lead to easily acceptable conclusions. In essence, we have to interpret

---

Ministry of Health [1965] AC 512. One's feeling is that any such transfer would have to be based on the existence of a non-contractual civil wrong involving the fetus – as in the Court's second option.

[181] Wrongful life actions have not been addressed as such in Scotland but it is suspected that a rather similar argument could be deployed there – and it might not be necessary to invoke the civil law *nasciturus* fiction: see *Hamilton* v. *Fife Health Board* 1993 SCLR 408.

[182] J. Hubben, quoted by Tony Sheldon, 'Court Awards Damages to Disabled Child for Having Been Born' (2003) 326 *British Medical Journal* 784.

[183] See the commentary on *McFarlane* v. *Tayside Health Board* at p. 123 above.

[184] n. 168 above.

[185] The quotation is from Morris and Saintier, n. 169 above, at 186.

causation in terms of liability not as the cause of the *disability* but as the cause of the *exhibition* of the disability – and this, we have seen, has been viewed as a bridge too far by the great majority of common law courts. Not only does it reopen the *McKay* court's fears as to the encouragement of abortion but it also goes a long way in justifying the intense opposition to the *Perruche* decision that was shown by the French medical profession. Consequently, the result of the further appeal to the Supreme Court of the Netherlands in *Molenaar* was bound to be of major jurisprudential importance.

And, in the end, the Supreme Court[186] stood firm and refused to be influenced either by the parliamentary reaction to *Perruche* in France or by the comparable domestic reaction to the Court of Appeal in *Molenaar*. It found that the midwife had been negligent in her management of the case and agreed that compensation should be available to the parents not only for the general and special costs of caring for Kelly but also in recognition of the emotional damage sustained and the cost of its treatment. More importantly in the present context, the viability of the child's action was confirmed primarily on the grounds that the parents contract with the hospital was undertaken partly on behalf of the child and, alternatively, that the hospital owed a duty of care to the child to act in her ultimate interests even though she was not a party to the agreement. It is, admittedly, difficult to unravel the ratio behind a very long judgment in the absence of a full and authoritative translation.[187] However, the court was adamant that it did not attribute Kelly's emotional damage, for which she was to be compensated, to her existence as such. The award of damages was justified solely on the basis that her condition was a foreseeable consequence of professional negligence – or a failure to act with reasonable competence. The 'consequence' was the birth of a disabled child which could have been prevented by timely intervention – that is, antenatal counselling to the effect that a legal termination of pregnancy was available. Thus far, we are in the well-trodden footsteps of the wrongful birth action. But, in attributing emotional damage to the neonate, the Supreme Court appears to have taken an incremental step forward in placing the 'choice' of termination in the hands of the fetus – albeit vicariously. My translation runs:

Admittedly, Kelly herself could not entertain the question of whether she wanted to be alive, but that decision could be taken on her behalf by her parents. Within

---

[186] LJN:AR5213, Hoge Raad, C03/206HR, 18 March 2005.
[187] I am grateful to Ms Claudia van Tooren, one of my students, for the partial translation that she undertook. See also Tony Sheldon, 'Dutch Supreme Court Backs Damages for Child for Having Been Born' (2005) 330 *British Medical Journal* 747.

the confines of the law, that decision could only be left to the parents and the fact that they may have chosen to have an abortion must be respected given the serious risks with which Kelly was faced at the time, and which have since materialised.

Thus, in placing the *choice* to live or die in the hands of the fetus, the Court seems to have allowed Kelly Molenaar compensation for emotional damage 'because of the fact she was born'[188] and, in doing so, has crossed the philosophical Rubicon and allowed a pure wrongful life action. That is a major step in a doubtful direction – but there is, as yet, no evidence of a popular or parliamentary backlash such as arose in France.

Conclusion

Confusing though they may be, the recent European cases confirm the suspicion that there is a movement, on a global scale, towards revision of our hitherto ingrained attitudes to the wrongful life action. The reasons for the existing antipathy are multiple but, as the individual cases demonstrate, each can be countered by acceptable argument – even though it may be in the form of minority opinion. The difficulty is to combine these separate arguments into a coherent whole by which to justify – or refute – the apparent change in attitude.

Fundamental to the discussion is the very nature of the action. The difficulty that has beset every jurisdiction is that the correlate of wrongful life is rightful death – and Stephenson LJ crystallised the consequent dilemma when he asked: 'How can there be a duty to take away life?' I am convinced that this question reveals an underlying misconception – the child bringing a wrongful life action is not complaining of being born but of being born disabled.[189] The action is, in reality, one for diminished life. He or she is not, thereby, claiming that an individual caused the disabilities. Rather, the action is of the nature: 'I sought your advice as to whether to choose to live a disabled life was in my interests. My interests would have been served had the advice been that I would be severely handicapped if I lived. Due to your negligence, I was deprived of a choice, I am severely handicapped and my interests in life are compromised. I need restitution for the loss of those interests'[190]

Accepting a diminished life construct assists us in several other aspects of the wrongful life debate. First, we are no longer grappling with the mysteries of non-existence and can return to the physical world we know.

[188] Sheldon, n. 187 above.

[189] It is to be noted that this concept was accepted by Lawson J in the trial phase of *McKay*, n. 65 above, [1982] QB 1166 at 1175, [1982] 2 All ER 771 at 777.

[190] Rethinking Mason, n. 74 above, at 157.

Second – and on much the same line – it allows the courts to assess the neonate's deficit in understandable terms; the 'intolerable and insoluble problem' of the assessment of damage, which Griffiths LJ saw as the most compelling reason for rejecting the cause of action,[191] no longer applies; the courts are perfectly able to assess the monetary equivalents that separate a normal and a disabled life. And, third, and, perhaps, conceptually most importantly, it firmly correlates recompense with suffering due to negligence – that is, negligent advice given to the fetus through its mother. It is the neonate who suffers and every instinct tells us that this should be recognised; recognition of a 'diminished life' spares us the uncomfortable, and often used, excuse that not all losses give rise to compensation in tort and that wrongful life is one of them.

Problems, of course, remain. High among these is the rule that the object of recompense is to restore the injured party as nearly as possible to his or her state before the injury which would, logically, be non-existence. Once again, however, this problem is, at least, reduced once it is appreciated that the injury is being born disabled – not being born. We are still left with the thorny problem of causation which I have partially addressed above. We will see, however, in the next chapter that the concept of neonatal refusal of treatment by way of parental decision is well-recognised by both the judiciary and the general public. Given the fact that, as we have already noted, an injury sustained *in utero* matures in a legal sense at birth, there is no reason why such proxy decision making should not extend to the fetus – and it is this concept that, I believe, lies at the heart of both the *Perruche* and *Molenaar* decisions. Effectively, the negligent health carer has denied the fetus the opportunity to choose between a continued life of suffering and withdrawal of treatment in the form of antenatal care. To describe an abortion in such terms may seem to many to be unacceptably euphemistic – but, then, the whole concept of infantile decision-making by parental proxy can be seen as little more than a sophistic fancy. How important is it, in fact, to establish an orthodox construct of causation in the circumstances? I admit to being greatly impressed by the judicial statement:

In attributing causation, the court is primarily making a value judgment on responsibility. In making this judgment the court will have regard to the purpose sought to be achieved by the relevant tort, as applied to the particular circumstances[192]

---

[191] In *McKay*, n. 65 above, at QB 1192, All ER 790.
[192] *Kuwait Airways* v. *Iraq Airways Co* [2002] 2 AC 883 per Lord Nicholls at [74]. I must acknowledge Morris and Saintier, n. 169 above at 187, for directing me to this citation. The authors also draw attention to the French rule of *équivalence des conditions* which

and one wonders whether wrongful life may not be a suitable case for adjusting principle so as to fit the circumstances.[193] Morris and Saintier point out[194] that Nicholas Perruche's disabled life has two causes: the rubella *and* the doctor's negligence. The doctor was not to blame for his having contracted rubella, but s/he is to blame for his having to live with the consequences.

The remaining objection to allowing a diminished life action lies, as noted above, in the suggestion that, given the uncertainty of definition as to severity and prognosis that is entailed in fetal diagnosis, it would lead to excessive defensive medicine and to an increased number of abortions. As to the latter, while conditions may differ in France and Great Britain, we have already noted that abortion is now commonplace in the latter and any consequent increase would be, at most, insignificant. As to the former, it has to be remembered that an action for wrongful birth will almost always be raised in parallel with one for wrongful life and the basic grounds on which each is argued will be similar.[195] Since, as we have seen, the former is likely to succeed, the seeds of self-protection on the part of health carers are already sown; opening the door to an action for diminished life would have no practical effect in this respect.

We are left with a penultimate question which, at the end of a long chapter, is a hard one to ask – essentially, it reduces to: 'does it matter?' The answer, it seems to me, lies, fundamentally, in equity; this, in turn, depends upon an assessment of the wrong done and this is clearly divisible. The parents have a recognised claim for the emotional and physical stress[196] caused by the negligent birth and the consequent rearing of a disabled child – this is the true nature of the wrongful birth action. As a result of the same negligence, the disabled child is suffering and, conditions being what they are, any attempt to restore him or her to

they illustrate as allowing that, while *a* cause of the damage is the rubella, the medical faults may be said to have contributed to it, hence a causal link can be established. The English courts also seem content to juggle with causation when necessary – e.g. *Chester* v. *Afshar* [2005] 1 AC 134, [2004] 4 All ER 587 for which see Kenyon Mason and Douglas Brodie, '*Bolam, Bolam* . . . Wherefore Art Thou *Bolam*?' (2005) 9 *Edinburgh Law Review* 298–306, where it is concluded that our causation rules are in something of a state of flux.

[193] 'The function of the law is to enable rights to be vindicated and to provide remedies when duties have been breached': *Chester* v. *Afshar*, n. 192 above, per Lord Hope at [87].

[194] n. 169 above, at 188.

[195] See Pearson J in *Harbeson*, n. 48 above, at 496: '[T]he policies which persuade [courts] to recognise parents' claims of wrongful birth apply equally to recognition of claims of wrongful life.'

[196] Which may have wider implications. Kennedy and Grubb, for example, point to the fact that the negligence not only deprives the woman of her choice as to abortion but also puts a very effective brake on her choice of having another, normal child: *Medical Law*, n. 29 above, at 1552.

'normality', or the *status quo ante* negligence, will cost money – and this is the purpose of the wrongful, or diminished, life action. Since the latter is not currently available, present practice is to acknowledge that economic burden by way of the damages payable under the heading of wrongful birth and, given the fact that the parents will, ultimately, sign the cheques, this is an understandably practical solution which has stood the test of time in many jurisdictions. But, is it conceptually correct? My argument suggests that it is not.

Once again, however, the pragmatist will ask 'does it matter?' – and, in my view, the cases have shown that there are good practical reasons for believing that it may do. In the first place, in the absence of special circumstances, an award to the parents for the upkeep of a child will cease on that child attaining majority; clearly, as we have already noted,[197] this is both unfair and illogical in respect of the child's permanent disabilities. Second, as was stressed in *Perruche*, not all parents are ideal parents. The majority of parents will, of course, act as responsible administrators but they should be no more than that. Equity demands that the child who is recompensed for disability should be in legal control of his or her remedial environment; and this, as we have seen, underlies the reasoning behind the *Perruche* and *Molenaar* judgments.

In the event, two persons – the mother and the neonate – have been injured and there is an acceptable argument for allowing dual actions – always provided that they are seen as being distinct actions based on different types of injury that result from a common cause. The difficulty is, of course, that establishing a commonality of cause involves the use of what many would regard as paralogic. The alternative, and probably better, conclusion is that, having eradicated the problem of causation along the lines that have been suggested above, we should treat both claims in terms of simple negligence.

---

[197] At p. 98 above.

7   The management of the disabled neonate

Introduction

As Hale LJ said in her memorable speech in *Parkinson*:[1]

[T]he invasion of the mother's personal autonomy does not stop once her body and mind have returned to their pre-pregnancy state ... The obligation to provide or make acceptable and safe arrangements for the child's care and supervision lasts for 24 hours a day, seven days a week, all year round, until the child becomes old enough to take care of himself.

And, if that be true of the normal child – and probably most of us would agree that it is – how much more does it apply to one who is disabled? Indeed, this compelling passage from Lady Hale convinces me that a study of the troubled pregnancy is incomplete without a consideration of its medico-legally most important aftermath – that is, the management of congenital disease. Thus, the rationale of this chapter, lies in the belief that there is a practical, as well as a conceptual, continuum between pregnancy and early motherhood. Given this premise, however, it will be appreciated that our remit can legitimately cover only those conditions which were present *in utero* or those in which the seeds of disablement were sown during fetal life – or, put another way, we will be considering only the child whose disability was foreseeable before he or she was born. As a corollary, we are not concerned directly with non-congenital diseases of childhood but we will use such cases when they are needed to illustrate a relevant point.

Many children suffering from congenital disability will be absorbed into a happy family relationship; for others, the strain on the family may be such as to dictate the help of the local authority – but, in either instance, the child will be cared for and its suffering will be correspondingly reduced. Inevitably, however, there will be some who are beyond such care and for whom it could be argued that, given the choice, they

---

[1] *Parkinson* v. *St James and Seacroft University Hospital NHS Trust* [2002] QB 266, (2001) 61 BMLR 100 at [69].

would prefer not to be maintained alive; the troubled pregnancy has developed into a troubled infancy or, put another way, the wrongful life hypothetical has become a reality.

And therein lies a major distinction which we have noted throughout the previous chapter – that, whereas we can only speculate, albeit often on good evidence, as to the extent of fetal disability, we can usually make an informed and objective assessment in the case of the disabled neonate. We have, significantly, introduced a new *person* into the doctor/patient equation which, in turn, raises a new, and major, ethical issue. As long ago as 1982, I wrote:

[I]t becomes clear that, in simple brutal logic, neonaticide[2] is scientifically preferable to abortion. Yet, in practice, such a concept is abhorrent and intolerable.[3]

Which last is an easy thing to say but, in practice, is more difficult to justify. Certainly, it is not easy to do so by appealing to history. The great majority of books dealing with this subject will point to the Roman penchant for abandoning disabled infants and, while we should not be over influenced by the mores of the Roman 'civilisation', there is little doubt that the practice has, at times, been recognised in many parts of the world.[4] Revulsion was probably fuelled in the United Kingdom by the extent of child murder in the eighteenth and early nineteenth centuries[5] and it was at about this time that the phrase, and the concept of, 'the sanctity of life' – often taken to mean that 'life' was always something to be preserved – became commonplace and well-established within the medical profession.

[2] Although it has been used before in various guises – e.g. to define the killing of a child in the first 24 hours of its birth – the word as used here is something of a neologism of my own to imply elective non-treatment of severe congenital disease. I used it so as to distinguish euthanasia, which involves activity, and infanticide which, in English law, is specifically defined as the killing of a child less than one year old by its mother when the balance of her mind was disturbed either by pregnancy or lactation (Infanticide Act 1938); the term is not so limited in other jurisdictions such as the United States. In Scotland, a similar offence would be described as child murder which is, paradoxically, treated as culpable homicide – just as infanticide is dealt with as manslaughter in England.

[3] J. K. Mason and R. A. McCall Smith, *Law and Medical Ethics* (London: Butterworths, 1982) at 88.

[4] For a full, and sometimes hair-raising, exposition, see the classic work in this area: Robert F. Weir, *Selective Non-treatment of Handicapped Newborns* (New York: Oxford University Press, 1984), chapter 1.

[5] Specific statutory prohibition of concealment of birth dates, in Scotland, from the still extant Concealment of Birth (Scotland) Act 1809 though there was earlier legislation in England dating from 1624. I have touched on the subject in *Medico-legal Aspects of Reproduction and Parenthood* (Aldershot: Ashgate, 2nd edn 1998), chapter 14. For fuller reviews see Katherine O'Donovan, 'The Medicalisation of Infanticide' [1984] *Criminal Law Review* 259–64; Mark Jackson, 'Infanticide: historical perspectives' (1996) 146 *New Law Journal* 416–20.

The sanctity of life

It would be purely speculative to attempt to identify the origin of the phrase or to say how it became so intimately attached to life and death decision making. It is generally regarded as a religious tenet, and is certainly ingrained in orthodox Judaism,[6] although it has been said that there is no scriptural basis for placing an absolute value on life itself.[7] This, of course, is not to say that we should not place an extremely high value on human life and there is no doubt that the law in this area will always start from a preference for life over death. This is probably a statement of the obvious but a single quotation will not be out of place:

[T]he court's high respect for the sanctity of human life imposes a strong presumption in favour of taking all steps capable of preserving it, save in exceptional circumstances.[8]

but, it was added, 'the problem is to define those circumstances' – and that, in turn, defines the purpose of this chapter.

At base, the problem lies in the interpretation of the word 'sanctity' which, on the face of things, is an absolute term which many would equate with 'inviolability'. Those who do so would understand the 'sanctity of life' to mean 'the sanctity of life at any price' which would, consequentially, dictate providing maximum treatment aimed at preservation of life irrespective of the quality of that life and of the adverse effects of aggressive therapy. This attitude, commonly known as vitalism or absolutism, was probably widely adopted in the Western world in the late nineteenth and early twentieth centuries and was tenable in that, on the one hand, relatively few severely disabled infants survived birth and, on the other, invasive and aggressive treatments capable of preserving disabled life were barely available; the problem of 'to treat or not to treat' the disabled neonate was, thereby, self-contained – in short, doing 'everything that could be done' resulted in not much being done at all.

The movement away from vitalism, which evolved fairly rapidly in the first half of the twentieth century was encouraged by two main developments. The first was in the field of philosophy where the concept of 'personhood' was widely canvassed. The gist of this is that a human being does not become a human person – and, thus, command the respect due to a human person – until he or she has developed the

---

[6] See *Re C (medical treatment)* [1998] 1 FLR 384, (1997) 40 BMLR 31, discussed at p. 263.
[7] For example, Kenneth Boyd, 'Euthanasia: Back to the Future' in John Keown (ed.), *Euthanasia Examined* (Cambridge: Cambridge University Press, 1991), chapter 7.
[8] *Re J (a minor) (wardship: medical treatment)* [1991] Fam 33, (1990) 6 BMLR 25 per Taylor LJ at Fam 53, BMLR 40.

intellectual capacity to exercise the rights of such a person.[9] Thus, abortion, neonaticide and infanticide in its wider sense are on a par. The dangers of such a construct – which commanded considerable, if only temporary, support at the time – are, I believe, self-evident and, as things stand, such a philosophy is unlikely to be adopted by the courts of any developed countries. Which, of course, does not mean it may not be revivified at some time.

The quality of neonatal life

Far more significant in the present context were developments in the practical world of neonatology where the work of Lorber, who had pioneered aggressive surgical treatment of spina bifida,[10] was particularly influential. A retrospective review of his results later convinced him that many of his cases were living lives of unacceptably poor and painful quality and he subsequently campaigned vigorously for non-treatment in many cases in the interests of the individual sufferers.[11] Quite clearly, these views were being widely accepted; by 1986 it was being openly reported that up to 30 per cent of deaths in neonatal intensive care units followed the deliberate withdrawal of life support[12] and this may, now, be an underestimate.[13] In a way, this is not so surprising as might appear insofar as infants must be extremely ill to be admitted to intensive care and death will have been inevitable in many cases. There are, however, a number of points to be gleaned from such figures. First, it is clear that the concept of 'futility' is now well accepted, despite the fact that its definition is imprecise; I will return to this problem shortly. Second, since

---

[9] This theory was particularly developed by Michael Tooley, 'In Defense of Abortion and Infanticide' in J Feinberg (ed.), *The Problem of Abortion* (Belmont: Wadsworth, 1973) 83–114 and later elaborated by Singer. See, Helga Kuhse and Peter Singer, *Should the Baby Live?* (Oxford: Oxford University Press, 1985).

[10] J. Lorber, 'Ethical Problems in the Management of Myelomeningocele' (1975) 10 *Journal of the Royal College of Physicians of London* 47–60.

[11] J. Lorber and S. A. Salfield, 'Results of Selective Treatment of Spina Bifida Cystica' (1981) 56 *Archives of Disease in Childhood* 822–30.

[12] Andrew Whitelaw, 'Death as an Option in Neonatal Intensive Care' (1986) 328 *Lancet* 328–31; C. H. Walker, '. . . Officiously to Keep Alive' 63 *Archives of Disease in Childhood* 560–6. For a general review, see A. G. M. Campbell and H. E. McHaffie, 'Prolonging Life and Allowing Death: Infants' (1995) 21 *Journal of Medical Ethics* 339–44.

[13] Ian M. Balfour-Lynn and Robert C. Tasker, 'Futility and Death in Paediatric Medical Intensive Care' (1996) 22 *Journal of Medical Ethics* 279–81 reported that two-thirds of the deaths in their very prestigious ICU resulted from limitation of treatment or withdrawal of mechanical ventilation. It is to be noted that the unit was paediatric rather than neonatal. The authors withheld the precise years of their study, leaving one to speculate as to the importance of the clarification of the law in the early part of the decade which is discussed in detail at p. 262.

only a minute number of such cases come to court, the vast majority of these decisions must be reached on the basis of agreement between the health care team and the parents – and it is almost impossible to over-emphasise the importance of involving the 'team', as opposed to the physician in charge, in the decision-making process. Third, and for much the same reason, it can be assumed that the law recognises the rights of the parent–health carers combination to make such decisions.[14] Finally – and, perhaps, most significantly – the number of such reports indicates that the 'sanctity of life' doctrine as a measure of good medical practice is now a matter of past history. And the law has followed the trend – as Lord Donaldson said in the basic case of *Re J*, 'the absolutist approach [is one] which I would in any event unhesitatingly reject'.[15]

Principles of management of severe congenital disease

What, then, is to replace it? In my view, there are two overarching concepts which govern the withholding or withdrawal of treatment from disabled neonates[16] – medical futility and the patient's best interests. These can be translated in practical terms as, on the one hand, the *effect* of treatment as objectively recognised and, on the other, as the *benefits* to the patient.[17] It is, however, inevitable that the two will overlap – and this is important in that the effect of a treatment is something that can properly be assessed by the medical profession, while the latter is a matter for the competent patient, for the child's parents or guardians or, in default of either, for the courts; it will be seen as we progress that the great majority of disputed cases derive from a conflicting interpretation of the position as seen from the medical and parental viewpoints.

---

[14] '[A] proper acknowledgement of the law [is] that parents, by virtue of ss. 2 and 3 of the Children Act 1989, hold parental responsibility; that includes the right to consent to or refuse treatment.' Per Hedley J in *Re Wyatt (a child) (medical treatment: parents' consent)* (2004) 84 BMLR 206 at [16]. See also Sir Mark Potter P in *Re K*, n. 227 below at [42].

[15] n. 8 above, at Fam 44 BMLR 32.

[16] It is, perhaps, unnecessary to re-emphasise that we are not concerned at this point with the positive killing of such infants which is unlawful and to which we will return at the end of the chapter. We are reminded of the words of Lord Mustill: 'If an act resulting in death is done without lawful excuse and with intent to kill it is murder. But an omission to act with the same result and the same intent is in general no offence' – *Airedale NHS Trust* v. *Bland* [1993] 1 All ER 821 at 890, (1992) 12 BMLR 64 at 137. For discussion of the moral dubiety of the law in this area, see Raanan Gillon, 'Euthanasia, Withholding Life-prolonging Treatment, and Moral Differences between Killing and Letting Die' (1988) 14 *Journal of Medical Ethics* 115–17.

[17] See L. J. Schneiderman and N. Jecker, 'Futility in Practice' (1993) 153 *Archives of Internal Medicine* 437–41.

Medical futility

Of course, the very word 'futility' carries its own complexities and contradictions and there is great force in Gillon's rejection of the term as a guide to decision making on the grounds that it is 'ambiguous, complicated and distressing'.[18] This is not the place for a major discussion of the philosophical issues involved – these can, in themselves, occupy a book at least as large as this.[19] My conclusion is that, if we are to retain the term – and at least some of the difficulties, including its potential rejection on religious grounds,[20] are removed if we substitute that of 'non-productive treatment' – we should restrict it in the present context to *medical futility*, for that is what the doctor has the expertise to assess. The definition provided by Schneiderman and Jecker is as useful as any:

A treatment which cannot provide a minimum likelihood or quality of benefit should be regarded as futile and is not owed to the patient as a matter of moral duty.[21]

The 'best interests' test

The concept of 'best interests' is closely bound to the welfare principle which originated in and dictated the governance of wardship[22] – to quote Thorpe LJ: 'There can be no doubt in my mind that the evaluation of best interests is akin to a welfare appraisal.'[23] We will see later that the concept of 'best interests' has come to dominate judicial thinking in all areas in which the courts are asked to settle disputes as to the management of incompetent patients – so much so that other approaches to the solution of the problems raised are, now, rejected not so much as a matter of

---

[18] Raanan Gillon, ' "Futility" – Too Ambiguous and Pejorative a Term?' (1997) 23 *Journal of Medical Ethics* 339–40.

[19] Such a work is Marjorie B. Zucker and Howard D. Zucker (eds.), *Medical Futility* (Cambridge: Cambridge University Press, 1997).

[20] Since the rigid sanctity of life doctrine is commonly associated with Roman Catholicism, it is well to remember the words of Pope Pius XII:

Man has a right and a duty in case of severe illness to take the necessary steps to preserve life and health . . . But he is obliged at all times to employ only ordinary means . . . that is to say those means which do not impose an extraordinary burden on himself or others.

(1957) 49 *Acta Apostolicae Sedis* 1027.

[21] n. 17 above.

[22] Wardship is no longer a function of the courts by virtue of the Children Act 1989. Appeal may be made, however, to the inherent jurisdiction of the court which is retained by s.100. Alternatively, a treatment dispute can be brought to the court as a specific issue and the court can provide a specific issue order (s.100(3)).

[23] In *Re A (medical treatment: male sterilisation)* [2000] 1 FLR 549 at 560. The fact that *Re A* was concerned with an adult incompetent is immaterial.

preference but, rather, are being virtually condemned as lying 'out of bounds'. A single example will suffice to show the extent of the shift of emphasis. A quarter of a century ago in *Re B (a minor) (wardship: medical treatment)*,[24] to which we will return, Templeman LJ implied that the watershed for non-treatment of disabled neonates should be that life was going to be 'so awful that in effect the child must be condemned to die' while Dunn LJ used the yardstick that 'the child's life is likely to be an intolerable one'. By 2005, however, that view had been rejected on a number of occasions and was firmly laid to rest by the Court of Appeal decision in *Wyatt v. Portsmouth Hospital*.[25] We will return to this important jurisprudential question in greater detail in discussion of that case later in this chapter.

How, then, will the court attempt to evaluate the child's best interests? We must turn, again, to Lord Donaldson in *Re J* where he laid down what have since become the ground rules by way of reference to the earlier case of *Re B*:[26]

Re B seems to me to come very near to being a binding authority for the proposition that there is a balancing exercise to be performed in assessing the course to be adopted in the best interests of the child. Even if it is not, I have no doubt that this should be and is the law.[27]

And he went on to say: '[A]ccount has to be taken of the pain and suffering and quality of life which the child will experience if life is prolonged. Account has also to be taken of the pain and suffering involved in the proposed treatment itself.' And finally, having paid full respect to the sanctity of human life, he rejected the vitalist doctrine:

But in the end there will be cases in which the answer must be that it is not in the interests of the child to subject it to treatment which will cause increased suffering and produce no commensurate benefit, giving the fullest possible weight to the child's, and mankind's, desire to survive.[28]

So far, so good. But it is appropriate to take a small diversion at this point and consider that part of Lord Donaldson's speech which is open to criticism but which is of considerable conceptual importance. Discussing how this balancing exercise is to be formulated, he quoted, with approval, the Canadian Justice McKenzie:

It is not appropriate for an external decision-maker to apply his standards of what constitutes a liveable life and exercise the right to impose death if that standard is

---

[24] [1982] 3 FLR 117, [1981] 1 WLR 1421.
[25] *Re Wyatt (a child) (medical treatment: continuation of order)* (2005) 86 BMLR 173, CA.
[26] n. 24 above.   [27] *Re J*, n. 8 above, at BMLR 34.   [28] ibid., at Fam 44, BMLR 35.

not met in his estimation. The decision can only be made in the context of the disabled person viewing the worthwhileness or otherwise of his life in its own context as a disabled person – and in that context he would not compare his life with that of a person enjoying normal advantages. He would know nothing of a normal person's life having never experienced it.[29]

To my mind, this is a very clear expression of what is known as the 'substituted judgment' test for treatment of the incompetent. This test, which is widely used in the courts of the United States, has been defined as 'donning the mental mantle of the incompetent'[30] – or, essentially, reading the patient's mind.

I confess to being in the minority in preferring the 'substituted judgment' to the 'best interests' test in that the former attempts to preserve respect for the personality of the patient while the latter is blatantly paternalistic. The majority argument to the contrary is, of course, that there should be some evidence of the patient's intentions when competent before a substituted judgment can be meaningfully applied – and this condition is impossible to fulfil in the case of a young child. My counter to this lies in suggesting that we would, in fact, be substituting the judgment of the reasonable child given the same circumstances. This, admittedly, comes very close to proposing a distinction without a difference and it is true that, in practice, the two tests reach the same conclusion in the great majority of cases.[31] This, however, may not be entirely true and we will revert to the point when discussing Dr Arthur's case below. Nonetheless, the English courts are imbued with the welfare principle and have consistently repudiated the substituted judgment test[32] since the House of Lords decision in Re F.[33]

Not only will the courts regularly apply the best interests test but they are, to an extent, jealous of its interpretation. The opinions of the interested parties are no more than factors in the balancing equation – something that has been made very clear in the Family Court and in the Court of Appeal under the influence of Lady Butler-Sloss. Thus, we have Thorpe LJ:

---

[29] *Superintendent of Family and Child Services and Dawson* (1983) 145 D LR (3d) 610 at 620 quoted in *Re J*, n. 8 above, at Fam 44, BMLR 32.

[30] *Superintendent of Belchertown State School* v. *Saikewicz* 370 NE 2d 417 (Mass., 1978).

[31] In passing, this may not apply in the case of the adult who has completed an advance directive. When it comes to decision time, his or her advance rejection of treatment may well be at odds with what can be seen objectively as his or her best interests. The advance directive is, however, now binding in England and Wales (Mental Capacity Act 2005, s.26).

[32] So much so that we find Brooke LJ being convinced of 'a *danger* of detecting a substituted choice test [in a quoted passage]' (my emphasis): *W Healthcare NHS Trust* v. *KH* [2005] 1 WLR 834, CA at [26]. In the same case, however, the court appeared to regret the non-availability of the test (at [23]).

[33] *Re F (mental patient: sterilisation)* [1990] 2 AC 1.

In deciding what is best for the disabled patient the judge must have regard for the patient's welfare as the paramount consideration. This embraces issues far wider than the medical . . . In my opinion *Bolam*[34] has no contribution to make to [the] second and determinative stage of the judicial decision.[35]

with Butler-Sloss P confirming:

[B]est interests is wider in concept than medical considerations . . . In my judgement best interests encompasses medical, emotional and all other welfare issues . . . It therefore falls to the judge to decide whether to accept or reject the expert medical opinion.[36]

One further commentary on the best interests test must be quoted because of the importance that has been attached to it in later cases:

[I]t seems to me that the first instance judge with a responsibility to make an evaluation of the best interests of a claimant lacking capacity should draw up a balance sheet. The first entry should be of any factor or factors of actual benefit . . . Then on the other sheet the judge should write any counterbalancing dis-benefits to the applicant . . . Then the judge should enter on each sheet the potential gains and losses in each instance making some estimate of the extent of the possibility that the gain or loss might accrue. At the end of that exercise the judge should be better placed to strike a balance between the sum of the certain and possible gains against the sum of the certain and possible losses.[37]

All of which may look like little more than sound common sense but which, nevertheless, now has immense jurisprudential significance. Effectively, in the event of dispute involving treatment of a child against the wishes of its parents, it is only the application of the best interests test that separates a lawful court decision from a breach of the child's human rights to his or her bodily integrity that are subsumed under Article 8 of the European Convention on Human Rights and incorporated in the Human Rights Act 1998, schedule 1.[38]

---

[34] *Bolam* v. *Friern Hospital Management Committee* [1957] 2 All ER 118, (1957) 1 BMLR 1. We have discussed this standard test for medical negligence and its evolution in Chapter 1.

[35] *Re S (adult patient) (sterilisation)* [2001] Fam 15, (2000) 55 BMLR 105 at 119.

[36] n. 35 above, at Fam 24, BMLR 113. See also, Dyson LJ speaking for the court in *R (on the application of N)* v. *Doctor M and others* [2003] 1 FLR 667, (2003) 72 BMLR 81 at [29]: '[T]he fact that there is a responsible body of opinion against the proposed treatment is relevant to the question whether it is in the patient's best interests or medically necessary, but it is no more than that'. Once again, the fact that these cases were all dealing with adult incompetents is immaterial to the concept.

[37] *Re A (medical treatment: male sterilisation)* [2000] 1 FLR 549 per Thorpe LJ at 560.

[38] *Glass* v. *United Kingdom* [2004] 1 FLR 1019, (2004) 77 BMLR 120. For extended commentary on this important case, see Richard Huxtable and Karen Forbes, '*Glass* v. *UK*: Maternal Instinct v. Medical Opinion' (2004) 16 *Child and Family Law Quarterly* 339–54.

Envoi. Finally, as a conclusion to this introduction to the law, we should note that Butler-Sloss P has recently found no difficulty in combining and reconciling the concepts of medical futility and the best interests of the disabled child. *Re L* concerned a child aged 9 months who suffered from Edwards' syndrome – a normally rapidly fatal chromosomal disease; the disputed problem was whether or not mechanical ventilation should be provided in the event of respiratory failure. The President summarised her position:

[T]he test is 'best interests' which are interpreted more broadly than 'medical interests' and include emotional and other factors. There is a strong presumption in favour of saving life, but not where treatment would be futile, and there is no obligation on the medical profession to give treatment which would be futile.[39]

One could have wished that Her Ladyship had used the term *medical* futility because, as has been intimated above, the definition of futility when unqualified depends so much on one's viewpoint.[40] To give what may seem an over-harsh example, facial movement in a brain-damaged infant may be, to the health carer, no more than a reflex muscular contraction that is irrelevant to an assessment of the child's condition; to the parents, it may be interpreted as a smile that is worth preserving at all costs. Even so, in the broad context of the case, Butler-Sloss P, who reverted with strong approval to Lord Donaldson in *Re J,*[41] can be interpreted as placing medical futility firmly in the ambit of Thorpe LJ's itemised balance sheet within which it will play a very significant role in the assessment of the patient's best interests.

The British cases

The particular intention of this review of some of the relevant British cases is to identify any evident trend that is being adopted by the courts in their decision-making. First, however, we must dispose of an interesting anomaly – that is, that, in practice, so few cases involving the

---

[39] *Re L (medical treatment: benefit)* [2005] 1 FLR 491 at [12].

[40] In my view, the best case illustrative of this conflict is *R* v. *Cambridge Health Authority, ex p B* [1995] 2 All ER 129, CA in which the extended treatment of a child with leukaemia, carrying a possible 2–10 per cent chance of success, was resisted by the Authority but regarded as essential by the parents. The difference in approach between the trial judge and the Court of Appeal, together with the interposition of problems of resource allocation, are particularly interesting. The nature of the case, however, in not being one of congenital disease, puts it beyond the parameters of the present discussion.

[41] n. 8 above.

management of congenital disease come to the courts when compared with the apparently large number of agreed non-treatment decisions which are taken in neonatal intensive care units without the need for judicial intervention, a matter to which attention has already been drawn (at p. 244).[42]

Hypothesis is a dangerous exercise but I suspect that, in the great majority of cases that give rise to doubts as to their correct management, the infant either goes home with the family and is cared for lovingly within the domestic ambience or is treated in hospital for varying lengths of time with full agreement between the parents and the health carers. In a minority of these cases, however, the health carers will, with time, begin to appreciate the increasing futility of their therapeutic efforts, no matter how great may be their dedication while, simultaneously, bonding between the parents and their child matures. As a result, a tension develops which, again, may often be resolved. But there remains a mercifully small residue of cases in which an agreed management plan becomes increasingly less possible and recourse to the courts is inevitable. The practical results are two-fold. In the first place, this process, if it occurs, takes time and, as a result, the majority of relevant cases, in fact, concerns infants rather than neonates. Secondly, and as a direct consequence, the vast majority of cases will be brought by the health carers wishing to withhold or terminate treatment; it is relatively unusual for the parents to attempt to prevent the use of life sustaining treatment[43] save in the well-known instance of doctrinaire religious objection brought, predominantly, by Jehovah's Witnesses.[44]

---

[42] The number is now very considerable. Most recently, relevant discussions with parents are said to occur in some 70 per cent of deaths in neonatal ICU's: Hazel McHaffie et al., *Crucial Decisions at the Beginning of Life* (Oxford: Radcliffe Medical Press, 2001).

[43] Cf. the less uncommon situation in respect of adults – e.g. *W Healthcare NHS Trust* v. *KH*, n. 32 above. This, among several others, was a reason given for advocating 'caution in the application to children of factors relevant to the treatment of adults' in *Re Wyatt (a child) (medical treatment: continuation of order)* (2005) 86 BMLR 173 at [90] – although some general statements of principle can plainly apply to both.

[44] Such cases will seldom relate to congenital disease and are, therefore, outwith our remit. A useful recent article is by Osamu Muramoto, 'Bioethical Aspects of the Recent Changes in the Policy of Refusal of Blood by Jehovah's Witnesses' (2001) 322 *British Medical Journal* 37–9 and, for a comparative view of the law, S. Woolley, 'Children of Jehovah's Witnesses and Adolescent Jehovah's Witnesses: What are their Rights?' (2005) 90 *Archives of Disease in Childhood* 715–19. There are, of course, other religious groups opposed to medical interference which attract less public attention. Modern cases have involved Christian Scientists and Rastafarians (Diana Brahams, 'Religious Objection versus Parental Duty' (1993) 342 *Lancet* 1189–90).

Exceptions will, however, occur and Hedley J has recently provided a most useful, albeit said to be tentative, classification of those cases which come, or may come, to court.[45] He identified four variations:

(i) Where a doctor advocated a treatment which the parents resisted and a failure to administer such treatment would be an affront to that doctor's conscience;

(ii) Where a doctor advocated treatment which the parents resisted on grounds that, whilst reasonable, were contrary to the clinician's view;

(iii) Where the parents wanted treatment, which the clinician could not advise, but the giving of which would not be an affront to conscience;

(iv) Where giving the treatment requested would be an affront to conscience.

As the judge pointed out, the vast majority of disagreements will fall within categories (ii) and (iii). The precise categorisation of individual cases is, admittedly, often a subjective exercise; nevertheless, his analysis affords a convenient template on which to build a collage of the British cases and, although it may involve a number of apparent diversions, I propose to do so rather than follow a strict chronological sequence. Even so, I believe it would be useful, first, to isolate what I regard as the 'original' cases that arose in 1981.

The 1981 cases

I have separated these cases as a pair, first, because they came to notice at much the same time and were, together, responsible for bringing the problems of the disabled neonate into the public domain.[46] Second, because the marked contrast between them virtually laid down the ground rules for the later extensive litigation in the field. And, thirdly – and not least – because they serve to illustrate the remarkable change in medical and lay attitudes to disability that has evolved over the last quarter of a century.

Re B (a minor) (wardship: medical treatment)[47] was a case with a turbulent history that demonstrates, inter alia, the confusion among medical

---

[45] In *Re Wyatt (a child) (medical treatment: parents' consent)* (2004) 84 BMLR 206 at [18]. I have, however, used the judge's revised wording in *Re Wyatt* (2005) 87 BMLR 183 at [30].

[46] I have compared the two cases previously in J. K. Mason and David W. Meyers, 'Parental Choice and Selective Non-treatment of Deformed Newborns: A View from Mid-Atlantic' (1986)12 *Journal of Medical Ethics* 67–71. For a recent overview, see R. J. Boyle, R. Salter and M. W. Arnander, 'Ethics of Refusing Parental Requests to Withhold or Withdraw Treatment from their Premature Baby' (2004) 30 *Journal of Medical Ethics* 402–5.

[47] [1990] 3 All ER 927, [1981] 1 WLR 1421.

practitioners as to the law at that time. Baby B was, unexpectedly, born with Down's syndrome complicated by intestinal atresia or blockage. It is important to note that, while death was inevitable in the absence of a reparative operation, the surgery of itself was a fairly routine procedure which, as was said at the time, would have been carried out as a matter of course in the case of a child who was otherwise normal; nonetheless, there was a conflict of opinion between the obstetricians and the paediatric surgeons – particularly in relation to the likelihood of post-operative cardiac complications.[48] In any event, while the surgeons were willing to operate, the parents 'did not wish to take the responsibility in the future for the baby if the operation took place' and refused their consent – a decision which Dunn LJ was later to regard as one which 'everybody accepts was an entirely responsible one'.[49]

Faced with an apparently emergency application, Ewbank J gave care and control to the local authority together with leave for the operation to proceed. Even so, the surgeons, apparently unaware of the extent of the court's jurisdiction, refused to operate and the case came up for further review four days later.[50] However, just as he was about to confirm his order, the judge decided – with, it appears, full justification – that the parents had not been adequately involved and the case was reopened. Essentially, the parents' position could be summed up as their believing that God or nature had 'given the baby a way out' and they asked the court to respect their wishes that surgery should not be undertaken. Ewbank J, who was committed to a decision based on the best interests of the child, was, however, able to subsume the parents' rejection of B within those interests and, in a remarkable volte face, determined that, on balance, the parents' decision was correct and was in the interests of the child.

Re B, of course, went to appeal but, before following the direct line, I propose changing course and, first, considering the case of *R* v. *Arthur*[51] which was heard some three months after *Re B*. In so doing, both the similarities and contrasts of the two cases become more easily appreciated.

---

[48] The judge at first instance was strongly influenced by one expert opinion that the risk of heart disease following the operation was normally 33 per cent but was double this in the case of mongoloid children. 'Therefore', he said, 'although the surgery itself is acceptable in an ordinary case, there are risks beyond the normal for a child with this mental disability.' To refuse the life-saving operation on these grounds appears to this writer to be a *non sequitur* of remarkable proportions.

[49] n. 47 above, at All ER 929, WLR 1424.

[50] Meantime, the local authority had not taken up the proffered chance of an operation at an alternative hospital.

[51] (1981) 12 BMLR 1, Crown Ct.

Baby John Pearson was, like baby B, unexpectedly found to be suffering from Down's syndrome when he was born and, as in the case of baby B, his parents rejected him.[52] The essential difference was that, whereas B had a physical complication that was potentially fatal, J was, to all appearances, anatomically normal; at the time of his rejection, he could anticipate the customary life span of a Down's syndrome person of some 20 to 30 years. Dr Arthur, as the consultant in charge, saw him some 4 hours after his birth and, after discussion with his mother – the details of which are unrecorded – wrote in the notes: 'Parents do not wish the baby to survive. Nursing care only.' Although there was some doubt among the staff as to the meaning of the latter phrase, it was generally assumed to mean that the baby was to be comforted and hydrated; he was not to be resuscitated in the event that infection supervened. Dr Arthur also prescribed the sedative drug DF118 (dihydrocodeine), presumably in an effort to limit the child's suffering from the effects of withholding nutrition. The dose prescribed, and the amount actually given, were, naturally, discussed at length during the trial. Suffice it to say, here, that the levels discovered in the tissue at post-mortem examination were very much higher than had been authoritatively reported as normal therapeutic concentrations. John Pearson died 69 hours after his birth, the cause of death being recorded following post-mortem examination by a duo of forensic and paediatric consultant pathologists as: Multilobular pneumonia due to lung stasis due to dihydrocodeine poisoning in an infant with Down's syndrome.[53] Dr Arthur was indicted for murder but, during the trial, further evidence was brought which indicated that John Pearson was not as physically sound as was first thought and that he might have died irrespective of the therapeutic regime to which he was subjected. The charge of murder was, therefore, withdrawn from the jury and Dr Arthur was, in the end, found not guilty of attempted murder.

This book is not about criminal law. Nonetheless, I feel as strongly about the *Arthur* case now as I did a quarter of a century ago and I cannot resist repetition of Farquharson J's definition of an attempt:

[F]or an act to amount to an attempt it must be one which is immediately connected with the crime which it is intended to be committed ... To be an

---

[52] It was written in the notes: 'Mum feels he will be a strain on the family and her daughter [and] is not anxious to keep him' (ibid., at BMLR 7). The insertion is mine – without it, the statement is even more bizarre and its omission must have been an error. John's mother was also reported as saying to her husband: 'I don't want it, duck' (ibid.).

[53] It is interesting that the forensic pathologist maintained his diagnosis of poisoning even after re-examination in the light of the further evidence adduced at the trial.

attempt the act must be so closely connected with the crime itself that anybody would regard the person concerned as trying to commit it[54]

which seems to me to describe the association between withholding nutrition from a baby and causing its death fairly adequately.

Be that as it may, it is of no present concern. Rather, I suggest there are three areas of social significance that are highlighted by these two first instance cases. The first is the remarkable deference shown by the courts to the medical profession in this era. Thus, we have Farquharson J saying, in his charge to the jury, first:

[T]he President of the Royal College of Physicians, with his colleagues, has a considerable say in the ethics of this profession. And so what he has to tell you, if you accept it, and I can think of no reason why you should not, must carry great weight[55]

and, later:

[W]hatever a profession may evolve as a system of standards of ethics, it cannot stand on its own, and cannot survive if it is in conflict with the law ... But, I imagine that you will think long and hard before deciding that doctors, of the eminence we have heard, representing to you what medical ethics are, and apparently have been over a period of time in that great profession, have evolved standards which amount to committing crime.[56]

Which, despite the original demurrer, seems to come perilously close to inviting the tail to wag the dog.

The second area of interest lies in its corollary – that is, the easy acceptance by the law of the medical profession's self-regulated role as arbiter of life and death. We have already noted the large number of deaths in neonatal intensive care units attributed to withdrawal of support and this was acknowledged, albeit on the smaller scale of 13 per cent, by Professor Campbell.[57] The difficulty in Dr Arthur's case is, of course, that the patient was not in intensive care and, indeed, so far as the staff were concerned at the time, he required no treatment other than normal baby care which must surely include nutrition. A policy based on the provision of intensive care was, thus, being applied in a wholly different ambience. The opinion of Sir Douglas Black sums up the resulting confusion:

Where there is an uncomplicated Down's case and the parents did not want the child to live, the child requires normal, healthy care, but I think there are circumstances where it would be ethical to put it on a course of management that would

---

[54] ibid., at BMLR 2.   [55] ibid., at BMLR 20.   [56] ibid., at BMLR 22.
[57] ibid., at BMLR 15.

end in its death ... I say that with a child suffering from Down's and with a parental wish that it should not survive, it is ethical to terminate life, providing other considerations are taken into account.[58]

And, as we have seen, Farquharson J accepted this, and other evidence in the same vein, without criticism. Which is, in some ways, surprising – in my view, the greater part of the expert evidence provided in the case is so full of contradictions and dissimulations as to defy logical analysis.

The third feature common to both *Arthur* and *Re B* at first instance that I find difficult to accommodate is the insouciance with which both courts were able to accept the apparent 'right' of parents to abandon their disabled children. Perhaps there is an element of *force majeure* involved for it is difficult to see how it is possible to compel a couple to care for a child they do not want. Although care is all the uncomplicated Down's syndrome child requires, it may, nonetheless, be demanding and, in the end, the use of compulsion of any sort on reluctant parents may certainly not be in the child's best interests. Criminal sanctions, say, by way of the Children and Young Persons Act 1933, s.1 (or the Children and Young Persons (Scotland) Act 1937) may serve to satisfy the public conscience but the abandoned child still remains in the arms of the local authority irrespective of what happens to its parents – and it is, in any event, arguable that for the parents to hand a child over to health or social carers does not constitute abandonment. Much the same is true of the application of the family law, for example, by the grant of a care and supervision order under the Children Act 1989, s.31 – for better or for worse, the child is still subject to institutional care. The insistence by Ewbank J on the 'reasonableness' of the parents' decision to let their child die, coupled with Dunn LJ's later description of it as being 'entirely responsible',[59] and Farquharson J's condemnation of any criticism of a conscious decision to reject a mongol baby, may leave one wondering as to the strict legal position – but, in the end, it may be that a *laissez faire* attitude is the best approach to the inevitable conclusion that good parenting cannot be enforced.[60]

---

[58] ibid., at BMLR 21.   [59] In the Court of Appeal in *Re B*, n. 47 above, at WLR 1424.

[60] The problem of the apparent use of adoption as the ideal solution lies in its uncertainty and the cases illustrate this well. The local authority was confident that, given she lived, B could be provided with a good adoptive environment; Ewbank J, however, appeared reluctant to put adoptive parents to the test – 'there are bound to be strains and problems in any family bringing up a mongol child and consideration must be given to that factor' (1982) 3 FLR 117. Farquharson J actually used the remoteness of the likelihood of 'the child ever being taken into another family either by adoption or fostering' as a partial reason why John Pearson should have been allowed to die (n. 51 above, at BMLR 5). The doctors will also take into consideration the likelihood of adoption when making their

Which might seem a tenable, albeit mellifluous, conclusion until we see the Attorney-General in Parliament less than one year later:

I am satisfied that the law relating to murder and to attempted murder is the same now as it was before the trial ... and that it is the same irrespective of the wishes of the parents or any other person having a duty to care for the victim.[61]

It is as well that, although not referred to at the *Arthur* trial,[62] *Re B* went to appeal and we can now return to that case.

The local authority appealed against the trial judge's decision 'that nature ought to be allowed to take its course', once it became clear that some surgeons advised that B should be treated and were prepared to proceed with the operation. Templeman LJ set out the options starkly in the Court of Appeal. Without surgery, B would die within a matter of days. Given that she had the operation, there was a possibility that she would suffer from heart disease and die within months. If, however, she survived the operation, she would live as a mongoloid child for some 20 to 30 years – in which case, no-one could say to what extent her handicaps would be apparent; even so, in what appears to be a contradictory statement, the Lord Justice held it as certain that she would be 'very severely mentally and physically handicapped'.[63] Pointing out that the 'decision' of the parents and the doctors was, now, no more than part of the evidence available, Templeman LJ went on to make his legendary judgment which, despite the doubts as to its authority that have been expressed recently (see p. 258 below), still merits repetition in full:

[A]t the end of the day it devolves on this court in this particular instance to decide whether the life of this child is demonstrably going to be so awful that in effect the child must be condemned to die, or whether the life of this child is still so imponderable that it would be wrong for her to be condemned to die. There may be cases, I know not, of severe proved damage where the future is so certain and where the life of the child is so bound to be full of pain and suffering that the court might be driven to a different conclusion, but in the present case the choice which lies before the court is this: whether to allow an operation to take place which may result in the child living for 20 or 30 years as a mongoloid or whether

---

life or death decisions (see Professor Campbell, ibid., at BMLR 16) – though how the prolonged negotiations associated with adoption are compatible with non-feeding as a 'holding operation' is not easy to understand.

[61] Official Reports, March 1982, Written answers, cols. 348–9.

[62] Although Farquharson J made it clear that he would have supported the first instance decision in *Re B* at least passively (see evidence of Professor Campbell, n. 51 above, at BMLR 17).

[63] The easy acceptance of a range of options indicates that the courts – and, presumably, society – had, at this time, abandoned any principle based on the 'sanctity of life' and had entered the far less certain domain of the quality of life. Indeed, this is implicit in the reliance on parental wishes and medical advice shown in *Arthur* and *Re B* at first instance.

(and I think this must be brutally the result) to terminate the life of a mongoloid child because she also has an intestinal complaint. Faced with that choice I have no doubt that is the duty of this court to decide that the child must live.[64]

In criticising the trial judge's reliance on the wishes of the parents, Templeman LJ emphasised that it was the duty of the court to decide whether it was in the interests of the child that the operation take place and he went on to say that it was not for the court to say that the life of a mongol child ought to be extinguished. In this, he was backed by Dunn LJ, quoting counsel: 'The child should be put into the same position as any other mongol child and must be given the chance to live an existence.'[65] The Court of Appeal was, thus, unanimous in deprecating the categorisation of learning disability per se as a reason for either parental or medical abandonment and this, again, draws attention to the uneasy relationship between the law on abortion and neonaticide which we have already considered.

This inconsistency draws attention to the last comparative aspect of *Re B* and *Arthur* that I would like to consider – that is, how would the cases be categorised in the light of Hedley J's classification described above at p. 252 and introduced some 25 years later? Does this serve to demonstrate a further difference between them? Judicial opinion in *Re B* was, as we have seen, unanimous in describing the parental view as 'reasonable'. The case must, therefore, be placed squarely in the judge's category (ii) in which the doctors advise treatment of the child that is refused by the parents on reasonable grounds. By contrast, I would place Dr Arthur's case in category (i) – the majority of the hospital staff would have 'treated' John Pearson as a matter of conscience had not this been refused by his parents on *un*reasonable grounds. This may be the reason why Dr Arthur was reported to the authorities and was singled out for prosecution; it may also be the reason why *Arthur* remains a stand-alone case. I feel confident that no future Dr Arthur would be as fortunate as was his or her role model; nonetheless, the same anomaly arises – it is hard to equate this prediction on moral grounds with society's ready acceptance of Down's syndrome as a sole ground for action under the Abortion Act 1967, section 1(1)(d).[66]

The Court of Appeal in *Re B* has subsequently been criticised, firstly, on the minor grounds of Templeman LJ's use of the phrase 'condemned

---

[64] n. 47 above, at WLR 1424.   [65] ibid., at WLR 1425.

[66] It is parenthetically interesting to note that nowhere was there a mention of the possibility of an action for wrongful birth. Would B's parents have accepted their child had they been aware that financial assistance for her upbringing might be available? One might equally wonder if it would be morally acceptable to dangle such a carrot in front of a couple in distress.

to die'.[67] Insofar as this can be taken as implying approval of infantile euthanasia one must agree with this. More importantly from the jurisprudential aspect, the opinion has been found suspect in its reliance on the 'awfulness' (Templeman LJ) or 'intolerability' (Dunn LJ) of a condition as a benchmark for its management. This has been interpreted as conflicting with the all-important and best interests test – a somewhat convoluted argument to which we return at p. 276 below.[68] But we can still ask[69] – is the 'best interests test' the 'best test' of treatment decisions? The assessment of the best interests of an incompetent infant will, ultimately, be subject to the experience of the adjudicator – and this will include experience of pain and discomfort. Thus, while we can apply such a test to physical disability, we cannot do so in the case of mental disorder as, in that case, the mentally 'ordered' decision maker is groping in the dark. The alternative, to which we have already drawn attention, is the substituted judgment test and we have also noted that, in normal circumstances, the effect of applying either test may well be the same. But we have here seen, particularly in *Arthur*, that they may also conflict. Stripped to its essentials, the expert evidence in that case tells us that the child's best interests were served by allowing it to die.[70] But there is no evidence whatsoever that that would have been John Pearson's judgment and we can look back to the Canadian case of *Dawson*[71] – and the importance of the patient's *own* ambience – for support of this view. The whole difficulty in the Arthur case lay in the astonishing inability of the witnesses – and the commentators at the time – to distinguish between physical and mental disability. The mental status of the Down's syndrome child may be a most appalling handicap to the observer[72] but there is nothing to suggest that it is to the patient. And the most important achievement of the Court of Appeal in *Re B* is to have, at least, drawn attention to that distinction.

Having said which, one must point to the possibly obvious – which is that we have been, here, concerned with mental disorder as evidenced by disorder of the *mind*. Mental disorder may also arise from disability of

---

[67] n. 8 above, at BMLR 25, 34.

[68] See, in particular, *Re Wyatt (a child) (medical treatment: continuation of order)* (2005) 86 BMLR 173, CA at [65]. As to intolerability, see also, though in an adult context: *R (on the application of Burke)* v. *General Medical Council* (2004) 79 BMLR 126, QBD – although, in the event, both courts appealed either to the interests or to the welfare of the particular patient.

[69] See p. 248 above.

[70] The fact that very few would now agree with that assessment does not affect the argument.

[71] n. 29 above.   [72] E.g. Farquharson J, n. 51 above, at BMLR 4.

the *brain*[73] such as that due to, say, hypoxic brain damage following complications during birth. Such cases can, however, be distinguished from those we have been discussing in that they will, very commonly, be associated with consequent physical disability which, as we have observed, can be assessed objectively; the 'best interests test' then becomes arguably the 'best test' of management. The same principle will, in general, attach to mental disorder associated with high neural tube defect although an accurate 'best interests' assessment may, in many such cases, be impossible until relatively advanced infancy. The extreme of this last condition is to be found in the anencephalic neonate. I know of no instance in the United Kingdom where the management of such a case has been contested in the courts. Were one to arise, I fancy the child would be adjudged to have 'no interests'; the condition would, I suggest, be regarded as analogous to the permanent vegetative state and the reasoning used in *Airedale NHS Trust* v. *Bland*[74] would be applied.[75]

Beyond this, one can only reiterate the words of Lord Donaldson to the effect that *Re B* provides near binding authority that a balancing exercise is to be performed in assessing the course to be adopted in the best interests of the child in this type of case.[76] We can now consider how this dictum has operated in the years that have followed.

Development of the jurisprudence since Re B

The doctor's conscience (1). Before proceeding to the mainstream cases, it will be helpful to consider Hedley J's two *uncommon* scenarios so as, hopefully, to establish the limits of doctor – parent cooperation. Category (iv), in which the parents are demanding treatment which the doctor cannot provide with good conscience, is the more important of these because it sets the benchmark for the whole spectrum of therapeutic conflict. The distinction between category (iii) and category (iv) cases is often uncertain and depends very much on the eye of the beholder. A short diversion to explore this track is justified although it is doubtful if it is, in fact, possible to reach a definitive solution.

---

[73] For proposed statutory definition of mental disorder, see Mental Health Bill 2004, c. 2(5). The new definitions are likely to survive the parliamentary mayhem that has surrounded the introduction of the Bill.

[74] [1993] 1 All ER 821, (1993) 12 BMLR 64, HL.

[75] This would contrast with the historic American case of *Re Baby K* 832 F Supp 1022 (FD Va., 1993), affd 16 F 3d 590 (4th Circuit, 1994) where the court ordered an anencephalic infant to be ventilated. The decision was, however, largely based on statute law and the 'ethical propriety' of providing treatment was not addressed specifically.

[76] *Re J (a minor)*, n. 8 above.

Hedley J put it this way, albeit a little tentatively:

Conscience (whether one believes it to be God-given or culturally conditioned) is not a wholly rational sense. It is more in the nature of intuition or a hunch as to whether something is right or wrong ... It seems to me ... that a case comes within (iv) above where a clinician concludes that a requested treatment is inimical to the best interest of the patient, and that his professional conscience, intuition or hunch, confirms that view. In those circumstances he may refuse to act and cannot be compelled to do so, though he should not prevent another from so acting, should that clinician feel able to do so.[77]

If, then, we are to follow Mr Justice Hedley's schema, we must, first, distinguish between conscience and clinical judgment – and the two are undoubtedly different. The latter is a matter of practical experience; in the doctor's opinion, a treatment is either *correct* or it is *incorrect* and the evaluation is reached by way of the patient's overall medical benefit. The distinction is, however, comparative rather than absolute. Thus, there may be two therapeutic possibilities and the doctor, in applying his or her clinical judgment, can choose one as being the better – or correct – but not necessarily reject the other in toto. In any event, the problem is a technical matter. Conscience, by contrast, is a matter of moral judgment – it is either *right* or *wrong* to provide a treatment. Thus, again, two doctors may make diametrically opposed decisions but, so long as the decision is based on conscience, both may be acceptable – for conscience is a *personal* and wholly subjective matter. In short, the concern is not so much related to the effect on the patient as on the doctor's appreciation of his or her own status – is he or she acting rightly or wrongly in a principled sense?

Put that way, conscience would seem to be the ultimate expression of autonomy. The difficulty, however, is that this can only be regarded as inviolable in respect of the conscientious individual; his or her views cannot be imposed on others or used to restrict the actions of others – and this second implication is demonstrated in Hedley J's final caveat. On the face of things, there is no reason why, for example, a doctor's conscience might not view abortion as so intrinsically *wrong* that he or she would not feel justified in referring a patient to another practitioner despite that patient's protestation of damage, say, to her mental health. Yet one feels that, in such circumstances, the rules of negligence would not be abrogated by an appeal to conscience. Thus, there are bound to be times when one's moral conscience conflicts with one's professional duties – and the dividing line may be less than bright and clear.

[77] n. 45 above, at 87 BMLR 183 [35], [36].

With these provisos in mind, I would regard *Re J (a minor) (wardship: medical treatment)* [78] – hereafter *Re J(2)* [79] – as the scene-setting case which defines the limits to which the doctor can be driven. It is, admittedly, not a case of congenital disease but the points it makes so clearly can be, and have been, applied so easily to the disabled neonate that its inclusion is well-nigh essential to the understanding of the whole picture.

In brief, J was a 16-month-old child who was severely handicapped both mentally and physically as a result of a fall when a baby – to such an extent that medical opinion was that it would be inappropriate, to the extent of it being cruel, to provide ventilation and other intensive care should he suffer a life threatening event. Nonetheless, the local authority, who had care of the child by way of some devoted foster parents, successfully invoked the inherent jurisdiction of the High Court [80] and obtained an interim order that J was to be treated aggressively should doing so serve to prolong his life. The health authority, supported by the Official Solicitor and the local authority, which had now changed its view, appealed against the order which, however, still represented the wishes of the child's mother.

A virtually unique feature of *Re J(2)* is that Waite J at first instance took the unusual step of questioning Lord Donaldson's opinion in the previous case of *Re J* [81] – going so far, in fact, as to describe judgments which the Master of the Rolls regarded as expressions of the law as obiter. As a result, the ratio of *Re J(2)* in the Court of Appeal was delivered in particularly strong language which leaves no room for doubt as to the correct position – 'The order of Waite J was wholly inconsistent with the law as so stated and cannot be justified upon the basis of any authority known to me.' [82] The significance of *Re J(2)* can be summed up in one quotation from the Master of the Rolls:

The fundamental issue in this appeal is whether the court in the exercise of its inherent power to protect the interests of minors should ever require a medical practitioner or health authority acting by a medical practitioner to adopt a course of treatment which in the bona fide clinical judgment of the practitioner concerned is contraindicated as not being in the best interests of the patient. I have to say that I cannot at present conceive of any circumstances in which this would be other than an abuse of power as directly or indirectly requiring the practitioner to act contrary to the fundamental duty which he owes to his patient. This . . . is to treat the patient in accordance with his own best clinical judgment, notwithstanding that other practitioners who are not called upon to treat the patient

[78] [1993] Fam 15, (1992) 9 BMLR 10, CA.
[79] To distinguish from *Re J* (1990), n. 8 above.
[80] Under the Children Act 1989, s.100.   [81] n. 8 above. We return to *Re J* below.
[82] Per Lord Donaldson MR, n. 78 above, at Fam 28, BMLR 18.

may have formed a quite different judgment or that the court, acting on expert evidence, may disagree with him.[83]

Balcombe and Leggatt LLJ provided concurring judgments that were equally firmly worded and dismissive of an order that 'purported to order a doctor to treat a patient in a particular way contrary to the doctor's will'[84] and there is little doubt that the spirit of *R J(2)* underpins the law – despite the recent emergence of some scepticism.[85]

The case of *Re C (medical treatment)*,[86] for example, involved another 16-month-old child, this time suffering from the genetic disease of spinal muscular atrophy. The rather unusual circumstances of the case involved a therapeutic test in which her ventilator support would be removed; should she, as a result, suffer another respiratory collapse – as was strongly anticipated – the ventilator would not be replaced and she would be allowed to die. Her parents, who, as orthodox Jews, held absolutist views as to the sanctity of life, were prepared to accept the test but insisted that the ventilator be replaced if that was necessary for the preservation of the child's life. I must confess, also, to some doubts as to the ethics of a test that, in effect, challenges a baby to 'fight for its life'; nevertheless, the President of the Family Division granted leave to the hospital to proceed accordingly – in the child's best interests. In so doing, he reiterated Lord Donaldson's dicta and summarised these:

[To follow the wishes of the parents] would be tantamount to requiring the doctors to undertake a course of treatment which they are unwilling to do. The court could not make an order which would require them to do so.[87]

And, whether or not you believe, as I do, that *Re C* is, by its nature, an incremental advance on *Re J(2)*, it served to confirm the limits of the paediatrician's duties – that is, at least, until almost the moment in time when this typescript was due for submission.[88]

However, before leaving those cases which have, albeit somewhat arbitrarily, been categorised as 'conscience cases', we should take another minor diversion and consider Balcombe LJ's opinion in *Re J(2)* which was especially interesting in that it paid particular attention to the parallel

---

[83] ibid., at Fam 26, BMLR 17.   [84] Per Leggatt LJ, ibid., at Fam 31, BMLR 21.
[85] A determined effort at first instance to undermine it – admittedly in an adult context – was made in *R (on the application of Burke)* v. *General Medical Council* [2005] QB 424, (2004) 79 BMLR 126 but this was peremptorily halted on appeal: (2005) 85 BMLR 1. We cannot, however, ignore the very contemporary results in *Wyatt* and *An NHS Trust* v. *MB* which are discussed in detail at pp. 275 et seq.
[86] (1997) 40 BMLR 31.   [87] ibid., at 37.
[88] See, now, *An NHS Trust* v. *MB*, n. 176 below.

concerns as to the health authority's duties and the problems of resource allocation. He had this to say:

> I would also stress the absolute undesirability of the court making an order which may have the effect of compelling a doctor or a health authority to make available scarce resources (both human and material) to a particular child, without knowing whether or not there are other patients to whom those resources might more advantageously be devoted ... The effect of the order of Waite J ... might have been to require the health authority to put J on a ventilator in an intensive care unit, and thereby possibly to deny the benefit of those limited resources to a child who was much more likely than J to benefit from them.[89]

Which seems the correct approach but the case was heard before the introduction of the Human Rights Act 1998. One must now wonder if the selectivity involved might be held to contravene Article 2 of Schedule 1 – the right to life.[90] There seems to be no reason why it should not, at least, be challenged on an individual basis.[91]

The doctor's conscience (2). It will also be convenient at this point to look at Hedley J's other uncommon category – that is, where the medical opinion is so strong, that the doctor's conscience must be stretched to the limit in the face of parental refusal to accept the treatment offered. We have already noted that, beyond those concerned with blood transfusion, such cases are extremely rare.

The case of Baby C[92] is atypical in that the child was 3½ years old by the time the court became involved. However, it involved a case of biliary atresia and, therefore, lies within the parameters of congenital disease. The circumstances were such that it can be regarded as a paradigm example of Lady Hale's 'continuing pregnancy'.[93]

C had already undergone surgery at the age of 3 weeks; it was unsuccessful and medical opinion, including that sought by his mother, was unanimous in recommending a liver transplant. C's mother, however,

---

[89] n. 78 above, at Fam 30, BMLR 20.

[90] 'No one shall be deprived of his life intentionally'. The very different case of *R (on the application of Rogers)* v. *Swindon NHS Primary Care Trust* [2006] EWCA Civ 392, which involved the provision of anti-cancer drugs, suggests that rationality in allotting scarce resources might be the basic criterion.

[91] This was proposed, at least in respect of Articles 3 and 8, in *R (on the application of Burke)* v. *General Medical Council*, n. 85 above, at [194]. However, that is of little assistance as that case was declared to be unconcerned with resource allocation on appeal.

[92] Almost perversely known as *Re T (a minor) (wardship: medical treatment)* [1997] 1 All ER 906, (1996) 35 BMLR 63. The case is well discussed in Marie Fox and Jean McHale, 'In Whose Best Interests?' (1997) 60 *Modern Law Review* 700–9; see also Andrew Bainham, 'Do Babies have Rights?' (1997) 56 *Cambridge Law Journal* 48–50.

[93] See n. 1 above.

mindful of the pain he had undergone following his earlier operation, was unwilling to repeat the experience and took him abroad when he was placed on the urgent transplant list. The local authority where the family normally lived then raised the matter as a special issue under the Children Act 1989, section 100(3). Connell J concluded that the refusal of treatment was not consistent with reasonable parenting and directed that the child be returned to the United Kingdom and be presented to a hospital to await a transplantation operation; C's mother, supported by his father, appealed against this direction.

The pleadings in the Court of Appeal are interesting in that counsel for the mother accepted the line taken in the court below and based his case on the assumption that the mother's decision was, in fact, 'within that band of reasonable decisions with which the court should not interfere and coerce the mother'. Counsel for the local authority and the guardian ad litem maintained that the correct test was the welfare of the child and not the reasonableness of the parents. Almost inevitably, the court agreed with the latter view: 'The consent or refusal of consent of the parents', said Butler-Sloss LJ, 'is an important consideration to weigh in the balancing exercise to be carried out by the judge. In that context the extent to which the court will have regard to the view of the parents will depend upon the court's assessment of that view.'[94]

And, then, surprisingly, the Lady Justice virtually reversed the pleadings and concluded that it was not in C's best interests to undergo the transplant operation. I fancy that this was, in the main, due to her deep conviction that:

The mother and this child are one for the purpose of this unusual case and the decision of the court to consent to the operation jointly affects the mother and son ... The welfare of the child depends upon its mother.[95]

And, again:

[T]he prospect of forcing the devoted mother of this young baby to the consequences of his major invasive surgery, leads me to the conclusion ... that it is not in the best interests of this child to give consent and require him to return to England for the purpose of undergoing liver transplantation. I believe that the best interests of this child require that his future treatment should be left in the hands of his devoted parents[96]

– who, it is to be noted, were health care workers, although we are not told in what capacity. Whether or not this was significant, it is, from no more than a paper reading of the case, difficult to equate so much parental

---

[94] n. 92 above, at All ER 913, BMLR 71.   [95] ibid., at All ER 914, BMLR 72.
[96] ibid., at All ER 916, BMLR 74.

devotion with a refusal to exchange a possibly difficult, though probably worthwhile, several years' life for their child for a certain and relatively rapid death. In the late 1990s, transplantation was a rapidly evolving specialty with improvements in, say, immunosuppression being regularly introduced; and, if we are looking at the dangers and discomforts of the operation, we must also remember that there were probably several dozen parents in England crying for the opportunity for their children at the time when C's parents were resisting it with such determination.

Re T is very unusual, if not unique, both in its origin as being very close to a category (i) case[97] and as to its disposal contrary to medical opinion. As a result, I feel we should not overestimate its significance. Against my obvious doubts as to the rightness of the outcome, it has to be noted that the decision was unanimous; the impression, thus, remains that there was, perhaps, far more in the case than appears in the written word. Possibly the main lesson to be learned from the case is that, no matter how determinedly the courts will take measures to avoid the impression, 'best interests' is, at heart, a subjective test – subject, that is, to the inevitable variations in individual human natures. We can leave it with the words of Professors Kennedy and Grubb: '*Re T* is a most unusual case indeed.'[98]

The mainstream cases. Having set the scene in 1981 and disposed of those cases which are mainly of interest in demonstrating the extremes, we can now concentrate on our search for any legal pattern directed to the management of the disabled neonate that may have evolved over the last quarter of a century.

The first apposite post-*Arthur* example is *Re C*,[99] a case which takes on an added significance in being the first of the series of relevant cases decided by Lord Donaldson MR whose influence in this field has been so profound.[100] *Re C* concerned a moribund infant with severe brain damage due to congenital hydrocephalus. She was, in fact, already a ward of court when a dispute arose based on the question: should she

---

[97] It certainly was not a 'pure' category (i) case as one surgeon, on whom the Court depended heavily, was not prepared to operate with the parents still objecting. This does not seem to be a throw-back to *Re B* in 1981 – where there was a misunderstanding of the relative roles of the parents and the Court – but was, rather, due to a fear that the operation would not succeed without adequate long-term post-operative care.

[98] *Medical Law* (London: Butterworths, 3rd edn 2000) at 802.

[99] *Re C (a minor) (wardship: medical treatment)* [1990] Fam 26, [1989] 2 All ER 782.

[100] I have reviewed the early cases elsewhere in J. K. Mason, 'Master of the Balancers: Non-Voluntary Therapy under the Mantle of Lord Donaldson' [1993] *Juridical Review* 115–32.

be treated as a non-handicapped child or should she receive 'such treatment as is appropriate to her condition'?

In deciding for the latter option, Ward J at first instance inadvertently made medico-legal history when he directed that leave be given to the hospital authorities 'to treat the ward to die with the greatest dignity and the least of pain, suffering and distress'. The concept of being 'treated to die' clearly opened the way to suggestions that C was being treated in a way *designed* to bring about her death and the judge was quick to amend his direction to read:

I direct that leave be given to the hospital authorities to treat the ward in such a way that she may end her life and die peacefully with the greatest dignity and with the least of pain, suffering and distress.[101]

None of the principals in the case objected to this but, nevertheless, the Official Solicitor, acting as guardian to C, appealed on the grounds, firstly, of the phrasing of the original direction and of the anxiety as to motive that this involved, and, secondly, as a way of questioning parts of the order that appeared to provide that in no circumstances should certain treatment be undertaken. In the end, the Court of Appeal unanimously allowed the appeal to the very narrow extent of deleting such of the judge's direction which might be misinterpreted as conflicting with the expert medical advice.[102] The general direction that the goal should be to ease C's suffering rather than to achieve a short prolongation of her life was, however, approved.

Insofar as no medical or surgical procedure could alter the fact that C was dying, it was a relatively easy case to decide. But it is to be noted that the only United Kingdom case available as a precedent was *Re B* in 1981 which, although being of very different type, was, nevertheless, dealt with on an opposing line. It can possibly be said that the decision in *Re C* contained nothing new; nonetheless, it laid down at least one parameter for the emerging jurisprudence to use as a sheet anchor – that a dying child can be allowed to die in peace.

The next case, *Re J*,[103] however, dealt with a child who was not dying. The problem was that of the management of J in the event that his condition deteriorated to the extent that, while he could be treated and, perhaps, resuscitated, he would die in the absence of such treatment. This was a novel situation for the courts at the time; it has, however, now

---

[101] n. 99 above, at Fam 35, All ER 787.
[102] Indeed, the underlying current of *Re C* is clearly devoted to nullifying what seems to have been a whispering campaign against the hospital.
[103] *Re J*, n. 8 above.

become what is virtually the standard scenario in disputed cases of neo-natal medicine. *Re J* can, therefore, be looked on as the foundation case which laid down the template for judicial decision-making and it has already been referred to on several occasions in this chapter. It is, however, such a milestone case that it is essential that its message is consolidated.

J was a 5-month-old ward of court[104] who had been severely brain damaged during birth following a 27-week gestation period. He was ventilated for a month but was then weaned off the ventilator. Subsequently, he suffered from multiple cardio-respiratory failures and was, at one time, returned to full ventilation; at the time of the trial, however, he was breathing independently. He was likely to be quadriplegic, blind and deaf but, at the same time would probably be able to feel pain to the same extent as a normal child. The problem was what to do in the event that J had another attack requiring ventilatory treatment and, in the event, Scott Baker J made an order indicating that it would not be in J's best interests to reventilate him in the event of his stopping breathing unless to do so seemed appropriate to the doctors caring for him at the time.

The precedental importance of *Re J* is emphasised by the fact that the Official Solicitor appealed the order – and he or she has never since done so in similar circumstances. In essence, the Official Solicitor based his appeal on two grounds. First he held that, lying between the extremes of *Re C*[105] and *Re B*,[106] J's case broke new jurisprudential ground and, second, he maintained that, while Scott Baker J was correct in acting in what he thought were the best interests of the child, he erred 'in that a court is never justified in withholding consent to treatment which could enable a child to survive a life-threatening condition, whatever the quality of the life which it would experience thereafter'.[107] Left like that, the case would have been a straightforward assessment of the vitalist or absolutist approach which we have discussed above at p. 243.[108] However, in the alternative, the Official Solicitor submitted that withholding treatment was only justified if the court was certain that life would be 'intolerable' or

---

[104] The wardship was for extraneous reasons. Thus, although there was no conflict between the doctors and the parents, the rights and duties as to treatment were vested in the court. The parents were not formally associated with the appeal but had, by that time, begun to doubt their decision to accept the order given at first instance. It is to be noted that, for present purposes, *Re J* is an exceptional case that is being used to demonstrate the general rule.

[105] See p. 266 above.   [106] See p. 252 above.

[107] At [1990] 3 All ER 930, 934, 6 BMLR 25, 29.

[108] The Solicitor depended to a large extent on the opinions given in *McKay* v. *Essex Area Health Authority* [1982] QB 1166 (for which, see p. 205 above) but Lord Donaldson, supported by the other members of the court, felt that the case provided neither guidance nor assistance – and I fancy that most people would agree that this was so.

so awful that, 'in effect, the child must be condemned to die';[109] this, he argued, had not been demonstrated in J's case.

Lord Donaldson, as we have already seen, was quick to reject the absolutist approach – 'In real life there are presumptions, strong presumptions and almost overwhelming presumptions, but there are few, if any, absolutes'[110] – and turned to the alternative submission. Here, having analysed the speeches in *Re B* in depth, he expressed the fundamental purpose of the hearing in J's and similar cases in two sentences:

What doctors and the court have to decide is whether, in the best interests of the child patient, a particular decision as to medical treatment should be taken which *as a side effect* will render death more or less likely . . . What can never be justified is the use of drugs or surgical procedures with the primary purpose of [hastening the moment of death].[111]

He then explained how this was to be done:

[A]ccount has to be taken of the pain and suffering and quality of life which the child will experience if life is prolonged. Account has also to be taken of the pain and suffering involved in the proposed treatment itself.[112]

And, significantly for the future:

I do not think that we are bound to, or should, treat Templeman LJ's use of the words 'demonstrably so awful' or Dunn LJ's use of the word 'intolerable' as providing a quasi-statutory yardstick.

And, in applying these generalisations to J's case, the court unanimously accepted medical advice as to the discomforts and dangers involved in further invasive treatment and affirmed the judge's decision, subject to some minor variations which need not concern us here.

Thus, *Re J* makes the position clear and, at the same time, provides a template for the future. The foregoing summary may not, however, emphasise the extreme caution with which the decision was reached. Two concluding quotations will, I think, suffice. We have already noted Taylor LJ on the presumption in favour of taking all reasonable steps to preserve human life save in exceptional circumstances.[113] And, finally, we have Balcombe LJ:

There is only one test: that is the interests of the ward are paramount. Of course the court will approach those interests with a strong predilection in favour of

---

[109] As per Templeman and Dunn LLJ in *Re B*, p. 259 above.
[110] n. 103 above at All ER 937, BMLR 32–33.
[111] ibid., at All ER 938, BMLR 34 (emphasis in the original). Lord Balcombe also noted that in none of the wardship cases had there been a proposal that a positive step should be taken to terminate life.
[112] Ibid.   [113] n. 8 above.

the preservation of life because of the sanctity of human life ... [But] to preserve life at all costs, whatever the quality of life to be preserved, and however distressing to the ward may be the nature of the treatment necessary to preserve life, may not be in the interests of the ward.[114]

Re J is slightly complicated by Taylor LJ's unconventional views as to substituted judgment when he said:

I consider that the correct approach is for the court to judge the quality of life the child would have to endure if given the treatment and decide whether in all the circumstances such a life would be so afflicted as to be intolerable to that child. I say 'to that child' because the test should not be whether the life would be tolerable to the decider. The test must be whether the child in question, if capable of exercising sound judgment, would consider the life tolerable.[115]

That divergence from mainstream jurisprudence lies, however, at the theoretical level. In practice, *Re J* is as good a piece of pragmatic reasoning as is likely to be found; it fully deserves its historic position and it still remains the authority in the field that is most consistently quoted with approval.

Later cases of particular interest. The courts' interest in the congenitally disabled baby seems, then, to have waned for some 15 years before there was a sudden burst of reactivity which is detailed later in the chapter. Meantime, I would like to look, briefly, at two somewhat isolated cases which provide links in the continuing development of the jurisprudence.

The first of these is *Re C (a baby)*.[116] C was a premature baby who developed meningitis and, as a consequence, was so disabled that Sir Stephen Brown P summed up her condition as being 'almost a living death'. She was wholly dependent on artificial ventilation and it was anticipated that she would suffer from increasing pain and distress if the circumstances remained as they were. There was no conflict, both the parents and the doctors agreeing that artificial ventilation should be withdrawn – in which case she would die almost immediately; C was, accordingly made a ward of court. Sir Stephen Brown P concluded that she did not have 'what can be described as an independent existence' and unhesitatingly granted leave that artificial ventilation should be discontinued.

Reading the bare bones of the very short report, it is, in fact, difficult to see why C's case could not have been dealt with as a simple matter of agreed medical futility and, therein, lies the interest of the case. Probably as a direct consequence, the President was asked to comment on when such cases should be brought to court for adjudication. He declined to do this, holding

---

[114] n. 103 above, at All ER 942, BMLR 39.   [115] ibid., at All ER 945, BMLR 42.
[116] [1996] 2 FLR 43, (1996) 32 BMLR 44.

that each case must be considered on its merits and, thereby, setting the pattern for future decision-making. Even so, it might have been useful had he explained why C was made a ward of court in the uncontroversial circumstances of her death; it was said to be appropriate that the parents should be relieved in some measure of their grave responsibility but many others must have shouldered similar responsibility with no such assistance. The case remains something of a medico-legal conundrum.

The second case I have singled out is that of *A National Health Service Trust* v. *D*.[117] ID was also born prematurely and suffered from multi-organ dysfunction.[118] At the age of 19 months, the Trust, supported by the Official Solicitor, applied for authority not to resuscitate him by artificial ventilation in the event of a future cardiac or respiratory collapse but to allow him to die with suitable palliative care. The application was strongly opposed by his parents who were, at the time, caring for him at home and who considered that there was improvement in his condition – including some response to his environment.[119] Thus far, then, ID's case was very similar to those that have gone before; the new twist was that the order was the first to consider the problems raised by the European Convention on Human Rights, now incorporated in the Human Rights Act 1998 – albeit that the Act was not yet in force at the time.

In giving his judgment, Cazalet J helpfully summarised the four principles that were now established as governing the law in this area. These were:

- The paramount consideration must be the best interests of the child;
- The court's respect for the sanctity of human life must impose a strong obligation in favour of taking steps capable of preserving life, save in exceptional circumstances;
- The court is concerned only with the circumstances in which steps should not be taken to prolong life; and
- The court cannot direct a doctor to provide treatment when to do so is contrary to his or her clinical judgment[120]

---

[117] [2000] 2 FLR 677, (2000) 55 BMLR 19.

[118] Estimates of the occurrence of disability in infants born between 23 and 28 weeks' gestation vary considerably but severe disability is most likely to be in the region of 20 per cent: C. de Garis, H. Kuhse, P. Singer and V. Y. Yu, 'Attitudes of Australian Neonatal Paediatricians to the Treatment of Extremely Preterm Infants' (1987) 23 *Australian Paediatric Journal* 223–6. The reference is old but is interesting because of its authorship; the actual figure is unlikely to be very different today.

[119] The situation was complicated in that, in addition to the universal medical opinion being that intensive care was inappropriate, there were no beds available in the hospitals with suitable units.

[120] n. 117 above, at FLR 685–6 BMLR 28. In addition, Cazalet J referred to the Court of Appeal's recommendation in *R* v. *Portsmouth Hospitals NHS Trust, ex p Glass* [1999] 2

and, having considered all these in the course of a detailed consideration of the evidence, he granted the declaration, subject to the clinical opinion of the paediatrician in charge should ID be readmitted to hospital.

Cazalet J relied heavily on *Re J*. However, as already mentioned, the novel aspect of the judgment related to the impact, if any, of the Convention rights on the legal position in the United Kingdom as it is defined by that case. Clearly, the most relevant item was Article 2,[121] which states:

Everyone's right to life shall be protected by law. No one shall be deprived of his life intentionally save in the execution of a sentence of a court ...

In the absence of any apposite ruling by the European Court of Human Rights, Cazalet J was forced to extemporise. First, he ruled that there could be no infringement of Article 2 given that the order was issued in the best interests of ID.[122] Second, he noted that Article 3, which requires that a person is not subjected to inhuman or degrading treatment, includes the right to die with dignity[123] – and a major purpose of the declaration made was to protect that right. He concluded that no breach of any Convention Article was shown in his ruling. This opinion has not been challenged; nevertheless it remains only an opinion. One feels that it is likely to be followed; it could be, however, that the increase in 'rights-based litigation' will dictate ever-increasingly meticulous examination of the facts in future cases that are conducted under the umbrella of the 1998 Act.

This detailed consideration of the past cases might suggest that a recognisable pattern of judicial action has been established. It could be supposed that the legal and ethical minefield of neonatal disability had been successfully cleared and that further litigation was both unnecessary and unlikely – each case was to be decided on its merits and the foundation 'merits' had been clarified. Yet the early 2000s produced a flurry of new, and hotly contested, cases that attracted considerable media

FLR 905, (1999) 50 BMLR 269 to the effect that it would be inappropriate for the court to grant a declaration in anticipation of circumstances that had not yet arisen. His Honour considered, however, that the two cases were distinct – an opinion with which most would agree. In passing, I should explain that *Glass* concerned a 12-year-old boy and that, accordingly the case lies outside the remit of this chapter.

[121] See, now Human Rights Act 1998, Schedule 1, part I.

[122] A similar ruling, also involving Article 8 (the right to respect for a person's private life) has been made in the adult context although the reasoning was rather different and is scarcely applicable to children: *NHS Trust A* v. *Mrs M, NHS Trust B* v. *Mrs H* [2001] 2 WLR 942, (2001) 58 BMLR 87.

[123] Relying on *D* v. *UK* (1997) 24 EHRR 423 although this case depended on *positive* action which caused suffering. A right to 'die with dignity' does not include right to have one's life terminated: *Pretty* v. *United Kingdom* [2002] 2 FLR 45, (2002) 66 BMLR 147.

attention. Quite why this should have happened is tantalisingly uncertain. Nevertheless, the cases form an interlocking group that is also defined by the unusual intensity of the emotions provoked. Insofar as they suggest at least an incremental change in judicial attitudes, they can usefully be discussed as a distinct group that provides its own lessons.

The recent cases

The case of Charlotte Wyatt. The saga of Baby Wyatt began in 2004 and is still ongoing as this typescript goes to press. Charlotte Wyatt weighed 1 lb when she was born after 26 weeks' gestation – which is very close to the limit of physiologically possible independent life. She had minimal lung function requiring 40–50 per cent oxygen delivered by way of a head box and her brain was very severely underdeveloped; even so, she could experience pain and distress. Her condition deteriorated following an infection at the age of 9 months and, at the age of one year, the NHS Trust, supported by a unanimous medical opinion, and that of the guardian appointed to supervise her interests, sought a declaration that the provision of artificial ventilation, if required, would be against her best interests; the Trust also requested relief to permit the doctors not to send her for artificial ventilation or similar aggressive treatment even though she might die sooner than she would if it were provided.[124] This was strongly opposed by the parents whose maximum concession to an otherwise 'life at all costs' stance was that they would contemplate withdrawal of ventilation after a few days' trial had shown it to be of no value to the child.

Hedley J's assessment was singularly sensitive and far-ranging. His introduction is a salutary reminder of the difficulties the courts accept when providing solutions to medical dilemmas:

This kind of dispute is to be resolved by a Judge of the Family Division and, whilst the judge will be more aware than anyone of his own limitations in deciding as profound an issue as this, decision there simply has to be. It may well be that an external decision in the end is a better solution than the stark alternatives of medical or parental veto.[125]

Even so, the decision in Charlotte Wyatt's case was, in this writer's opinion, virtually dictated by precedent. The judge quoted Hoffmann

---

[124] *Re Wyatt (a child) (medical treatment: parents' consent)* [2005] 1 FLR 21, (2004) 84 BMLR 206. This stage of the case has been reviewed by David W. Meyers, '*Wyatt* and *Winston-Jones*: Who Decides to Treat or Let Die Seriously Ill Babies?' (2005) 9 *Edinburgh Law Review* 307–16.

[125] *Re Wyatt*, n. 124 above, at [4].

LJ's firm opinion as to the current attitudes to the sanctity of life doctrine and how, in particular, it can be modified by respect for the dignity of the individual human being.[126] He reviewed the best interests test along the lines we have done in this chapter and, of course, relied heavily on Lord Donaldson and Taylor LJ in *Re J*.[127] Faced with the anxiety for a 'good', inevitable death for Charlotte and a uniformly adverse prognosis as to her quality of life, if any,[128] it is difficult to see that he had any real alternative to granting the relief requested – despite the fact that *The Times* asserted that the judge's 'decision was wrong'.[129] It is, however, to be noted that the relief given was, perforce, only permissive[130] and that is where the complexity of the case appears to lie. The declaration ran:

In the event that the responsible paediatric medical consultants reach a decision that Charlotte's medical condition shall have deteriorated to such an extent that she is unable to maintain oxygen and carbon dioxide exchange, it shall be lawful for responsible paediatric medical consultants to reach a decision that she should not be intubated and/or ventilated.

A similar declaration was made as to the provision of continuous positive airways pressure. Thus, there was nothing final about the orders which merely stated that the doctors were acting lawfully should they take a given action in what their clinical acumen indicated to be the best interests of the patient.

To the surprise of almost everyone concerned, Charlotte's condition also appeared to be fluid rather than static – at least in respect of visible signs. Accordingly an application was made to stay the orders pending further investigations into her condition.[131] Hedley J refused this on several grounds, the most significant of which were, first, that the order did not derogate from the duty of the doctors to treat the child in what they saw as its best medical interests and, second, because there was no

---

[126] In *Airedale NHS Trust* v. *Bland* [1993] AC 789 at 826. This, as is well known, was the primary case on the management of the permanent vegetative state. Although it went to the House of Lords, Hoffman LJ's speech in the Court of Appeal is probably the most illuminating of the many opinions recorded in that case as to its moral dimensions.

[127] n. 8 above.

[128] Prophetically, Hedley J did say:' Yet no-one can say for absolute certain that she will not survive for another year however much the probabilities are against it' (*Re Wyatt*, n. 124 above, at [29]). Charlotte is, in fact, still alive – and adopted – in 2007.

[129] Leading Article 'Life and Law' (2004) 8 October, p. 15. Margot Brazier, 'Times of Change?' (2005) 13 *Medical Law Review* 1–16 points out that such disputes are not novel; the difference between 1993 and 2005 is that they are now conducted in a glare of publicity.

[130] Injunctive relief was precluded by the decision in the Court of Appeal in *Re J(2)*, n. 78 above, while the difficulties involved in granting positive declaratory relief become apparent in the later hearings.

[131] *Portsmouth Hospitals NHS Trust* v. *Wyatt and ors* [2005] EWHC 117.

evidence of any significant change in Charlotte's *underlying* condition and her ability to withstand aggressive or invasive treatment. This judgment was appealed but, before that came to court, a third High Court hearing was undertaken three months later.[132]

Here, the goal-posts were again shifted and the obligation to show that the declarations should continue passed to the NHS Trust. Certainly there was a change in Charlotte's condition since the orders were made; it could no longer be described as being intolerable. She still, however, suffered from a chronic respiratory disease that was expected to be fatal and, in essence, the matter was one of quite narrow disagreement between the Trust and the parents. The former was prepared to give treatment up to but not including invasive intensive care which was likely, should she survive, to cause deterioration in her condition and would certainly imperil a peaceful death; at least two specialists inferred that aggressive treatment would be contrary to their professional conscience. The latter maintained that all available treatment should be given. In favouring the majority medical opinion, Hedley J went, perhaps, one stage further and, rather than wait until a crisis occurred, made an immediate order to continue his declarations.[133] In doing so, he stressed again that the order was permissive only – the Trust was under no obligation to follow it should the circumstances indicate that aggressive treatment was, in fact, appropriate; he also mandated that the order was not open-ended but was subject to compulsory review.

The matter then went to the Court of Appeal,[134] the application being, in fact, one seeking permission to appeal to that court. The issue lay not so much in the substance of the declarations as in the propriety of continuing them in the absence of an immediate need for their application – basically, 'if declarations are capable of becoming unlawful due to changes of circumstances, was it appropriate to make them in the first place?'[135] The main finding of the Court – that the judge was entitled to continue the declarations and right to order a review – are, therefore, of comparatively little interest in the medico-ethical context which provides the substance of this book. Nonetheless,

---

[132] *Wyatt v. Portsmouth Hospitals NHS Trust and Wyatt (by her guardian) (No. 3)* [2005] EWHC 693, [2005] 2 FLR 480.
[133] Relying on the exceptional circumstances of the case and on the advice of Lord Woolf MR in *R v. Portsmouth Hospitals NHS Trust, ex p Glass* [1999] 2 FLR 905 – the general rule is that declarations should be sought and considered in the light of circumstances as they are and not as they may be.
[134] *Re Wyatt (a child) (medical treatment: continuation of order)* (2005) 86 BMLR 173.
[135] ibid., at [113].

the Court of Appeal decision in *Wyatt* is, in the writer's opinion, of major medico-legal significance on two main counts. First, it and later companion cases[136] stress the case specificity of decisions such as these; I have always emphasised what I see as the impossibility of laying down either a legal policy or a single ethical imperative by which to dictate 'good medical practice'[137] – and this is particularly so in the case of life or death decision-making.[138] Secondly, the Court took the opportunity to examine and define the 'best interests' test in depth with the clear intention that the judgment would define the law at least for some time to come.[139] Despite the fact that we have already looked at 'best interests' in general, it will not be inappropriate to take time-out in which to examine what was said in particular.

Cut down to the bare bones, the argument as to the test to be applied in deciding non-treatment cases lies between, on the one hand, a conclusion as to the 'intolerability' of continued life and, on the other, an assessment of whether the patient's 'interests' – as widely defined – are 'best served' by continued or discontinued treatment, which, in the great majority of cases, means, perforce, life or death.

The former 'test' owes its origin to Templeman LJ's allusion to it in *Re B* which we have already discussed.[140] The Court of Appeal in *Wyatt* took the view that Lord Templeman's opinion, which was backed by Dunn LJ[141] but which was, of necessity, given very hurriedly, had been disapproved by the majority in the undoubtedly seminal case of *Re J*.[142] I, personally, feel that is overstating the case to an extent – such criticism as there was was directed mainly to the somewhat emotive language involved. Certainly, Taylor LJ in his *concurring* speech, was prepared to accept that the 'correct approach' to this type of decision-making was to ask and

---

[136] See, for example, *An NHS Trust* v. *MB (a child represented by CAFCASS as guardian ad litem)* [2006] 2 FLR 319 per Holman J at [106], [107].

[137] Most recently in J. K. Mason, 'Ethical Principles and Ethical Practice' (2006) 1 *Clinical Ethics* 3–6.

[138] Although they are dealing with adult situations it is interesting and instructive to compare *W Healthcare NHS Trust* v. *H and another* [2005] 1 WLR 834 (treatment authorised against wishes of the family) with *An NHS Trust* v. *D* (2006) 87 BMLR 119 (non-treatment authorised against the wishes of the family). The courts seem to be moving gradually to the recognition of 'a PVS state' as the benchmark of futility in treatment.

[139] '[I]n cases of this sensitivity and difficulty, the guidelines which the experienced judges of the Family Division have to follow should be both as clear and as simple as is consistent with the serious issues which they engage' (n. 134 above, at [85]).

[140] At p. 257 above.

[141] 'There is no evidence that this child's short life is likely to be an intolerable one' (n. 47 above at WLR 1424).

[142] The relevant passages are quoted in *Re Wyatt*, n. 134 above at [68]–[74].

answer the question 'whether in all the circumstances such a life would be so afflicted as to be intolerable to the child'.[143] More recently, Brooke LJ has said:

Normally the approach that the law should adopt is whether, in the judgment of the court, the continuation of life would be intolerable,[144]

a statement that the Court of Appeal in *Wyatt* was quick to interpret as being, at best, obiter.

It is, in fact, not entirely clear why the concept of an intolerable life has become so unpopular in the eyes of the law. Many would say that intolerability is a term that is easily understood and, therefore, descriptively useful.[145] On the other hand, it has shades of meaning that vary from one observer to another[146] and, more importantly, its assessment carries overtones of a substituted judgment which the courts, as we have seen, are anxious to avoid. The *particular* impetus to its rejection as a test, however, probably stems not from a generality but from the nature of the pleadings in *Wyatt* itself. Intolerability is an absolute;[147] anything short of it must be tolerable to a degree. Counsel for Charlotte's parents argued that, since there had been some objective improvement in her condition between the first and second hearings, her life could no longer be said to be intolerable and, therefore, the judge had been wrong to continue the declarations.[148] The use of the word 'intolerable' was, thus, transformed from being a subject for quiet academic analysis to one of immediate practical importance on which the whole case hinged.

---

[143] *Re J*, n. 8 above, at 42. Also adopted by Sir Stephen Brown P in *Re R (adult: medical treatment)* (1996) 31 BMLR 127 at 136.

[144] In *W Healthcare Trust*, n. 138 above, at [26]. This may have been prompted by the statement of Munby J 'The touchstone of best interests in this context is intolerability' in *R (on the application of Burke)* v. *General Medical Council* (2004) 79 BMLR 126 at [113]. Munby J's decision was, however, somewhat tersely disapproved in the Court of Appeal: *R (on the application of Burke)* v. *General Medical Council* (2005) 85 BMLR 1 and is, as a result, a doubtful authority.

[145] Professor Margaret Brazier has said: 'With respect to Mr Justice Hedley the prevailing factor knitting together most of the diverse judicial reasoning in these tragic cases is intolerability: is the treatment proposed likely to render the continued life of the child demonstrably awful?' – M. Brazier, 'Letting Charlotte Die' (2004) 30 *Journal of Medical Ethics* 519–20.

[146] One is reminded of Lord Donaldson MR: 'Even very severely handicapped people find a quality of life rewarding which to the unhandicapped may seem manifestly intolerable' in *Re J* (n. 8 above, at Fam 46 All ER 938).

[147] Indeed, it is arguable that 'an intolerable life' is a contradiction in terms. Much the same view is put by Holman J in *An NHS Trust* v. *MB*, n. 136 above, at [17].

[148] n. 134 above, at [60].

Hedley J, in his original judgment,[149] reviewed the case law described in the earlier part of this chapter and, particularly, those cases which raised the criterion of an intolerable life. He concluded:

Helpful though these passages are, it is in my view essential that the concept of 'intolerable to that child' should not be seen as a gloss on, much less a supplementary test to, best interests. It is a valuable guide in the search for best interests in this kind of case.[150]

He was, later, supported in this by Butler-Sloss P who said, in a parallel case:

[T]he court should be focusing on best interests rather than on the concept of intolerability, although the latter may be encompassed within the former.[151]

He was also fully supported by the Court of Appeal who had this to say:

[T]he forensic debate should, in our judgment, be unfettered by any contentious glosses on the best interests test which are likely either inappropriately to shift the focus of the debate, or to restrict the broad exercise of the judicial discretion involved in balancing the multifarious factors in the case.[152]

We do not, however, dismiss 'intolerability' as a factor altogether. As we have already stated, we agree with Hedley J that whilst 'intolerable to the child' should not be seen either as a gloss on or a supplementary guide to best interests, it is, as he said, a valuable guide in the search for best interests in this kind of case.[153]

And, at this point, we might pause and wonder just what do these passages mean? I must express my sympathy with Holman J who, in a later case, ruminated:

I avoid reference to the concept of 'intolerability'... In any event, the most recent word from the Court of Appeal on the concept of 'intolerability' ... [says] that the concept of 'intolerable to the child' should not be seen as a gloss on, much less a supplementary test to, best interests. Although they continue by saying the concept is 'a valuable guide in the search for best interests in this kind of case', I doubt my own intellectual capacity on the one hand to exclude it even as a 'gloss on', much less supplementary test to, best interests; and yet on the other hand treat it as a 'valuable guide'.[154]

It is very difficult to disagree with these sentiments which drive one to ask whether we are not, again, becoming involved in a non-existent argument. All those who have been quoted as advocating 'intolerability' as a test for discontinuing treatment have seen the degree of the tolerability of

[149] n. 124 above.   [150] ibid., at [24].
[151] In *Re L (medical treatment: benefit)* [2005] 1 FLR 491 at [12].
[152] n. 134 above, at [86].   [153] ibid., at [91].
[154] In *An NHS Trust* v. *MB*, n. 136 above, at [17].

pain and suffering as no more than a feature of the child's overall interests. We have, for example, noted Butler-Sloss P's simple relegation of 'intolerability' to no more than an aspect of 'best interests', and we have Brooke LJ taking a very similar line – if only by implication.[155]

And this, surely, is the correct approach. The long discussion of the phrase and the ambiguous conclusion of the Court of Appeal in *Wyatt* serve only to muddy the waters. It may have been necessary for the solution of that particular case but, as to generality, one must agree with Holman J that, effectively, the passage adds nothing to the existing law.[156] As an analysis, it fails in its object of providing guidelines of clarity and simplicity.

The same cannot be said of the second consideration – that is, as to the determination of the disabled infant's interests as a whole. Here, the guidelines, based on a number of so-called intellectual milestones, provide an extended and particularised framework of the existing jurisprudence which has been followed with approval in later cases.[157] It will be convenient to tabulate these:[158]

- The welfare of the child is paramount and the judge must look at the question from the assumed point of view of the patient;[159]
- There is a strong presumption in favour of a course of action which will prolong life, but that presumption is not irrebuttable;
- The term 'best interests' encompasses medical, emotional, and all other welfare issues;[160]
- The court must conduct a balancing exercise in which all the relevant factors are weighed;
- A helpful way of undertaking this exercise is to draw up a balance sheet.[161]

And quite clearly, the degree of suffering involved, not only in the disability itself, but also that associated with the treatment of the disability – e.g. mechanical ventilation, intubation and the like – can, and will, be subsumed within these parameters.

---

[155] n. 144 above.

[156] In *An NHS Trust* v. *MB*, n. 136 above, discussed in detail at p. 284.

[157] ibid. While this list is very helpful, it is, in effect, little more than an amplification of the principles set out by Cazalet J in *A National Health Service Trust* v. *D*, n. 117 above.

[158] n. 134 above, at [87].

[159] As has already been discussed, it is difficult not to read an element of substituted judgment into this guideline. It is, however, very pertinent to the neonatal condition as the neonate will have *known no other condition*. See McKenzie J in *Dawson*, n. 29 above.

[160] And, surely, it is easy, perhaps obligatory, to include 'tolerability' under this head.

[161] Following Thorpe LJ's detailed advice in *Re A (medical treatment: male sterilisation)* [2000] 1 FLR 549 at 555.

It remains only, to consider the final phases of the saga of Charlotte Wyatt as at the time of writing – and, here, the procedural issues do assume a medico-ethical significance in that the policy behind the granting of declarations in this type of case was fully explored. The Court of Appeal had mandated a further hearing should her circumstances change and, by the time Hedley J was impelled to give his fourth judgment, Charlotte's consultant paediatrician had, in his own words, 'crossed an invisible line whereby I can say to the court that there are now circumstances where ... it would be justifiable for Charlotte to be ventilated'. Having said which, he went on to make it 'crystal clear that it was quite impossible to define in advance what these circumstances might be'.[162] What had become equally plain was that the attitudes of the parents to the Trust had become so polarised that the staff were fearful of the outcome should they be required to take a non-treatment decision – so much so that, in the words of Hedley J, they were asking to be granted the last word in the event of an irreconcilable disagreement.[163] Declarations are, however, normally granted on an all or nothing basis in order to deal with a *particular* situation. It is possible to make such declarations on the basis of clearly anticipated facts, as had been done in Charlotte's case, but the facts on which the declaration depended were now no longer sustainable. In essence, the case could be seen as veering from Hedley J's category (iv) – a matter of conscience – to that of category (iii), depending on clinical judgment; the boundary was, however, indefinite with much depending on Charlotte's uncertain clinical progress.

It is clear from the report that the case had now become so sensitive that Hedley J was obliged to pick his words with particular care; while this was entirely praiseworthy, it has to be said that it led to some loss of clarity. I have, therefore, done my best to extract from his latest judgment[164] what I see as the main pointers as to the law as it stands in the absence of any declaration:

- The proposition that the doctors would have to follow the instructions of the parents against their own judgment of the patient's best interests does *not* represent the law (at [28]);
- The duty of the clinician is to act in the patient's best interests albeit while working in partnership with a child's parents whenever that is possible (at [29]);
- A doctor cannot be required to act contrary to his or her conscience though he should take a second opinion and not prevent another from so acting should that clinician feel able to do so (at [32] and [36]);

---

[162] *Re Wyatt* (2005) 87 BMLR 183 at [8] and [10].
[163] n. 162 above, at [14].   [164] n. 162 above.

- Somewhat tentatively, Hedley J suggests that a doctor would be being required to act contrary to his or her conscience if he or she concluded that the requested treatment was inimical to the patient's best interests and that his or her professional 'conscience, intuition or hunch confirms that view' (at [36]).[165]

So much for the generality. Returning, however, to the particularity of *Wyatt*, Hedley J concluded that, while it was possible to use a declaration to resolve a future dispute, the court should be careful in doing so when the medical opinion was unanimous – to do so would, in effect, be providing the treating clinician with a therapeutic veto. It was, he thought, impossible to frame a conventional declaration. His judgment had set out the law in the given circumstances in a way 'comprehensible to all' and, as a consequence, no further declaratory relief was required.[166] One can sympathise with the judge when he pointed out, with regret, that there was really no way in which he could preclude future litigation.[167]

The sheer volume of litigation provoked by the case of Charlotte Wyatt dictated that many of the issues involved, and generally accepted as being finalised, were rehearsed in depth; the case took on its own measure of importance and, to an extent, introduced an element of confusion. However, a further case was being heard at much the same time which, I believe, demonstrates more typically the flavour of the jurisprudence relating to the management of severe congenital disease in the early twenty-first century.

Re L – *the case of Baby Winston-Jones*. *Re L*[168] concerned a child born 9 months previously with trisomy 18 (Edwards' syndrome). He had multiple heart defects, suffered from epilepsy and had sustained numerous cardio-respiratory arrests; he was fed by nasogastric tube and was requiring increasing amounts of supplementary oxygen. The two hospital Trusts dealing with him sought a declaration that it would be lawful not to provide further aggressive treatment in the artificial ventilation and cardiac massage should the need recur but this was strongly

---

[165] In setting out the intellectual process (ibid., at [34]) by which the doctor reaches his or her decision, Hedley J is, in my respectful submission, confusing conscience (which is primarily of a spiritual dimension) with intuition (which is founded on experience). He does, however, agree that conscience is not a wholly rational sense and that it, too, has a truly individual aspect (at [35]).

[166] There are overtones here of Sir Stephen Brown P in *Re C (a baby)* [1996] 2 FLR 43, (1996) 32 BMLR 44 and his insistence on dealing with the particularity of these cases within the existing law.

[167] n. 162 above, at [42]. See now *Re Wyatt* [2006] EWHC 319, [2006] 2 FLR 111.

[168] *Re L (medical treatment: benefit)* [2005] 1 FLR 491, first reported as *Re Winston-Jones (a child) (medical treatment: parent's consent)* [2004] All ER (D) 313.

opposed by L's mother who considered that they had established a strong bonding relationship; moreover, she maintained he had defied the odds by remaining alive and that the best of his life lay before him.

In a relatively short judgment, Butler-Sloss P relied on the well-known words of Lord Donaldson in *Re J* – which have been recorded at p. 269 – and supported Hedley J in *Wyatt* in applying a best interests test while, at the same time, relegating the concept of intolerability to no more than one aspect of those interests. In summary, there was a strong presumption in favour of preserving life, but not where treatment would be futile, and there is no obligation on the medical profession to give treatment which would be futile.[169] In the end, Dame Elizabeth granted the declaration in respect of mechanical ventilation but not as to cardiac massage and her reasons for so doing are instructive. As to the former, there were serious risks associated with giving the general anaesthetic which would be required for the insertion of the endotracheal tube; in addition, the child had a 75–100 per cent chance of becoming ventilator dependent:

> The consequences of remaining permanently on an artificial ventilator would ... be to deprive him, as I understand it, of any closeness with his mother ... and she has said herself it would not be for him a life of sufficient value.[170]

Which seems to me to be a very good a example of the so-called 'broad interpretation' of best interests that was pioneered by Butler-Sloss P and Thorpe LJ.[171]

As to cardiac massage, the President pointed out that it had already twice been used successfully on the patient. Despite the fact that almost all the experts opposed its further use, she considered it should remain an option for use depending on the clinical judgment of the treating doctors – and a strong message was given to the effect that they should think long and hard before rejecting that option.[172] Dame Elizabeth was so emphatic on this point as to draw attention to her basic reason for distinguishing the two procedures in this way. It is clear that this lies in the inherent dangers of mechanical ventilation and, looking back over the various cases, it is apparent that the 'danger' of an aggressive

---

[169] *Re L* n. 168 above, at [12]. The President does not define futility (see p. 246 above for discussion). It could be, in the present case, because there was no curative treatment – a purely medical assessment. The impression gained, however, is that her reasons were wider and based on treatment serving no useful purpose in a more general sense. Certainly, as explained, much of her final analysis rested on the actual damage that aggressive treatment could cause.

[170] ibid., at [23]. And at [25]: 'that would not make his life worth living'.

[171] See p. 249 above.   [172] n. 168 above, at [30].

treatment is a frequent reason for its omission being declared lawful. At first glance, it seems illogical to use its dangerousness as a reason for excluding a treatment without which the patient will certainly die – and this paradox has never, to my knowledge, been addressed by the judges concerned. It may, in fact, provide something of a safety net for the medical profession. A death *due to* aggressive therapy is likely to attract adverse publicity, a coroner's inquiry and even, in these litigious days, to litigation. While such factors should not affect, let alone determine, treatment decisions, they can rightly be included in Butler-Sloss's balance of advantages and disadvantages when other factors serve to render a procedure futile.

Be that as it may, *Re L* takes us from the maelstrom of *Wyatt* into calmer waters[173] and, in following the reasoning of Lord Donaldson so closely, restores the status quo as first established in *Re J*. But, even a cursory look at the cases decided subsequent to that landmark decision is sufficient to draw attention to the undoubted fact that, given a conflict between doctors and parents as to the management of disabled children, the courts have almost invariably sided with the experts – the case of *Re T*[174] standing out as a glaring exception. In a way, this is bound to be so. Most judges have been parents – they can agree or disagree with other parents on the basis of experience; it is far harder – although it can, of course, be quite properly done – effectively, to say to a consultant paediatrician: 'I know more medicine than you do', particularly when, as is so often the case, the medical opinion is unanimous.[175] This is not in any way to decry the dedication and intensity of effort shown by the Family Courts – it is simply to state the obvious: that, when a decision is going to be based on expert opinion, the experts have a head start on the laypersons, just as the experts who have been managing a case have the edge on those who are called in to give an opinion. The reader, and, it has to be said, the author, may suspect that the recent cases presage a change in attitude that is more than subtle. There is a strong indication that what were once regarded as purely medical matters are now being decided on a far wider base. With this in mind, what will be the last case to be discussed within this series may acquire a special interest.

---

[173] Though, perhaps, fortuitously. Baby L died shortly after the case was heard and, despite Butler-Sloss P's exhortations to reduce the level of conflict, his mother took the matter to the police: (2004) *The Times*, 13 November, p. 11.

[174] n. 92 above.

[175] It is clearly for this reason that the family courts have rejected a purely medicalised *Bolam* test as a benchmark and have moved to the concept of widely based 'best interests'.

The case of Baby MB. An NHS Trust v. *MB*[176] concerned an 18-month-old child, MB, who had suffered from the age of six weeks from spinal muscular atrophy. The condition, which is genetically determined and is untreatable, had progressed steadily until, at the time of the hearing, he could move only his eyebrows, the corner of his mouth, his thumb and his toes. A gastrostomy tube was in position and he could breathe only by way of positive pressure ventilation through an endotracheal tube. The prognosis was that he would deteriorate and the opinion of his doctors was that it was unethical, even cruel, to keep him alive. Accordingly, and notwithstanding the parents' opposition, the Trust sought a declaration that it would be lawful to withdraw all forms of ventilation from M and, in general, only to palliate him and allow him to die peacefully.[177] On the other hand, the court was dealing with a child who was described as having awareness and to have 'the normal thoughts and thought processes of a small child of 18 months'.[178] Holman J's dilemma could, therefore, be summed up:

So far as I am aware, no courts has yet been asked to approve that, against the will of the child's parents, life support may be withdrawn or discontinued, with the predictable, inevitable and immediate death of a conscious child with sensory awareness and assumed normal cognition and no reliable evidence of any significant brain damage[179]

– and my researches, together with the cases discussed in this book, indicate that this is true, subject to the synchrony of the important phrases: 'against the will of the parents' and 'a child with sensory awareness'.[180] At least, however, MB's case was unusual in that the great majority of previous cases dealt with the withholding of invasive treatment in the event that it was needed. The judge was, therefore, faced with a problem which we have not had occasion to consider thus far – is there any distinction to be made between withholding and withdrawing treatment?

The question has, of course, both legal and ethical dimensions and the answer depends very much on whether removal from ventilator support is to be regarded as an act or an omission. It is now widely

---

[176] *An NHS Trust* v. *MB (a child represented by CAFCASS as guardian ad litem)* [2006] 2 FLR 319.

[177] In direct contrast, the parents issued a cross application making it lawful to perform a tracheostomy by means of which to carry our long-term ventilation.

[178] n. 176 above, at [10].   [179] ibid., at [11].

[180] Holman J, himself, drew attention to what one would see as the two most likely contenders to precedence: *Re C (a baby)*, n. 116 above (sustained entirely by artificial ventilation but severely brain damaged and parental agreement to removal), and *Re C (a minor)* (1997), n. 86 above (the only disagreement with the parents related to re-establishing ventilation after an attempt to wean the child off the support).

agreed that there is no logical ethical distinction to be drawn between the two so long as the objective is the same in either case. Most would, however, agree that to say there is no moral difference is not to say there is a moral equivalence; there are, indeed good consequentialist arguments in favour of retaining an ethical distinction between killing by act and killing by inactivity.[181]

By contrast to what is a somewhat pedantic argument, such a distinction is critical to the criminal law – actively causing death can scarcely avoid an implication of unlawful homicide whereas causing death by omission will be regarded as such only in well-defined circumstances.[182] The issue in respect of withdrawal of treatment has been examined in detail in *Airedale NHS Trust* v. *Bland*[183] from which Holman J also drew inspiration. The House of Lords in that case which, as is well known, concerned the management of a 21-year–old man in a permanent vegetative state, concluded that removal of life support was an omission – this being, in general, on the rather unsatisfactory grounds that, were it to be held otherwise, it would be impossible to accept the equivalence of withholding and withdrawing treatment.[184] It was this second essential that was to concern the court in *MB* most crucially and Holman J again turned to *Bland* and, in particular, Lord Lowry who said in that case:

I do not believe that there is a valid distinction between the omission to treat a patient and the abandonment of treatment which has been commenced, since to recognise such a distinction could quite illogically confer on a doctor who had refrained from treatment an immunity which did not benefit a doctor who had embarked on treatment in order to see whether it might help the patient and had abandoned the treatment when it was seen not to do so.[185]

---

[181] There is a mass of literature on the subject. A concise appreciation is to be found in Gillon, n. 16 above. For the present author, perhaps the main distinction to be made is that the latter does not necessarily lead to the former.

[182] In particular, when the relationship is such that the 'omitter' has a duty to act. The doctor may be exonerated by way of a rather circular application of the *Bolam* principle – that he has no duty to act if a responsible body of medical opinion would have failed to act on grounds of futility – *Airedale NHS Trust* v. *Bland*, n. 183 below per Lord Keith at AC 858–9 BMLR 106–7.

[183] [1993] AC 789, (1993) 12 BMLR 64.

[184] ibid., per Lord Goff at AC 866, BMLR 113. I have to say that I find the idea of regarding the dismantling of ventilator support as 'inactivity' to be sophistic: see J. K. Mason and G. T. Laurie, *Mason and McCall Smith's Law and Medical Ethics* (Oxford, Oxford University Press, 7th edn 2005) at para. 17.104. Nonetheless, the inner pragmatist must be grateful to the House of Lords for grasping the nettle. It is true that *Bland* dealt with the removal of a nasogastric tube; the step between that and removal of a ventilator is, however, not great – see Lord Browne-Wilkinson (n. 183 above, at AC 882, at BMLR 128).

[185] ibid., at AC 875, BMLR 121.

Once again, the circularity of the argument is unsatisfactory but, perhaps, inevitable. It was, however, the unanimous view of the House. The judge was also able to draw on the medical profession for ethical support:

There is no significant ethical difference between withdrawing (stopping) and withholding treatments, given the same ethical objective[186]

– 'the best interests test', Holman J concluded, 'applies equally to both situations'.

Having, thus, dealt with the relatively novel aspects of the case, Holman J considered that the law in this area was now well-established and could be encompassed within ten propositions.[187] All of these have been considered in the course of this chapter. Nevertheless, *MB*, being the last case in the series, can conveniently provide a summary of all that has gone before. Accordingly, despite the element of repetition, I think it will be useful to recapitulate Holman J's ten propositions in full. They are:[188]

i) When asked by one or both parties to arbitrate on a treatment decision, it is the role and duty of the court to do so and to exercise its own independent and objective judgment;

ii) This right and power only arises because the patient lacks the capacity to make a personal decision;

iii) Substituted judgment has no place in decision making, nor does the court decide on the reasonableness of the doctors' or parents' decisions;

iv) The matter must be decided on the basis of an objective approach or test;

v) That test is the best interests of the patient – best interests being used in the widest sense;

vi) The court must do its best to balance all the conflicting considerations in a particular case and see where the final balance of the best interests lies;

vii) Considerable weight must be attached to the prolongation of life but the principle is not absolute and may be outweighed if the pleasures and the quality of life are sufficiently small and the pain and suffering or other burdens of living are sufficiently great;

viii) The principal authority for these considerations lies in the words of Lord Donaldson in *Re J (a minor) (wardship: medical treatment)*;[189]

---

[186] Royal College of Paediatrics and Child Health, *Withholding or Withdrawing Life Sustaining Treatment in Children: A Framework for Practice* (2nd edn 2004) at para. 2.3.2.1.

[187] n. 176 above, at [16].

[188] The wording is my own summarised interpretation of the original.

[189] n. 8 above, at Fam 46.

ix) All these cases are very fact specific;

x) The views and opinions of both the doctors and the parents must be carefully considered. The parents *wishes*, however, are wholly irrelevant to consideration of the objective best interests of the child save to the extent that they may illuminate the quality and value to the child of the child/parent relationship.

As to the last of these propositions, the judge was confronted with 'a very formidable body of medical evidence of very high quality' which was unanimous that, if only M's interests were being considered, then withdrawing ventilation and allowing him to die would be in his best interests,[190] this being, largely on the dual grounds that his condition was deteriorating and that the medical procedures to which he was exposed caused a mixture of discomfort, distress and pain. The medical evidence was, in fact, that of an appalling condition. M's mother, on the other hand, while admitting that he showed evidence of pain and distress, pointed out that he also showed evidence of pleasure from visual and aural stimuli; both she and her husband thought the experts were unduly pessimistic.

Accordingly, Holman J turned to the lists of benefits and burdens introduced by Thorpe LJ in *Re A*[191] – and advocated by the Court of Appeal in *Wyatt* as being the best and safest way of balancing all the factors involved in the assessment of best interests – and reproduced such a list in his judgment.[192] Again, this is a novel aspect of *MB* which merits brief discussion. It is notable that Holman J clearly appreciated that, useful as they might be, such lists should be used with care. In particular, he identified 'the huge difficulties' in formulating:

[a]n overall appraisal of the weight to be attached to so many varied considerations which cannot be weighed 'mathematically', and so arrive at the final balance and decision[193]

– and it is precisely that 'mathematical' concept which, in my view, renders such 'profit and loss' balance sheets less ideal than might seem at first glance. The guardian's list of benefits derived from continuing ventilation occupies 7½ inches of A4 paper; the comparable list of disbenefits runs to 46½ inches. While it is very unlikely that anyone would, in practice, be deluded into interpreting a qualitative analysis in quantitative terms, the temptation to believe that the disbenefits are,

---

[190] n. 176 above, at [30].   [191] n. 161 above.

[192] n. 176 above, at [60]. The list was, in fact, one prepared on behalf of the guardian by Ms Caroline Thomas, counsel for the child. As far as I know, it is the first, and excellent, example of compliance with *Re A* (n. 161 above) to be reported.

[193] n. 176 above, at [62].

accordingly, some six times greater than the benefits is strong.[194] Holman J considered (at [58]) that such balance sheets should be drawn up by both parties in any future case of this nature; that may well be appropriate, but only if their use is confined to what they are – aide-memoires.

Be all that as it may, Holman J concluded that it was not in the best interests of M that ventilation should be discontinued with the result that he die immediately and he refused the declaration sought by the Trust. In fact, he went further in considering that it was positively in M's best interests to continue with continuous pressure ventilation – including persistence with the very invasive nursing it involved.[195] Nonetheless, he was prepared to declare that it would be lawful to withhold certain painful procedures – including cardio-pulmonary resuscitation and its adjuncts and the prescription of parenteral antibiotics – in the event that the need arose, the reason being that the fact of the need would indicate that M was moving closer to death despite being ventilated.

So what was it that induced Holman J to turn so dramatically against not only the general tide of decisions in this area but also against what was unanimous medical opinion – something which we have seen to be very rare indeed? He gave his reasons in a fairly lengthy passage[196] which I hope to summarise without destroying its particular immanence:

I accept that there is almost relentless discomfort . . . It is indeed a helpless and sad life. But that life does in my view include within it the benefits that I have tried to describe . . . [I] must proceed on the basis that M has age appropriate cognition, and does continue to have a relationship of value to him with his family, and does continue to gain other pleasures from touch, sight and sound . . . [These benefits] are precious and real and they are the benefits, and only benefits, that M was designed to gain from his life. I do not consider that from one day to the next all the routine discomfort, distress and pain [that he suffers] outweigh these benefits so that . . . life itself should immediately end. On the contrary, I positively consider that as his life does still have benefits, and is his life, it should be enabled to continue . . .

The time may come when he has further deteriorated to such an extent . . . that the balance changes. But I do not consider that the future, however awful it may become, yet justifies that today, tomorrow or the next day his current burdens outweigh the benefits and he should be allowed to die.

The doctors all consider that there is a positive benefit to M [being enabled to die what is] called a 'good death' . . . Some people . . . might strongly desire to

[194] In point of fact, the guardian supported the Trust.
[195] ibid., at [90]. Although adding the all-important proviso: 'Although that is my opinion, I cannot and do not make an order or declaration to that effect. I merely state it.' Holman J was not, therefore, dictating medical treatment – indeed, as he implied, the long line of precedents, forbade him to do so.
[196] ibid., at [100]–[105].

achieve a good death even at the expense of a shorter life. But not all. The instinct to survive is so strong that others may endure great and prolonged suffering in the struggle to survive ... I do not think that on the facts of this case the perceived advantage of a good death can yet tip the scales so that the benefits of survival and life itself are outweighed.

It is difficult to criticise such a compassionate decision and many would say that it is presumptuous to do so. Nonetheless, perhaps because of my medical training, the evidence on behalf of the Trust seems so over-whelming as to make the decision seem not so much as a balancing act as a search for straws on which to hang the ethics of the sanctity of life. Despite Holman J's insistence that his judgment was not designed to have 'implications',[197] one has to look for the basic reason behind it and its effect, if any, on the existing jurisprudence. In a nutshell, is there a distinction to be drawn between the contemporaneous case of baby L – for which see p. 281 above – and M, both of whom were equally loved by their mothers?

The significant factor lies in Holman J's concentration on M's cogni-tive ability which, as we have seen, he did not doubt was that of a normal 18-month-old child. MB, therefore, effectively presented the same extreme ethico-legal problems as those that have been met in the several well-known cases of progressive neuro-muscular disease in adults and which form a distinctive category of cases within the euthanasia debate.[198] The great majority of apposite infantile cases which we have discussed have been severely brain damaged; I read Holman J as placing MB in the far more difficult category of *mens sana in corpore insano*. To that extent, he was not moving against the emerging stream but was considering a rare, if not unique, set of circumstances. Accordingly, *An NHS Trust* v. *MB* may, indeed, have significant impli-cations – not the least of which lies in the overhanging question: was it the right decision? It is feasible to suggest that, in contrast to brain damaged children – who we can hope do not appreciate or feel their status – it is unkinder to subject the sensate child to 'relentless discom-fort' by preserving its life. It is, however, difficult to see the alternative as other than a step towards child euthanasia which we will consider as a finale to this book. Holman J's decision will be tested to the limit should there be another MB. (See Addendum to this Chapter.)

---

[197] ibid., at [107].

[198] The case of *Pretty* v. *United Kingdom* [2002] 2 FLR 45 will probably spring first to the mind of the UK reader but perhaps the more relevant is the New Zealand case *Auckland Area Health Board* v. *Attorney-General* [1993] 1 NZLR 235, [1993] 4 Med LR 239 because it concerned an *incompetent* adult – in that case, the decision went the other way.

Professional guidelines

The courts of the United Kingdom are, as we have seen, traditionally reluctant to interfere with clinical judgment – a departure from the norm is likely to result in a *cause célèbre*. Equally, of course, professional bodies can only advise their members as to what constitutes good professional practice or, in our particular ambience, what is to be regarded as an adequate standard of care. The route commonly adopted in the United Kingdom when the common or statute law is unclear as to detail is by way of the creation of 'guidelines' by an authoritative body. These generally do not have the force of law but their non-observance will reflect adversely on the person who fails to follow them – and this is particularly so when the guidelines take the form of a Code of Practice issued by a body that is itself created by statute or by secondary legislation.[199] The situation is less clear, however, when there is no statutory backing and when guidelines remain just that. Kennedy and Grubb, while agreeing that the courts, when 'wrestling with legal/moral issues arising from clinical practice, should be able to refer to a professional view', have, in fact suggested that 'unofficial' guidelines may be controversial within the profession and, consequently, may attract an undeserved significance.[200]

Of the several documents relating to paediatric practice that are now available,[201] those of significance in the present context clearly include that produced by the Royal College of Paediatrics and Child Health,[202]

---

[199] A classic example is the establishment of the Human Fertilisation and Embryology Authority by way of the Human Fertilisation and Embryology Act 1990, s.5 and its proposed merger with the Human Tissue Authority to form the Regulatory Authority for Fertilisation and Tissue. Guidelines issued by the General Medical Council, which is bound to provide advice under the Medical Act 1983, would have similar authority and are subject to judicial review: 'Having produced the Guidance, the task of the GMC . . . is to ensure that it is vigorously promulgated, taught, understood and implemented at every level and in every hospital' – *R (on the application of Burke)* v. *General Medical Council* (2005) 85 BMLR 1, CA at [83].

[200] Kennedy and Grubb, *Medical Law* (3rd edn 2000), pp. 2175–6. J. H. Tingle, 'Do Guidelines Have Legal Implications?' (2002) 86 *Archives of Disease in Childhood* 387–8 believes that professional autonomy will always set the legal standard and that guidelines cannot be seen as a shield.

[201] For example, British Medical Association, *Withholding and Withdrawing Life-prolonging Medical Treatment* (2001) and General Medical Council, *Withholding and Withdrawing Life-prolonging Treatments: Good Practice in Decision-making* (2002). See also BMA *Parental Responsibility* (2004). The Report of the Nuffield Council on Bioethics, *Critical Care Decisions in Fetal and Neonatal Medicine: Ethical Issues* (2006), was issued during the last phase of the publication of this book. It seems to do little more than reiterate current medical practice though it is unambiguous in its recommendations

[202] Royal College of Paediatrics and Child Health, *Withholding or Withdrawing Life Sustaining Treatment in Children: A Framework for Practice* (2nd edn 2004).

the first edition of which was quoted with approval in *Re C (a minor)*.[203] Whether or not these guidelines represent a consensus,[204] they are the most definitive available and they merit recording. In its summary, the Royal College suggests there are five conditions in which consideration might be given to withholding or withdrawing treatment:

- *The 'brain dead' child*. Once the diagnosis of brain death has been made, it is agreed within the profession that treatment in such circumstances is futile and withdrawal is appropriate.[205]

- *The 'permanent vegetative' state*. In this situation it may be appropriate to withdraw or withhold life sustaining treatment.[206]

- *The 'no chance' situation*. The child has such severe disease that life sustaining treatment simply delays death without significant alleviation of suffering. Treatment to sustain life is inappropriate.[207]

- *The 'no purpose' situation*. Although the patient may be able to survive with treatment, the degree of physical or mental impairment will be so great that it is unreasonable to expect him or her to bear it. The child in this situation may not be capable now or in the future of taking part in decision making or other self directed activity. If it is likely that future life will be 'impossibly poor' then treatment might reasonably be withheld or withdrawn.

- *The 'unbearable' situation*. The child and/or family feel that in the face of progressive and irreversible illness further treatment is more than can be borne. They may wish to have a particular treatment withdrawn or to refuse further treatment irrespective of the medical opinion that it may be of some benefit.[208]

---

[203] n. 86 above.

[204] And it is fair to note that the College itself recognises that this may not be so at para. 1.

[205] I regard this as tautologous. A brain dead child is dead and there is no ethical or legal justification for continuing to treat a dead child: *Re A* [1992] 3 Med LR 303. The College recognises this in the body of the report at para. 3.1.3.

[206] It is to be noted that the rule under which virtually all cases in which it is proposed to withdraw artificial nutrition and hydration should be referred to the High Court applies only to adults who lack capacity; the extensive nature of parental responsibilities is thereby endorsed: *Practice Note (Official Solicitor: declaratory proceedings: medical and welfare decisions for adults who lack capacity)* [2001] 2 FLR 158.

[207] It is said that the knowing continuance of futile treatment may constitute an assault or 'inhuman and degrading treatment' under Article 3 of the European Convention on Human Rights at para. 3.1.3. This, I suggest, would be, at least, very difficult to show – one person's futility may be another's heroic effort. See, for example, *Simms* v. *Simms, A* v. *A* [2003] 1 All ER 669, (2003) 71 BMLR 61 – although, in this case, the judge made it a condition of her judgment that treatment involved no risk of increasing the patients' suffering.

[208] This last category sits uneasily in a discussion that is founded upon cooperation between the hospital and the parents. The final situation postulated seems to cry out for a court decision given that the medical opinion was firmly held. Cf. the case of *Glass* v. *UK*

In situations that do not fit these five categories, or where there is uncertainty about the degree of future impairment or disagreement, the child's life should be safeguarded in the best way possible until the issues are resolved.

One could spend a great deal of time discussing these guidelines. For present purposes, however, there are three aspects which merit consideration in the light of the foregoing discussion. First, it is clear that the profession, as represented by the College's Ethics Advisory Committee, has abandoned any reliance on the 'sanctity of life' principle and relies on a quality of life analysis. This is confirmed by the British Medical Association which recommends[209] that intervention may be unjustified if the child's condition is incompatible with survival or where there is broad consensus that the condition is so severe that treatment would not provide a benefit in terms of being able to restore or maintain the patient's health. Moreover, where treatments would involve suffering or distress to the child, these and other burdens must be weighed against the anticipated benefit, even if life cannot be prolonged without treatment.

Second, the recommendations are, perhaps inevitably, based on a medical assessment – the child's 'best interests' receive very little attention. While 'best interests' will certainly lie at the heart of any medical recommendations,[210] the lacuna tends to strengthen the Court of Appeal's repeated insistence that the latter represent only a part of the evidence to be used in the determination of the former.[211] Finally, it is noteworthy that neonatal euthanasia – defined by the College as 'causing death by intended lethal action, but for the relief of suffering' – is not listed as a recognized treatment option.[212] That is not, however, to say

---

(2004) 77 BMLR 120 in which the United Kingdom was found in breach of Article 8 of the Convention for having delayed a court hearing in a case of disputed therapy.

[209] n. 201 above.

[210] The Foreword to the first edition emphasises the fundamental aim 'to consider and serve the best interests of the child'. This is repeated in the second edition at para. 1.

[211] The BMA, for example, adds: 'Where there is genuine uncertainty about which treatment option would be of most clinical benefit, parents are usually best placed and equipped to weigh the evidence and apply it to their child's own circumstances' – n. 201 above at para. 15.1. For an empirical study of how decisions are made in the hospital setting, see Hazel E. McHaffie, Ian A. Laing, Michael Parker and John McMillan 'Deciding for Imperilled Newborns: Medical Authority or Parental Autonomy?' (2001) 27 *Journal of Medical Ethics* 104–9.

[212] Para. 2.4.3. The Guidelines make it clear that the College does not support euthanasia as defined. A recent press report suggests that this may not now be so: Sarah-Kate Templeton, 'Doctors: Let Us Kill Disabled Babies' (2006) *Sunday Times*, 5 November, p. 1. The wording of the College's statement, however, makes it difficult to justify the emotive newspaper heading; it is only suggested that the problem should be considered in depth.

that that will always be the case nor that there are not, even now, supporters of active euthanasia for selected categories of disabled newborns. We will make this our last port of call.

Neonatal euthanasia

We have already looked, briefly, at the proposition that controlled neonaticide could be seen as a preferable alternative to late abortion in the case of severe fetal disability and have discarded it.[213] Yet the matter cannot be left there. We are concerned, now, with children who have been born into a life which, on occasion, may be intolerable in the true sense of the word and, if it is arguable – as it *is* widely argued[214] – that an adult in such a condition has a right to have his or her life ended, then it is also arguable that the neonate has a similar right. The difference between the two cases is, of course, that, whereas the former is contingent upon a considered decision by an autonomous individual with the capacity to make such a decision, no such exculpation is available to the infant. A surrogate decision, based on either a fictional substituted judgment or made in the child's best interests, would have to be taken in the latter case – and the legal and moral difficulties in equating death with best interests are so great that the conditions justifying such a conclusion would have to be quite exceptional.

If there were to be a genuine movement towards neonatal euthanasia, one would expect it to arise in a jurisdiction that has already accepted it in the adult ambience and such an initiative has, in fact, recently been taken in the Netherlands by way of the so-called Groningen Protocol.[215] This, coming from a single University Department of Paediatrics, has now been endorsed on a national scale by Dutch doctors and has been accepted as representing good medical practice by the government.[216] In simple terms, the Groningen Protocol, first, divides those children for whom 'end-of-life decisions' might be made into three categories: those with no chance of survival, those who have a very poor prognosis and are dependant on intensive care and, finally, those with a hopeless prognosis who are

---

[213] See p. 242 above.

[214] Clearly, this is no place to attempt to revisit the euthanasia debate. Of the mass of available literature, there can be few works more helpful than Margaret Otlowski, *Voluntary Euthanasia and the Common Law* (Oxford: Oxford University Press, 2000).

[215] Eduard Verhagen and Pieter J. J. Sauer, 'The Groningen Protocol – Euthanasia in Severely Ill Newborns' (2005) 352 *New England Journal of Medicine* 959–62.

[216] Tony Sheldon, 'The Netherlands Regulates Ending the Lives of Severely Ill Neonates' (2005) 331 *British Medical Journal* 1357.

experiencing what parents and medical experts deem to be unbearable suffering. The Protocol is concerned with this last group and presupposes that five medical requirements must be fulfilled before the life of such an infant can be deliberately terminated:

- The diagnosis and prognosis must be certain;[217]
- Hopeless and unbearable suffering must be present;
- The diagnosis, prognosis and unbearable suffering must be confirmed by at least one independent doctor;
- Both parents must give informed consent; and
- The procedure must be performed in accordance with the accepted medical standard.

And a number of practical and supportive conditions which will help to clarify the decision-making process are listed.

Neonatal euthanasia is still not legal in the Netherlands but is governed by the rather unusual medical jurisprudence adopted in the Low Countries[218] whereby a decision to prosecute in the case of an unnatural death depends on whether or not the requirements of accepted medical practice have been met – which, on the face of things, looks rather like the application of a super-*Bolam* test.[219] This *post hoc* process contrasts vividly with the United Kingdom policy whereby, as we have seen, the courts will be asked for a declaration as to the lawfulness of a medical action *before* the event. Which makes one wonder, in passing, whether the Groningen Protocol has done much more than raise a storm in a teacup. Verhagen and Sauer[220] reported that 22 cases of euthanasia involving infants with spina bifida had been reported to the public prosecution service since 1997; it was held in all that the requirements of 'careful practice' were fulfilled and no prosecutions followed. The Protocol may well be attempting to do not more than tidy up an uncertain law which is already being widely flouted.[221]

---

[217] Whether or not a prognosis can ever be *certain* is open to question; in my view it is a matter of the degree of probability which can only achieve *near* certainty. See also T. K. Koogler, B. S. Wilfond and L. F. Ross, 'Lethal Language, Lethal Decisions' (2003) 33 *Hastings Center Report* 37–41.

[218] History suggests that, where the Netherlands has trod, Belgium will follow – see Luc Deliens, Freddy Mortier, Johan Bilsen et al. 'End of Life Decisions in Medical Practice in Flanders, Belgium: A nationwide Survey' (2000) 356 *Lancet* 1806–11. Also, a note by Jane Burgermeister, 'Doctor Reignites Euthanasia Row in Belgium after Mercy Killing' (2006) 332 *British Medical Journal* 382.

[219] See p. 10 above. It seems that the assessment will be made by a committee of three doctors and an ethicist (n. 217 above).

[220] n. 215 above.

[221] Tony Sheldon, 'Killing or Caring?' (2005) 330 *British Medical Journal* 560.

Needless to say, the Groningen proposals have attracted considerable criticism. The majority of these will be well known to anyone who has considered the euthanasia debate in general. The counter-arguments are amplified in the case of children and have been well described in a short, but telling, article from the Israeli Center for Medical Ethics.[222] The gravamen of the argument lies in the fact that, whereas the case for adult euthanasia is founded on respect for human autonomy, no such justification is available in the case of the infant who has not reached the age of capacity. Conversely, even the Dutch currently repudiate surrogate consent to euthanasia in adults. Why, then, should we countenance it in infants?[223] Significantly, in my view, Jotkowitz and Glick question the whole ethos of guidelines and protocols:

[A] detailed protocol with internal checks and balances tends to minimise the impact of what we feel is a morally unacceptable act.[224]

Or, in other words, given such a protocol, the temptation is to ask if a child fits within its terms rather than to consider that child's condition as an individual problem *ab initio*. In the end, however, they resort to the 'slippery slope' argument – and who should blame them, given the suspect history of adult euthanasia in the Netherlands?[225]

At the time of writing, neonatal euthanasia has not been seriously mooted in the United Kingdom nor has a declaration of its lawfulness been sought from any court. Were such a case to be brought, it would, in present circumstances, have to be rejected. The problem remains as to what would be the outcome were criminal charges to be brought against a paediatrician who, say, followed the Groningen Protocol. Would he or she follow the path of Dr Arthur – whose case we have discussed at length at p. 254 – or that of Dr Cox,[226] who injected his suffering adult patient with potassium chloride and was found guilty of attempted murder?

---

[222] A. B. Jotkowitz and S. Glick, 'The Groningen Protocol: Another Perspective' (2006) 32 *Journal of Medical Ethics* 157–8. It is only fair, however, to refer to a very recent article that is strongly supportive of the protocol: B. A. Manninen, 'A Case for Justified Non-voluntary Active Euthanasia: Exploring the Ethics of the Groningen Protocol' (2006) 32 *Journal of Medical Ethics* 643–51.

[223] The BMA (n. 201 above) firmly believes that parents are generally the best judges of their young children's, and the family's, interests; this, however, cannot be applied to euthanasia which is not considered as a management option.

[224] n. 222 above, at 157.

[225] See, for example, the disquieting article by L. Pijnemborg, P. J. van der Maas, J. J. M. van Delden and C. W. M. Looman, 'Life Terminating Acts without Explicit Request of Patient' (1993) 341 *Lancet* 1196–9 – the reason for concern lies in the title.

[226] *R* v. *Cox* (1992) 12 BMLR 38.

Fortunately, the question is hypothetical. Nonetheless, I should, perhaps, fly my colours for the last time and quote again, and with approval, from Jotkowitz and Glick:

> We agree that in certain circumstances it is reasonable and desirable to limit the level of care in these severely disabled and suffering infants: but the direct taking of human life crosses a major boundary line.

Addendum

The case of *Baby K*[227] has been reported as this book is at the page-proofing stage and justifies the forewarning offered in the last lines of p. 289. K was a child aged 5½ months suffering from congenital myo-tonica dystrophy – a severe muscle wasting disease. Her situation was, therefore, very comparable to that of Baby MB which we have discussed at p. 284. She was very severely disabled, lying somewhere between categories 3 and 4 of those set out by the Royal College of Paediatrics and Child Health as justifying consideration of withdrawal of treatment – for which, see p. 291. The responsible NHS Trust sought a declaration enabling the withdrawal of nutrition and fluids and this was granted by the court as being in the child's best interests. Since this decision seems to be one in direct contrast to that reached in *A NHS Trust v. MB*, it is worth outlining some preliminary thoughts as to the points which might distinguish the cases. These include: K was considerably younger than M; she was being fed by total parenteral nutrition rather than by way of a less invasive and less technically complicated feeding by gastrostomy; she was undoubtedly dying from a combination of septicaemia and liver failure; due to the nature of her condition, she had less, if any, evidence of cognitive function than had MB; and, unusually, the parents, the guardian and the local authority were in complete agreement with the Trust as to the course to be adopted. Sir Mark Potter P very appropriately reiterated (at para [51]) the widely agreed comment that 'all cases of this king are highly fact sensitive'.

---

[227] *Re K (A child) (Medical treatment: Declaration)* [2006] EWHC 1007, [2006] 2 FLR 883.

8   Conclusion

The abiding impression following the completion of this book is that the analysis of the legal approach to the management of the troubled pregnancy discloses a mix of well-established patterns which, nonetheless, include some difficult anomalies.

Patterns and anomalies

In general, the decisions reached by the courts on an international scale have demonstrated a surprising consistency over the years which is only now being challenged. Surprising, first, because the various jurisdictions that we have considered have approached the available actions either *de novo* or have relied heavily on experience in the United States which, inevitably in view of the large number of separate judiciaries involved and the wide cultural differences imposed by the size of the country, has provided a number of possible solutions to virtually every problem raised. And, second, because many of the landmark decisions made, have turned as much on the judicial interpretation of the moral issues involved as on anything else. A remarkable corollary to this has been the way in which public opinion, in the form of elected parliaments, has responded quickly whenever the courts have stepped out of the established line in the name of legal principle. Thus, we have seen a knee-jerk reaction on the part of the French Parliament to the acceptance by the highest court of a 'wrongful life' action on the part of a disabled neonate.[1] Similarly, the Parliaments of New South Wales and Queensland rapidly closed the door on actions involving wrongful pregnancy after the High Court of Australia had opened it widely in a case involving a negligent failure to sterilise a woman.[2]

Yet, as I have suggested, this apparently regular pattern contains a number of anomalies which, ultimately, derive from the difficulty of

---

[1] See p. 233.   [2] *Cattanach* v. *Melchior* (2003) 199 ALR 131 (see p. 128).

accommodating the normal principles of tort law within a setting that is charged with emotions ranging from an ingrained respect for the 'sanctity' of human life to an equally ingrained resistance to its 'commodification'. Courts across the world have struggled with this problem and, as a result, we are left with a jurisprudence which, although it cannot be said to be 'bad law', still demonstrates a lack of coherence.

My strong impression is that, because of this ambivalence, courts have a tendency to look at the end results of negligence rather than at the primary reasons for actions that result from a troubled pregnancy. An example lies in the simple situation of the wrongful pregnancy. As things stand, if each of two 'sterilised' women unwillingly bears a child and one of the children is healthy while the other is, unexpectedly, disabled, the mother of the latter stands to receive some recompense while the former is left to her own devices. Yet the negligence is the same in each case. There may be a case for a differential assessment of the quantum of damages but such an exercise becomes illogical if the basic quantum is nil – as it was established in *McFarlane*.[3] This anomaly may be, at least, smoothed over by Lord Bingham's 'conventional award' – which I have attributed to 'the conscience of the Lords'.[4] We will have to wait and see if that will materialise for, even if it is applied across the whole spectrum, there is still the hurdle of the level of the award to overcome.

We can also point the finger at the seemingly bizarre distinction that is drawn between wrongful birth and wrongful life actions. How can it be anything other than anomalous that we should compensate the person who is given the wrong message to carry – the mother who is misinformed as to the risk of a disabled fetus – and yet to deny the claims of one who was never given any warning message – that is, the consequently disabled neonate? The conceptual difficulty here is that, while there are two offended parties, there has been only one offence – the failure to deliver the correct message. Can it, then, be seen as fair to place the tortfeasor in double jeopardy? Currently, insofar as the wrongful birth action is widely accepted and that for wrongful life is equally widely refused, the answer is 'no'. But, again, one can ask – is this right when, in fact, the 'injuries' are quite distinct? The parents are claiming for the costs of rearing a disabled child. The neonate, however, as we have seen, is claiming compensation for the pain and suffering of a diminished life resulting from negligent advice. Provided the heads of damage are kept quite distinct, it seems

---

[3] *McFarlane* v. *Tayside Health Board* (2000) 2 AC 59, 2000 SC 1 which occupies the greater part of Chapter 4.
[4] *Rees* v. *Darlington Memorial Hospital NHS Trust* [2004] AC 309, see p. 176.

right that the recompense should be allocated appropriately – but only the European continental courts seem, thus far, to have acknowledged that.[5]

Conflicts of values

The fetal status – again

Deep down, at source, I suggest that there are two main concerns that combine to confuse the courts in their search for coherent solutions to the troubles of pregnancy. First is what many would regard as the prime anomaly – the legal insistence that the fetus has 'no rights'. It is a truism that one marker of the civilisation of a society is the quality of the protection it provides for its vulnerable citizens. This, of course, has been evident over the past decades throughout advanced societies within which such protection has been provided progressively to those groups in need – that is, until we come to possibly the most vulnerable of all sections of society, the unborn child, whose survival is still determined by seventeenth-century jurisprudence.[6]

The case of *Vo* v. *France*[7] must surely be convincing evidence that some protection of the fetus against the negligent or criminal antenatal carer is a requisite for the twenty-first century – the step between the 'no interests' of the fetus and the paramountcy of the 'best interests' of the neonate spans too great a divide. Mrs Vo's case emphasises that the barrier to the recognition of fetal interests lies in the abortion issue. The impregnability of that barrier is, however, founded on a misconstruction of the motives behind the call for review. The target is not the repeal of the Abortion Act which, like it or not, is here to stay. What is needed is a change in the 'mind-set' to abortion which would recognise that the fetus has at least *some* interests, or even rights, which need to be placed in the balance pan. Our main concern here is with termination of pregnancy on the grounds of fetal disability and, while we have considered the position of the fetus whose interests *are unlikely to be served by being born* at considerable length under the rubric of wrongful life, we have, to all intents, ignored that of the one who *might well wish to be born* irrespective of physical imperfection – and the 1967 Act, section 1(1)(d) makes no allowance for such a possibility. In essence, this is something of a plea that we should approach the section 1(1)(d) case from a different angle and, rather than asking the

---

[5] See p. 233.
[6] See Lord Mustill in *Attorney General's Reference (no. 3 of 1994)* [1998] AC 245 quoting Co. Inst., Part III, ch.7, p. 50.
[7] (2004) 79 BMLR 71.

pregnant woman: 'do you want to abort this pregnancy?', we should, first, look to the option: 'would you consider offering your unwanted baby for adoption when it is born?'[8] The choice would always be the woman's, but attitudes might well be changed for the better. In fact, it is surprising how little adoption features in the cases that have been studied here – possibly because the outcome of an offer for adoption is so uncertain, especially at the fetal stage of development.[9] Where, it *is* taken up, it is mentioned as an alternative to abortion but on an equal footing; in fact, of course, abortion and adoption are widely distinct concepts – the former actively destroys life, the latter preserves it. They should not be regarded as being on a par either as to morality or as a practical refuge.

All of which relates, in the end, to one of the main problems within the 1967 Act – that of the failure of demarcation as to 'substantial risk' of 'serious handicap' in section 1(1)(d).[10] There is no 'bright ring' to guide us – nor is there likely to be given the current wording of the Act. This is, surely, a matter which Parliament ought to, and could, look at urgently without reopening controversy. Having said which, it is, perhaps para-doxical that I should go on to isolate the wrongful birth action as being one aspect of litigation in this field that stands out as having been solved logically in the courts of the United Kingdom. The essential distinguish-ing feature of such an action is that the parents concerned *wanted* a child; they did not, however, want a *disabled* child which they now have as a result of the antenatal carers' negligence. It, therefore, seems to be as fair as is possible[11] to both sides in such a situation that the parents should accept the child but that the carers should recompense them fully for the difference in the costs of rearing a disabled rather than a healthy child – and there need be no difficulty in assessing such costs.[12] Almost

---

[8] This is not an entirely original script but was first suggested, albeit in the context of terminations under s.1(1)(a), by Sheila A. M. McLean, 'Abortion Law: Is Consensual Reform Possible?' (1990) 17 *Journal of Law and Society* 106–23.

[9] And even in the case of the neonate. See, for example *Re B (a minor) (wardship: medical treatment)* [1981] 1 WLR 1421, [1982] 3 FLR 117, discussed at p. 256, n. 60.

[10] An interesting article has been published while this book was being processed which considers the problem of mental handicap and the treatment of the disabled neonate which I have addressed in Chapter 7. As part of the solution, it introduces the concept of 'reduced benefits of life' in assessing such infants: D. Wilkinson, 'Is it in the Best Interests of an Intellectually Disabled Infant to Die?' (2006) 32 *Journal of Medical Ethics* 454.

[11] Although it is almost impossible to accommodate the *emotional* cost within the envelope of 'fairness' – so many variables are involved.

[12] It has been reported recently that another European country, Austria, has, for the first time, allowed such an action. The Supreme Court does appear from the brief report available, however, to have muddied the waters by ordering *full* support of a Down's syndrome child: Bojan Pancevski,'Doctor Must Pay Child Support after Inadequate Warning of Disability' (2006) 333 *British Medical Journal* 168.

perversely, however, the current UK jurisprudence on wrongful birth was founded inaccurately on analyses of *McFarlane*,[13] the case of wrongful pregnancy which forms the hub of this book and which leads to what I see as the second main reason behind the courts' anxieties – that is, the conflict between human emotion and legal principle that is such a feature of cases involving the uncovenanted birth of a healthy child.

We have seen the development of this struggle on an international scale throughout this book – demonstrated by, on the one hand, a reluctance to see the birth of a child as anything other than something to be welcomed and, on the other, taking the black-letter view that wrongful pregnancy, in particular, is as much a matter of negligence as of reproduction and that the normal rules of medical negligence must apply. And although it may seem trite to remind the reader, this conflict is epitomised by the unanimous support for the former view by the House of Lords in the Scottish case of *McFarlane* and the majority opinion in favour of the latter in the Australian case of *Cattanach*, both of which have been extensively reviewed in Chapter 4.

Legal or moral principle?

This is no place to recapitulate the arguments employed on each side which have already been reviewed in detail. In summary, however, it seems to me that the whole discourse is based on a fundamental misconception. I have tried to emphasise throughout this book that the basis of the uncovenanted pregnancy action implies no disrespect of the fetus that has been unwittingly conceived or for the child that it has become. It is the *consequences* of a new addition to the family that are in issue and these may go deeper than has, perhaps, been portrayed up till now. Looking back over the previous chapters, I feel I may have concentrated too much on the pure financial costs of a new baby. But there is more at stake than this. It has to be remembered that the uncovenanted child is not simply *unplanned* – rather, positive plans have been made and positive steps have been taken *not* to have an addition to the family. In the event, the whole *modus vivendi* of the family as an item has been distorted. What is being asked in an action for wrongful pregnancy, and to much the same effect in that for wrongful birth, is that the family ambience should be restored so far as is possible to what was planned before the plans were disrupted by the negligence of another. To what extent, if any, then, should the ordinary rules of tort be modified in order to accommodate a

---

[13] n. 3 above.

very particular aspect of negligence? The answer is, perhaps, not so simple as appeared when the first of the articles on which this book is founded was written.[14]

The majority decision in *Cattanach* was, on a subjective view, a triumph for anyone who believed that *McFarlane* was wrong on the grounds that the decision flew in the face of the established law of negligence. Why, then, does it take on the mantle of a Pyrrhic victory? The minority in *Cattanach* appear to have thrown legal principle to the winds and the answer to that question can only lie in an intuitive – and, arguably, unreasonable – preference for their idiosyncratic and undoubtedly emotional approach over the attempts in the House of Lords to achieve a rational reason for an irrational decision. In short, what *Cattanach* does is to emphasise that, as we all know, there are two sides to every question – and to the question of recompense for wrongful pregnancy in particular. But, it has to be said, the train stops there; on pure legal principle, Mr and Mrs McFarlane deserved more than they got and one must save some sympathy for those who have to follow in their footsteps. At least in my view, the House of Lords recognised that in *Rees*,[15] even if only *sub silentio*.

Thus, the final question remains – should matters such as these, which are so fundamental to societal morality, be decided on the basis of judicial activism or should they be left to Parliament? Perhaps it would be best to leave the answer to that question for another day.

---

[14] J. K. Mason, 'Unwanted Pregnancy: A Case of Retroversion?' (2000) 4 *Edinburgh Law Review* 191–206.
[15] See p. 174 above.

Bibliography

Alfirevic, Zarko and James P. Neilson, 'Antenatal Screening for Down's Syndrome' (2004) 329 *British Medical Journal* 811–12

Anonymous, 'Informed Consent: A Proposed Standard for Medical Disclosure' (1973) 48 *New York University Law Review* 548–63

Atiyah, P. S., *The Damages Lottery* (Oxford: Hart Publishing, 1997)

Bainham, Andrew, 'Do Babies Have Rights?' (1997) 56 *Cambridge Law Journal* 48–50

Balfour-Lynn, Ian M. and Robert C. Tasker, 'Futility and Death in Paediatric Medical Intensive Care' (1996) 22 *Journal of Medical Ethics* 279–81

Baugher, Patricia, 'Fundamental Protection of a Fundamental Right: Recovery of Child-rearing Damages for Wrongful Pregnancy' (2000) 75 *Washington Law Review* 1205–36

Beauchamp, Tom L. and James F. Childress, *Principles of Biomedical Ethics* (New York: Oxford University Press, 5th edn 2001)

Beaumont, Patricia M. A., 'Wrongful Life and Wrongful Birth' in S. A. M. McLean (ed.), *Contemporary Issues in Law, Medicine and Ethics* (Aldershot: Dartmouth Publishing, 1996), chapter 6

Bickford-Smith, Margaret, 'Failed Sterilisation Resulting in the Birth of a Disabled Child: The Issues' (2001) 4 *Journal of Personal Injury Law* 404–10

Booth, Penny, 'A Child is a Blessing – Heavily in Disguise, Right?' (2001) 151 *New Law Journal* 1738

Boyd, Kenneth, 'Euthanasia: Back to the Future' in John Keown (ed.), *Euthanasia Examined* (Cambridge: Cambridge University Press, 1991), chapter 7

Boyle, R. J., R. Salter and M. W. Arnander, 'Ethics of Refusing Parental Requests to Withhold or Withdraw Treatment from their Premature Baby' (2004) 30 *Journal of Medical Ethics* 402–5

Brahams, Diana, 'Religious Objection versus Parental Duty' (1993) 342 *Lancet* 1189–90

Brazier, Margaret, *Medicine, Patients and the Law* (London: Penguin Books, 3rd edn 2003)

Brazier, Margaret and José Miola, 'Bye-bye *Bolam*: A Medical Litigation Revolution?' (2000) 8 *Medical Law Review* 85–114

Brazier, M., 'Letting Charlotte Die' (2004) 30 *Journal of Medical Ethics* 519–20

Brazier, Margot, 'Times of Change?' (2005) 13 *Medical Law Review* 1–16

'Human(s) (as) Medicine(s)' in Sheila A. M. McLean (ed.), *First Do No Harm: Law, Ethics and Health Care* (Aldershot: Ashgate Publishing, 2006), chapter 12

BBC News, 'Cardinal Urges Abortion Rethink', 21 June 2006 at http://news.bbc.co.uk/2/hi/health/5099362.stm.

British Medical Association, *Withholding and Withdrawing Life-prolonging Medical Treatment* (London: B.M.A., 2001)

Parental Responsibility (London, B.M.A., 2004)

Brody, Baruch, *Abortion and the Sanctity of Human Life: A Philosophical View* (Cambridge, MA: MIT Press, 1985)

Brown, M. T. 'A Future Like Ours Revisited' (2002) 28 *Journal of Medical Ethics* 192–5

Burgermeister, Jane, 'Doctor Reignites Euthanasia Row in Belgium after Mercy Killing' (2006) 332 *British Medical Journal* 382

Callahan, Daniel J., *Abortion, Law, Choice and Morality* (New York: Macmillan, 1970)

Callus, Thérèse, '"Wrongful Life" a la Francaise' (2001) 5 *Medical Law International* 117–26

Cameron, C. and R. Williamson, 'Is there an Ethical Difference between Preimplantation Genetic Diagnosis and Abortion?' (2003) 29 *Journal of Medical Ethics* 90–2

Cameron-Perry, J. Ellis, 'Return of the Burden of the "Blessing" ' (1999) 149 *New Law Journal* 1887–8

Campbell, A. G. M. and H. E. McHaffie, 'Prolonging Life and Allowing Death: Infants' (1995) 21 *Journal of Medical Ethics* 339–44

Cane, Peter, 'Another Failed Sterilisation' (2004) 120 *Law Quarterly Review* 189–93

Capron, Alexander Morgan, 'Tort Liability in Genetic Counselling' (1979) 79 *Columbia Law Review* 618–84

Chalmers, Don and Robert Schwartz, '*Rogers* v. *Whitaker* and Informed Consent in Australia: A Fair Dinkum Duty of Disclosure' (1993) 1 *Medical Law Review* 139–59

Clarke, Angus, 'Is Non-directive Genetic Counselling Possible?' (1991) 338 *Lancet* 998–1001

(ed.), *Genetic Counselling: Practice and Principles* (London, Routledge, 1994)

De Garis, C., H. Kuhse, P. Singer and V. Y. Yu, 'Attitudes of Australian Neonatal Paediatricians to the Treatment of Extremely Preterm Infants' (1987) 23 *Australian Paediatric Journal* 223–6

Deliens, Luc, Freddy Mortier, Johan Bilsen et al. 'End of Life Decisions in Medical Practice in Flanders, Belgium: A Nationwide Survey' (2000) 356 *Lancet* 1806–11

Department of Health, *A Guide to Consent for Examination or Treatment* (HC (90) 22 amended by HSG (9) 32)

Our Inheritance, Our Future (2003), Cm 5791-II

Devaney, Sarah, 'Autonomy Rules OK' (2005) 13 *Medical Law Review* 102–7

Dickens, Bernard, 'Wrongful Birth and Life, Wrongful Death before Birth and Wrongful law' in Sheila A. M. McLean (ed.), *Legal Issues in Human Reproduction* (Aldershot: Dartmouth, 1989), chapter 4

Dixon, Clare, 'An Unconventional Gloss on Unintended Children' (2003) 153 *New Law Journal* 1732–3

Dorozynski, Alexander, 'Highest French Court Awards Compensation for "Being Born"' (2001) 323 *British Medical Journal* 1384

Drife, James Owen, 'Deregulating Emergency Contraception' (1993) 307 *British Medical Journal* 695–6

Duguet, A.M., 'Wrongful Life: The Recent French Cour de Cassation Decisions' (2002) 9 *European Journal of Health Law* 139–49

Dyer, Clare, 'Gynaecologist Acquitted in Hysterectomy Case' (1996) 312 *British Medical Journal* 11–12

    'HFEA Widens its Criteria for Pre-implantation Genetic Diagnosis' (2006) 332 *British Medical Journal* 1174

Earle, Murray, 'The Future of Informed Consent in British Common Law' (1999) 6 *European Journal of Health Law* 235–48

Ferguson, Pamela R., *Drug Injuries and the Pursuit of Compensation* (London: Sweet & Maxwell, 1996)

Fleming, J. G., *The Law of Torts* (London: LBC Information Services, 9th edn 1998)

Ford, Norman M., *When Did I Begin?* (Cambridge: Cambridge University Press, 1991)

Fortin, Jane E. S., 'Is the "Wrongful Life" Action Really Dead?' [1987] *Journal of Social Welfare Law* 306–13

Fovargue, Sara and José Miola, 'Policing Pregnancy: Implications of the Attorney-General's Reference (No. 3 of 1994)' (1998) 6 *Medical Law Review* 265–96

Fox, Marie and Jean McHale, 'In Whose Best Interests?' (1997) 60 *Modern Law Review* 700–9

Francome, Colin, *Abortion in the USA and the UK* (Aldershot: Ashgate Publishing, 2004)

Furedi, Ann, 'Wrong but the Right Thing to Do: Public Opinion and Abortion' in Ellie Lee (ed.), *Abortion Law and Politics Today* (London: Macmillan Press, 1998), chapter 10

General Medical Council, *Good Medical Practice* (2001)

    Withholding and Withdrawing Life-prolonging Treatments: Good Practice in Decision-making (2002)

Gillam, Lynn, 'Prenatal Diagnosis and Discrimination against the Disabled' (1999) 25 *Journal of Medical Ethics* 163–71

Gillon, Raanan, 'Euthanasia, Withholding Life-prolonging Treatment, and Moral Differences between Killing and Letting Die' (1988) 14 *Journal of Medical Ethics* 115–17

    '"Futility" – Too Ambiguous and Pejorative a Term?' (1997) 23 *Journal of Medical Ethics* 339–40

    'Is there a "new ethics of abortion"?' (2001) 27 *Journal of Medical Ethics* supp. II:ii5–ii9

Gledhill, Ruth, 'Curate Loses Legal Challenge over "Cleft-palate" Abortion', (2005) *The Times*, 17 March, p. 14

Golder, Ben, 'From *McFarlane* to *Melchior* and beyond: Love, Sex, Money and Commodification in the Anglo-Australian Law of Torts' (2004) 12 *Torts Law Journal* 128

Green, J. M., 'Obstetricians' views on Prenatal Diagnosis and Termination of Pregnancy: 1980 Compared with 1993' (1995) 102 *British Journal of Obstetrics and Gynaecology* 228–32

Grey, Alice, '*Harriton v Stephens*: Life, Logic and Legal Fictions' (2006) 28 *Sydney Law Review* 545–60

Grubb, Andrew, 'Damages for "Wrongful Conception"' (1985) 44 *Cambridge Law Journal* 30–2

'Abortion Law in England: The Medicalization of a Crime' (1990) 18 *Law, Medicine & Health Care* 146–61

Harris, John, 'Consent and End of Life Decisions' (2003) 29 *Journal of Medical Ethics* 10–15

House of Commons Science and Technology Committee, *Human Genetics: The Science and its Consequences*, Third Report (1995)

Hoyano, Laura C. H., 'Misconceptions and Wrongful Conceptions' (2002) 65 *Modern Law Review* 883–906

Hugh-Jones, G., 'Commentary on *Taylor* v. *Shropshire HA*' [2000] Lloyd's Rep Med 107

Huxtable, Richard and Karen Forbes, '*Glass* v. *UK*: Maternal Instinct v. Medical Opinion' (2004) 16 *Child and Family Law Quarterly* 339–54

Jackson, Anthony, 'Wrongful Life and Wrongful Birth. The English conception' (1996) 17 *Journal of Legal Medicine* 349–81

Jackson, Emily, 'Abortion, Autonomy and Prenatal Diagnosis' (2000) 9 *Social & Legal Studies* 467–94

Regulating Reproduction: Law, Technology and Autonomy (Oxford: Hart Publishing, 2001)

Jackson, Mark, 'Infanticide: Historical Perspectives' (1996) 146 *New Law Journal* 416–20

Jotkowitz, A. B. and S. Glick, 'The Groningen Protocol: Another Perspective' (2006) 32 *Journal of Medical Ethics* 157–8

Kashi, Joseph S., 'The Case of the Unwanted Blessing: Wrongful Life' (1977) 31 *University of Miami Law Review* 1409–32

Kennedy, B., 'The Trend Toward Judicial Recognition of Wrongful Life: A Dissenting View' (1983) *UCLA Law Review* 473–501

Kennedy, I., 'Legal and Ethical Implications of Postcoital Birth Control' in *Treat Me Right* (Oxford: Oxford University Press, 1988), chapter 3

Kennedy, I. and A. Grubb, *Medical Law* (London: Butterworths, 3rd edn 2000)

Keown, I. J., '"Miscarriage": A Medico-Legal Analysis' [1984] *Criminal Law Review* 604–14

Keown, J., *Abortion, Doctors and the Law* (Cambridge: Cambridge University Press, 1988)

Keown, John, 'Reining in the *Bolam* test' (1998) 57 *Cambridge Law Journal* 248–50

Koogler, T. K., B. S. Wilfond and L. F. Ross, 'Lethal Language, Lethal Decisions' (2003) 33 *Hastings Center Report* 37–41

Kuhse, Helga and Peter Singer, *Should the Baby Live?* (Oxford: Oxford University Press, 1985)

Laurie, Graeme T., 'In Defence of Ignorance: Genetic Information and the Right not to Know' (1999) 6 *European Journal of Health Law* 119–32

Law Commission, *Report on Injuries to Unborn Children* (1974, Law Com. No 60) (Cmd. 5709)

Leading Article 'Life and Law' (2004) *The Times*, 8 October, p. 15

Lewis, Penney, 'The Necessary Implications of Wrongful Life Claims: Lessons from France' (2005) 12 *European Journal of Health Law* 135–52

Lorber, J., 'Ethical Problems in the Management of Myelomeningocele' (1975) 10 *Journal of the Royal College of Physicians of London* 47–60

Lorber, J. and S. A. Salfield, 'Results of Selective Treatment of Spina Bifida Cystica' (1981) 56 *Archives of Disease in Childhood* 822–30

McHaffie, Hazel et al., *Crucial Decisions at the Beginning of Life* (Oxford: Radcliffe Medical Press, 2001)

McHaffie, Hazel E., Ian A. Laing, Michael Parker and John McMillan, 'Deciding for Imperilled Newborns: Medical Authority or Parental Autonomy?' (2001) 27 *Journal of Medical Ethics* 104–9

Maclean, Alasdair, 'Beyond *Bolam* and *Bolitho*' (2002) 5 *Medical Law International* 205–30

McLean, Sheila A. M., *A Patient's Right to Know: Information Disclosure, the Doctor and the Law* (Aldershot: Dartmouth, 1989)

'Abortion Law: Is Consensual Reform Possible?' (1990) 17 *Journal of Law and Society* 106–23

McLean, Sheila, *Old Law, New Medicine* (London: Pandora Press, 1999)

McLean, S. A. M. and J. K. Mason, *Legal and Ethical Aspects of Healthcare* (Cambridge, Cambridge University Press, 2003)

McLean, Sheila A. M. and J. Kenyon Mason, 'Our Inheritance, Our Future: Their Rights?' (2005) 13 *International Journal of Children's Rights* 255–72

Manninen, A. B., 'A Case for Justified Non-voluntary Active Euthanasia: Exploring the Ethics of the Groningen Protocol' (2006) 32 *Journal of Medical Ethics* 643–51

Marquis, Don, 'Why Abortion is Immoral' (1989) 86 *Journal of Philosophy* 183–202

'Abortion and the Beginning and End of Human Life' (2006) 34 *Journal of Law and Medical Ethics* 16–25

Mason, J. K., 'Master of the Balancers: Non-Voluntary Therapy under the Mantle of Lord Donaldson' [1993] *Juridical Review* 115–32

Medico-Legal Aspects of Reproduction and Parenthood (Aldershot: Ashgate, 2nd edn 1998)

'A Lords' Eye View of Fetal Status' (1999) 3 *Edinburgh Law Review* 246–50

'Unwanted Pregnancy: A Case of Retroversion?' (2000) 4 *Edinburgh Law Review* 191–206

'Wrongful Pregnancy, Wrongful Birth and Wrongful Terminology' (2002) 6 *Edinburgh Law Review* 46–66

'Wrongful life: The problem of causation' (2004) 6 *Medical Law International* 149–61

'A Turn-up Down Under: *McFarlane* in the Light of *Cattanach*' (2004) 1 SCRIPT-ed, at http://www.law.ed.ac.uk/ahrb/script-

'From Dundee to Darlington: An End to the *McFarlane* Line?' [2004] *Juridical Review* 365–86

'What's in a Name? The Vagaries of *Vo v France*' (2005) 17 *Child and Family Law Quarterly* 97–112

'Ethical Principles and Ethical Practice' (2006) 1 *Clinical Ethics* 3–6

Mason, J. K. and G. T. Laurie, *Mason and McCall Smith's Law and Medical Ethics* (Oxford: Oxford University Press, 7th edn 2005)

Mason, J. K. and R. A. McCall Smith, *Law and Medical Ethics* (Butterworths: London, 1982)

Mason, J. K. and David W. Meyers, 'Parental Choice and Selective Non-treatment of Deformed Newborns: a View from mid-Atlantic' (1986) 12 *Journal of Medical Ethics* 67–71

Mason, Kenyon and Douglas Brodie, '*Bolam, Bolam* ... Wherefore Art Thou *Bolam?*' (2005) 9 *Edinburgh Law Review* 298–306

Meyers, David, '*Chester* v. *Afshar*: Sayonara, Sub Silentio, *Sidaway?*' in Sheila A. M. McLean (ed.), *First Do No Harm* (Aldershot: Ashgate, 2006), chapter 16

Meyers, David W., '*Wyatt* and *Winston-Jones*: Who Decides to Treat or Let Die Seriously Ill Babies?' (2005) 9 *Edinburgh Law Review* 307–16

Miola, José, 'Autonomy Rued OK?' (2006) 14 *Medical Law Review* 108–14

Morris, Anne and Severine Saintier, 'To Be Or Not To Be: Is That The Question? Wrongful Life and Misconceptions' (2003) 11 *Medical Law Review* 167–93

Mueller, Robert F. and Ian D. Young, *Emery's Elements of Medical Genetics* (Edinburgh, Churchill Livingstone, 11th edn 2001)

Muramoto, Osamu, 'Bioethical Aspects of the Recent Changes in the Policy of Refusal of Blood by Jehovah's Witnesses' (2001) 322 *British Medical Journal* 37–9

Norrie, Kenneth McK., 'Damages for the Birth of a Child' 1985 *Scots Law Times* 69–74

Norrie, Kenneth, 'Post-Coital anti-pregnancy techniques and the law' in A. Allan Templeton and Douglas Cusine (eds.), *Reproductive Medicine and the Law* (Edinburgh: Churchill Livingstone, 1990), chapter 2

Nuffield Council on Bioethics, *Genetic Screening: Ethical Issues* (1993)

Nys, H. F. L. and J. C. J. Dute, 'A Wrongful Existence in the Netherlands' (2004) 30 *Journal of Medical Ethics* 393–4

O'Donovan, Katherine, 'The Medicalisation of Infanticide' [1984] *Criminal Law Review* 259–64

'Taking a Neutral Stance on the Legal Protection of the Fetus' (2006) 14 *Medical Law Review* 115–23

O'Donovan, Katherine and Roy Gilbar, 'The Loved Ones: Families, Intimates and Patient Autonomy' (2003) 23 *Legal Studies* 332–58

O'Neill, Onora, *Autonomy and Trust in Bioethics* (Cambridge: Cambridge University Press, 2002)

Otlowski, Margaret, *Voluntary Euthanasia and the Common Law* (Oxford: Oxford University Press, 2000)

Pace, P. J. 'Civil Liability for Pre-natal Injury' (1977) 40 *Modern Law Review* 141–58

Pancevski, Bojan, 'Doctor Must Pay Child Support after Inadequate Warning of Disability' (2006) 333 *British Medical Journal* 168

Pedain, Antje, 'Unconventional Justice in the House of Lords' (2004) 63 *Cambridge Law Journal* 19–21

Perry, Michael J., *Under God?* (Cambridge: Cambridge University Press, 2003)

Pijnemborg, L., P. J. van der Maas, J. J. M. van Delden and C. W. M. Looman, 'Life Terminating Acts without Explicit Request of Patient' (1993) 341 *Lancet* 1196–9

Plomer, Aurora, 'A Foetal Right to Life? The Case of *Vo v France*' (2005) 5 *Human Rights Law Review* 311–36

Pradel, Jean, 'Violences involontaires sur femme enceinte et délit d'homicide involontaire' (2004) 7/7148 *Recueil Dalloz* 449–50

Priaulx, Nicky, 'Parental Disability and Wrongful Conception' [2003] *Family Law* 117–20

'That's One Heck of an "Unruly Horse"! Riding Roughshod over Autonomy in Wrongful Conception' (2004) 12 *Feminist Legal Studies* 317–31

Priaulx, Nicolette M., 'Damages for the "Unwanted" Child: Time for a Rethink?' (2005) 73 *Medico-Legal Journal* 152–63

Radley-Gardner, Oliver, 'Wrongful Birth Revisited' (2002) 118 *Law Quarterly Review* 11–15

Rogers, Lois, 'Fifty Babies a Year are Alive after Abortion' (2005) *Sunday Times*, 27 November

Rotkin, Jeffrey R. and Maxwell J. Mehlman, 'Wrongful Birth: Medical, Legal and Philosophical Issues' (1994) 22 *Journal of Law, Medicine and Ethics* 21–8

Royal College of Obstetricians and Gynaecologists, *Termination of Pregnancy for Fetal Abnormality in England, Wales and Scotland* (1996)

Royal College of Obstetricians and Gynaecologists, *The Care of Women Requesting Induced Abortion: Guideline* (2000)

Royal College of Paediatrics and Child Health, *Withholding or Withdrawing Life Sustaining Treatment in Children: A Framework for Practice* (2nd edn 2004)

Rudman, Stanley, *Concepts of Person and Christian Ethics* (Cambridge: Cambridge University Press, 1997)

Russell, Eleanor J., 'Is Parenthood an "Unblemished Blessing" in Every Case?' 1998 *Scots Law Times* 191–7

Sanger, Carol, 'Regulating Teenage Abortion in the United States' (2004) 18 *International Journal of Law, Policy and the Family* 305–18

Savulescu, J., 'Abortion, Embryo Destruction and the Future of Value Argument' (2002) 28 *Journal of Medical Ethics* 133–5

Schneiderman, L. J. and N. Jecker, 'Futility in Practice' (1993) 153 *Archives of Internal Medicine* 437–41

Scott, Rosamund, 'The English Fetus and the Right to Life' (2004) 11 *European Journal of Health Law* 347–64

Seneviratne, Mary, 'Pre-natal Injury and Transferred Malice: The Invented Other' (1996) 59 *Modern Law Review* 884–92

Shapira, Amos, ' "Wrongful life" Lawsuits for Faulty Genetic Counselling: Should the Impaired Newborn be Entitled to Sue?' (1998) 24 *Journal of Medical Ethics* 369–75

Sheldon, Sally and Stephen Wilkinson, 'Termination of Pregnancy for Reasons of Foetal Disability: Are There Grounds for a Special Exception in Law?' (2001) 9 *Medical Law Review* 85–109

Sheldon, Tony, 'Court awards Damages to Disabled Child for Having Been Born' (2003) 326 *British Medical Journal* 784

'Dutch Supreme Court Backs Damages for Child for Having Been Born' (2005) 330 *British Medical Journal* 747

'The Netherlands Regulates Ending the Lives of Severely Ill Neonates' (2005) 331 *British Medical Journal* 1357

'Killing or Caring?' (2005) 330 *British Medical Journal* 560

Singer, Peter, *Rethinking Life and Death* (New York: St. Martin's Press, 1995)

Singer, S., '*Rees v. Darlington Memorial Hospital NHS Trust* [2004] 1 AC 309' [2004] 26 *Journal of Social Welfare and Family Law* 403–15

Smith, J. C., D. Cranston, T. O'Brien et al., 'Fatherhood without Apparent Spermatozoa after Vasectomy' (1994) 344 *Lancet* 30

Spriggs, M. and J. Savulescu, 'The Perruche Judgment and the "Right Not to Be Born"' (2002) 28 *Journal of Medical Ethics* 63–4

Steinbock, Bonnie, *Life before Birth: The Moral and Legal Status of Embryos and Fetuses* (New York: Oxford University Press, 1992).

Stewart, Angus, 'Damages for the Birth of a Child' (1995) 40 *Journal of the Law Society of Scotland* 298–302

Stirrat, G. M. and R. Gill, 'Autonomy in Medical Ethics after O'Neill' (2005) 31 *Journal of Medical Ethics* 127–30

Strasser, Mark, 'Yes, Virginia, There Can Be Wrongful Life: On Consistency, Public Policy, and the Birth-Related Torts' (2004) 4 *Georgetown Journal of Gender and Law* 821–61

Stretton, Dean, 'The Birth Torts: Damages for Wrongful Birth and Wrongful Life' (2005) 10 *Deakin Law Review* 310–64

Suter, Sonia Mateu, 'The Routinization of Prenatal Testing' (2002) 28 *American Journal of Law and Medicine* 233–70

Teff, Harvey, 'The Action for "Wrongful Life" in England and the United States' (1985) 34 *International and Comparative Law Quarterly* 423–41

Temkin, Jennifer, 'Pre-natal Injury, Homicide and the Draft Criminal Code' (1986) 45 *Cambridge Law Journal* 414–29

Templeton, Sarah-Kate, 'Doctors: Let Us Kill Disabled Babies' (2006) *Sunday Times*, 5 November, p. 1.1

Templeton, Sarah-Kate and Lois Rogers, 'Babies that Live after Abortion Are Left to Die' (2004) *The Sunday Times*, 20 June, p. 1.3

Thomson, Joe, 'Abandoning the Law of Delict?' 2000 *Scots Law Times* 43–5

Thomson, Judith Jarvis, 'A Defense of Abortion' (1971) 1 *Philosophy and Public Affairs* 47–66

Tingle, J. H., 'Do Guidelines Have Legal Implications?' (2002) 86 *Archives of Disease in Childhood* 387–8

Todd, Stephen, 'Wrongful Conception, Wrongful Birth and Wrongful Life' (2005) 27 *Sydney Law Review* 525–42

Tooley, Michael, 'In Defense of Abortion and Infanticide' in J. Feinberg (ed.), *The Problem of Abortion* (Belmont: Wadsworth, 1973), pp. 83–114

Abortion and Infanticide (Oxford: Clarendon Press, 1983)

Treneman, A., 'Sex and Relationships Muddy the Debate' (2005) *The Times*, 20 July, p. 28

Trotzig, Marten A., 'The Defective Child and the Actions for Wrongful Life and Wrongful Birth' (1980) 14 *Family Law Quarterly* 15–40

Tunkel, Victor, 'Modern Anti-Pregnancy Techniques and the Criminal Law' [1974] *Criminal Law Review* 461–71

Verhagen, Eduard and Pieter J. J. Sauer, 'The Groningen Protocol – Euthanasia in Severely Ill Newborns' (2005) 352 *New England Journal of Medicine* 959–62

Verkuyl, Douwe A. A., 'Two World Religions and Family Planning' (1993) 342 *Lancet* 473–5

Wald, N. J., H. C. Watt and A. K. Hackshaw, 'Integrated Screening for Down's Syndrome on the Basis of Tests Performed During the first and Second Trimesters' (1999) 341 *New England Journal of Medicine* 461–7

Walker, C. H., '. . . Officiously to Keep Alive' 63 *Archives of Disease in Childhood* 560–6

Warden, John, 'Abortion and Conscience' (1990) 301 *British Medical Journal* 1013

Warnock, Dame Mary (Chairman), *Report of the Committee of Inquiry into Human Fertilisation and Embryology* (1984), Cmd. 9314

Watson, Penelope, 'Wrongful Life Actions in Australia' (2002) 26 *Melbourne University Law Review* 736–49

Weir, Robert F., *Selective Non-treatment of Handicapped Newborns* (New York: Oxford University Press, 1984)

Weir, Tony, 'The Unwanted Child' (2000) 59 *Cambridge Law Journal* 238–41

'The Unwanted Child' (2002) 6 *Edinburgh Law Review* 244–53

Wennberg, R. N., *Life in the Balance* (Grand Rapids: W. B. Eerdmans, 1985)

Whitelaw, Andrew, 'Death as an Option in Neonatal Intensive Care' (1986) 328 *Lancet* 328–31

Whitfield, Adrian, 'Common Law Duties to Unborn Children' (1993) 1 *Medical Law Review* 28–52

Wicks, Elizabeth, Michael Wyldes and Mark Kilby, 'Late Termination of Pregnancy for Fetal Abnormality: Medical and Legal Perspectives' (2004) 12 *Medical Law Review* 285–305

Wilkinson, D., 'Is it in the Best Interests of an Intellectually Disabled Infant to Die?' (2006) 32 *Journal of Medical Ethics* 454–9

Williams, Glanville, *Textbook of Criminal Law* (London: Stevens & Sons, 2nd edn 1983)

Woolley, S., 'Children of Jehovah's Witnesses and Adolescent Jehovah's Witnesses: What are their Rights?' (2005) 90 *Archives of Disease in Childhood* 715–19

Wyatt, John, 'Medical Paternalism and the Fetus' (2001) 27 *Journal of Medical Ethics* suppl. II:ii15–ii20

Zucker, Marjorie B. and Howard D. Zucker (eds.), *Medical Futility* (Cambridge: Cambridge University Press, 1997)

Index